W9-DHM-020

MODELING TRADE POLICY

Applied general equilibrium (AGE) models have received considerable attention and scrutiny in the public debate over NAFTA. This
collection brings together the leading AGE models constructed to
analyze NAFTA. A variety of approaches are taken, including mul-
ticounty and multisectoral models, models that focus on institutional
features of particular sectors (agricultural, autos, steel, textiles, and
apparel), such as multinational firms and rules of origin, and models
with some intertemporal structure. Further, theoretical linkages that
drive numerical results in the larger AGE models are identified
through stylized models. The volume provides a unique opportunity
to assess, in the context of a closely related set of policy experiments,
the current status and direction of research on AGE modeling of trade
policy. The volume also assesses what can be learned about the likely
economic effects of NAFTA from the collection of studies taken as
a whole. Areas in need of further study have been highlighted.

Modeling trade policy

Applied general equilibrium assessments of North American free trade

Edited by

JOSEPH F. FRANCOIS
General Agreement on Tariffs and Trade

CLINTON R. SHIELLS
International Monetary Fund

CAMBRIDGE
UNIVERSITY PRESS

Published by the Press Syndicate of the University of Cambridge
The Pitt Building, Trumpington Street, Cambridge CB2 1RP
40 West 20th Street, New York, NY 10011-4211, USA
10 Stamford Road, Oakleigh, Melbourne 3166, Australia

First published 1994

Printed in the United States of America

Library of Congress Cataloging-in-Publication Data

Modeling trade policy : applied general equilibrium assessments of NAFTA /
    [edited by] Joseph F. Francois, Clinton R. Shiells.
        p.   cm.
    Includes index.
    ISBN 0-521-45003-9 (hc)
    1. Free trade – North America – Mathematical models.   2. Canada.
Treaties, etc. 1992 Oct. 7.   3. Equilibrium (Economics) – Mathematical models.
I. Francois, Joseph F.   II. Shiells, Clinton R.
HF1746.M63   1994
382'.71'097–dc20   93-43808
                                                                        CIP

A catalog record for this book is available from the British Library.

ISBN 0-521-45003-9 hardback

Contents

List of Contributors

Drusilla K. Brown, *Tufts University*

Mary E. Burfisher, *Economic Research Service, U.S. Department of Agriculture*

David J. Cox, *University of Waterloo*

Joseph F. Francois, *GATT Secretariat*

Timothy J. Kehoe, *University of Minnesota and Federal Reserve Bank of Minneapolis*

Santiago Levy, *Boston University*

Florencio López-de-Silanes, *Harvard University and National Bureau of Economic Research*

James R. Markusen, *University of Colorado, Boulder, and NBER*

Kenneth A. Reinert, *Kalamazoo College*

Sherman Robinson, *Department of Agricultural and Resource Economics, University of California, Berkeley*

David W. Roland-Holst, *OECD Development Center and Mills College*

José Romero, *El Colegio de México*

Thomas F. Rutherford, *University of Colorado, Boulder*

Clinton R. Shiells, *International Monetary Fund*

Horacio E. Sobarzo, *El Colegio de México*

Karen E. Thierfelder, *Economics Department, U.S. Naval Academy*

Irene Trela, *University of Western Ontario*

Sweder van Wijnbergen, *World Bank and CEPR*

John Whalley, *University of Western Ontario and NBER*

Leslie Young, *University of Texas, Austin*

The views expressed herein are those of the authors and should not be attributed in any way to the institutions with which they are affiliated.

PART I

Introduction

1

AGE Models of North American Free Trade

Joseph F. Francois
GATT Secretariat

Clinton R. Shiells
International Monetary Fund

The North American Free Trade Agreement (NAFTA) has been the subject of a protracted and acrimonious public debate in the United States about its overall economic benefits as well as its impact on labor and the environment. In the context of this debate, applied general equilibrium (AGE) models of trade liberalization between Canada, Mexico, and the United States have emerged as the tools of choice for analyzing NAFTA.

The NAFTA debate has provided a common focus for economists working on AGE modeling of trade policy. As this volume went to press, the final outcome of the debate and the fate of the NAFTA agreement had not been resolved; regardless of the outcome, however, the essays collected in this volume provide a unique opportunity to assess, in the context of a closely related set of policy experiments, the current status and direction of research on AGE modeling of trade policy. The chapters reflect both the sometimes impressive progress made to date in AGE modeling and the significant shortcomings of the current generation of models.

I. Background

Compared to the enactment of the U.S.-Canada Free Trade Agreement (CAFTA), the movement toward trade liberalization between Mexico and its North American neighbors has been relatively rapid. As recently as 1990, many analysts viewed the prospect of a U.S.-Mexico free trade area as having little chance of passage in either country. The United States and Mexico

3

have a long history of strained relations. In the commercial realm, tension dates both from the presence of U.S. multinationals in the petroleum extraction sector and from Mexico's 1917 expropriation of its natural resource assets, which was cemented in the Mexican constitution. More recently, further strains in commercial relations have developed regarding the legal rights of businesses and individuals in Mexico, especially as regards contract enforcement.

Because "fast track" negotiating authority was due to expire during proposed NAFTA negotiations, the debate over fast track in the spring of 1991 brought out the main elements of the debate over NAFTA.[1] While fast-track authority allowed for negotiation of both NAFTA and the Uruguay Round, the Uruguay Round was essentially forgotten in the discourse over NAFTA. Instead, discussion on the bill extending fast track was focused almost exclusively on the economic benefits of a U.S.-Mexico FTA, as well as further issues related to labor and environmental standards. The main issue raised was the effect of a U.S.-Mexico FTA on U.S. jobs. Labor unions, especially through the AFL-CIO, argued that vast differences in wages would induce massive job losses as U.S. firms shut down plants located in the United States and opened new plants in Mexico. Organized labor also emphasized the need to prevent low-wage international competition from eroding levels of labor standards to the lowest common denominator. At the same time, environmentalist groups expressed concern that U.S. firms would move operations to Mexico in order to take advantage of more lax environmental standards. Many pointed to the adverse environmental conditions in the U.S.-Mexico border region and argued that an FTA would enlarge the scope of this problem.

There are several reasons for the level of interest shown in economic models of NAFTA (including both AGE and macroeconometric models) on the part of U.S. policymakers. The first is historical accident. Mexican Secretary of Commerce and Industrial Development Jaime Serra-Puche wrote his Ph.D. dissertation in economics at Yale University on an AGE model of Mexico and made a big push at the outset of the negotiations for development of AGE models of NAFTA, based on his academic connections. His encouragement was instrumental in initiating several of the models included in this volume. Given Serra's interest and involvement and Ambassador Carla Hills' propensity for detailed economic homework, AGE model results were featured prominently in early public discussion of a U.S.-Mexico FTA by officials from both countries.

The Bush administration was pushed during the fast-track process to show why an FTA with Mexico was in the national interest. Its response to Congress (USTR, 1991) was designed to address these concerns; in its statement, the administration cited three major economic analyses of NAFTA: the IN-FORUM-CIMAT study (Almon, 1990), the KPMG Peat Marwick study (1991), and the February 1991 study by the U.S. International Trade Commission (ITC). Almon's study employed two separate macromodels, one for Mexico and one for the United States, and linked them through the trade accounts. The Peat Marwick project constructed separate AGE models of Mexico and the United States, linking them through the balance of payments. The reported results of the ITC study were qualitative rather than quantitative but drew upon both partial equilibrium models of particular industrial sectors and a simple AGE model constructed to assess the implications of migration effects for U.S. workers.

These three studies, and the ITC study in particular, created a veritable firestorm of criticism within organized labor groups in the United States. One of the more heated elements of this controversy concerned AGE assessments of wage effects. In one of the first government assessments of the proposed US.-Mexico Free Trade Agreement, the ITC reported that NAFTA might result in a "slight" depression or a slight increase in average wage levels for unskilled labor. However, regardless of sign, the effects on average wage rates were projected to be very small. Later public clarifications quantified "slight" as essentially indistinguishable from zero (ranging from -0.002 to $+0.01$ percent of annual earnings per worker per year).[2] Notwithstanding the order of magnitude of these effects, a lively and emotional argument continued. For some parties, the order of magnitude was not important, but rather the sign. Still others argued, in congressional testimony and elsewhere, that the ITC's "slight" really meant "massive" and that "unskilled" really covered 60 percent of the U.S. work force. In a subsequent study, Hinojosa-Ojeda and Robinson (1991) later reported wage changes for unskilled U.S. labor that were larger than the ITC estimates, though generally positive, in the range of -0.1 to $+1.8$ percent of annual earnings per year. Within this range, unskilled urban labor wage rates fell in only one of four FTA implementation scenarios examined. The Hinojosa-Ojeda and Robinson results were added to the arsenal of estimates cited by both sides prior to the fast-track vote. In some quarters, the one set of estimates (out of four) showing that unskilled wages would fall was drawn on as the definitive assessment of likely economic effects.

With AGE-based model results being employed to support the full spectrum of positions on NAFTA, the resulting confusion over the merit of model results debased the value of the more rigorous assessments of NAFTA to policymakers. To clear the air and assess the general sense of the emerging empirical literature on NAFTA, Ambassador Hills requested that the U.S. International Trade Commission hold a public symposium to bring together all economy-wide models of NAFTA, AGE-based and otherwise. For the first time in the United States, the AGE trade policy–modeling community found itself in the limelight, providing direct input for the government's trade policy process. Several of the chapters in the current volume are extensions of the papers delivered at the ITC symposium.[3] Ambassador Hills employed these studies in her frequent statements in favor of the agreement before the Congress and the public.

Another reason for the focus of policymakers on AGE models is that they provide numerical results for the main economic variables of policy interest while avoiding many of the problems of alternative methodologies. The main competing methodology is the macroeconometric model, which is not ideally suited to modeling NAFTA. The agreement consists primarily of changes in trade and direct investment restrictions at the sectoral level. NAFTA will therefore lead to a change in the structure of goods and factor prices and is perhaps best analyzed using AGE models based firmly on microeconomic theory. Macroeconometric models omit many of the effects that trade theorists view as important, namely, gains from trade due to cross-country differences in factor proportions and increasing returns to scale. They also miss the advantages of two-way trade and specialization at the intermediate product level.

At the same time, NAFTA is likely to have important macroeconomic repercussions, such as positive shocks to investor expectations. Macromodels would be ideal for assessing such effects. In particular, NAFTA may lead to increased capital flows, in the form of portfolio as well as direct investment, into Mexico. Although investment flows induced by NAFTA are likely to be at least as important as its direct effects due to changes in trade flows, neither the AGE models nor the current stock of workhorse macroeconometric models are capable of determining the effect of NAFTA on investor expectations, and hence investment flows, endogenously. Given this, we would argue that the macromodels of NAFTA omit the potentially important macroeconomic effects, thus carrying many of the same weaknesses and shortcomings attributed to the AGE models, without offering alternative strengths. Macroeconomic modelers had the potential to make important innovative contributions regarding NAFTA, but no such analyses actually emerged during the policy debate.

Finally, a version of Say's law applies here: the abundant supply of AGE models of NAFTA can be said to have helped to create a demand for them in policy circles. The Bush administration was pressed during the fast-track debate to show how an FTA with Mexico would benefit the United States. Upon taking office, the Clinton administration set about formulating its own position on the desirability of NAFTA, as negotiated by the Bush administration. There were few degrees of freedom for the new administration, due both to the concerns of labor and environmentalist groups concerning the desirability of the agreement and the abundance of research studies on it. The Clinton administration was constrained in formulating its position on the benefits of NAFTA by the results of the AGE models presented in this volume. While it could not credibly claim that NAFTA was a losing proposition for the United States, neither could it claim that NAFTA would yield a million new jobs. The middle ground, emphasized by these models, is that the effects on the United

States are relatively slight in aggregate. In our view, both the potential costs and benefits of NAFTA for the United States and Canada have been greatly exaggerated; the greatest impact will be in Mexico.

It is safe to say that the public policy debate has been most intense in the United States. The debate in Canada really opened new fronts on old issues, rather than opening up new issues. As a result, most of the models presented in this volume are concentrated on the United States and/or Mexico. At the same time, the use of the models has varied by country. While U.S. negotiators were generally lawyers, Mexican negotiators, for their part, were mostly Ph.D. economists from leading U.S. universities. The Mexicans approached the FTA as they would an academic exercise, using AGE studies to familiarize themselves with the economic implications of major policy issues and to assess the potential benefits of an FTA. Even in Canada, the use of AGE models was a long-standing one in the trade policy process. It was their emergence in the U.S. debate that was a truly novel phenomenon. Consequently, the results of AGE analysis played substantially different roles in Mexico and the United States. In Mexico, they were used by economists to formulate the policy positions they were negotiating. In the United States, negotiations were directed by attorneys trained to broker the positions of interested parties, so the AGE models were featured in the public debate over the general merits of the proposed NAFTA agreement rather than in the formulation and assessment of actual negotiating positions.

Although AGE models provide a wealth of information on the allocative and distributional effects of NAFTA, ironically it is their aggregate results that have become the focus of attention in the U.S. policy process. General equilibrium models are very useful for analyzing the changes in sectoral output, product prices, factor usage, and factor prices as well as changes in national welfare measures consequent to changes in trade regimes. They also highlight the importance of resource constraints and factor markets. Such models are not usually developed simply to assess the aggregate effects of trade liberalization.

The macrowelfare measures that AGE models do provide are those dictated by microeconomic theory, such as equivalent variation changes and related national income measures. In general, estimates of sectoral employment effects are a poor substitute at best for the measures of aggregate welfare effects featured in AGE models. Yet policymakers and interest groups have demonstrated an almost singular obsession with loosely defined concepts of job gains or losses while often rejecting empirical evidence concerning these effects that violates their own positions. We would argue that they are not asking the right set of questions. However, in the heat of public policy debate, such conceptual points of order tend to be lost, and the quality of trade policy analysis is often measured in the end by the yardstick of political expediency.

II. **The North American Economies**

Although CAFTA furthered the integration of very similar economies, NAFTA represents a step toward the economic integration of countries with widely disparate income levels. Mexico is a relatively poor, labor-abundant country. Wage rates are relatively low, and a large stock of labor is employed in inefficient agricultural production. The Mexican economy is also much smaller than the combined CAFTA market. These issues, and in particular the implication of NAFTA for wages in the United States, have been at the forefront of the public policy debate. In this section, we briefly examine the North American economies in light of the issues featured in this discourse; a relatively detailed (and certainly more structured) discussion of the formal structure of these economies is provided in Chapter 2.

Figure 1.1 presents a comparison of some basic macroeconomic indicators for the North American economies. In 1990, Mexican GDP was $236 billion, or $2,680 (U.S.) per capita. U.S. real per-capita income levels were almost ten times larger, at $21,800. Overall, the U.S. economy is almost 20 times larger than the Mexican economy, in terms of GDP. In 1990, U.S. GDP was valued at $5,465 billion, while the Mexican GDP was valued at $236 billion. These simple relationships lie at the root of the findings of practically all of the AGE studies of NAFTA. The relative size of the combined CAFTA economies and the Mexican economy imply that most of the pressure for adjustment will be on the Mexican side of the border. At the same time, relative income and wage levels imply greater adjustment in U.S. and Canadian wage rates than that which has accompanied CAFTA. Of these two factors (relative scale and factor endowments), the dominant one in assessing the immediate- to medium-term relative impacts of the NAFTA proves to be country size. In all of the static AGE studies in this volume, adjustment pressures are focused on Mexico. Even for unskilled labor, the impact of closer integration of the Mexican economy with one many times its size is, not surprisingly, concentrated in the smaller economy.[4]

Because of the disparity in wage rates, some of the greatest concerns about NAFTA have been raised by organized labor interests. Trade theory suggests that U.S. wages may fall in response to NAFTA, both in absolute terms and relative to the rental fee on capital services. The effect of NAFTA on U.S. wages, especially for low-wage workers, should be greater than that of CAFTA. The actual magnitude of the effect is an empirical question and depends on a number of factors, including the potential complementarity of U.S.-Mexican production, terms-of-trade effects, and intercountry differences in total factor productivity.

While Mexico is certainly a lower-wage country, this is not solely due to the availability of private capital. Current wage differences are the result of a number of additional, interrelated factors, including education, productivity,

Gross Domestic Product -- 1990
(billions of $US)

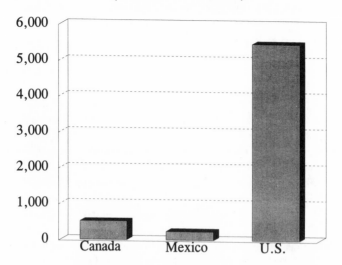

1990 Per-capita Incomes

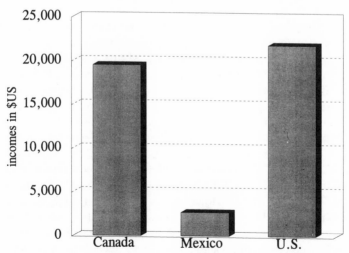

Figure 1.1. The Structure of the North American Economies – 1990

and the quality of infrastructure. To highlight such differences, Figure 1.2 illustrates the current disparity in the level of infrastructural development in the three countries, which is at least as striking as the wage differences and potentially at least as important. This implies that capital flows or trade alone cannot lead to an equalization of wage rates. These disparities are implicitly incorporated into AGE models through social accounting data, which reflect relative factor productivity.

The dynamic structure of the North American economies is also important. Although the United States' and Canada's are larger, the Mexican economy has recently been the most dynamic and the fastest growing. Figure 1.3 illustrates these patterns. As of 1990, population growth was 2.2 percent per year in Mexico, compared to 0.8 percent in the United States and 1.1 percent in Canada. Mexico's population was also relatively young, with roughly one person in three under the age of 15; this compares to one in five in the United States and Canada. The nonworking population per 100 workers in Mexico was 69 in 1990, compared to 51 in the United States and 48 in Canada. Real GDP growth was 3.9 percent in Mexico, 1.0 percent in the United States, and 0.9 percent in Canada. On a per capita basis, the growth rate was 1.1 percent in Mexico, compared to 0.2 percent in the United States and -0.2 percent in Canada.

Trade patterns reflect both the relative scale of the NAFTA economies and the extent to which integration has already taken place. The United States is Mexico's most important trading partner, accounting for over 70 percent of Mexican exports and imports in 1989. At the same time, from a U.S. perspective, Mexico ranks behind Canada and Japan, with 6 percent of U.S. imports and 7 percent of exports in 1989. With regard to Canada, its trade with the United States in 1989 amounted to $163 billion. In contrast, Canadian trade with Mexico accounted for only $2 billion of 1989 imports and exports.

The extent to which integration has already taken place, especially under CAFTA, the U.S-Canada auto pact, and the offshore assembly provisions of the U.S. tariff code, is reflected in the current level of intra-industry trade and shared production arrangements. This trade is reported under HTS tariff headings 9802.00.60 and 9802.00.80, which provide for production sharing. Auto imports from Canada would enter duty-free anyway under the Automotive Products Trade Act (APTA). However, the extension of a U.S. Customs user fee, first imposed in 1986, motivates the importers of duty-free vehicles from Canada to declare eligibility under 9802.00.80. According to Customs data, $19.5 billion dollars worth of automobiles and parts entered the United States from Canada in 1990 under the production sharing headings. Of the imports from Canada, $7.2 billion represented U.S. components, a 36 percent value share. In the case of Mexico, $3.9 billion was imported, with a U.S. components value share of 47 percent. To a large extent, the pattern of U.S. trade in

Highways
(km per 1,000 population)

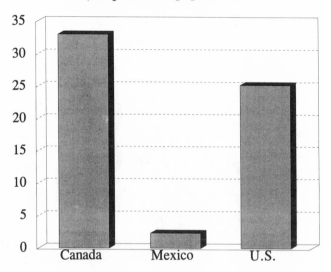

Telephone lines
(per-capita)

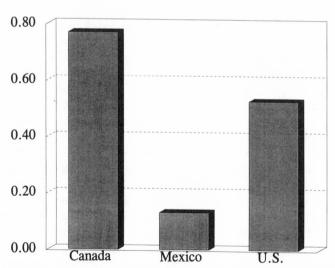

Figure 1.2. The Structure of the North American Economies – 1990

Growth in Canada, Mexico and the U.S.

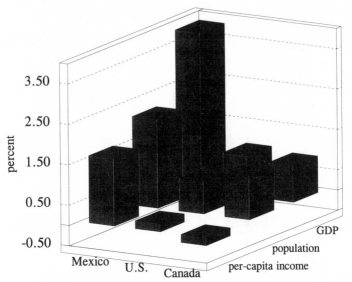

Figure 1.3. The Structure of the North American Economies – 1990

automobiles with Mexico involves a high degree of integration and already reflects relative labor cost differences.

In manufacturing sectors, another important factor is the existence of potential scale economies. Industries with fixed costs, such as autos, can produce at lower cost per unit if the scale of production is increased. Trade theory suggests that trade barriers may support too large a number of product varieties, each of which is produced at too low a volume. This is arguably the case, for example, for the portion of the Mexican auto industry located near Mexico City. Chapter 2 in this volume offers evidence that, due in part to relatively low volume, Mexican production costs for domestic consumption are substantially higher than comparable costs in the United States and Canada. Trade liberalization may therefore lead to economic gains through rationalization of the domestic industry. These rationalization gains, whereby inefficient plants are closed and the remaining plants operate at more efficient levels, may be an important part of NAFTA's effects, especially for Mexico.

III. Structure of the Models

The rigorous empirical literature on NAFTA can be placed in three groups: AGEs, linked macroeconometric models, and econometric studies. In principle, it would be best to employ models that incorporate all three approaches. One would ideally like to specify a complete general equilibrium system based on microeconomic theory, collect time-series data on all pertinent variables in a way that satisfied all relevant accounting identities, and econometrically estimate the complete structural equation system utilizing all of the constraints and other information implied by economic theory. Relevant macrofeatures (such as investment dynamics and the formation of expectations) should also be incorporated into the overall model structure.

In actual practice, there are insufficient data to do this, and so there is a trade-off between theory and econometric estimation. In most AGEs, theory is used to "calibrate" some share parameters based on estimated parameters and base-year data. Thus, the balance is struck in favor of a rigorously specified theoretical system. In econometric studies, subsystems of equations are estimated for particular sectors or actors in the economy, but it is impossible to generalize from results for particular sectors to the economy as a whole, and it is often difficult to compare results across sectors. In these studies, a rigorous and comprehensive theoretical model is sacrificed to an extent in order to base the analysis as solidly as possible upon disaggregated time-series data. Macroeconometric models represent a sort of middle ground; in order to incorporate many traditional concerns from macroeconomics, such as the influence of fiscal and monetary policy on aggregate income, the price level, and unemployment, they forgo the rigorous, microtheoretic basis inherent in AGEs. More of the macroeconometric equation system is usually estimated econometrically than with AGEs, but these equations are often "adjusted" by the modeler if implied model forecasts do not make sense.

Of the three modeling methods, AGEs have received the most attention in the public policy debate on NAFTA. There are a number of reasons for this. Econometric studies have been done on Californian agriculture and NAFTA, automobile manufacturing and NAFTA, locational aspects of U.S. exports, and the environmental effects of NAFTA, among others. However, it is not possible to compare the results of sectoral studies across sectors or to evaluate the transmission of trade policy changes across sectors. Yet the complete picture of NAFTA hinges on the very interactions missed in single-sector econometric studies. Although the broad sectoral coverage of NAFTA translates into strong demand by policymakers for sectoral details of its effects, there is not a good supply of econometric studies of each and every major sector that is likely to be affected by NAFTA. Coverage is instead rather spotty. For these reasons, policy makers have tended to focus on the AGE models.

In principle, macroeconometric modeling has much to offer even for the analysis of multisectoral structural reforms such as trade policy. Trade liberalization may affect the capital account as well as the current account through positive shocks to investor expectations. The induced effects of NAFTA on capital flows and, hence, the exchange rate are likely to be very important. A dynamic, forward-looking model of North American trade and investment flows, incorporating general equilibrium linkages between goods, asset, and factor markets, would thus appear to have much to recommend it. In practice, however, extant macroeconometric models that have been applied in the context of NAFTA have been rather different from what we have just described. The models employed have been in use for many years, in some cases reflecting over 20 years of poorly documented, ad hoc evolution of their original structure. Moreover, the models were designed for very different purposes than the analysis of multisectoral trade liberalization. As a result, additional ad hoc modifications must be appended in order to analyze NAFTA. Although it is sometimes hard to see what drives certain AGE model results, this problem is much more severe with the larger, more established workhorse macromodels, for which it is not even feasible to list all of the model equations. Chapters 5 and 7 in this volume present a diagnostic view of the workings of typical AGE model specifications that is complemented by Chapter 2, which highlights the empirical implications of different theoretical approaches.

AGE models of trade policy have evolved from a number of different traditions, ranging from the developing country models used at the World Bank by Dervis, de Melo, and Robinson to the multicountry models of developed countries constructed by Whalley, Deardorff and Stern, and others.[5] The first generation of models was based on the assumption of perfect competition and Armington-style national product differentiation. Harris added imperfect competition, developing an AGE model of Canadian trade that incorporated scale economies and imperfect competition. The models in this volume draw substantially from this tradition of AGE modeling. (Chapter 4 in this volume, for example, extends Cox's work with Harris on CAFTA.)

In the remainder of this section, we attempt to describe the broad structural features of these models, starting with some key dimensions, important structural elements, and the set of available policy instruments.

Model Dimensions

A distinction can be drawn between AGE models of NAFTA that give more or less equal attention to all sectors of the economy, which we shall refer to as "multisector models," and models that highlight one or a few sectors in the economy, which we shall refer to as "sector-focused models." Table 1.1 gives some information on the dimensionality and degree of sectoral detail in each model. There are a variety of reasons why the technical complexity of models may decline as their dimensionality increases, including limits in computer hardware, difficulties in assembling a detailed benchmark data set, and complexity of model solution and interpretation. Given this, there is a trade-off between increasing the number of industrial sectors and modeling important institutional features of particular sectors. In view of this trade-off, we view the multisector and sector-focused models as complementary.

The models by Brown (whose chapter in this volume is a stylized version of the larger Brown et al. (1992) model), Cox, Roland-Holst et al., Sobarzo, and Young and Romero may be characterized as multisector models. They contain between 12 and 27 industrial sectors, including agriculture, mining, manufacturing, and services. In most respects, all sectors are modeled in the same way. An exception is the specification of market structure, where most of the NAFTA models in this volume assume that some sectors are imperfectly competitive while others are perfectly competitive.

The Brown and Roland-Holst et al. models (Chapters 5 and 2) explicitly represent production and demand behavior in all three North American economies. This approach permits all bilateral trade flows to be determined endogenously within the models. Cox's model (Chapter 4) extends his earlier work with Harris, essentially abstracting from the production structure in all countries other than Canada. This is a useful benchmark for assessing the effects of NAFTA because the model has been featured prominently in the analysis of the U.S.-Canada FTA. Sobarzo adopts a modeling framework that is very similar to Cox's. Again, the focus is on just one country: Mexico, in this instance.

Young and Romero (Chapter 10) attempt to capture some of the dynamic effects of NAFTA on Mexico via increased investment. They distinguish capital- and intermediate-goods sectors from final-goods sectors and point out that trade protection on Mexican capital and intermediate goods is relatively high as compared to protection on final goods. Further, they allow investment in one period to expand production in future periods. None of the other models in this volume include this link because of their static structures. As a result, Young and Romero are able to capture the induced effect of tariff liberalization on capital accumulation and output, which results in an increase in output during the transition to a new steady-state equilibrium. Their model, however, is firmly grounded in the older, neoclassical growth literature. In contrast to recent endogenous growth models, there is therefore no room for analysis of changes in steady-state output growth.

There are a number of sector-focused models, including those of Burfisher et al. (Chapter 7), Levy and van Wijnbergen (Chapter 6), Lopez-de-Silanes et al. (Chapter 8), and Trela and Whalley (Chapter 9). The first two of these models focus on agriculture. Burfisher et al. have detailed and realistic specifications of the Mexican and U.S. domestic agricultural programs. They model migration linkages between a number of segmented labor markets, both domestically and internationally. Levy and van Wijnbergen focus on Mexico to model its agricultural programs and internal migration links. In addition, they allow for several different representative household types, characterized by

Table 1.1. *Summary of Demand and Production Structure*

Model	Country(ies)	Demand Side		Production Side	
		Demand Functions	Disaggregation	Production Functions	Disaggregation
Multisector Models					
Brown	Home and Foreign	2-level utility functions: 1-Cobb-Douglas between composite goods 2-CES between firm varieties	1 consumer in each country	CES function of capital and labor for fixed and variable inputs	2 composite goods
Cox	Canada	Domestic final demand: 2-level utility functions 1-Cobb-Douglas between composite goods 2-CES between national varieties Foreign final demand: Derived from CES utility functions between national varieties	1 consumer in each region (Canada, U.S., Mexico, and ROW) buys goods from each region	Fixed costs in imperfectly competitive industries are linear functions of labor and capital input prices Unit variable costs are Cobb-Douglas functions of labor, capital, and intermediate inputs	19 production sectors in Canada
Roland-Holst, Reinert, and Shiells	Canada Mexico U.S.	2-level utility functions 1-LES between composite goods 2-CES between national varieties	1 consumer in each country	CES value-added functions of labor and capital inputs; gross output is a CET function of domestic sales and exports to each region; fixed coefficient use of intermediate goods	26 production sectors in each country
Sobarzo	Mexico	2-level utility functions 1-Cobb-Douglas between composite goods 2-CES between national varieties (Mexico, other North America, and ROW)	1 consumer	Cobb-Douglas value-added functions of labor and capital inputs; fixed coefficient use of intermediate goods; fixed coefficients between intermediate inputs and value added	27 production sectors in Mexico

Young and Romero	Mexico	Cobb-Douglas preferences between consumption goods sectors; imports and domestic products are perfect substitutes	1 consumer	2-level cost functions 1-translog function of prices of labor and composite intermediate goods and rental fee on composite capital 2-composite capital price is a translog function of capital goods prices; composite intermediate price is a Cobb-Douglas function of intermediate goods prices	9 consumption goods and 3 capital goods sectors
Sector-Focused Models					
Burfisher, Robinson, and Thierfelder	Mexico U.S.	2-level utility functions 1-Cobb-Douglas between composite goods 2-Almost ideal demand system between national varieties (Mexico, U.S., and ROW)	1 consumer in each country	CES value-added functions of primary factors (4 labor types, capital, and agricultural land); domestic output is a CET function of domestic sales and exports to each region; fixed coefficient use of intermediate goods	11 production sectors (4 farm and 1 food processing) in each country
Levy and van Wijnbergen	Mexico	3-level utility functions 1-Cobb-Douglas between 3 goods (industry, services, and a composite agricultural good) 2-CES between 5 rural goods 3-CES between raw corn and tortillas Imports and domestic goods are perfect substitutes	6 household types	Cobb-Douglas value-added functions of primary factors (2 labor types, 2 capital types, and 3 land types); mostly fixed coefficient use of intermediate goods; exogenous rate of Hicks-neutral technical change	7 production sectors (5 agricultural)

Table 1.1. (*cont.*)

| Model | Country(ies) | Demand Side | | Production Side | | |
		Demand Functions	Disaggregation	Production Functions	Disaggregation

Multisector Models

Model	Country(ies)	Demand Functions	Disaggregation	Production Functions	Disaggregation
Lopez-de-Silanes, Markusen, and Rutherford	Canada Mexico U.S. ROW	3-level utility functions 1-Cobb-Douglas between composite autos and a composite of other goods 2-CES between composites of autos produced by different firm types (U.S. and ROW ownership) 3-CES between varieties of autos produced by different firms of each type	1 consumer in each region (Canada, Mexico, U.S., and ROW)	Final assembly of autos: Multinational producers; fixed cost plus constant marginal cost Auto parts: 2-level CES 1-CES production function between national composites 2-CES production function between firm varieties; fixed cost plus constant marginal cost Engines: One engine per car; engines are produced using capital and labor at constant cost	4 production sectors (final assembly, parts, engines, and other goods) in each of 4 regions (Canada, Mexico, U.S., and ROW)
Trela and Whalley: Steel	Canada Mexico U.S. ROA	CES utility function between 3 goods (steel producing sector, steel consuming sector, and all other goods); domestic production and imports from each of 3 regions (Canada, Mexico, and ROA, a 22-country aggregate of other non-VRA countries) are perfect substitutes	1 consumer for each region (Canada, Mexico, U.S., and ROA)	Domestic production: CES value-added functions of labor and capital inputs; fixed coefficients between intermediate inputs and value added Foreign production: CET function between output of 3 production sectors	3 production sectors (steel producing, steel consuming, and other) in each region

18

Trela and Whalley: Textiles and Apparel	Canada Mexico U.S. ROA	3-level utility functions 1-CES between a composite of all textile and apparel products and a composite of all other goods 2-CES between a composite of all textile goods and a composite of all apparel goods 3-CES between MFA-restricted and unrestricted goods Domestic production and imports from each of 3 regions (Canada, Mexico, and ROA, a 33-country aggregate of other supplying MFA countries) are perfect substitutes	1 consumer for each region (Canada, Mexico, U.S., and ROA)	3-level production possibilities frontiers 1-CET between a composite of all textile and apparel products and a composite of all other goods 2-CET between a composite of all textile goods and a composite of all apparel goods 3-CET between MFA-restricted and unrestricted goods	4 production sectors in each region

19

their ownership shares of several different factors of production. They also include exogenous population growth and technical change. They are able to obtain rich insights into the adjustment problems posed by agricultural trade liberalization for Mexico.

López-de-Silanes et al. (Chapter 8) focus on the automotive industry in North America, analyzing the local content and trade-balancing provisions under the Mexican auto decrees as well as rules of origin under NAFTA. To do this, they model the behavior of multinational firms who may own plants in all three countries in North America. In addition, they have disaggregated final auto assembly from engines and parts.

Trela and Whalley (Chapter 9) provide two sector-focused models. The steel model examines the effect of NAFTA within the context of the existing U.S. system of voluntary restraint arrangements (VRAs). The textiles and apparel model incorporates quantitative U.S. import restrictions under the Multifiber Arrangement (MFA). Both models assume that workers face adjustment costs external to the firm if they move from one sector to another.

Theoretical Structure

To assess AGE model simulation results, it is very important to understand how the structure of the model influences the simulation results. These models have rightly been criticized for lack of transparency in this regard. The research done on NAFTA using AGEs brought forth an astounding variety of models, each constructed a bit differently in accordance with the respective modelers' understanding of how the North American economy is structured. Some, such as Brown and Burfisher et al. in this volume, have stripped down the big models to isolate the key features driving some of the results. In addition, other modelers, such as Roland-Holst et al., have performed simulations under a variety of different market structure assumptions and using different measures of trade protection. The plethora of research on NAFTA using AGEs has significantly expanded our knowledge of what the key structural features in such models are. We proceed now to highlight the role of demand structure (Armington versus monopolistic competition, choice of functional form), market structure (perfect competition versus imperfect competition), closure rules (international capital mobility, migration, full employment versus fixed wage, and the trade balance), and intertemporal structure (static versus dynamic). Many of the structural features are summarized in Tables 1.1 and 1.2. Basic data sources are also presented in Table 1.3.

Demand Specifications: Modelers have found that results are sensitive to the specification of demand behavior. These models generally assume that the pattern of national expenditure is determined via a multistage budgeting process. In the first stage, total expenditure is allocated between all of the production sectors in the model. First-stage preferences are generally either based on Cobb-Douglas preferences or on the Stone-Geary linear expenditure system. In the second stage, expenditure for each industrial sector is allocated between imports and competing domestic production. Specifications of second-stage preferences vary more widely than that of first-stage preferences. Some models employ the "Armington assumption"; some assume firm-level product differentiation; and some use flexible, functional forms such as the almost ideal demand system (AIDS).

The Armington assumption consists of national product differentiation combined with the constant elasticity of substitution (CES) functional form. If German cars are perceived as different from U.S. and Japanese cars by consumers, then products are differentiated at the national level. If the utility function for the car industry has constant (and equal) elasticities between all national varieties, then preferences satisfy the Armington assumption. Many of the AGE models in this volume employ the Armington assumption, including Cox, Roland-Holst et al., and Sobarzo; by doing so, modelers are able to draw on the body of empirical literature on trade elasticities. [See Shiells and Reinert (1993).]

Generally, the elasticities of substitution between varieties will not be constant, but will vary over time due to changes in relative prices and will not be equal between different pairs of varieties. On the latter point, Winters has argued that it is unreasonable to suppose, for example, that Japanese cars are equally substitutable with German and U.S. cars.[6] A way of generalizing the specification of second-stage preferences, while maintaining the assumption that there is national product differentiation, is to use flexible, functional forms, such as the AIDS. Such forms do not impose constancy and pair-wise equality of substitution elasticities, thus avoiding some of the restrictiveness of the Armington assumption. Burfisher et al. employ an AIDS specification to model NAFTA, emphasizing the possibility that income elasticities may exceed unity, causing income effects of trade liberalization to be more substantial than in models based on the CES functional form (which implicitly assume unitary income elasticities) for second-stage preferences.[7]

An alternative way of modifying the Armington specification of second-stage preferences is to assume firm-level, rather than national, product differentiation. The idea behind firm-level product differentiation is that Fords and Hondas are perceived as different varieties, not as U.S. and Japanese cars. Combined with the constant elasticity of substitution form for the utility function, firm-level product differentiation has been incorporated into some AGE models of NAFTA, such as the Brown and López-de-Silanes et al. models. (Incidentally, the important and innovative twist in the López-de-Silanes et al. model is that firms are multinational, owning plants in all three North American economies.)

Table 1.2. *Summary of Market Structure and Model Closure*

| Model | Market Structure | | | Model Closure | |
	Firm Behavior	Entry and Exit	Balance of Payments	Capital Market	Labor Market
Multisector Models					
Brown	Monopolistic competition with Bertrand pricing	Free	Walras' Law implies the current account is in equilibrium	Fixed aggregate capital stock; perfectly mobile between sectors; immobile internationally	Fixed aggregate labor supply; perfectly mobile between sectors; immobile internationally
Cox	Imperfectly competitive industries use a weighted average of Eastman-Stykolt and monopolistically-competitive pricing	Free	Walras' Law implies the current account is in equilibrium	Fixed rental rate on capital services; perfectly mobile between sectors and internationally	Fixed aggregate labor supply; perfectly mobile between sectors; immobile internationally
Roland-Holst, Reinert, and Shiells	Perfect competition, average cost pricing due to contestable markets, or Cournot markup pricing	Free under Cournot	Trade balance is equal to net foreign borrowing	Fixed aggregate capital stock; perfectly mobile between sectors; immobile internationally	Fixed wage rate; perfectly mobile between sectors; immobile internationally
Sobarzo	Imperfectly competitive industries use monopolistically-competitive pricing	Free	Variable trade balance and fixed real exchange rate	Fixed world rental rate on capital services; perfectly mobile between sectors and internationally	Fixed aggregate labor supply; perfectly mobile between sectors; immobile internationally

Young and Romero	Perfect competition	Free	Walras' Law implies the current account is in equilibrium	Exogenous world prices of machines and vehicles, use transferable between sectors and internationally; exogenous supply of buildings, use transferable between sectors but not internationally	Exogenous aggregate labor supply; mobile between sectors within specified bounds; immobile internationally
Sector-Focused Models					
Burfisher, Robinson, and Thierfelder	Perfect competition	Free	Current account balance is equal to net foreign savings	Fixed aggregate capital stock; perfectly mobile between sectors; immobile internationally	Fixed aggregate supply of each labor type; perfectly mobile between sectors; labor markets are segmented and linked through migration
Levy and van Wijnbergen	Perfect competition	Free	Walras' law implies that trade is balanced in equilibrium	Exogenous rate of growth of sector-specific capital; immobile internationally	Exogenous rate of growth of rural and urban labor types; labor markets are segmented and linked through migration

23

Table 1.2. *(cont.)*

Model	Market Structure			Model Closure		
	Firm Behavior	Entry and Exit	Balance of Payments	Capital Market	Labor Market
Multisector Models					
Lopez-de-Silanes, Markusen, and Rutherford	Final assembly: Multinational firms employ a Cournot markup rule Parts: Monopolistic competition with Bertrand pricing Engines: Intra-firm production under constant costs	Free	Walras' law implies that trade is balanced in equilibrium	Capital used in parts and other goods differs from capital used in auto assembly and engine production Capital is perfectly mobile between parts and other goods but immobile internationally Capital used in auto assembly and engines has some mobility between sectors and internationally	"Labor" is a composite of all factors that are perfectly mobile between sectors and immobile internationally
Trela and Whalley: Steel	Perfect competition	Free	Trade balance is zero and steel exports to the U.S. are quota-constrained	Fixed aggregate capital stock; perfectly mobile between sectors; immobile internationally	Fixed aggregate labor supply; partially mobile between sectors, with external adjustment costs of moving between sectors; immobile internationally
Trela and Whalley: Textiles and Apparel	Perfect competition	Free	Trade balance is zero and some categories of textile and apparel trade are quota-constrained	Capital market is implicit only, due to use of the CET production possibilities frontier	Labor market is implicit only, due to use of the CET production possibilities frontier

Table 1.3. *Sources of Data and Elasticities in the Models*

Model	Year(s) Replicated	Extraneous Use of Elasticities	Production Data	Demand Data	Trade Data
Multisector Models					
Cox	1981	Elasticities of substitution between national varieties (4 specifications for sensitivity analysis), and inverse scale elasticities	Statistics Canada input-output tables, Statistics Canada data on number of firms, capital stocks, and non-capital variable costs	Input-output tables	Input-output tables
Roland-Holst, Reinert, and Shiells	1988	Elasticities of substitution between national varieties (own estimates), elasticities of substitution between capital and labor, elasticities of transformation between domestic supply and exports, and cost disadvantage ratios	Social accounting matrix (own construction)	Social accounting matrix	Social accounting matrix
Sobarzo	1985	Elasticities of substitution between national varieties, export demand elasticities, and inverse scale elasticities	Social accounting matrix (own construction)	Social accounting matrix	Social accounting matrix
Young and Romero	1992-2002	Translog cost function parameters (own estimates)	INEGI National Accounts and input-output tables, Banco de Mexico capital stocks	National Accounts	National Accounts

Table 1.3. (cont.)

Sector-Focused Models					
Burfisher, Robinson, and Thierfelder	1988 (Mexico) 1987 (U.S.)	Almost ideal import demand system calibrated based on expenditure and substitution elasticities, elasticities of transformation between domestic supply and exports, export demand elasticities for the rest of the world	Social accounting matrices (own construction)	Social accounting matrices	Social accounting matrices
Levy and van Wijnbergen	1991-2000	Elasticity of substitution between corn and basic grain in livestock production, aggregate supply elasticity for maize, elasticities of substitution between 5 rural goods in household demand, elasticities of substitution between raw corn and tortillas in household demand, rural-urban migration elasticities, inter-temporal substitution elasticity	Social accounting matrix (own construction)	1984 Income-Expenditure Survey and social accounting matrix	Social accounting matrix
Lopez-de-Silanes, Markusen, and Rutherford	1989	Elasticities of labor supply to firms, elasticities of scale (from engineering studies)	Labor shares of value-added, production of autos, engines, and parts by region, and GDP	Consumer auto price indices	Matrix of trade flows between regions in autos, engines, and parts

Model	Year(s) Replicated	Extraneous Use of Elasticities	Production Data	Demand Data	Trade Data
Multisector Models					
Trela and Whalley: Steel	1986	Elasticities of substitution between labor and capital are based on a literature search, CES and CET parameters are set to 1 (6 specifications for sensitivity analysis)	UN, U.S. Department of Commerce, UNIDO, USITC	Consumption is determined as a residual, from production and net trade data	U.S. Department of Commerce, USITC
Trela and Whalley: Textiles and Apparel	1986	Elasticities of substitution and transformation at each of 3 levels (7 specifications for sensitivity analysis)	UN, U.S. Department of Commerce, World Bank	Consumption is determined as a residual, from production and net trade data	U.S. Department of Commerce and Canadian Department of External Affairs

Note: Brown's model is not included in this table because it is not calibrated to the actual world economy.

27

A fourth alternative specification of second-stage preferences is to assume that imports and competing domestic goods are perfect substitutes. In the first three alternative specifications, it was implicitly assumed that imports and domestic goods are imperfect substitutes, so that a 1 percent change in the relative price of imports would result in a less than 1 percent change in the relative price of domestic substitutes. If imports and domestic goods are perfect substitutes, then they must have identical prices in equilibrium, causing their prices to move proportionately. Therefore, trade liberalization results in larger domestic price changes under the perfect-substitutes assumption than under the imperfect-substitutes assumption. Typically, then, the effects of trade liberalization on domestic production are substantially greater under the perfect-substitutes assumption. Of the essays in this volume, Young and Romero, Levy and van Wijnbergen, and Trela and Whalley make the assumption that imports and domestic goods are perfect substitutes. As a result, their models find bigger effects from NAFTA than the other, imperfect-substitutes models contained in this volume.[8]

Considerable debate has taken place in the literature on the appropriate specification of second-stage preferences. Brown and Norman have, independently, argued that the Armington assumption should be abandoned in favor of firm-level product differentiation with CES preferences and Helpman-Krugman–style monopolistic competition.[9] AGE modelers originally started with traditional trade theory, which assumes perfect interchangeability of imported and domestic substitutes, but modified it by making the Armington assumption to account for two-way trade and pervasive violation of the law of one price. Brown argues that the terms-of-trade effects are too large in Armington-style AGE models, at least relative to the prior expectations of modelers, whereas Norman argues that relative outputs change too little. Bearing in mind that large relative price movements are associated with small relative output effects, we note that Brown and Norman are making the same theoretical point.

Norman maintains that relative outputs in perfect-substitutes AGE models are too responsive to changes in tariffs due to imperfectly competitive behavior on the supply side. To dampen output responses, again based on prior expectations, modelers have made the Armington assumption. This, he argues, is a feature of the demand side that is widely viewed as implausible for the reasons discussed above. Norman asks why modelers want to modify the demand side, using the Armington assumption, when the problem lies on the supply side. He argues that AGE modelers should instead incorporate imperfect competition based on firm-level product differentiation. Brown does exactly that in her chapter in this volume.

Should we abandon the Armington or national product differentiation assumptions for purposes of AGE modeling, particularly for purposes of modeling trade? We argue, based on the evidence and a bit of rumination, that this question should be answered in the negative. Laying aside the important question of functional form, the use of firm-level in place of national product differentiation boils down to a slight modification of the firm's markup rule and in addition allows for free entry and exit of firms.

Under a national product differentiation assumption with monopoly pricing, each country (indexed by i) produces a unique and differentiated variety and charges a monopoly markup over marginal cost:

$$P_i = \frac{MC_i}{[1 + (1/\eta_i)]} \tag{1.1}$$

In equation 1.1, P_i is the price of country i's product, MC_i is the marginal cost of production, and η_i is the elasticity of demand for country i's product. This elasticity is determined from the following demand function:

$$Q_i = E \frac{\omega_i P_i^{-s}}{\sum_i \omega_i P_i^{1-s}} \tag{1.2}$$

where E is total expenditure on this industrial sector, Q_i is the quantity of country i's product demanded, s is the elasticity of substitution between country varieties (assumed constant), and ω_i represents CES aggregation weights.

Under the firm-level product differentiation assumption, there are n_i different product varieties in country i. Making the usual Spence-Dixit-Stiglitz assumption regarding preferences, the demand for each firm's product variety is given by the following equation:

$$q_i = E \frac{\omega_i P_i^{-s}}{\sum_i (n_i \omega_i) P_i^{1-s}} \tag{1.3}$$

Here P_i and q_i are the (identical) price and quantity of a representative firm in country i, E is expenditure on this industrial sector, and s is the elasticity of substitution between product varieties. Total demand for the products produced in country i will be

$$Q_i = E \frac{(n_i \omega_i) P_i^{-s}}{\sum_i (n_i \omega_i) P_i^{1-s}} \tag{1.4}$$

The representative firm maximizes profits by setting price equal to a markup over marginal cost:

$$P_i = \frac{MC_i}{[1 + (1/\eta_i)]} \tag{1.5}$$

Here MC_i is the marginal cost of a representative firm in country i, and η_i is the firm's perceived elasticity of demand as determined by the preceding representative firm's demand equation. Brown assumes free entry and exit so that the markup rule is combined with a zero profit condition in order to obtain monopolistically competitive equilibrium.

The important point is that the Armington and monopolistic competition specifications are identical if the number of domestic and foreign product varieties is unchanged in equilibrium, allowing for free entry and exit. (This outcome appears quite likely, based on Brown's analysis in Chapter 5.) The similarity of the two approaches, in reduced form, is apparent from the markup rules and demand equations shown above. With the strong symmetry that is usually applied in AGE models with monopolistic competition, equations 1.2 and 1.4 are identical, apart from the interpretation of the aggregation weights. At the same time, the aggregate demand elasticities are also identical. Because scale economies can be incorporated into both specifications, the difference can be reduced, essentially, to the choice of a price markup rule.

As is common in AGE models with monopolistic competition, Brown does not impose integer constraints on the number of firms so that n_i can assume any real value. In her model simulations of NAFTA, the number of firms changes by less than integer amounts. Were integer constraints imposed in the simulations, it is likely that the number of firms would remain unchanged; we strongly suspect that this conclusion would generalize to other situations.

Market Structure: A variety of different assumptions are made in this volume regarding market structure. A combination of constant returns to scale (CRTS) and perfect competition is simplest to model but omits potentially important gains from trade. The Young and Romero, Burfisher et al., Levy and van Wijnbergen, and Trela and Whalley models assume perfect competition in all sectors. The remaining chapters apply models that assume increasing returns to scale (IRTS) and combine this with one or more forms of imperfect competition. The choice of market structure and behavioral hypothesis concerning the imperfectly competitive firm's behavior can significantly influence the model simulation results obtained.

If there are increasing returns to scale, it is necessary to modify the standard assumption that firms take prices as given. Some form of imperfect competition must be assumed. The following types of imperfect competition are specified in the models found in this volume: Bertrand, Cournot, contestable markets, Eastman-Stykolt, and monopolistic competition specifications. Bertrand pricing means that firms set prices to maximize profits, taking prices charged by competitors as given, and Bertrand equilibrium occurs when each firm's price is equal to the price that other firms expect it to choose. Cournot quantity-setting means that firms set quantities to maximize profits, taking quantities selected by competitors as given; Cournot equilibrium occurs when each firm's quantity is equal to the quantity that other firms expect it to choose. Under the contestable markets specification, firms set price equal to average cost, which is just low enough to deter entry by potential competitors. Under the Eastman-Stykolt specification, domestic firms all charge a focal price, which is assumed to equal the landed price of imports inclusive of duties. The Chamberlin-Cournot monopolistic competition specification assumes that all firms in an industry produce different varieties of a good using the same technology, that cross-price elasticities of demand between varieties are equal, and that entry is free. Under most forms of imperfect competition, it is possible to hold a fixed number of firms in the market or, alternatively, to allow costless entry and exit. The form of imperfect competition chosen and whether or not there is free entry (and exit) can affect the simulation results in a complex manner. Market structure in each model is summarized in Table 1.2.

Closure Rules: The AGE models in this volume also make a variety of assumptions regarding aggregate wage or employment determination, international mobility of capital, and exchange rate determination. These assumptions are referred to as *closure rules* and are summarized in Table 1.2.

A number of assumptions are also made regarding the labor market. The simplest specification is to assume that labor is homogeneous, perfectly mobile between sectors within a country, and immobile internationally, as in the Brown, Cox, Roland-Holst et al., Sobarzo, and Young and Romero chapters. Given this, trade liberalization essentially shifts the labor demand schedules for different industrial sectors. Import-competing sectors generally face declining demand for labor, whereas exportable- and nontraded-goods sectors generally face increasing labor demand. In the aggregate, labor demand generally shifts out in these models in response to North American free trade.

Much emphasis has been placed in the policy debate over NAFTA and the AGEs concerning the full-employment assumption. Given the shift in the aggregate labor demand schedule, it is possible to specify the labor market in these AGEs either by assuming constant aggregate employment (which generally will not be "full employment"), thereby allowing the wage to adjust, or to assume that wages are sticky, thereby allowing aggregate employment to adjust. A large body of economic theory implies that there should be no aggregate employment response to tariff liberalization in the long run.[10] At the same time, however, many economists disagree with this view. A strong sentiment emerged in the policy debate on NAFTA, among economists and non-economists alike, that trade liberalization may influence aggregate employment in the longrun (or at least for as long as mattered for the current generation of policymakers). The sticky wage approach provides some assessment (though admittedly crude) of likely employment effects in such conditions.

Because of their roots in classical trade theory, all but one AGE model in this volume assume that wages are flexible and labor markets clear. The exception is the Roland-Holst et al. model, which assumes that the average wage rate is fixed so that aggregate employment adjusts to restore equilibrium in the labor market following a policy change. Even so, the simulation results imply that trade liberalization would lead to an increase in aggregate employment in all three North American economies, in contrast to the view of some policy-makers. These employment gains result from increased efficiency of resource allocation associated with trade liberalization.[11] Viewed as a whole, the wage and employment results presented in this volume all point to increased aggregate employment and wage effects for the United States, Mexico, and Canada.

Standard labor market closure must be modified in models that feature segmented labor markets. The Burfisher et al. model, for example, assumes that there is enough migration to fix (1) the rural/urban-unskilled wage differential within Mexico and (2) the rural/rural and urban-unskilled/urban-unskilled wage differentials between Mexico and the United States (expressed in a common currency). An implication of this closure rule is that an exchange rate change will lead to international labor migration. Burfisher et al. assess the relative importance of migration and traditional Stolper-Samuelson effects on factor prices, finding that migration effects dominate, and examine a number of extensions to the behavioral specification of migration that have been used in previous studies, including their own.[12]

With regard to capital mobility, there is a choice between fixing the rental rate on capital, thereby allowing for imports of capital, and fixing the aggregate capital stock, thereby allowing the rental on capital to adjust. If the aggregate capital stock is assumed to be determined exogenously, then it is possible to combine an increase in the aggregate capital stock with a trade liberalization experiment. Because both methods of allowing for capital imports are ad hoc, a more acceptable alternative would be to model the effect of trade liberalization on firms' investment decisions. This approach has been taken by Young and Romero.

Finally, there is a choice between fixing the exchange rate and allowing the trade balance to adjust to restore equilibrium in the foreign exchange market or, alternatively, fixing the trade balance and allowing the exchange rate to adjust to clear the foreign exchange market. Most models rely on the latter. This would be appropriate, for example, if the capital account were determined exogenously, by asset market equilibrium. Ideally, the current and capital accounts and the exchange rate would be determined endogenously.[13] However, none of the models adopt this more complex approach.

Dynamics: The remaining element of the AGE models of NAFTA that we need to discuss is their intertemporal structure, or rather their lack thereof. Most models are exercises in comparative statics. Starting with an economy in long-run equilibrium, we make a change in one of the exogenous variables in the model. The economy will adjust, which may take time, conceivably many years. Yet the length of adjustment is unspecified in comparative statics exercises. Ultimately, the economy adjusts to the exogenous shock and attains a new equilibrium. By comparing the initial and final static equilibrium solutions for prices and quantities of all goods in the economy, we obtain the long-run or steady-state effect of an exogenous policy change. In this case, the policy variables are tariff changes contemplated under NAFTA.

There are many reasons to be concerned with the dynamic path by which an economy moves from the initial to the final equilibrium position. For one thing, policymakers are very concerned with costs of adjustment. For another, a static model may omit some potentially important dynamic effects of trade liberalization. Static gains from trade due both to specialization in accordance with comparative advantage and scale economies lead to increased aggregate output. In dynamic models, this induces additional savings, leads to capital accumulation, and increases output in the future. In neoclassical growth models, capital accumulation due to induced savings leads to an increase in economic growth only in the transition from one steady state to another. Young and Romero model this transitional increase in growth, which can be very important quantitatively.

In addition to the transitional effects, there are potentially important steady-state growth effects tied to trade liberalization as well. However, while such effects are emphasized in the new growth theories, the theoretical foundations do not yet exist for rigorous empirical implementation. [See Francois and Shiells (1993).] In the open-economy endogenous growth models often associated with Grossman, Helpman, Lucas, Romer, Stokey, Young, and many others,[14] trade liberalization may change incentives for learning by doing, investment in research and development or schooling, or incentives to specialize the production process by acquiring differentiated capital or intermediate inputs. If there are dynamic externalities or spillovers associated with these activities, it is theoretically possible for trade liberalization to increase the rate of economic growth in the steady state. Kehoe's chapter in this volume explores these dynamic growth effects, in a highly stylized manner, as applied to NAFTA and Mexico in particular. While there are as yet no rigorous, dynamic AGEs that incorporate endogenous growth effects in the spirit of the recent literature on the subject, his preliminary calculations indicate that such effects may dwarf static welfare calculations, at least for a small, developing economy like Mexico.

IV. Model Results

Having considered the policy context and model structures in some detail, we now assess the results of the models presented in this volume, highlighting areas of convergence and divergence and what implications these results have for policymakers. There are now many papers and reports that offer surveys of results from these models. Generally, the focus of these surveys is on obtaining ranges of results for a few aggregate variables, such as employment, wages, output, trade, and welfare. It is our view that one of the primary strengths of AGE models is their ability to sort through the different channels by which various components of NAFTA will affect the North American economy. By focusing instead on quantitative predictions for macrovariables, extant surveys sell AGE-based results short. We shall, therefore, depart considerably from previous surveys by refraining from forming these sorts of ranges. Instead, we assess what can be said about the effects of various elements of NAFTA, what are the important and distinctive results obtained in each of the studies in the present volume, and why these results are important in the context of the policy debate concerning NAFTA. These comparisons are summarized in Table 1.4.

The main conclusions that can be drawn from the large, multisector AGE models of NAFTA are as follows. First, models that incorporate some form of imperfect competition obtain larger impact effects than models that assume perfect competition. The chapter by Roland-Holst et al. is noteworthy in its reporting of alternative simulations using a variety of market structures; these simulations show the influence that these assumptions have on model simulation results. Second, nontariff barriers (NTBs) are potentially as important as tariff barriers, as shown in the López-de-Silanes, Roland-Holst et al., Sobarzo, and Trela and Whalley chapters. Third, international capital mobility induced by NAFTA is potentially more important than trade liberalization contained in NAFTA, especially for Mexico. This is apparent from Brown's larger model, as well as from those of Sobarzo and Young and Romero. Finally, real wages in Canada and the United States are expected to rise as a result of NAFTA, in sharp contrast to what would be expected based on the Stolper-Samuelson theorem. Brown's chapter does an impressive job of stripping down her larger model and then identifying the key theoretical linkages that drive especially the increase in real wages, concluding that economies of scale in Mexico and terms-of-trade gains in the United States lead to increases in real returns to the scarce factor in each country.

The sector-focused models contain a rich array of insights and often employ important methodological innovations in the AGE literature. These models have the advantage of capturing some key institutional features of a sector that are, of necessity, omitted from most large models. Both of the models of agriculture, for example, incorporate labor migration and domestic agricultural programs. If Mexican maize were liberalized, the models suggest that large numbers of farmers would be displaced. These studies show the importance of timing, income distribution, and incentives for adjustment for the design of · public policy. A noteworthy insight from these papers is that induced migration

Table 1.4. *Synthesis of Major Policy Findings of the Models*

Model	Details of Policy Simulations	Policy Data Used	Policy Conclusions
Multisector Models			
Cox	1. Impact of CAFTA on Canada 2. Impact of NAFTA on Canada 3. Impact of CAFTA and a separate U.S.-Mexico FTA (hub and spoke arrangement or HASP)	Ad valorem tariff rates for Canada, Mexico, and the United States	1. Canada gains significantly from CAFTA, largely due to rationalization within manufacturing 2. Given CAFTA, a NAFTA would have little added effect on Canada 3. Given CAFTA, a HASP would have virtually no effect on Canada
Roland-Holst, Reinert, and Shiells	1. Removal of tariffs within North America 2. Removal of tariffs and non-tariff barriers within North America 3. Sensitivity to choice of market structure 4. Sensitivity to inter-country price differences	Ad valorem tariff rates and non-tariff barrier (NTB) coverage ratios for Canada, Mexico, and the United States	1. Removal of NTBs is potentially more important than tariff liberalization within North America 2. NAFTA would raise aggregate employment in all three countries if there is excess supply of labor 3. Market structure and increasing returns to scale matter for AGE simulations of NAFTA 4. Inter-country price differences are important for analyzing resource shifts between sectors due to NAFTA

Table 1.4. (cont.)

Model	Details of Policy Simulations	Policy Data Used	Policy Conclusions
Multisector Models			
Sobarzo	Impact of NAFTA on Mexico	Ad valorem tariff rates and NTB coverage ratios for Mexico	1. NAFTA would have a more substantial effect on Mexican GDP than on welfare due to an influx of foreign-owned capital 2. Mexican exports of apparel, rubber, leather, tobacco, and textiles to North America would increase strongly 3. Mexican imports of agriculture, food, and beverages from North America would increase substantially 4. Large inter-sectoral labor movements within Mexico would result from NAFTA
Young and Romero	1. Impact of tariff elimination on Mexico 2. Given zero tariffs, impact of a real interest rate reduction on Mexico	Ad valorem tariff rates for Mexico	1. Mexico levies relatively high tariffs on capital and intermediate goods 2. Elimination of tariffs leads to capital accumulation and a transitory but substantial increase in economic growth for Mexico 3. NAFTA may lower uncertainty and reduce Mexican real interest rates, which would raise real Mexican GDP by much more than free trade alone
Sector-Focused Models			

36

| Burfisher, Robinson, and Thierfelder | 1. Removal of all bilateral tariffs and quotas between Mexico and the U.S. (free trade)
2. Free trade plus rural-urban migration in Mexico (internal migration)
3. Free trade, internal migration, and migration between Mexico and the U.S. (international migration)
4. Effects of a Mexican tariff in a distortion-free base model (Stolper-Samuelson effects of a Mexican tariff)
5. Effects of a U.S. tariff in a distortion-free base model (Stolper-Samuelson effects of a U.S. tariff)
6. International migration and Stolper-Samuelson effects of a U.S. tariff | 1. Ad valorem tariff rates for Mexico and the United States
2. Agricultural import quota for Mexico and the United States
3. Input subsidies to producers and processors in agricultural sectors for Mexico and the United States
4. Mexican tortilla subsidies
5. U.S. agricultural deficiency payments | 1. With no migration, agricultural trade liberalization within NAFTA reduces Mexican rural wages and increases U.S. rural wages
2. With migration, wage effects of agricultural trade liberalization within NAFTA are reversed, as rural labor supply falls in Mexico and rises in the U.S.
4. NAFTA raises urban unskilled wages in Mexico by increasing demand and, via rural-urban migration, by reducing supply in the urban unskilled labor market
5. NAFTA reduces wages of U.S. urban unskilled workers due to increased migration from Mexico
6. Migration is very sensitive to the wage differential and to the treatment of the exchange rate in the migration equation |

Table 1.4. (cont.)

Model	Details of Policy Simulations	Policy Data Used	Policy Conclusions
Multisector Models			
Levy and van Wijnbergen	1. Immediate liberalization of Mexican taxes and subsidies (including trade protection) on Mexican corn and tortillas 2. Gradual liberalization of Mexican corn and tortillas, over 5 years 3. Supplement liberalization of Mexican corn and tortillas with a program of improvements in irrigation of rain-fed agricultural land 4. Supplement liberalization of Mexican corn and tortillas and land improvements with improved market access to the U.S. fruit and vegetable market	1. Ad valorem tariff rates for Mexico 2. Urban and rural corn prices, given Mexico's corn tax and subsidy configuration 3. Value added tax rates for manufacturing and services 4. Direct tax rates on productive factors and households 5. Average cost, internal rate of return, and labor requirements for irrigation projects	1. Efficiency gains of Mexican corn liberalization are substantial but unevenly distributed 2. Gradualism does not greatly reduce efficiency gains but barely mitigates welfare losses for affected groups 3. Irrigation investments increase demand for rural labor and the value of rain-fed land, thereby mitigating the welfare losses caused by Mexican corn liberalization 4. Combining improved access to the U.S. fresh fruits and vegetables market, with Mexican corn liberalization and irrigation investments, yields improved welfare for all Mexican household groups
Lopez-de-Silanes, Markusen, and Rutherford	NAFTA: North American free trade in autos, engines, and parts, with no content or trade-balancing provisions CR: North American free trade in autos, engines, and parts, with a 62% North American content provision on parts, engines, and labor CR/TB: Adds the existing Mexican trade-balancing restriction to the CR scenario	1. Ad valorem tariff rates on autos, engines, and parts for Canada, Mexico, and the U.S. 2. Premia due to existing Mexican and Canada-U.S. content restrictions 3. Premia due to existing Mexican trade-balancing restriction	1. Mexico receives a significant welfare benefit from North American free trade in autos, while the rest of the world experiences no welfare change 2. Canada and the U.S. experience small gains in auto employment, while Mexican auto employment falls significantly (5-8%) 3. With a North American content provision, North American firms increase auto and engine production (about 5%), while foreign firms incur very large losses (25% for autos, 50% for engines) 4. Allowing Mexico to retain its trade-balancing restriction makes little difference

38

| Trela and Whalley: | 1. Bi-lateral U.S.-Mexico agreement with liberalization of U.S. tariffs and NTBs in steel, textiles and apparel.
2. Same as scenario 1, but with only U.S. NTBs being liberalized.
3. Same as scenario 1, but with only U.S. tariffs being liberalized.
4. Similar to scenario 2, with a doubling of U.S. quotas for Mexico.
5. Tri-lateral agreement with liberalization of U.S. tariffs and NTBs for steel, textiles, and apparel and Canadian tariffs and NTBs for textiles and apparel. (Canada is a net steel exporter in the model). | 1. Ad valorem tariff rates and tariff equivalents for quotas, based on unit cost comparisons, are used for steel.
2. Ad valorem tariff rates and tariff equivalents for quotas, based on Hong Kong auction prices, are used for textiles and apparel. | 1. Liberalization is jointly advantageous to Mexico and the United States, though adverse for third countries. Most gains accrue to Mexico. For the U.S., welfare gains are magnified by the opportunity to reduce rent transfers to quota-restricted third countries.
2. For Canada, the benefits of tri-lateral liberalization in textiles and apparel are also dominated by rent transfers from quotas. Increased rent transfers from Canada outweigh the gains from increased market access.
3. The form of liberalization is important. It is best for the U.S. if tariff liberalization is accompanied by quota liberalization. This minimizes the potential for increased quota rent transfers to Mexico. |

Note: Brown's model is not included in this table because it is not calibrated to the actual world economy.

effects have a very real potential to swamp the direct effects of trade liberalization on wages.

In the auto sector, market structure may have important implications for trade liberalization. Auto plants in Mexico currently operate at inefficient levels and produce too many models. The rationalization induced by NAFTA may be very significant in the Mexican auto industry. In addition, the multinational nature of North American auto firms influences how firms may respond to NAFTA.

The Trela and Whalley chapter highlights the significance of the institutional aspects of textile trade for the gains from trade liberalization. In their simulations, tariff liberalization alone results in the transfer of MFA quota rents to Mexico, hurting the United States. However, if the United States relaxes the quotas as well, quota rents are recaptured. Such a process would benefit the United States. In general, the type of liberalization matters.

V. Conclusions and Implications for Future Research

Within the United States, there has been unprecedented interest by the general public, the Clinton administration, and Congress in formal economic models of NAFTA. In view of this, it is important not to oversell their results. Trade negotiators often are concerned with very detailed product categories and policies. Even a general equilibrium model that focuses on one sector may not be sufficiently detailed to capture the matters of most immediate concern to negotiators. At the same time, however, the alternatives are at least as problematic.

The AGE models featured in this volume fall into three broad categories. First, there are static models of one or more countries that examine liberalization of trade barriers in all sectors simultaneously but whose sectoring schemes are fairly broad. These big models often incorporate some form of imperfect competition, which allows for the possibility that trade liberalization will lead to rationalization of the previously protected industry. Without exception, simulations based on these models show that Canada, Mexico, and the United States all stand to gain from NAFTA, although the welfare gains are modest as a percent of GDP. Mexico appears to have the most to gain, with percentage changes in welfare on the order of 1 to 5 percent. It is also apparent that worker dislocation in Canada or the United States is generally not very substantial in a static AGE model with only 20 or 30 industrial sectors.

A second set of models focuses on a particular sector such as agriculture or autos. These models have a number of advantages over applied partial equilibrium (PE) models and case studies. In contrast to PE models, AGE models incorporate factor-market and balance-of-payments equilibrium conditions. This feature is important for studying large sectors for which trade liberalization will have significant effects on labor markets in other sectors and on the country's overall trade balance.

A third category of models consists of the dynamic AGEs. The first generation of trade AGEs were perfectly competitive and static in nature. Imperfect competition was then introduced into the static AGEs. Based on early evidence, the emerging generation of AGEs would appear to involve more sophisticated dynamic processes. The dynamic gains from trade liberalization are typically greater than the static gains emphasized in the current generation of AGEs. For example, liberalization of capital goods leads to increased investment, which leads to accumulation of capital and to welfare gains over time.

In addition to the dynamic effects related to capital accumulation, trade liberalization may lead to an increase in the rate of technical change. These gains are associated with "dynamic economies of scale." [See Francois and Shiells (1993).] If there is learning by doing, for example, firms may lower their costs if the country is opened up to trade, due to specialization in accordance with comparative advantage. Alternatively, trade liberalization may make a broader array of specialized capital goods available to the domestic industry. In either case, trade liberalization can lead to an increased rate of economic growth, whose welfare gains dwarf those obtained in other models. While even the theory of endogenous innovation and trade is in a state of flux, to say nothing of its quantification, there is little doubt that dynamic gains from trade liberalization are of great importance.

In general, the different paths taken to model the aggregate effects of NAFTA all seem to lead to similar qualitative conclusions. Dominating practically all of the model results is the relative sizes of the Canadian, Mexican, and U.S. economies. The potential complementarity of the U.S. and Mexican economies is also important. Combined with the fact that the highest tariff and nontariff barriers are in Mexico, intercountry differences in the level of economic activity imply that NAFTA may induce large-scale rationalization and adjustment there. For the United States, by contrast, effects should prove to be relatively mild. The largest gains for the United States will follow from liberalization of Mexican NTBs. The greatest benefit may, therefore, be the opportunity to secure a relatively prosperous and politically stable southern neighbor at little cost. NAFTA may also strike at the economic roots of migration from Mexico to the United States.

An important difference between NAFTA as it may actually come to pass and the policy experiments conducted by the AGE modeling projects presented here is one of timing. With few exceptions, the experiments conducted generally contemplate immediate liberalization. Because many, if not most, NTBs will be phased out over a 10–15-year time period, the annual effects of NAFTA's implementation may be less noticeable for all parties than the findings presented here would suggest, but if these findings are combined with some casual empiricism regarding the political economy of liberalization, then it becomes clear that the potential exists for adverse effects and (not necessarily related) pressure for adjustment assistance, especially on a sectoral level. This is particularly true for agriculture in Mexico and for unskilled labor in the United States.

Canadian public perception of CAFTA suggests strongly that NAFTA will be blamed, at least in some circles, for most – if not all – negative economic shocks experienced during or following implementation. Because this "scapegoat" effect is not necessarily linked to real effects or developments, governments in all three countries need to be prepared to deal with pressure for adjustment assistance and related trade remedies, not only for NAFTA-induced structural adjustment, but also for those blamed erroneously on NAFTA. To support this point, one only needs to look to Canada, where mainstream parties have blamed the global recession on CAFTA. In a similar vein, structural adjustments in the United States associated with basic macroimbalances are often attributed to "unfair trade" in individual sectors, rather than to the broader macroenvironment.

Endnotes

1. The president notified the Congress of his decision to proceed with free trade negotiations with Mexico under fast-track negotiating authority on September 25, 1990. Following further discussions with Mexico and Canada, the President notified Congress on February 5, 1991 of the decision of all three governments to broaden the negotiations to include Canada, and so to work towards a NAFTA. Fast track provides for congressional consultation during negotiations, followed by formal notification of an agreement and a simple yes or no vote on the agreement. It is meant to add credence to the U.S. negotiating position by ensuring against congressional amendment after an agreement has been negotiated.

2. Congress had originally requested that the Commission's study be strictly qualitative. This made the later public clarifications of actual magnitudes necessary once the report's findings were cited in congressional testimony.

3. See U.S. International Trade Commission (1992).

4. In hindsight, this should not be surprising. Even in the basic Ricardian and Hecksher-Ohlin frameworks, economic integration tends to focus adjustment on the smaller economy.

5. For a survey of these models, see Shoven and Whalley (1984). A comprehensive collection and evaluation of AGE trade models is contained in Srinivasan and Whalley (1986).

6. See Winters (1984).

7. For an attempt to estimate the AIDS for North American tradable demands econometrically, see Shiells, Roland-Holst, and Reinert (1993).

8. Actual trade data reflects a great deal of two-way trade. While this is consistent with Armington and monopolistic competition specifications, it is not consistent with the perfect-substitutes assumption. For this reason, perfect-substitutes models usually employ specifications of *net* trade flows.

9. See Brown (1987) and Norman (1990). For econometric evidence that suggests large terms-of-trade effects in Armington models of North American free trade, see Shiells and Reinert (1993).

10. We realize that these issues are far from settled. We refer the reader to Greenwald and Stiglitz (1993) for some further discussion.

11. This result has been obtained by other modelers in connection with NAFTA that are not contained in the present volume. Analytically, this result appears to have much in common with the ORANI model results contained in Srinivasan and Whalley (1986). Comments by Feenstra and Harris in this same volume analyze the theoretical mechanism that underlies the positive association between trade liberalization and aggregate employment, emphasizing its counter-intuitive but plausible nature. Their analyses appear to be directly relevant to the Roland-Holst et al. model contained in this volume as well.

12. Levy and van Wijnbergen also assume segmented labor markets and allow for migration but only within Mexico.

13. See Goulder and Eichengreen (1992).

14. See Grossman and Helpman (1991).

References

Almon, C. 1990. *Industrial effects of a free trade agreement between Mexico and the U.S.A.* Research report prepared for the U.S. Department of Labor, Bureau of International Labor Affairs, under Contract J-9-K-9-0077, September.

Brown, D.K. 1987. "Tariffs, the terms of trade, and national product differentiation." *Journal of Policy Modeling* 9(3):503–26.

Brown, D.K., A.V. Deardorff, and R.M. Stern. 1992. "A North American free trade agreement: analytical issues and a computational assessment." *World Economy* 15: (January): 11–29.

Francois, J.F., and C.R. Shiells. 1993. *Dynamic effects of trade liberalization: a survey.* U.S. International Trade Commission, Publication 2608, February.

Goulder, L.H., and B. Eichengreen. 1992. "Trade liberalization in general equilibrium: Intertemporal and inter-industry effects." *Canadian Journal of Economics* 25(2):253–80.

Greenwald, B., and J. Stiglitz. 1993. "New and old Keynesians." *Journal of Economic Perspectives* 7(1):23–44.

Grossman, G.M., and E. Helpman. 1991. *Innovation and growth in the global economy.* Cambridge, MA: MIT Press.

Hinojosa-Ojeda, R., and S. Robinson. 1991. "Alternative scenarios of U.S.-Mexican integration: A computable general equilibrium approach." Department of Agriculture and Resource Economics, Division of Agriculture and Natural Resources, University of California, Working Paper No. 609, April.

KPMG Peat Marwick. 1991. "Analysis of economic effects of a free trade area between the United States and Mexico." KPMG Peat Marwick Policy Economics Group, prepared for the U.S. Council of the Mexico-U.S. Business Committee, Washington, DC.

Norman, V.D. 1990. "Assessing trade and welfare effects of trade liberalization: A comparison of alternative approaches to CGE modeling with imperfect competition." *European Economic Review* 34:725–45.

Shiells, C.R., D.R. Roland-Holst, and K.A. Reinert. 1993. "Modeling a North American free trade area: Estimation of flexible functional forms." *Weltwirtschaftliches Archiv* 129(1):55–77.

Shiells, C.R., and K.A. Reinert. 1993. "Armington models and terms-of-trade effects: Some econometric evidence for North America." *Canadian Journal of Economics* 26(2):299–316.

Shoven, J.B., and J. Whalley. 1984. "Applied general-equilibrium models of taxation and international trade: An introduction and survey." *Journal of Economic Literature* 22(3):1007–51.

Srinivasan, T.N., and J. Whalley, eds. 1986. *General equilibrium trade policy modeling.* Cambridge, MA: MIT Press.

U.S. Trade Representative. 1991. *Response of the administration to issues raised in connection with the negotiation of a North American free trade agreement.* Transmitted to Congress by the president on May 1.

U.S. International Trade Commission. 1991. *The likely impact on the United States of a free trade agreement with Mexico.* Publication 2353, February.

———1992. *Economy-wide modeling of the economic implications of a FTA with Mexico and a NAFTA with Canada and Mexico.* Publication 2516, May.

Winters, L. A. 1984. "Separability and the specification of foreign trade preferences." *Journal of International Economics* 17(3/4):239–63.

PART II

Multisector Models

2

A General Equilibrium Analysis of North American Economic Integration*

David W. Roland-Holst
OECD

Kenneth A. Reinert
Kalamazoo College

Clinton R. Shiells
International Monetary Fund

I. Introduction

The North American Free Trade Agreement (NAFTA) is representative of a worldwide trend toward regionalism in trade negotiations. This shift
away from multilateralism is a result of both the strengths and weaknesses of
the GATT framework. On one hand, GATT has been quite successful at demonstrating once and for all that relatively low tariff protection can greatly
expand global trade opportunities. At the same time, however, these norms
have lowered the stakes for regionalists, who can now remove residual protection with their neighbors secure in the knowledge that severe retaliation is
not individually rational for other trading partners. The success of GATT in
reducing average tariff protection has also narrowed the negotiating agenda
down to its more stubborn elements, such as trade in agricultural and textile
products.

GATT's weaknesses have also become more apparent and problematic over
time. In its early days, the multilateral negotiating framework faced a relatively
easy task, with a few dominant economies leading the way by leveling tariff
barriers on a dominant share of international trade. Now the family of influ-
ential traders is much larger, their geographic and economic interests are more
diverse, and consensus is much more difficult to achieve or even approximate.
Finally, an emphasis on multilateral negotiations on tariff protection has led

---

* The opinions expressed here are those of the authors and should not be attributed to
 their affiliated institutions.

to proliferation of nontariff trade control measures that in many instances threaten to reverse the long-term trend toward a more liberalized global trading regime. A prominent example of this is the Multi-Fiber Arrangement governing textile and apparel trade.

As it is currently under negotiation, NAFTA is a partial response to the shortcomings that each North American country might perceive in the Uruguay Round. This chapter examines the potential impact of more complete North American economic integration using a general equilibrium simulation model, calibrated to a three-country social accounting matrix (SAM) that details 26 sectors of production and is estimated for 1988. The chapter has two main objectives. The first is to describe the structure of the North American economy using information contained in the 1988 SAM to set the stage for the model simulations of this and subsequent chapters. The second objective is to highlight the role of assumptions concerning market structure and conduct and intercountry relative prices on the aggregate and sectoral results of applied general equilibrium (AGE) model simulations of North American economic integration.

Our results indicate that all three countries stand to gain substantially from the reduction of trade barriers. It is apparent, however, that the pattern of adjustment in domestic production, factor use, demand, and trade in all three countries differs significantly, depending upon the assumptions made about domestic industry structure and conduct and intercountry relative prices. Unless greater account is taken of these detailed features of the three economies, current regional negotiations can only partially fulfill the stated objectives of greater economic efficiency and gains from trade. More seriously, policy makers who omit these considerations will be ill prepared for the domestic and international issues that will inevitably arise during the adjustment process.

In the next section, we provide an overview of domestic economic structure and trade relations among the three North American countries. Section III summarizes the information we have obtained on regional protection patterns and relative prices. The fourth section discusses the structure and conventions of the AGE model, followed in section V by the simulation results we obtained with it. A sixth and final section presents concluding remarks.

II. The Structure of North American Production, Demand, and Income

Our model is calibrated to a detailed three-country social accounting matrix estimated for the year 1988 for Canada, the United States, and Mexico, which is described in greater detail in Reinert, Roland-Holst, and Shiells (1993). The first step in its construction was to transform the macroaccounts of the three countries into a North American macroeconomic SAM. This was accomplished using data from Statistics Canada (March 1991 and April 1991),

Reinert and Roland-Holst (1992), and Estados Unidos Mexicanos (1990). Trilateral trade flows were taken from U.S. Department of Commerce (1988), Globerman and Bader (1991), and U.S. International Trade Commission (1991). Factor service and capital flows were taken from U.S. Department of Commerce (1991). The second stage in the construction of the North American SAM was estimation of detailed sectoral accounts, including value added, domestic final demand, import, export, and interindustry transactions. Each of these were estimated for 26 production sectors. For value added, this was done using 1988 Canadian input-output accounts from Statistics Canada, 1988 U.S. data from Reinert and Roland-Holst (1992), and 1988 and 1985 Mexican data from Estados Unidos Mexicanos (1990) and Sobarzo (1992), respectively. For Canada, domestic final demand was taken from the 1988 Canadian input-output accounts. For the United States, sectoral domestic final demands were taken directly from Reinert and Roland-Holst (1992); for Mexico, these were estimated based on 1985 shares from Sobarzo (1992). Sectoral trade flows were estimated with SITC trade data from the United Nations, while domestic sectoral flows were estimated from individual country sources. Canadian interindustry flows for 1988 were rebalanced slightly to row and column controls calculated from the new sectoral data using the RAS procedure.[1] U.S. interindustry flows were taken directly from Reinert and Roland-Holst (1992). Mexican interindustry flows from Sobarzo (1992) were updated from 1985 using row and column controls calculated with the estimated 1988 sectoral data and an RAS procedure.

Although the structural detail of the 90 × 90 three-country SAM is the essential information set for the AGE model, it is too large to be readily interpreted by inspection. In the following three tables, we summarize the data from the SAM in a more accessible format. This information on the general structure of production, demand, income, and trade in each country will facilitate understanding of the simulation results reported later in the chapter.

Table 2.1 presents structural information on the United States. For each of the 26 sectors and three aggregate sectoral categories (primary, manufacturing, and services), the base-year data for shares of gross output (column 1), value added (2), demand (3), exports (4), and imports (5) are given. These columns provide a snapshot of the sectoral composition of production, income, supply, demand, and trade in the United States. Services obviously dominate the production side of this economy, generating 63 percent of gross output and 77 percent of total value added. Manufacturing's share of gross output (31 percent) far exceeds its value-added share (19 percent) because of its higher degree of intermediate use. Demand includes imports, and these raise the overall share of manufactures while lowering that of services. U.S. exports constitute a higher share of output in agriculture (8 percent) and manufacturing (10 per-

Table 2.1. *Structure of Production, Demand, Income, and Trade for the United States, 1988 (all figures in percentages)*

		1 X	2 VA	3 D	4 E	5 M	6 VL/Vk	7 E/X	8 M/D	9 Mr/M	10 Mc/M	11 Mu/M	12 Mm/M	13 Er/E	14 Ec/E	15 Eu/E	16 Em/E
1	Agriculture	2	2	3	5	1	55	10	7	75	11	0	15	87	6	0	7
2	Mining	0	0	0	1	0	180	18	30	85	9	0	5	47	51	0	2
3	Petroleum	3	2	4	2	7	28	4	29	70	20	0	10	88	8	0	4
	All Primary	5	4	6	9	9	56	8	20	72	18	0	10	82	13	0	6
4	Food Processing	3	2	6	3	2	130	4	5	84	12	0	5	80	13	0	6
5	Beverages	1	0	1	0	0	149	1	9	81	11	0	8	83	14	0	2
6	Tobacco	0	0	0	1	1	41	9	4	94	3	0	4	100	0	0	0
7	Textiles	1	1	1	1	1	294	4	10	90	7	0	2	55	34	0	11
8	Apparel	1	1	2	0	2	312	1	35	96	2	0	2	60	12	0	28
9	Leather	0	0	0	0	1	137	3	67	98	0	0	2	16	47	0	37
10	Paper	2	2	3	3	1	211	5	9	33	64	0	3	72	20	0	8
11	Chemical	2	1	3	8	4	109	15	12	91	3	0	7	84	12	0	4
12	Rubber	2	1	2	4	2	240	14	13	88	9	0	4	84	10	0	6
13	NonMetMinProd	1	1	2	1	3	298	3	17	95	4	0	0	58	37	0	5
14	Iron and Steel	1	0	2	1	3	403	16	19	86	12	0	2	90	7	0	4
15	NonFerMetals	3	2	4	3	4	485	5	16	68	24	0	7	17	67	0	15
16	WoodMetal Prod	1	1	3	1	3	310	3	13	67	27	0	6	67	27	0	6
17	NonElecMach	2	2	3	6	6	359	14	24	87	11	0	2	45	41	0	14
18	ElectricalMach	4	3	6	11	17	274	13	33	88	5	0	8	76	13	0	11
19	TransportEqp	5	2	7	16	12	274	17	31	57	39	0	4	59	38	0	3
20	Other Manufact	1	1	2	2	7	154	8	39	90	7	0	3	73	24	0	2
	All Manufactures	31	19	46	63	71	170	10	20	78	18	0	5	69	24	0	7
21	Construction	7	5	9	0	0	622	0	0	0	0	0	0	100	0	0	0
22	Electricity	4	4	4	0	0	42	0	29	100	0	0	0	100	0	0	0
23	Commerce	11	13	7	10	11	258	4	0	0	0	0	0	100	0	0	0
24	TransptCommun	5	6	4	6	6	173	6	18	100	0	0	0	100	0	0	0
25	FinInsRlEstate	14	16	9	6	3	43	2	3	100	0	0	0	100	0	0	0
26	OtherServices	24	33	15	6	1	366	1	0	100	0	0	0	100	0	0	0
	All Services	63	77	48	28	20	267	2	4	100	0	0	0	100	0	0	0
	Economy-wide	100	100	100	100	100	240	5	13	81	15	0	4	79	16	0	5

Notes: Columns 1–5 contain totals, and columns 6–16 contain denominator-weighted averages. The letters r, c, u, and m in columns 9–16 denote the rest of the world, Canada, the United States, and Mexico, respectively.

cent) than in services (2 percent), whereas the majority of imports are in manufacturing (71 percent).

Column 6 lists the ratios of labor to capital value added in percentage terms, and these vary widely across sectors. Agriculture has a weighted average of 56 percent labor to capital value added, while manufacturing spends nearly twice as much on labor as capital and services two and a half times as much. Ferrous metals (sector 14) are dominated by returns to labor, which get over ten times the value added accruing to capital in 1988. Value-added ratios in services vary widely, from lows of 42 and 43 percent in the capital-intensive electricity and finance sectors to over 600 percent in construction.

Column 7 presents measures of overall trade dependence, and Column 8 lists exports as a share of gross output and imports as a share of total demand. Generally speaking, average sectoral import dependence is greater than export dependence in 1988. The U.S. economy exports only 5 percent of gross output overall but imports 13 percent of total demand. The most export-intensive sectors in the current aggregation are mining (18 percent), transport equipment (17 percent), iron and steel (16 percent), and chemicals (15 percent). Together these sectors account for 28 percent of exports (column 4). The most import-dependent sectors are leather goods (67 percent), other manufactures (39 percent), apparel (35 percent), and electrical machinery (33 percent), together accounting for 31 percent of all imports (column 5).

The last eight columns of Table 2.1 contain import (9–12) and export (13–16) shares for each trading partner in total imports or exports. It is apparent from columns 9 and 13 that the United States relies upon markets outside North America for most of its import supply and export demand, with economywide averages of 81 percent for imports and 79 percent for exports. Thus, the potential for trade diversion by the United States in response to North American economic integration may be considerable. The United States and Canada do, however, maintain the world's largest bilateral trade relationship, with U.S.-Japan trade in second place, and U.S. trade shares with respect to its northern neighbor are significant in many sectors. About two-thirds (64 percent) of U.S. paper imports and 39 percent of transport equipment imports come from Canada. Canada in turn buys two-thirds of U.S. nonferrous metal product exports, over half (51 percent) of its mining exports, and over one-third of its exports of leather (47 percent), nonelectric machinery (41 percent), transport equipment (38 percent), nonmetal mineral products (37 percent), and textiles (34 percent). Generally speaking, the United States had significantly higher export dependence on Canada than import dependence under 1988 protection patterns.

United States' trade dependence on Mexico is generally lower than its dependence on Canada, as would be expected given the relative sizes of the three economies. Import dependence averages only 10 percent in primary sectors and 5 percent in manufacturing (column 12) but is as high as 15 percent in agriculture and 8 percent in beverages. As an export market, Mexico is more attractive to some U.S. sectors (column 16), although the averages for primary and manufacturing are only 6 and 7 percent, respectively. U.S. leather producers direct 37 percent of their exports to Mexico, and 28 percent of U.S. apparel exports were destined there in 1988. The lower economywide averages for U.S.-Mexico trade shares indicate that considerable scope may exist for trade creation within, and diversion to, a North American customs union.

Table 2.2 presents comparable structural information for Canada, and close inspection reveals interesting contrasts with its main trading partner. Canada's economy is more concentrated in primary (8 percent) and manufacturing (38 percent) than the United States, with significantly greater relative shares for mining, paper, and transport equipment and less concentration on service sector activities. The value-added distribution also reflects this but is again skewed toward services. Canadian demand exhibits similar compositional differences, and exports are even more primary and manufacturing dependent than demand. Canada is more than twice as export dependent (13 percent) as the United States, nearly three-quarters (73 percent) of its exports are in manufacturing, and it has less than half the service export concentration (13 percent) of the United States.

The ratio of labor to capital value added in Canada varies significantly from comparable sectors in the United States. In many cases (for example, mining, petroleum, and construction), this may be due to differing products or technologies, but the differences here are generally greater than one might reasonably expect from these sources alone.[2] Broad sectoral and economywide averages are more similar, but labor still receives substantially more in Canadian primary and manufacturing sectors and less in services.

Generally, Canada appears to be about twice as trade dependent as the United States, with 13 percent of output going to exports and 25 percent of demand met by imports. Further, over half of both its import (56 percent) and export (61 percent) activity was with the United States. This represents almost fourfold greater bilateral dependence on the part of Canada. In some sectors, the United States holds a dominant or near monopoly/monopsony position in Canadian trade. Examples of the former are Canadian import market shares of over 70 percent in agriculture, mining, paper, rubber, nonferrous metals, wood and metal products, nonelectrical machinery, and transport equipment. The United States also buys more than three-quarters of Canadian exports of petroleum, beverages, apparel, iron and steel, electrical machinery, and other manufactures.

Nearly three-quarters of all Canadian manufacturing goods are directed to the U.S. market, indicating quite limited scope for bilateral trade diversion on the part of Canada as a result of North American economic integration. Indeed,

Table 2.2. *Structure of Production, Demand, Income, and Trade for Canada, 1988 (all figures in percentages)*

	1 X	2 VA	3 D	4 E	5 M	6 VL/Vk	7 E/X	8 M/D	9 Mr/M	10 Mc/M	11 Mu/M	12 Mm/M	13 Er/E	14 Ec/E	15 Eu/E	16 Em/E
1 Agriculture	3	3	4	4	1	53	17	9	26	0	72	2	99	0	0	1
2 Mining	2	3	1	3	1	91	20	91	17	0	80	4	92	0	7	1
3 Petroleum	3	2	4	7	6	60	28	18	77	0	21	2	4	0	96	0
All Primary	8	8	9	14	7	68	22	20	45	0	53	3	50	0	50	0
4 Food Processing	4	2	6	2	3	174	8	13	50	0	49	1	52	0	46	2
5 Beverages	1	1	1	0	0	111	8	16	83	0	14	3	15	0	85	0
6 Tobacco	0	0	0	0	0	65	4	3	48	0	52	0	75	0	25	0
7 Textiles	1	1	1	1	2	272	11	43	50	0	49	1	50	0	50	1
8 Apparel	1	1	1	0	4	431	5	33	93	0	7	0	25	0	75	0
9 Leather	0	0	0	0	2	648	6	57	77	0	23	0	84	0	16	1
10 Paper	4	4	4	12	1	172	39	15	18	0	82	0	42	0	58	0
11 Chemical	2	2	3	1	4	94	4	44	32	0	67	0	45	0	55	0
12 Rubber	1	1	1	1	1	385	17	38	22	0	78	0	36	0	63	0
13 NonMetMinProd	1	1	2	1	1	156	13	34	39	0	60	1	72	0	27	2
14 Iron and Steel	1	1	2	2	2	302	15	26	54	0	45	0	20	0	78	0
15 NonFerMetals	1	1	1	3	2	121	32	36	21	0	78	1	32	0	68	2
16 WoodMetal Prod	4	3	5	8	3	388	24	23	28	0	71	0	35	0	65	0
17 NonElecMach	3	1	5	6	7	279	24	59	26	0	72	2	52	0	47	0
18 ElectricalMach	3	2	5	4	4	270	19	51	32	0	66	2	27	0	72	1
19 TransportEqp	9	3	15	31	6	314	44	42	18	0	81	1	6	0	93	0
20 OtherManufact	1	3	2	2	10	358	20	51	56	0	43	1	23	0	77	0
AllManufactures	38	24	52	73	54	251	25	36	31	0	68	1	26	0	74	0
21 Construction	9	9	8	0	0	351	0	0	0	0	0	0	0	0	0	0
22 Electricity	2	4	1	1	0	41	4	4	100	0	0	0	100	0	0	0
23 Commerce	11	18	5	3	2	340	4	4	100	0	0	0	100	0	0	0
24 TransptCommun	7	8	6	6	5	185	10	9	100	0	0	0	100	0	0	0
25 FinInsRlEstate	8	10	6	1	13	168	1	30	100	0	0	0	100	0	0	0
26 OtherServices	17	20	13	3	18	71	2	15	100	0	0	0	100	0	0	0
AllServices	54	68	39	13	39	203	3	11	100	0	0	0	100	0	0	0
Economy-wide	100	100	100	100	100	204	13	25	43	0	56	1	39	0	61	0

Notes: Columns 1–5 contain totals, and columns 6–16 contain denominator-weighted averages. The letters r, c, u, and m in columns 9–16 denote the rest of the world, Canada, the United States, and Mexico, respectively.

Mexico may have more potential as a diversionary source of Canadian imports and destination for exports. As of 1988, Mexico only met 1 percent of Canada's import needs and bought a negligible amount of the latter's exports. These levels are well below their potential, as indicated by the observed Mexican shares in U.S. trade.

The Mexican economy is summarized in Table 2.3, and these figures clearly delineate structural differences vis-à-vis its northern trading partners. As one might expect, Mexico is two to three times more primary intensive than the more industrialized countries. Its manufacturing concentration is more comparable largely because of a relatively smaller service economy. Demand is also more oriented toward subsistence and manufacturing necessities (for example, food processing) and less toward services.

Trade shares are also consistent with intuition about Mexico's comparative advantage, with almost half (44 percent) of exports from primary sectors and 87 percent of imports in manufacturing. One conspicuous but similarly intuitive difference is the ratio of labor to capital value added, which in some sectors is an order of magnitude less than in the more affluent countries. Mexico is generally more trade dependent overall than the United States but less so than Canada, with 12 percent exports in gross output and 24 percent imports in total demand. The sectoral patterns of this dependence vary considerably from the other two countries, with much greater primary export dependence and more variation in manufacturing import dependence.

Although Mexico exhibits U.S. bilateral trade dependence comparable to Canada, its composition is quite different. The United States has an even more dominant position in selected Mexican manufacturing sectors than in Canadian ones, with a more than 80 percent share in six Mexican import markets and nine Mexican export markets. Overall, 81 percent of Mexican manufacturing exports went to the United States in 1988. Again, this implies that trade diversion as a result of increased economic integration is more likely within, rather than from outside, the North American region.

The structural data reviewed in this section provide considerable detail on the three domestic economies and their trade linkages, and the impressions given are generally consistent with what one would expect. We see the United States at the center of a regional economy, the largest and most self-sufficient member. Canada shares many attributes as a relatively affluent and industrialized country but exhibits considerably more bilateral trade dependency and less diversity in production and trade structure. Mexico is the most distinctive of the three, with a large subsistence sector, low value-added shares for labor across the economy, even higher trade dependency, and less diversity.

All these structural features will have important implications for the adjustment patterns ensuing from North American economic integration. Even this detailed information cannot be considered in isolation, however, because

Table 2.3. *Structure of Production, Demand, Income, and Trade for Mexico, 1988 (all figures in percentages)*

	1 X	2 VA	3 D	4 E	5 M	6 Vl/Vk	7 E/X	8 M/D	9 Mr/M	10 Mc/M	11 Mu/M	12 Mm/M	13 Er/E	14 Ec/E	15 Eu/E	16 Em/E
1 Agriculture	8	8	8	3	8	23	5	22	43	2	55	0	9	3	87	0
2 Mining	1	2	1	3	2	44	26	28	69	4	27	0	77	11	11	0
3 Petroleum	8	3	11	38	2	12	61	5	42	0	58	0	72	0	28	0
All Primary	17	13	21	44	13	23	32	13	46	2	52	0	67	1	31	0
4 FoodProcessing	8	6	12	3	7	19	4	10	53	3	44	0	43	4	53	0
5 Beverages	1	1	2	1	1	30	7	6	91	0	9	0	3	5	92	0
6 Tobacco	0	0	0	0	0	31	5	0	0	0	100	0	41	0	59	0
7 Textiles	1	1	2	1	1	43	7	19	18	1	81	0	42	10	48	0
8 Apparel	1	1	2	1	0	35	14	15	12	0	88	0	3	1	96	0
9 Leather	1	1	1	1	0	53	9	15	0	0	100	0	6	1	93	0
10 Paper	2	2	2	1	3	27	8	41	27	3	70	0	10	1	90	0
11 Chemical	4	3	6	4	11	29	14	32	54	0	46	0	33	1	66	0
12 Rubber	1	1	1	1	1	38	11	49	13	1	86	0	5	0	95	0
13 NonMetMinProd	1	2	2	0	1	25	11	17	41	2	57	0	82	11	8	0
14 Iron and Steel	2	1	3	1	14	37	3	53	79	1	19	0	26	4	70	0
15 NonFerMetals	1	1	1	2	3	28	7	39	24	0	76	0	6	1	94	0
16 WoodMetal Prod	3	1	4	3	11	34	29	24	35	0	64	0	3	2	95	0
17 NonElecMach	1	1	4	3	8	41	16	85	30	1	69	0	9	22	69	0
18 ElectricalMach	4	1	6	19	8	51	65	70	19	0	81	0	8	3	89	0
19 TransportEqp	5	2	7	12	22	41	31	54	58	2	41	0	20	4	76	0
20 OtherManufact	1	1	2	3	5	23	34	39	74	0	26	0	11	3	86	0
AllManufactures	40	25	58	56	87	31	17	37	40	1	59	0	15	4	81	0
21 Construction	6	4	8	0	0	184	0	0	0	0	0	0	0	0	0	0
22 Electricity	1	2	1	0	0	50	0	0	0	0	0	0	0	0	0	0
23 Commerce	15	25	0	0	0	23	0	0	0	0	0	0	0	0	0	0
24 TransptCommun	5	8	4	0	0	39	0	0	0	0	0	0	0	0	0	0
25 FinInsRlEstate	5	8	2	0	0	29	0	0	0	0	0	0	0	0	0	0
26 OtherServices	10	16	5	0	0	116	0	0	0	0	0	0	0	0	0	0
AllServices	43	63	21	0	0	60	0	0	0	0	0	0	0	0	0	0
Economy-wide	100	100	100	100	100	48	12	24	41	1	58	0	38	3	59	0

Notes: Columns 1–5 contain totals, and columns 6–16 contain denominator-weighted averages. The letters r, c, u, and m in columns 9–16 denote the rest of the world, Canada, the United States, and Mexico, respectively.

market conduct in every one of the countries and sectors will also have a decisive influence on the adjustment process. It is on this point where the specification in the AGE model can make a significant contribution, particularly in light of the U.S. market share dominance in many Canadian and Mexican sectors.

III. North American Patterns of Import Protection and Relative Prices

Any attempt to evaluate regional economic liberalization must begin with a clear appraisal of existing barriers to trade as well as price differentials that arise from these and other sources. Most general equilibrium studies of trade reform or liberalization focus on the removal of ad valorem–equivalent price distortions against imports.[3] This is also the primary focus in the present study, and in this section we summarize the estimates of North American protection levels used to calibrate our AGE model.[4]

In addition to tariffs, a wide variety of other import restraints exert themselves upon bilateral trade flows in North America. Nontariff barriers (NTBs) to imports include a variety of real and implicit (contingent) quantity constraints, content requirements, rules of origin, and supervisory measures such as registration and inspection requirements. In a separate paper, Roland-Holst, Reinert, and Shiells (1992) have estimated the composite ad valorem effect of these trade barriers within North America, and part of these results are presented in Table 2.4. Our estimates are a composite of three sources: the observed sectoral tariff collection rates in the 1988 North American SAM, independent sectoral estimates by other researchers, and the combined UNCTAD-GATT data base of four-digit SITC trade control measures, the latter containing information up through 1989. Table 2.4 details two protection levels for each trade flow, tariffs and the estimated composite (tariff and nontariff) ad valorem import price distortion.

As the first nine columns indicate, North American tariff protection is relatively low by world standards. Some sectoral flows are significantly distorted, at least in nominal terms; that is, they make no allowance for protection of intermediates. As the trade-weighted averages in the table indicate, however, these constitute a relatively small share of total trade. When other import control measures are taken into account, both the composition and economy-wide averages of import distortions increase significantly for all three economies. This information not only reveals higher levels of North American protection but also indicates how narrow the basis may be for current NAFTA negotiations if NTBs are not addressed. The averages reveal a few noteworthy general features. First, Canadian exporters face the highest barriers from their regional trading partners. Both the United States and Mexico tend to discriminate more against Canada than against the rest of the world and least so against

Table 2.4. *Ad Valorem Estimates for North American Import Protection (percentages and averages are weighted by domestic sectoral output)*

	Tariff Rates USA			Canada			Mexico			Composite Protection Rates USA			Canada			Mexico		
	ROW	Canada	Mexico	ROW	USA	Mexico	ROW	USA	Canada	ROW	Canada	Mexico	ROW	USA	Mexico	ROW	USA	Canada
1 Agriculture	1	1	2	0	0	0	0	0	0	24	14		42	81	99	84	84	100
2 Mining	0	1	6	1	1	0	0	1	0	4	6		37	1	0	0	2	0
3 Petroleum	1	0	0	0	0	0	1	2	0	92	65		98	25	7	86	89	0
All Primary	1	1	2	0	0	0	0	1	0	77	60	20	86	28	31	69	79	75
4 Food Processing	4	2	6	4	4	5	1	3		27	23	78	58	58	35	95	101	82
5 Beverages	3	3	2	35	35	35	0	0	0	97	97	35	35	35	35	100	100	0
6 Tobacco	10	17	8	8	8	12	0	0	0	21	81	0	8	8	0	100	100	0
7 Textiles	10	6	7	12	12	20	3	2	2	51	6	103	85	79	12	3	3	0
8 Apparel	19	9	16	18	18		5	1	1	19	9	20	18	18	20	5	2	0
9 Leather	9	22	5	13	14	0	0	2	0	9	22	39	105	103	39	2	3	0
10 Paper	1	0	2	4	4	0	2	3	3	1	0	0	5	4	0	64	66	0
11 Chemical	5	17	2	5	5	8	2	1	0	7	18	8	14	12	8	9	7	87
12 Rubber	6	10	4	7	7	8	4	8	0	11	17	0	9	4	0	4	1	9
13 NonMetMinProd	6	1	0	5	5	8	1	4	0	9	1	11	19	14	11	7	11	0
14 Iron and Steel	4	3	3	4	4	0	2	4	0	83	48	95	86	74	95	47	43	0
15 NonFer Metals	1	1	0	2	2	6	4	3	0	2	1	0	1	2	0	2	4	0
16 WoodMetal Prod	4	1	2	6	6	2	5	3	0	13	5	9	16	14	9	4	3	0
17 NonElec Mach	3	1	1	2	2	6	7	7	0	11	2	9	3	2	9	7	4	0
18 Electrical Mach	3	2	3	4	4	4	1	2	0	13	7	2	5	6	2	13	8	5
19 Transport Eqp	3	0	2	7	7	7	2	10	0	71	65	83	68	57	83	13	19	15
20 Other Manufact	4	1	3	4	4	5	10	2	5	28	3	17	30	17	17	3	11	1
All Manufactures	5	1	3	7	3	5	3	2	2	28	38	32	10	36	31	25	15	26
21 Construction	0	0	0	0	0	0	0	0	0	0	0	0	0	0	0	0	0	0
22 Electricity	0	0	0	0	0	0	0	0	0	0	0	0	0	0	0	0	0	0
23 Commerce	0	0	0	0	0	0	0	0	0	0	0	0	0	0	0	0	0	0
24 TransptCommun	0	0	0	0	0	0	0	0	0	0	0	0	0	0	0	0	0	0
25 FinInsRlEstate	0	0	0	0	0	0	0	0	0	0	0	0	0	0	0	0	0	0
26 Other Services	0	0	0	0	0	0	0	0	0	0	0	0	0	0	0	0	0	0
All Services	0	0	0	0	0	0	0	0	0	0	0	0	0	0	0	0	0	0
Economy-wide	3	1	3	4	2	4	2	2	2	32	41	28	28	33	31	30	22	36

Source: Roland-Holst, Reinert, and Shiells (1992).

each other. These two (the United States and Mexico) are also very protectionist in primary sectors on average, whereas Canada and Mexico are most protectionist against agricultural imports. The United States maintains the highest average import barriers against its neighbors of the three, and Canada maintains the lowest.

Once initial trade distortions have been calibrated, researchers are usually content to remove them and evaluate the adjustment process under various behavioral assumptions about the domestic and international economies. Although this may be appropriate in single-country analysis, it may not be so in a multicountry setting. Trade barriers are not the only source of divergence in prices between countries, particularly for goods or services with limited tradability. To assume that goods are homogeneous and prices are equalized across North America, except for ad valorem trade distortions, is to neglect a large body of evidence indicating substantial and persistent differences in purchasing power parity (PPP) values for individual Canadian, U.S., and Mexican goods and services. Likewise, differences in prices for goods with limited tradability between countries translate into differences in relative prices of tradables and nontradables within countries. Ultimately, the relative and absolute levels of sectoral demand and supply are distorted by assuming intercountry price homogeneity. If such price differentials are assumed away in the calibration procedure by choosing units so that all prices are unity in the base case, estimates of general equilibrium effects of trade liberalization can be seriously distorted. To account for such intercountry differences in relative prices, we have calibrated the general equilibrium model using base-year differentials in domestic relative prices for the three North American economies. We believe that this represents an innovation in the applied general equilibrium trade-modeling literature.

Using 1988 data based on Summers and Heston (1991), we compiled the sectoral indices of PPP prices reported in Table 2.5. The PPP price indices in this table are given in terms of unitary 1977 U.S. prices for the same sectors. This choice of sector-specific price indices allows us to correct for sectoral size distortions that would arise from assuming price equalization. These values were in turn calibrated into the base prices of the AGE model described in the next section. It is apparent from casual inspection that, even at this relatively aggregated level of 26 sectors, prices across the three North American economies are far from identical. Assuming such price homogeneity (except for import distortions) could thus seriously distort the relative magnitudes of demand and supply and, hence, their response to multilateral trade liberalization. Consider the Mexican commerce sector, for example, which accounts for 25 percent of the country's total value added, according to Table 2.3. Comparing its PPP price (.41) with the Mexican average (.84) indicates that,

Table 2.5. *Domestic Prices Based on Purchasing Power Comparison*
(averages are weighted by domestic sectoral output)

		USA	Canada	Mexico
1	Agriculture	1.30	1.28	0.87
2	Mining	0.83	0.81	0.86
3	Petroleum	1.45	1.25	1.79
	All Primary	1.35	1.17	1.29
4	Food Processing	1.22	1.24	0.92
5	Beverages	1.23	1.08	1.12
6	Tobacco	1.49	1.60	0.87
7	Textiles	1.14	0.90	0.75
8	Apparel	1.02	1.08	0.66
9	Leather	0.91	1.18	0.61
10	Paper	0.98	1.25	0.76
11	Chemical	0.89	1.03	0.81
12	Rubber	1.48	2.66	0.99
13	NonMetMinProd	1.00	1.00	1.00
14	Iron and Steel	1.00	1.00	1.00
15	NonFer Metals	1.00	1.00	1.00
16	WoodMetal Prod	1.28	0.77	0.45
17	NonElec Mach	1.18	1.10	1.40
18	Electrical Mach	1.22	1.12	1.56
19	Transport Eqp	1.26	1.17	1.66
20	Other Manufact	1.08	1.22	0.94
	All Manufactures	1.16	1.14	1.04
21	Construction	1.15	1.21	0.72
22	Electricity	1.02	0.40	0.94
23	Commer	0.82	1.11	0.41
24	TransptCommun	0.79	1.20	0.28
25	FinInsRlEstate	1.10	1.55	0.48
26	Other Services	0.79	1.38	0.54
	All Services	0.91	1.14	0.56
	Economy-wide	1.01	1.21	0.84

Source: Summers and Heston (1991).

by international valuation, commerce represents over half of Mexico's real value added.

IV. An Applied General Equilibrium Model for Trade Policy Analysis

The three-country applied general equilibrium (AGE) model described here is in most respects typical of comparative static, multisectoral, economywide models in use today.[5] Generally speaking, all these models simulate price-directed resource allocation in commodity and factor markets. They maintain detailed information on sectoral prices, output, trade, consumption, and factor use in a consistent framework that also accounts for aggregates such as income, employment, revenue, and so on. The present model (the analytics of which are summarized in Table 2.6) differs from the mainstream of AGE specifications in three important ways. First, it is a detailed three-country model, so domestic supply, demand, and bilateral trade for the United States, Canada, and Mexico are fully endogenous at a 26-sector level of aggregation.[6] The three countries maintain six pairs of bilateral sectoral trade flows between them, governed by six endogenous price systems (U.S.-Canada, U.S.-Mexico, and Canada-Mexico imports and exports). Six more trade flows and price systems are also endogenous [U.S.-ROW (rest of the world), Canada-ROW, and Mexico-ROW, imports and exports].

A second important feature of the model is its differentiated product specification of the demand and supply for tradable commodities. Domestic demand comprises goods that are differentiated by origin (domestic goods, imports from North American trading partners, and imports from ROW), and domestic production is supplied to differentiated destinations (domestic market, exports to North American trading partners, and exports to ROW). Similar devices appear elsewhere in the AGE literature; the present model uses a nonnested CES specification for demand and a nonnested CET for supply.[7]

Third, the AGE model allows for some appraisal of the role of industry structure and conduct in determining the ultimate effects of trade policy. A number of authors have demonstrated that the presence of scale economies, realized or unrealized, can significantly influence the gains from trade liberalization.[8] The direction and magnitude of this influence generally depends upon the direction and magnitude of the induced scale adjustments, with aggregate efficiency and welfare, on the one hand, and average costs, on the other hand, moving in opposite directions. The sign of average cost adjustment depends on the specification of industry conduct, which is partly a methodological and partly an empirical issue. The magnitude of cost adjustments is purely an empirical question, which depends on the shape of average cost curves.

Given the diversity of the domestic markets involved and the absence of a clear methodological consensus on modeling firm behavior, we have chosen a very simple and parsimonious specification of both structure and conduct. We hope this will facilitate interpretation of our results as general indicators of scale effects.

Increasing returns are specified with one parameter, the cost disadvantage ratio, which measures the share by which average total cost exceeds marginal cost: $(ATC - MC)/ATC$. This is in turn calibrated to an equivalent fixed cost for the observed output and factor use in each sector.[9] For firm conduct, two possibilities are considered. First, we assume that domestic firms are Cournot oligopolists that price according to the endogenous, perceived demand elasticity, but that free market entry and exit keep profits in each sector equal to zero.

Table 2.6. *Equations for the North American AGE Model*

Equations

Consumer Behavior (Linear Expenditure System)

$$P_{ij}^Q C_{ij} = P_{ij}^Q \mu_{ij} + s_{ij}(Y_j - \sum_i P_{ij}^Q \mu_{ij}) \quad \forall i, j \tag{2.1}$$

Cost Equations and Production (Constant Elasticity of Substitution with Leontief Intermediates)

$$F_{ij} = (r_j KF_{ij} + w_j LF_{ij})(n_{ij}/n0_{ij}) \quad \forall i, j \tag{2.2}$$

$$V_{ij} = (X_{ij}/a_{ij})[b_{ij}^{\phi_{ij}} w_j^{(1-\phi_{ij})} + (1-b_{ij})^{\phi_{ij}} r_j^{(1-\phi_{ij})}]^{1/(1-\phi_{ij})} \quad \forall i, j \tag{2.3}$$

$$T_{ij} = F_{ij} + V_{ij} + \sum_h P_{hj}^Q io_{hij} X_{ij} \quad \forall i, j \tag{2.4}$$

Factor Demands

$$L_{ij} = V_{ij}^{\phi_{ij}} X_{ij}^{(1-\phi_{ij})} b_{ij}^{\phi_{ij}} w_j^{-\phi_{ij}} a_{ij}^{(\phi_{ij}-1)} \quad \forall i, j \tag{2.5}$$

$$K_{ij} = V_{ij}^{\phi_{ij}} X_{ij}^{(1-\phi_{ij})} (1-b_{ij})^{\phi_{ij}} r_j^{-\phi_{ij}} a_{ij}^{(\phi_{ij}-1)} \quad \forall i, j \tag{2.6}$$

Factor Markets

$$\sum_i K_{ij} + \sum_i KF_{ij}(n_{ij}/n0_{ij}) = K_j \quad \forall j \tag{2.7}$$

$$w_j = w0_j \quad \forall j \tag{2.8}$$

Commodity Demands, Supplies, and Allocation of Traded Goods (Constant Elasticity of Substitution and Constant Elasticity Transformation)

$$Q_{ij} = \alpha_{ij}[\sum_k \beta_{ijk} D_{ijk}^{(\sigma_{ij}-1)/\sigma_{ij}}]^{\sigma_{ij}/(\sigma_{ij}-1)} \quad \forall i, j \tag{2.9}$$

Table 2.6. (*cont.*)

$$(D_{ijk}/D_{ijj}) = [(\beta_{ijk}/\beta_{ijj})(P^D_{ijj}/P^D_{ijk})]^{\sigma_{ij}} \quad \forall\, i,\, j,\, k \tag{2.10}$$

$$X_{ij} = \gamma_{ij}[\sum_k \delta_{ijk} S^{(\tau_{ij}+1)/\tau_{ij}}_{ijk}]^{\tau_{ij}/(\tau_{ij}+1)} \quad \forall\, i,\, j \tag{2.11}$$

$$(S_{ijk}/S_{ijj}) = [(\delta_{ijk}/\delta_{ijj})(P^S_{ijj}/P^S_{ijk})]^{-\tau_{ij}} \quad \forall\, i,\, j,\, k \tag{2.12}$$

Commodity Prices

$$P^Q_{ij}Q_{ij} = \sum_k P^D_{ijk}D_{ijk} \quad \forall\, i,\, j \tag{2.13}$$

$$P^X_{ij}X_{ij} = \sum_k P^S_{ijk}S_{ijk} \quad \forall\, i,\, j \tag{2.14}$$

$$P^D_{ijk} = (1+t_{ijk})(1+\rho_{ijk})er_j PW^D_{ijk} \quad \forall\, i,\, j,\, k \tag{2.15}$$

$$P^S_{ijk} = er_j PW^S_{ijk} \quad \forall\, i,\, j,\, k \tag{2.16}$$

$$PW^D_{ijk} = PW^S_{ikj} \quad \forall\, i,\, j,\, k \tag{2.17}$$

$$P^D_{ijj} = P^S_{ijj} \quad \forall\, i,\, j \tag{2.18}$$

$$PW^D_{ijR} = PW0^D_{ijR} \quad \forall\, i,\, j \tag{2.19}$$

$$PW^S_{ijR} = PW0^S_{ijR} \quad \forall\, i,\, j \tag{2.20}$$

Commodity Market Equilibrium

$$Q_{ij} = C_{ij} + \sum_h io_{ihj}X_{hj} \quad \forall\, i,\, j \tag{2.21}$$

$$D_{ijk} = S_{ikj} \quad \forall\, i,\, j,\, k \tag{2.22}$$

Table 2.6. (*cont.*)

Income and Government Revenue

$$YL_j = w_j \sum_i [LF_{ij}(n_{ij}/n0_{ij}) + L_{ij}] \quad \forall j \tag{2.23}$$

$$YK_j = r_j \sum_i [KF_{ij}(n_{ij}/n0_{ij}) + K_{ij}] \quad \forall j \tag{2.24}$$

$$RT_j = \sum_i \sum_k t_{ijk} er_j PW^D_{ijk} D_{ijk} \quad \forall j \tag{2.25}$$

$$RQ_j = \sum_i \sum_k \beta_{ijk}(1 + t_{ijk}) er_j PW^D_{ijk} D_{ijk} \quad \forall j \tag{2.26}$$

$$Y_j = YL_j + YK_j + RT_j + RQ_j + \sum_i \pi_{ij} \quad \forall j \tag{2.27}$$

Perfectly Competitive Behavior

$$P^D_{iij} = (V_{ij} + \sum_h P^Q_{hij} io_{hij} X_{ij})/X_{ij} \quad \forall i, j \tag{2.28}$$

Cournot Behavior

$$\pi_{ij} = P^X_{ij} X_{ij} - T_{ij} \quad \forall i, j \tag{2.28'}$$

$$\pi_{ij} = \pi 0_{ij} \quad \forall i, j \tag{2.29'}$$

$$\{P^D_{iij} - [(V_{ij} + \sum_h P^Q_{hij} io_{hij} X_{ij})/X_{ij}]\}/P^D_{iij} = \Omega_{ij}/(n_{ij}\epsilon^D_{ij}) \quad \forall i, j \tag{2.30'}$$

$$\Omega_{ij} = 1 \quad \forall i, j \tag{2.31'}$$

$$\epsilon^D_{ij} = \sigma_{ij} + \beta^{\sigma_{ij}}_{iij}(P^Q_{ij}/P^D_{ij})^{(\sigma_{ij}-1)}[(\mu_{ij}/Q_{ij})(s_{ij}-1) + (C_{ij}/Q_{ij}) - q_{ij}] \quad \forall i, j \tag{2.32'}$$

Table 2.6. (*cont.*)

══

Contestable Markets Behavior

$$P_{ij}^X = T_{ij}/X_{ij} \quad \forall i, j \tag{2.28''}$$

$$n_{ij} = n0_{ij} \quad \forall i, j \tag{2.29''}$$

Foreign Balance

$$\sum_{k \neq j} \sum_i (PW_{ijk}^S S_{ijk} - PW_{ijk}^D D_{ijk}) = 0 \quad \forall j \tag{2.33}$$

Sets

$I = \{1,...,26\}$ sectors
$J = \{Canada(C), Mexico(M), United States(U)\}$ North American countries
$K = \{C,M,U, Rest of World(R)\}$ world countries

Indices

$h, i \in I$
$j \in J$
$k \in K$

Quantity Variables

C_{ij} = final demand for composite consumption good i in country j

D_{ijk} = demand for good i in country j from source country k

K_{ij} = variable capital used in sector i of country j

L_{ij} = variable labor used in sector i of country j

n_{ij} = number of firms in sector i of country j

Q_{ij} = final plus intermediate demand for composite consumption good i in country j

S_{ijk} = supply of good i from country j to destination country k

X_{ij} = gross domestic output of sector i of country j

Price and Elasticity Variables

er_j = exchange rate in country j

P_{ijk}^D = domestic purchaser price of good i in country j demanded from country k

Table 2.6. *(cont.)*

P^Q_{ij} = domestic purchaser price of composite consumption good i in country j

P^S_{ijk} = domestic producer price of good i in country j supplied to destination country k

P^X_{ij} = domestic producer price of composite production good i in country j

PW^D_{ijk} = world price of good i in country j demanded from source country k

PW^S_{ijk} = world price of good i in country j supplied to destination country k

r_j = rental rate on capital in country j

w_j = wage rate in country j

ϵ^D_{ij} = perceived elasticity of final demand in sector i of country j

Ω_{ij} = conjectural variations parameter in sector i of country j

Nominal Variables

F_{ij} = fixed costs in sector i of country j

RQ_j = quota rents in country j

RT_j = tariff revenue in country j

T_{ij} = total costs in sector i of country j

V_{ij} = variable costs in sector i of country j

Y_j = income in country j

YL_j = labor income in country j

YK_j = capital income in country j

π_{ij} = profits in sector i of country j

Behavioral, Policy and Other Parameters

a_{ij} = intercept parameter in CES production function in sector i of country j

b_{ij} = share parameter in CES production function in sector i of country j

io_{ijh} = input of sector h needed per unit of sector i output in country j

K_j = total capital stock in country j

KF_{ij} = fixed capital in sector i of country j

LF_{ij} = fixed labor in sector i of country j

Table 2.6. (*cont.*)

$n0_{ij}$ = number of firms in benchmark equilibrium in sector i of country j

$PW0^D_{ijR}$ = world price of good i in country j demanded from the rest of the world in the benchmark equilibrium

$PW0^S_{ijR}$ = world price of good i in country j supplied to the rest of the world in the benchmark equilibrium

s_{ij} = consumption share for composite good i in country j

t_{ijk} = ad valorem tariff on imports of good i into country j from source country k

$w0_j$ = wage rate in country j in benchmark equilibrium

α_{ij} = intercept parameter in CES product aggregation function for sector i of country j

β_{ijk} = share parameter in CES product aggregation function for product i in country j from source country k

δ_{ijk} = share parameter in CET allocation function from sector i in country j to destination country k

γ_{ij} = intercept parameter in CET allocation function for sector i in country j

μ_{ij} = subsistence minimum for composite consumption good i in country j

$\pi0_{ij}$ = profits in sector i of country j in benchmark equilibrium

ϕ_{ij} = elasticity of substitution between variable labor and variable capital in sector i production in country j

ρ_{ijk} = ad valorem equivalent quota on imports of good i into country j from country k

σ_{ij} = elasticity of substitution among sources of product i in country j

τ_{ij} = elasticity of transformation among destinations for sector i of country j

---

In this case, efficiency gains depend on entry/exit behavior, and there is no direct correspondence between aggregate sectoral output and efficiency.

In the second case, we simply assume a contestable market form of monopolistic competition where firms price at average cost and remain fixed in number during the period under consideration. This implies that efficiency varies directly with industry output.[10] Our estimates of the magnitude of unrealized scale economies in the base case are obtained from a variety of sources and are reproduced in Table 2.7.

The North American AGE model was calibrated to the 1988 SAM discussed

Table 2.7. *Structural Parameter Estimates*

	CDR (Percent)			Phi			Sigma			Tau		
	USA	Canada	Mexico	USA	Canada	Mexico	USA	Canada	Mexico	USA	Canada	Mexico
1 Agriculture	0	0	0	0.680	0.768	0.680	1.500	1.500	2.250	3.786	3.786	3.786
2 Mining	5	5	5	0.900	0.950	0.900	1.062	1.062	0.781	1.050	1.050	1.050
3 Petroleum	10	10	8	0.861	0.861	0.861	0.660	0.660	0.580	0.892	0.892	0.892
4 Food Processing	18	18	12	0.710	1.100	0.710	0.889	0.889	1.007	0.752	0.752	0.752
5 Beverages	13	13	18	0.710	1.100	0.710	0.326	0.326	0.726	0.492	0.492	0.492
6 Tobacco	7	7	24	0.708	1.100	0.708	1.008	1.008	1.008	0.784	0.784	0.784
7 Textiles	9	9	14	0.900	1.100	0.900	0.918	0.918	1.022	0.394	0.394	0.394
8 Apparel	6	6	13	0.900	1.100	0.900	0.479	0.479	0.802	0.129	0.129	0.129
9 Leather	2	2	14	0.900	1.100	0.900	1.007	1.007	1.066	1.164	1.164	1.164
10 Paper	16	16	22	0.900	1.100	0.900	0.967	0.967	0.734	0.425	0.425	0.425
11 Chemical	12	12	19	0.960	1.100	0.960	0.903	0.903	0.702	0.367	0.367	0.367
12 Rubber	13	13	18	0.960	1.100	0.960	1.026	1.026	0.763	0.276	0.276	0.276
13 NonMetMinProd	25	25	16	0.901	1.100	0.901	1.152	1.152	0.826	0.216	0.216	0.216
14 Iron and Steel	14	14	13	0.740	1.100	0.740	0.931	0.931	0.716	0.424	0.424	0.424
15 NonFer Metals	14	14	20	0.740	1.100	0.740	0.825	0.825	0.663	0.499	0.499	0.499
16 WoodMetal Prod	9	9	14	0.811	0.811	0.811	0.888	0.888	0.594	0.541	0.541	0.541
17 NonElec Mach	8	8	9	0.740	0.740	0.740	1.012	1.012	0.694	0.379	0.379	0.379
18 Electrical Mach	8	8	28	0.867	0.867	0.867	1.035	1.035	0.705	0.311	0.311	0.311
19 Transport Eqp	10	10	27	0.740	0.740	0.740	0.982	0.982	0.679	1.010	1.010	1.010
20 Other Manufact	9	9	12	0.900	0.500	0.900	0.550	0.550	0.463	0.411	0.411	0.411
21 Construction	0	0	0	0.521	0.300	0.521	1.500	1.500	1.200	0.500	0.500	0.500
22 Electricity	0	0	0	0.800	0.300	0.800	1.500	1.500	1.200	0.500	0.500	0.500
23 Commerce	0	0	0	0.502	0.300	0.502	1.500	1.500	1.200	1.100	1.100	1.100
24 TransptCommun	0	0	0	0.800	0.800	0.800	1.500	1.500	1.200	1.100	1.100	1.100
25 FinInsRlEstate	0	0	0	0.800	0.800	0.800	1.500	1.500	1.200	1.100	1.100	1.100
26 Other Services	0	0	0	0.800	0.800	0.800	1.500	1.500	1.200	1.100	1.100	1.100

Notes: CDR is the cost disadvantage ratio taken from sources described in Roland-Holst, Reinert, and Shiells (1992). Phi is the elasticity of substitution between labor and capital taken from Reinert and Roland-Holst (1991) for the United States and Mexico and from Delorme and Lester (1990) for Canada. Sigma is the elasticity of substitution between imports and domestic competing goods taken from Shiells and Reinert (1993) for the United States and Canada and from Sobarzo (1992) for Mexico. Tau is the elasticity of transformation between domestic supply and exports taken from Reinert and Roland-Holst (1991).

in section II. Structural parameters of the model were obtained by calibration, direct estimation, or imputation from other sources. Share parameters, input-output coefficients, ad valorem taxes, and tariffs were calibrated from the SAM itself. Employment and capital stock data were obtained from official publications. The basic data source for behavioral parameters was a weighted aggregation of detailed parameters compiled for the United States by Reinert and Roland-Holst (1991). The U.S. parameters were applied to Canada and Mexico, except for those cases where alternatives were available. Elasticities of substitution between labor and capital for Canada were taken from Delorme and Lester (1990). Nonnested Armington elasticities for the United States and Canada were taken from Shiells and Reinert (1993) and for Mexico from Sobarzo (1992). Some of the important behavioral parameters are presented in Table 2.7.

V. Simulation Results

This section presents the results of a variety of simulation experiments with the North American model described above. We consider economic integration scenarios that entail the removal of tariff protection and nontariff barriers, with each North American trading partner maintaining its existing protection with respect to the rest of the world.[11] Our results indicate that all three countries could realize substantial gains from regional economic integration and that each economy would undergo significant shifts in its trade patterns. These simulations also make it apparent that the pattern of adjustment would vary significantly, depending upon how information about intercountry price differences and industry structure and conduct is incorporated.

In the presence of unrealized scale economies of the type described in the previous section, the welfare gains from North American trade liberalization can be magnified, but their scope and composition depend upon whether firms are Cournot oligopolists or price-taking competitors in contestable markets. Further, the effect of base-price differences can be particularly interesting. Calibration of base-price differentials has only a modest influence on the aggregate welfare effects of the various integration scenarios. In contrast, sectoral adjustments vary dramatically from those observed with respect to a homogeneous price base. The first result is due to the fact that, despite changes in base-relative prices, the resource endowments of each country and thus its overall potential to gain from trade are invariant with respect to the price calibration. Changes in the sectoral composition of real output, on the other hand, are extremely sensitive to the measurement of relative prices in the benchmark equilibrium.

Thus, the aggregate gains from economic liberalization are relatively easy to predict, while sectoral composition of those gains, as well as the process of structural adjustment which integration might entail, is more uncertain. Given the weight of evidence indicating price disparities between countries, it is unlikely that simulations based on homogeneous prices will reveal the course of economic adjustment with an acceptable degree of accuracy. Failing to do so may undermine the political sustainability of the integration process.

Description of the Simulation Experiments

The aggregate results below were obtained in a total of eight simulation experiments. First, we simulated economic integration as a removal of tariffs in a domestic industry regime of constant returns to scale and perfect competition. In experiment 1, domestic prices were assumed to be homogeneous (that is, equal to unity) in the base, while experiment 2 was identical except for the calibration of base prices to the PPP values in Table 2.5. Experiments 3 and 4 are analogous, except that they simulate removal of both tariff and nontariff protection (second half of Table 2.4) under constant returns and perfect competition. Experiments 5 and 6 are the homogeneous and calibrated price (respectively) simulations of removing all protection under increasing returns to scale with Cournot oligopoly pricing (see section IV) and costless domestic market entry and exit. The last two experiments (experiments 7 and 8) use the same price regimes, liberalization, and increasing returns to scale. In these two cases, however, firms price at average cost, as in contestable markets, and the number of firms in each domestic industry is fixed.

Before presenting the experimental results, a word about closure of the AGE model. For a simulation model of this type to be fully determined, assumptions must be made about the adjustment process in domestic factor markets, commodity markets, and the market for foreign exchange. In the experiments that follow, we assume that labor in all three countries is perfectly mobile between sectors and in excess supply in the aggregate. Thus, the domestic aggregate wage is fixed, and aggregate employment varies to meet demand.

In each domestic product market, we assume prices are normalized to a fixed numeraire price index weighted by the base composition of sectoral final demand. In half the experiments, we assume base prices are homogeneous and equal to unity in the base. In the other half, we use the purchasing power parity price comparison information in Table 2.5 to estimate adjusted levels of domestic demand and output. On the external accounts, we assume that ROW exchange rates are flexible while trade balances are fixed.[12]

Discussion of the experimental results is divided into two parts. Aggregate economywide results are discussed first, followed by more detailed examination of sectoral adjustments in a smaller number of liberalization experiments. In a disaggregated neoclassical model such as the one used here, the most interesting results are at the sectoral level, where the real structural adjustments and reallocations occur in response to policy changes. Aggregate results are of interest but tend to be more homogeneous. Because commercial policy is usually formulated from the bottom up, much of the discussion below is devoted to sectoral effects.

Aggregate Results

The aggregate results of eight experiments are summarized in Table 2.8. As described in the previous section, the top two blocks of numbers in the table correspond to four integration experiments each, under two types of base price calibration. The first set of four corresponds to homogeneous base prices, assumed to be unity in each country and sector, whereas the second set of simulations calibrated the PPP information from Table 2.5 into base prices. The bottom block of numbers in Table 2.8 contains the percent differences of the second set of four experiments with respect to the first, that is, the percent change in aggregate results due to calibrating base prices based on PPPs. It is immediately apparent that North American economic integration is

Table 2.8. *Aggregate Effects of North American Economic Integration (percentages)*

Homogeneous Prices:

	Experiment 1 CRTS, Tariffs Only			Experiment 3 CRTS, All Protection			Experiment 5 IRTS, Cournot			Experiment 7 IRTS, Contestable		
	USA	Canada	Mexico	USA	Canada	Mexico	USA	Canada	Mexico	USA	Canada	Mexico
1 EV Welfare	0.08	0.34	0.13	1.87	6.45	2.45	1.66	5.14	2.54	2.55	6.75	3.29
2 Real GDP	0.06	0.50	0.14	1.51	9.01	2.30	1.36	7.08	2.64	2.07	10.57	3.38
3 Employment	0.09	0.80	0.37	2.14	12.16	1.90	1.88	9.38	1.88	2.47	11.02	2.40
4 Rental Rate	0.10	0.93	0.45	2.44	14.49	5.18	2.50	13.76	5.79	3.40	20.74	6.57
5 Real Exch Rate	-0.10	0.73	-0.21	-0.47	5.30	-3.57	-0.34	3.73	-2.74	-1.04	6.89	-4.20
6 Total Imports	0.38	0.70	1.17	9.37	20.51	14.97	8.58	19.35	15.13	12.34	24.18	17.70
7 Total Exports	0.28	1.30	1.13	8.29	31.36	13.22	7.97	27.70	14.45	10.43	39.83	16.72
8 NAFTA Imports	1.37	1.34	1.57	37.18	29.95	21.34	34.53	28.51	21.35	46.44	35.07	23.82
9 NAFTA Exports	1.38	1.20	2.00	27.96	44.05	14.47	26.82	40.27	15.64	32.47	55.22	17.29
10 Import Diversion	0.28	0.71	0.46	8.19	8.86	6.25	7.62	8.65	6.11	9.82	9.91	5.84
11 Export Diversion	0.36	0.13	1.03	6.25	11.62	1.20	5.98	11.84	1.13	6.90	13.26	0.58
12 Employment Adj	0.01	0.06	0.17	0.72	3.78	5.02	0.46	1.93	4.71	0.71	3.22	5.21

Price Calibration Based on PPPs:

	Experiment 2 CRTS, Tariffs Only			Experiment 4 CRTS, All Protection			Experiment 6 IRTS, Cournot			Experiment 8 IRTS, Contestable		
	USA	Canada	Mexico	USA	Canada	Mexico	USA	Canada	Mexico	USA	Canada	Mexico
1 EV Welfare	0.08	0.36	0.15	1.65	6.61	2.52	1.53	5.79	2.71	2.06	6.55	2.92
2 Real GDP	0.06	0.56	0.08	1.15	10.00	1.90	1.01	9.15	2.14	1.39	11.20	2.25
3 Employment	0.09	0.87	0.34	1.86	13.22	1.63	1.63	11.35	1.58	1.95	11.67	1.58
4 Rental Rate	0.09	1.00	0.39	2.09	15.69	4.79	2.14	16.58	5.24	2.65	21.68	5.41
5 Real Exch Rate	-0.10	0.80	-0.43	-0.87	7.00	-4.68	-0.90	6.65	-4.80	-1.42	8.75	-5.69
6 Total Imports	0.36	0.69	1.02	8.56	19.19	13.08	8.49	18.82	13.40	10.66	21.62	14.27
7 Total Exports	0.25	1.34	0.85	7.05	31.13	10.56	6.87	30.91	11.41	8.25	38.26	11.66
8 NAFTA Imports	1.33	1.34	1.43	35.32	28.25	19.62	35.51	27.79	19.87	42.48	31.65	20.82
9 NAFTA Exports	1.34	1.19	1.84	26.26	42.18	12.67	25.95	42.31	13.05	29.16	51.20	13.54
10 Import Diversion	0.28	0.71	0.46	7.97	8.59	6.53	8.04	8.54	6.43	9.36	9.34	6.43
11 Export Diversion	0.36	0.17	1.17	6.17	10.14	2.15	6.13	10.48	1.63	6.68	11.27	1.88
12 Employment Adj	0.01	0.16	0.10	0.55	3.50	6.21	0.36	1.96	6.21	0.50	3.12	6.43

Percent Change using PPPs:

	Difference CRTS, Tariffs Only			Difference CRTS, All Protection			Difference IRTS, Cournot			Difference IRTS, Contestable		
	USA	Canada	Mexico	USA	Canada	Mexico	USA	Canada	Mexico	USA	Canada	Mexico
1 EV Welfare	0	6	15	-12	2	3	-8	13	7	-19	-3	-11
2 Real GDP	0	12	-43	-24	11	-17	-26	29	-19	-33	6	-33
3 Employment	0	9	-8	-13	9	-14	-13	21	-16	-21	6	-34
4 Rental Rate	-10	8	-13	-14	8	-8	-14	20	-9	-22	5	-18
5 Real Exch Rate	0	10	105	85	32	31	165	78	75	37	27	35
6 Total Imports	-5	-1	-13	-9	-6	-13	-1	-3	-11	-14	-11	-19
7 Total Exports	-11	3	-25	-15	-1	-20	-14	12	-21	-21	-4	-30
8 NAFTA Imports	-3	-1	-9	-5	-6	-8	3	-3	-7	-9	-10	-13
9 NAFTA Exports	-3	-1	-8	-6	-4	-12	-3	5	-17	-10	-7	-22
10 Import Diversion	0	0	2	-3	-3	4	6	-1	5	-5	-6	10
11 Export Diversion	0	31	14	-1	-13	79	3	-11	44	-3	-15	224
12 Employment Adj	0	0	-41	-24	-7	24	-22	2	32	-30	-3	23

beneficial to the regional economies in every case. Equivalent variation aggregate welfare gains vary from about 0.1 percent of base GDP to over 6 percent, depending upon the degree of liberalization and the extent of scale economies realized in the adjustment process but irrespective of the base price system. In every case, increases in aggregate employment and average rental rates are accompanied by extensive sectoral reallocation of labor and capital. Our factor market closure assumptions are somewhat restrictive, and a more likely result would be some combination of increased employment and wages on one hand and foreign capital inflows on the other. Trade for all three countries increases in each experiment, both within the region and with the rest of the world, with the former significantly outweighing the latter because of strong trade diversion effects.[13]

Comparison of experiments 1 and 3 (or 2 and 4) indicate dramatic differences in the implications of simple tariff removal and economic integration policies that would entail more comprehensive trade liberalization. The aggregate effects generally differ by more than an order of magnitude and, as inspection of Table 2.4 would suggest, the sectoral differences are more extreme both in level and composition. It is thus questionable whether the experience of tariff liberalization over the past few years gives reliable indications for those contemplating a more complete realization of the gains from North American economic integration. This is true of the magnitude of gains, of which tariff liberalization can give only a foretaste, and of the structural adjustments more complete integration would necessitate, about which tariff induced adjustments provide minimal guidance.

Experiments 5 and 7 (6 and 8) are companions to 3 (4), simulating more complete North American economic integration under increasing returns to scale. Judging from these, it is apparent that the aggregate effects of liberalization can differ considerably, depending upon the extent of unrealized scale economies and the conduct of domestic firms. If firm entry and exit is limited and pricing is contestable, the gains from integration can be up to 50 percent greater in some countries than under perfect competition. If entry and exit are unrestricted and Cournot pricing prevails, aggregate gains are reduced in most countries because "crowding in" by new market entrants drives incumbent firms up their average cost curves. This appears to be a serious problem in Canada, whose gains are eroded about 25 percent by inefficient market entry. The other two countries achieve comparable gains under Cournot to those they would enjoy with constant returns and perfect competition. Tariff removal under increasing returns was also simulated, but the results differed little from experiment 1 (2). Again, this occurs because North American tariffs are relatively low, and little in the way of scale adjustments was occasioned by their removal.

The ranking of countries by percentage aggregate gains from liberalization is of particular interest. As one might naturally expect, the United States gains the least because it is by far the largest and also the least trade dependent of the three. Our evidence (Table 2.4) also indicates that U.S. goods face lower import barriers than this country has erected against imports from its neighbors. Mexico gains substantially because of its smaller size, higher trade dependence, and relatively higher barriers against its exports to both the United States and Canada. The Canadian result may seem surprising at first sight. Results vary with the degree of liberalization and the specification of domestic market structure and conduct, but Canada generally enjoys two to three times its neighbor's gains from economic integration as a percentage of its own GDP. Closer inspection reveals two important reasons for this, however. First, Canada is the most trade dependent of the three, both in overall and bilateral terms. Second, Canada faces much higher barriers against its exports to either Mexico or the United States than it maintains against imports from these neighbors.

Trade diversion and creation play an important role in all the experiments, with regional trade increasing by a larger percentage in every case than total trade (rows 6–9). The diversion measures in rows 10 and 11 give a normalized index of the extent to which each country's composition of trade has changes between partners.[14] Because the countries have different trade shares, there is no natural correspondence between trade diversion and aggregate gains from trade.

The employment diversion index, item 12 in each block, gives an indication of the degree of domestic resource reallocation and structural adjustment induced by economic integration.[15] Generally speaking, the smaller the economy, the greater the induced adjustment, trade shares and prior protection being equal. Even though the latter are not equal, it appears that Mexico will experience at least five times the amount of structural adjustment as a result of integration as will the United States. Canadian adjustment will fall somewhere between the two in magnitude.

The aggregate results for different relative price calibrations are generally comparable. This is particularly the case for aggregate real variables, which differ by more than 10 percent in only a few experiments, and mainly when the underlying variation is small (as for the United States) in any case. Real exchange rate differences are most substantial, because they are correcting for larger domestic price disparities in experiments 2, 4, 6, and 8. Mexico, and Mexican exports in particular, appear to be relatively sensitive to the base-price calibration, because Mexican PPP prices are much more dispersed than in the other two countries and because Mexican domestic prices of exportables are lower.

The dramatic welfare increases estimated here for more comprehensive integration actually represent a lower bound, because we have not incorporated dynamic effects such as capital accumulation and learning effects in these comparative static experiments.[16] The removal of significant trade distortions stimulates efficiency, reducing real costs and prices, promoting domestic and external demand and employment, and ultimately fueling a broadly based expansion of domestic demand and real living standards in all three countries. The aggregate income effects of this are significant enough that nearly every sector expands in all three countries. Thus, economic integration appears to be individually rational for most sectors if it can be implemented multilaterally, although this may not have been true for unilateral liberalization. We turn next to a closer examination of sectoral results, with particular attention to the specification of base relative prices.

Sectoral Results

The aggregate simulation results are relatively homogeneous and intuitive because removing import distortions leads to expanded trade, intensified comparative advantage, and greater economywide and global efficiency, all of which contribute to aggregate welfare. All these factors contribute to aggregate welfare but rarely play a decisive role in the formulation of trade policy. It is individual sectors that seek import protection. For this reason, aggregate real income or equivalent variation measures have little to say about the real forces influencing trade policy. Beneath the smooth veneer of the social welfare function, dramatic sectoral adjustments and tradeoffs generally take place when trade policies are altered. This section discusses the consequences of North American economic integration for individual sectors, with particular reference to the calibration of base relative prices.

Tables 2.9–2.11 present sectoral results for experiment 3, economic integration by removal of all estimated import protection under constant returns to scale and perfect competition with homogeneous prices calibrated into the base situation. Tables 2.12–2.14 present comparable sectoral information for domestic prices that are calibrated to the national differences in purchasing power parity given in Table 2.5.

The results for the United States are almost uniformly expansionary, with real output growing several percentage points in most sectors. The strongest expansion is in the Transport Equipment sector (17.60 percent), which has high levels of prior protection but enjoys a sharp increase in domestic and external demand (mainly via trade diversion) that more than offsets increased imports. The combined (falling) price and (rising) income effects of integration increase domestic real consumption by 20.70 percent, while exports to the ROW, Canada, and Mexico increase by 21.70, 55.50, and 23.50 percent, respectively. Other leading U.S. sectors are ferrous and nonferrous metals, leather, nonelectric machinery, and textiles.

The experience of U.S. transport equipment is typical of other nonservice sectors. Although the expansionary effects of full liberalization bid up average

Table 2.9. *Sectoral Results for Full Liberalization, U.S. Experiment 3:*
Constant Returns to Scale, Homogeneous Base Prices (figures in
percentages)

		Real Output	Real Cons	LD	KD	Mr	Mc	Mm	Er	Ec	Em
1	Agriculture	2.40	0.60	3.80	1.60	2.30	15.70	38.50	-2.20	87.90	129.30
2	Mining	2.70	1.20	3.50	1.30	2.90	8.30	18.60	1.40	8.10	8.10
3	Petroleum	0.40	4.90	2.10	-0.09	-0.30	29.60	38.20	0.80	21.20	35.20
4	Food Processing	1.20	0.80	2.10	-0.06	1.30	12.80	8.70	0.60	22.00	37.90
5	Beverages	0.50	1.00	1.40	-0.70	0.70	21.80	19.10	-0.20	9.90	43.60
6	Tobacco	-0.60	-0.20	1.80	-1.20	1.70	35.10	10.40	-2.00	2.80	0.80
7	Textiles	3.40	1.20	4.00	1.70	2.90	9.60	43.50	2.70	40.90	5.70
8	Apparel	1.00	1.00	1.50	-0.70	1.20	7.30	4.70	0.40	8.50	4.40
9	Leather	5.30	2.10	6.30	4.00	2.10	19.00	1.30	4.70	55.80	7.40
10	Paper	1.30	1.00	2.00	-0.20	1.90	3.30	0.70	0.10	5.40	28.20
11	Chemical	1.90	1.20	3.00	0.80	2.20	14.40	4.00	1.00	12.10	6.80
12	Rubber	3.30	1.40	4.00	1.80	3.70	21.50	2.70	2.60	15.80	4.40
13	NonMetMinProd	2.10	1.10	2.60	0.40	2.50	6.20	27.80	1.20	14.90	9.90
14	Iron and Steel	5.40	3.80	5.60	3.30	4.00	41.10	42.40	5.10	54.50	25.30
15	NonFer Metals	4.70	2.20	5.20	2.90	4.50	8.90	-0.10	4.00	19.80	7.40
16	WoodMetal Prod	2.80	1.00	3.20	1.00	2.90	10.30	6.20	2.10	14.10	5.20
17	NonElec Mach	3.70	2.00	4.20	2.00	3.50	8.30	3.30	3.10	6.70	8.60
18	Electrical Mach	2.00	0.90	2.50	0.30	2.40	10.90	4.00	1.10	8.70	6.30
19	Transport Eqp	17.60	20.70	18.30	15.80	6.50	79.10	10.30	21.70	55.50	23.50
20	Other Manufact	1.90	1.80	2.80	0.60	2.10	5.20	10.80	0.70	12.00	9.70
21	Construction	1.00	1.00	1.30	-0.80	0.00	38.50	2.30	0.70	129.30	-2.20
22	Electricity	1.10	0.80	2.70	0.50	2.50	18.60	2.90	0.01	8.10	1.40
23	Commerce	1.00	0.50	1.70	-0.50	0.00	38.20	-0.30	-0.20	35.20	0.80
24	TransptCommun	1.10	0.90	1.90	-0.30	2.50	8.70	1.30	0.10	37.90	0.60
25	FinInsRlEstate	0.01	-0.30	1.50	-0.60	3.00	19.10	0.70	-2.20	43.60	-0.20
26	Other Services	0.90	0.80	1.40	-0.80	2.30	10.40	1.70	-0.07	0.80	-2.00

Table 2.10. *Sectoral Results for Full Liberalization, Canada. Experiment 3:*
Constant Returns to Scale, Homogeneous Base Prices (figures in
percentages)

		Real Output	Real Cons	LD	KD	Mr	Mu	Mm	Er	Eu	Em
1	Agriculture	-2.30	4.00	5.80	-6.40	-3.00	87.90	92.30	-3.50	15.70	155.50
2	Mining	10.00	0.04	17.20	3.80	13.70	8.10	4.60	7.30	8.30	9.70
3	Petroleum	17.30	9.10	26.60	12.10	7.20	21.20	14.00	17.90	29.60	0.00
4	Food Processing	3.80	4.60	9.60	-5.60	0.70	22.00	26.60	5.50	12.80	35.70
5	Beverages	3.80	1.90	11.30	-4.10	1.90	9.90	9.40	3.70	21.80	0.00
6	Tobacco	1.80	1.20	11.40	-4.00	1.60	2.80	48.50	1.20	35.10	8.30
7	Textiles	4.20	9.50	8.40	-6.60	-2.10	40.90	7.60	11.70	9.60	8.20
8	Apparel	6.10	5.20	9.10	-6.00	3.30	8.50	17.60	13.20	7.30	0.00
9	Leather	7.30	7.80	9.40	-5.70	1.70	55.80	1.30	12.40	19.00	38.30
10	Paper	4.60	3.20	10.50	-4.80	4.90	5.40	7.40	5.00	3.30	9.60
11	Chemical	8.30	3.30	16.80	0.70	8.50	12.10	6.20	7.50	14.40	10.20
12	Rubber	18.70	4.40	22.40	5.40	16.00	15.80	7.90	20.80	21.50	8.00
13	NonMetMinProd	9.60	2.90	16.10	0.05	10.10	14.90	63.40	9.30	6.20	11.80
14	Iron and Steel	23.50	11.60	28.20	10.40	16.90	54.50	13.50	26.20	41.10	8.80
15	NonFer Metals	19.00	-2.80	27.30	9.70	27.70	19.80	9.00	14.80	8.90	7.10
16	WoodMetal Prod	10.50	3.90	13.30	0.30	7.90	14.10	5.80	14.20	10.30	11.90
17	NonElec Mach	9.00	4.80	12.60	-0.30	6.90	6.70	8.00	11.20	8.30	12.70
18	Electrical Mach	9.90	2.60	13.60	0.60	8.40	8.70	61.80	11.20	10.70	34.40
19	Transport Eqp	63.10	35.70	68.00	48.70	22.30	55.50	11.50	85.70	79.10	7.90
20	Other Manufact	7.10	7.00	10.00	-2.60	6.70	12.00	-3.00	9.30	5.20	-3.50
21	Construction	4.80	4.60	7.70	-4.90	4.00	0.00	0.00	0.00	0.00	0.00
22	Electricity	4.70	-1.10	14.20	1.10	11.40	0.00	0.00	-0.10	0.00	0.00
23	Commerce	6.30	4.80	9.30	-3.20	3.60	0.00	0.00	8.20	0.00	0.00
24	TransptCommun	7.00	3.30	11.70	-1.10	5.70	0.00	0.00	7.80	0.00	0.00
25	FinInsRlEstate	4.80	3.00	9.70	-2.90	4.90	0.00	0.00	4.70	0.00	0.00
26	Other Services	4.90	1.60	12.70	-0.20	7.30	0.00	0.00	3.20	0.00	0.00

Table 2.11. *Sectoral Results for Full Liberalization, Mexico. Experiment 3: Constant Returns to Scale, Homogeneous Base Prices (figures in percentages)*

		Real Output	Real Cons	LD	KD	Mr	Mu	Mc	Er	Eu	Ec
1	Agriculture	-9.30	4.90	-5.90	-10.10	-3.90	129.30	155.50	-24.10	38.50	92.30
2	Mining	3.10	-0.80	6.40	1.70	11.30	8.10	9.70	-4.90	18.60	4.60
3	Petroleum	19.40	12.30	24.30	18.80	11.80	35.20	0.00	16.30	38.20	14.00
4	Food Processing	0.70	3.90	4.60	-0.02	3.40	37.90	35.70	-1.60	8.70	26.60
5	Beverages	2.50	1.60	6.10	1.40	3.70	43.60	0.00	-3.80	19.10	9.40
6	Tobacco	1.90	1.60	5.50	0.80	0.00	0.80	8.30	-0.60	10.40	48.50
7	Textiles	3.60	2.30	7.00	2.20	5.80	5.70	8.20	-3.60	43.50	7.60
8	Apparel	1.80	1.50	5.30	0.60	5.30	4.40	0.00	-4.40	4.70	17.60
9	Leather	1.00	1.60	4.10	-0.50	0.00	7.40	38.30	-5.10	1.30	1.30
10	Paper	-1.10	12.60	2.50	-2.10	0.10	28.20	9.60	-3.80	0.70	7.40
11	Chemical	1.30	3.70	4.90	0.30	4.40	6.80	10.20	-4.50	4.00	6.20
12	Rubber	1.00	3.30	4.40	-0.30	4.40	4.40	8.00	-4.90	2.70	7.90
13	NonMetMinProd	1.10	-0.20	4.90	0.20	7.10	9.90	11.80	-6.90	27.80	63.40
14	Iron and Steel	7.30	10.20	10.90	6.00	5.20	25.30	8.80	1.70	42.40	13.50
15	NonFer Metals	0.90	2.00	4.60	-0.06	6.30	7.40	7.10	-8.40	-0.10	9.00
16	WoodMetal Prod	2.90	2.60	6.50	1.80	4.50	5.20	11.90	-3.10	6.20	5.80
17	NonElec Mach	5.50	6.60	8.90	4.10	8.20	8.60	12.70	1.20	3.30	8.00
18	Electrical Mach	3.50	6.40	6.70	1.90	2.90	6.30	34.40	1.80	4.00	61.80
19	Transport Eqp	10.50	16.10	14.10	9.00	10.70	23.50	7.90	7.00	10.30	11.50
20	Other Manufact	7.30	6.50	11.40	6.40	7.40	9.70	-12.00	-0.30	10.80	-12.00
21	Construction	1.90	1.90	3.50	-1.10	0.00	0.00	0.00	0.00	0.00	0.00
22	Electricity	5.90	0.70	9.10	4.30	0.00	0.00	0.00	0.00	0.00	0.00
23	Commerce	0.20	-1.60	4.00	-0.60	0.00	0.00	0.00	0.00	0.00	0.00
24	TransptCommun	2.10	-0.10	5.50	0.80	0.00	0.00	0.00	0.00	0.00	0.00
25	FinInsRlEstate	0.09	-1.10	3.70	-0.90	0.00	0.00	0.00 *	0.00	0.00	0.00
26	Other Services	2.40	0.70	4.60	-0.06	0.00	0.00	0.00	0.00	0.00	0.00

Table 2.12. *Sectoral Results for Full Liberalization, U.S. Experiment 4: Constant Returns to Scale, Calibrated PPP Base Prices (figures in percentages)*

		Real Output	Real Cons	LD	KD	Mr	Mc	Mm	Er	Ec	Em
1	Agriculture	2.10	0.50	3.30	1.40	2.40	17.60	36.80	-3.20	86.40	128.40
2	Mining	2.20	1.30	2.80	0.90	2.70	9.50	17.10	0.50	7.40	7.50
3	Petroleum	-0.40	3.50	1.10	-0.80	-1.00	29.70	35.30	-0.06	20.60	30.90
4	Food Processing	1.00	0.70	1.80	-0.05	1.40	13.60	7.70	0.20	21.30	37.40
5	Beverages	0.40	0.80	1.10	-0.70	0.60	22.20	18.70	-0.70	9.80	43.40
6	Tobacco	-0.50	-0.07	0.80	-1.00	2.00	35.80	10.10	-2.10	2.20	1.00
7	Textiles	2.90	1.10	3.30	1.40	2.60	10.60	42.60	1.80	40.90	5.80
8	Apparel	0.90	1.00	1.40	-0.50	1.20	7.90	4.60	0.09	8.40	5.00
9	Leather	5.30	2.30	6.10	4.20	2.20	20.10	1.40	4.40	55.20	8.40
10	Paper	1.10	1.10	1.70	-0.20	2.00	4.60	-0.30	-0.40	4.90	26.70
11	Chemical	1.60	1.30	2.50	0.60	2.20	15.30	3.30	0.40	11.80	6.40
12	Rubber	2.50	0.90	3.00	1.10	3.20	21.90	1.70	1.40	14.40	3.90
13	NonMetMinProd	1.60	1.00	2.10	0.20	2.40	7.20	27.40	0.50	14.00	10.30
14	Iron and Steel	4.10	3.60	4.20	2.30	3.00	41.40	40.20	3.40	52.90	23.70
15	NonFer Metals	3.70	2.20	4.10	2.20	3.70	9.00	-1.40	2.60	18.70	6.90
16	WoodMetal Prod	2.10	0.80	2.40	0.60	2.50	11.10	5.50	1.00	13.50	5.50
17	NonElec Mach	2.90	1.70	3.30	1.40	3.00	8.80	2.00	2.00	6.30	6.50
18	Electrical Mach	1.40	0.80	1.80	-0.09	2.20	11.70	3.30	0.20	8.10	4.80
19	Transport Eqp	13.80	16.50	14.30	12.20	2.90	74.30	5.50	17.50	52.00	17.50
20	Other Manufact	1.60	1.80	2.40	0.50	2.00	5.70	10.10	0.10	11.70	8.60
21	Construction	0.80	0.90	1.10	-0.80	0.00	36.80	2.40	0.40	128.40	-3.20
22	Electricity	1.00	0.90	2.30	0.40	2.60	17.10	2.70	-0.30	7.50	0.50
23	Commerce	0.90	0.60	1.50	-0.40	0.00	35.30	-1.00	-0.60	30.90	-0.06
24	TransptCommun	1.00	0.90	1.60	-0.20	2.80	7.70	1.40	-0.30	37.40	0.20
25	FinInsRlEstate	0.09	-0.10	1.40	-0.50	3.30	18.70	0.60	-2.30	43.40	-0.70
26	Other Services	1.00	0.90	1.40	-0.50	2.80	10.10	2.00	-0.40	1.00	-2.10

Table 2.13. *Sectoral Results for Full Liberalization, Canada. Experiment 4: Constant Returns to Scale, Calibrated PPP Base Prices (figures in percentages)*

		Real Output	Real Cons	LD	KD	Mr	Mu	Mm	Er	Eu	Em
1	Agriculture	-0.60	3.80	8.30	-5.00	-3.70	86.40	88.90	1.70	17.60	160.70
2	Mining	11.30	1.00	19.20	4.50	13.20	7.40	3.10	9.90	9.50	10.50
3	Petroleum	17.50	8.40	27.60	11.90	6.90	20.60	11.90	19.00	29.70	0.00
4	Food Processing	4.20	4.60	10.40	-5.90	-0.02	21.30	25.10	6.80	13.60	36.40
5	Beverages	4.20	2.20	12.40	-4.30	2.00	9.80	9.10	5.70	22.20	0.00
6	Tobacco	1.70	1.10	12.00	-4.60	0.40	2.20	48.40	1.90	35.80	10.00
7	Textiles	5.80	11.10	10.40	-5.90	-1.50	40.90	7.50	14.80	10.60	9.80
8	Apparel	6.70	5.60	10.00	-6.30	3.40	8.40	17.30	15.30	7.90	0.00
9	Leather	8.10	7.80	10.40	-5.90	1.20	55.20	-0.10	14.60	20.10	38.40
10	Paper	6.00	3.80	12.40	-4.20	4.40	4.90	6.70	8.20	4.60	10.10
11	Chemical	9.10	3.90	18.50	0.90	8.50	11.80	4.70	9.70	15.30	10.80
12	Rubber	18.80	2.80	22.70	4.50	14.60	14.40	7.10	22.50	21.90	9.60
13	NonMetMinProd	10.30	3.80	17.40	0.02	9.20	14.00	61.10	11.50	7.20	11.60
14	Iron and Steel	24.00	13.20	29.00	9.90	16.10	52.90	12.10	28.60	41.40	9.30
15	NonFer Metals	19.40	-2.30	28.30	9.30	26.80	18.70	8.50	16.90	9.00	8.60
16	WoodMetal Prod	11.70	5.90	14.80	0.70	7.70	13.50	4.80	17.40	11.10	10.80
17	NonElec Mach	10.00	4.80	13.90	-0.10	7.10	6.30	7.20	13.00	8.80	12.10
18	Electrical Mach	10.70	2.80	14.70	0.60	8.00	8.10	56.50	13.30	11.70	28.70
19	Transport Eqp	59.60	33.60	64.80	44.50	20.80	52.00	10.80	82.20	74.30	7.50
20	Other Manufact	7.60	7.00	10.80	-2.80	6.60	11.70	-3.70	11.20	5.70	1.70
21	Construction	5.20	4.90	8.30	-5.00	0.00	0.00	0.00	0.00	0.00	0.00
22	Electricity	5.00	-1.20	15.30	1.10	10.20	0.00	0.00	1.20	0.00	0.00
23	Commerce	7.20	5.70	10.40	-3.20	2.30	0.00	0.00	10.60	0.00	0.00
24	TransptCommun	7.80	3.80	12.90	-1.00	4.30	0.00	0.00	10.20	0.00	0.00
25	FinInsRlEstate	5.00	2.80	10.30	-3.20	3.30	0.00	0.00	6.40	0.00	0.00
26	Other Services	5.30	1.90	13.70	-0.20	6.00	0.00	0.00	4.80	0.00	0.00

Table 2.14. *Sectoral Results for Full Liberalization, Mexico. Experiment 4: Constant Returns to Scale, Calibrated PPP Base Prices (figures in percentages)*

		Real Output	Real Cons	LD	KD	Mr	Mu	Mc	Er	Eu	Ec
1	Agriculture	-10.80	3.40	-7.60	-11.50	-3.90	128.40	160.70	-27.40	36.80	88.90
2	Mining	1.60	0.50	4.60	0.30	10.90	7.50	10.50	-7.30	17.10	3.10
3	Petroleum	15.00	4.70	19.40	14.50	6.60	30.90	0.00	11.60	35.30	11.90
4	Food Processing	-0.50	2.80	3.10	-1.10	2.90	37.40	36.40	-3.30	7.70	25.10
5	Beverages	2.00	1.10	5.30	1.00	3.70	43.40	0.00	-5.30	18.70	9.10
6	Tobacco	1.70	1.40	5.00	0.60	0.00	1.00	10.00	-1.40	10.10	48.40
7	Textiles	3.50	2.40	6.60	2.20	6.70	5.80	9.80	-4.70	42.60	7.50
8	Apparel	2.20	2.10	5.40	1.10	6.60	5.00	0.00	-4.90	4.60	17.30
9	Leather	1.90	2.70	4.80	0.50	0.00	8.40	38.40	-5.20	1.40	-0.10
10	Paper	-2.90	9.20	0.40	-3.70	-1.30	26.70	10.10	-6.40	-0.30	6.70
11	Chemical	0.50	3.50	3.80	-0.40	4.10	6.40	10.80	-6.10	3.30	4.70
12	Rubber	0.30	2.70	3.40	-0.90	4.30	3.90	9.60	-6.50	1.70	7.10
13	NonMetMinProd	1.50	0.80	5.00	0.60	8.30	10.30	11.60	-7.50	27.40	61.10
14	Iron and Steel	5.50	6.50	8.80	4.30	4.00	23.70	9.30	-0.90	40.20	12.10
15	NonFer Metals	-0.04	2.30	3.30	-1.00	6.10	6.90	8.60	-10.40	-1.40	8.50
16	WoodMetal Prod	3.10	3.90	6.40	2.00	5.30	5.50	5.50	-4.10	5.50	4.80
17	NonElec Mach	3.20	4.40	6.30	1.90	5.80	6.50	12.10	-1.20	2.00	7.20
18	Electrical Mach	2.60	3.80	5.50	1.10	1.10	4.80	28.70	0.60	3.30	56.50
19	Transport Eqp	4.80	8.20	8.00	3.50	4.50	17.50	7.50	1.00	5.50	10.20
20	Other Manufact	6.20	5.10	9.90	5.30	6.30	8.60	-13.40	-2.40	10.10	-13.40
21	Construction	2.60	2.60	4.10	-0.10	0.00	0.00	0.00	0.00	0.00	0.00
22	Electricity	4.60	1.40	7.60	3.10	0.00	0.00	0.00	0.00	0.00	0.00
23	Commerce	1.20	0.40	4.70	0.40	0.00	0.00	0.00	0.00	0.00	0.00
24	TransptCommun	3.40	2.70	6.60	2.20	0.00	0.00	0.00	0.00	0.00	0.00
25	FinInsRlEstate	1.30	0.80	4.70	0.30	0.00	0.00	0.00	0.00	0.00	0.00
26	Other Services	3.30	2.30	5.30	0.90	0.00	0.00	0.00	0.00	0.00	0.00

factor prices and increase import penetration, increased efficiency and demand growth outweigh these, and 19 out of 20 nonservice sectors expand in real terms. Employment also increases in every sector under our labor surplus, fixed-average wage closure, while the fixed and fully employed aggregate stock of capital is reallocated between sectors. It might be more realistic to expect both factors to exhibit a combination of these adjustments, and indeed the asymmetric choice of closures was intended to illustrate both the growth and reallocation effects simultaneously.

Because of its higher degree of trade dependence and higher prior protection against its regional exports, Canada's adjustment is considerably more dramatic than that of the United States. The same basic processes are at work, but this time some sectors expand so much that capital becomes quite scarce and over half the expanding sectors are forced to substitute away from this factor. This is, of course, a boon for domestic employment, but it is reasonable to ask if this degree of transformation to more labor-intensive techniques would be feasible. The sectoral output, consumption, and trade results for Canada are similar to the United States in qualitative terms, but this economy expands by over twice as much in real GDP percentage terms.

Mexico's results are in a sense intermediate between the other two in percentage terms. Expansion is again broadly based but more focused on primary and tertiary sectors than is the case for its two industrialized neighbors. Manufacturing capacity does expand in Mexico, especially in transport equipment, but domestic and external demand also drive significant relative expansion of mining, petroleum, and services (infrastructure). One arresting result is the 9.30 percent contraction of Mexican agriculture, arising from a combination of increased import penetration by the United States and Canada and reduced ROW export opportunities. The problem here is the inability of this sector to hold onto factors that are bid away by sectors [especially petroleum, transport equipment (vehicles), and other manufacturing] expanding to meet domestic and external demand. As was already mentioned in the context of the aggregate results, Mexico undergoes the most extensive structural adjustment in the region, even though it experiences neither the largest gains nor the greatest individual sector expansions.

Tables 2.12–2.14 tell the same story, regarding the country- and sector-specific effects of regional economic integration, from the perspective of calibrated base prices. Because different relative prices imply different sectoral real output levels and factor productivities, the PPP price calibration causes different sectoral adjustments. As the aggregate results indicate (Table 2.8), the United States gains less under the calibrated price scenario, largely because its average PPP prices for tradables (Table 2.5) are higher than its two trading partners, so its exports are less competitive under PPP prices. Likewise, sectoral output expands less in tradable sectors and more in two nontradable sectors when prices are calibrated to PPP values. The same forces are at work to alter sectoral import and export responses. In the homogeneous base, domestic producer prices are unity in all three countries, while they differ in the PPP-calibrated base. Depending upon the price advantages or disadvantages these differences confer, imports or exports will behave differently when protection is removed. The same is true of domestic factor reallocation, which depends upon the real output and productivity values calibrated into the base.

The changes due to price calibration are generally smallest for the United States, which has the most homogeneous PPP prices. In the case of Canada, output effects are altered by as much as 74 percent, in the case of agriculture, whose PPP price is relatively high and therefore less competitive than homogeneity would imply. On average, however, Canadian real output and aggregate welfare expand more in the PPP base. This is largely because Canadian exports are more competitive under PPP prices, at least with respect to the United States and ROW. In the case of Canadian exports to the rest of the world in particular, the assumption of price homogeneity leads to substantial underestimation of the expansionary effects of economic integration.

Canadian exports to Mexico expand much less under PPP prices because the calibrated PPP price of tradables is generally lower in Mexico. Table 2.14 reveals this to be part of a larger phenomenon. Mexican gains from integration in the calibrated base are greater, but they rely less on growth in regional trade and more on increased exports to ROW. This is again because Mexico's relatively low PPP prices for tradables imply lower opportunity costs for Mexican exporters than for their counterparts in the United States or Canada. Mexico has the highest dispersion of PPP relative prices, so it exhibits the sharpest difference in sectoral output adjustments and factor reallocation. Using homogeneous prices in this kind of general equilibrium trade policy simulations would in some sectors lead to a tenfold miscalculation of the induced adjustments in Mexican commodity and factor markets.

One could reasonably conclude from both the homogeneous and calibrated PPP price approaches that economic integration is beneficial to the North American economies. The difference in these two approaches becomes quite important, however, when one seeks to identify the components of the domestic adjustment process, especially the winners and losers, within each country. For better or worse, these details are generally the essential determinants of the political economy of trade policy. Thus, greater effort must be directed toward improving our information on intercountry price differentials and explicitly incorporating this information into policy simulations.

VI. Conclusions and Extensions

As stated in the introduction, this chapter had two primary objectives: to describe the structure of the North American economy and to demonstrate the importance of market structure and conduct and intercountry price comparison data in accurately estimating the adjustments occasioned by North American economic integration.

The first objective has been met by constructing a detailed three-country SAM for 1988 and using it to appraise the composition of production, demand, and trade among the United States, Canada, and Mexico. Generally speaking, our results bear out the conventional wisdom about these economies. The United States is the largest and most self-sufficient member at the center of the regional economy. Canada is a relatively affluent and industrialized country like the United States, but it is more dependent on bilateral trade and less diverse in domestic structure and trade. Mexico is distinctive for its large subsistence sector, low value-added shares for labor across the economy, high trade dependence, and relatively limited diversity in current production activities.

The evidence we have compiled on regional protection indicates that, while it appears to be low in terms of tariffs, extensive nontariff barriers exist to seriously distort bilateral trade. Canada faces the highest barriers to its regional exports, the United States the lowest. In terms of purchasing power parity, the three countries have widely differing relative prices. The United States generally has the highest prices for tradables, whereas Mexico has the lowest for both tradables and nontradables. Individual sector disparities are in some cases considerable. For services, which accounts for at least half of GDP in all three countries, Mexican PPP prices are less than half those in Canada, with the United States somewhere in between.

To test the real significance of both the structural and price differentials between these three countries, we simulated regional economic integration with the AGE model. Our results indicate that the North American economies each have much to gain from greater integration of their markets and activities. These benefits are realized under a variety of specifications for domestic market structure and conduct, although the aggregate welfare effects change moderately. Even in this comparative static framework, where the cumulative effects of investment, innovation, and endogenous growth effects are not taken into account, the regional economies experience gains from 1.65 to 6.75 percent of base real GDP.

When explicit account is taken of intercountry differences in relative prices, the aggregate results remain relatively similar but the sectoral results change dramatically. It is apparent even from this limited set of simulation experiments that accounting for price differences of this kind is essential to understand clearly the complex resource reallocations and other structural adjustments which are occasioned by trade policy initiatives of this significance. By the same token, neglecting this information undermines the simulation analysis at the sectoral level, where the sustainability of most trade policy is ultimately determined.

Endnotes

1. The RAS procedure is described in Stone and Brown (1965).

2. For Canada, the capital and labor components of value added came directly from the 1988 Canadian input-output accounts. Unfortunately, data availability is less current in the United States. Therefore, the value-added data from Reinert and Roland-Holst (1992) are less precise than the Canadian data. However, the Reinert and Roland-Holst study made use of the most recent value-added data available at the time.

3. For notable exceptions, see López-de-Silanes et al. and Trela and Whalley, this volume.

4. The detailed construction of these estimates is given in Roland-Holst, Reinert, and Shiells (1992).

5. Dervis, de Melo, and Robinson (1982) provide an introduction to this methodology.

6. The only other general equilibrium model that models both consumption and production in a disaggregated fashion for all three countries in North America is that of Brown, Deardorff, and Stern (1992). In this volume, Brown reports results from the earlier paper and examines the key theoretical linkages in the earlier model using a stylized version.

7. The CES specification for demand is used provisionally in this model. The shortcomings of this usage are now well known, and the authors are presently at work on estimating more flexible functional forms for tradeable demand (Shiells, Roland-Holst, and Reinert, 1993). In defense of the present model, it does not exhibit the strong terms-of-trade effects sometimes associated with CES demand systems.

8. An example is Harris (1986).

9. In the calibration of the model, the cost disadvantage ratio for sector i of country j is used to establish the fixed costs in sector i of country j (F_{ij} in Table 2.6). Suppressing subscripts, CDR = (ATC − MC)/ATC, because there are constant returns to scale in the model, MC = AVC. Therefore, CDR = (ATC - AVC)/ATC or FC = CDR × TC. This approach is explained more thoroughly in Chapter 7 of de Melo and Tarr (1992).

10. de Melo and Tarr (1992) and de Melo and Roland-Holst (1991) compare a variety of specifications for firm conduct.

11. It is possible that harmonization of ROW protection would alter the results given here, but such policies are not presently under consideration.

12. The adjustment in ROW exchange rates is dictated by the exchange rate arbitrage condition, so there is really only one ROW exchange rate. We experimented with other foreign closures, but the results did not change significantly.

13. Trade diversion is measured by items 10 and 11 in Table 2.8. This trade diversion index is a nomalized measure of the shift in composition of trade between the region and the rest of the world. It essentially measures the percent of imports or exports diverted from one market to another. Positive values indicate diversion into the region and away from the rest of the world. Another index in the table is item 12, measuring the normalized reallocation of labor between domestic production activities.

14. In the case of imports for example, the diversion measure is given by $100\|m_1/\|m_0|-m_0\|/\|m_0\|$, where, for example, $m_1 = (m_{ic}, m_{im}, m_{ir})$ denotes the 3-tuple of partner (for the United States, for example) and ROW imports and $\|.\|$ and $|.|$ denote the Euclidean and simplex norms, respectively.

15. Defined as $100\|l_1 - l_0\|/\|l_0\|$, where the vectors l_0 and l_1 denote sectoral employment before and after integration. The larger the value, the more resource reallocation and structural adjustment the economy undergoes.

16. See Kehoe, this volume.

References

Brown, D.K, A.V. Deardorff, and R.M. Stern. 1992. "A North American free trade agreement: Analytical issues and a computational assessment." *The World Economy* 15(1):11–30.

Delorme, F., and J. Lester. 1990. "The structure of production in ten Canadian industries." *Empirical Economics* 15(4):315–46.

de Melo, J., and D.W. Roland-Holst. 1991. "Industrial organization and trade liberalization: Evidence from Korea." In *Empirical studies of commercial policy*, edited by R.E. Baldwin, Chicago: University of Chicago Press, 287–306.

de Melo, J., and D. Tarr. 1992. *A general equilibrium analysis of U.S. foreign trade policy.* Cambridge, MA: MIT Press.

Dervis, K., J. de Melo, and S. Robinson. 1982. *General equilibrium models for development policy.* Washington, D.C.: The World Bank.

Globerman, S., and M. Bader. 1991. "A perspective of trilateral economic relations." In *Continental accord: North American economic integration*, edited by S. Globerman. Vancouver: The Fraser Institute, 153–74.

Harris, R.G. 1986. "Market structure and trade liberalization: A general equilibrium assessment." In *General equilibrium trade policy modeling*, edited by T.N. Srinavasan and John Whalley. Cambridge, MA: MIT Press, 231–50.

Hunter, L., J.R. Markusen, and T.F. Rutherford. 1991. "Trade liberalization in a multinational-dominated industry: A theoretical and applied general equilibrium analysis." Mimeo, June.

Reinert, K.A., and D.W. Roland-Holst. 1991. "Parameter estimates for U.S. trade policy analysis." Unpublished manuscript, April.

Reinert, K.A., and D.W. Roland-Holst. 1992. "A detailed social accounting matrix for the United States: 1988." *Economic Systems Research*, 4(2):173–87.

Reinert, K.A., D.W. Roland-Holst, and C.R. Shiells. 1993. "Social accounts and the structure of the North American economy." Paper presented at the Annual Meetings of the American Economic Association, Anaheim, California, January.

Roland-Holst, D.W. 1991. "Estimaciones de equilibrio general de los efectos de la eliminación de tarifas entre México y los Estados Unidos." *Cuadernos Económicos* 48:197–213.

Roland-Holst, D.W., K.A. Reinert, and C.R. Shiells. 1992. "North American trade liberalization and the role of nontariff barriers." In U.S. International Trade Commission, *Economy-wide modeling of the economic implications of a FTA with Mexico and a NAFTA with Canada and Mexico.* USITC Publication 2508, 523–80.

Salinas de Gortari, C. 1990. *Segundo informe de gobierno*, Poder Ejecutivo Federal, Estados Unidos Mexicanos.

Shiells, C.R., and K.A. Reinert. 1993. "Armington models and terms-of-trade effects: Some econometric evidence for North America." *Canadian Journal of Economics* 26(2):299–316.

Shiells, C.R., D.W. Roland-Holst, and K.A. Reinert. 1993. "Modeling a North American free trade area: Estimation of flexible functional forms." *Weltwirtschaftliches Archiv* 129(1):55–77.

Sobarzo, H.E. 1992. "A general equilibrium analysis of the gains from trade for the Mexican economy of a North American free trade agreement." *World Economy* 15(1):83–100.

Statistics Canada. 1991. *Canada's balance of international payments.* Ottawa, March.

Statistics Canada. 1991, *National income and expenditure accounts.* Ottawa, April.

Stone, R., and A. Brown. 1965. "Behavioral and technical change in economic models." In E.A.G. Robinson, ed. *Problems in economic development.* London: Macmillan, 428–39.

Summers, R., and A. Heston. 1991. "The Penn world table (mark 5): An expanded set of international comparisons, 1950–1988." *Quarterly Journal of Economics* 106(2):327–68.

UNCTAD. 1987. *Handbook of trade control measures of developing countries.* UNCTAD/DDM/ Misc.2, UNCTAD, Geneva.

U.S. Department of Commerce. 1988. *Highlights of U.S. export and import trade* FT 990, December.

U.S. Department of Commerce. 1991. *Survey of Current Business* 71(6), June.

U.S. General Accounting Office. 1990. *U.S.-Mexico trade: Trends and impediments in agricultural trade.* January.

U.S. International Trade Commission. 1991. *The likely impact on the United States of a free trade agreement with Mexico.* USITC Publication 2353, February.

3

The Gains for Mexico from a North American Free Trade Agreement – An Applied General Equilibrium Assessment

Horacio E. Sobarzo
El Colegio de México

I. Introduction

This chapter attempts to evaluate the effects that an eventual North American Free Trade Agreement (NAFTA) between Mexico, Canada, and the United States would have on the Mexican economy, in the presence of economies of scale in the Mexican industry. For that purpose, we show the results of an applied general equilibrium model for Mexico, in which the treatment of economies of scale follows the lines of the Harris (1984) model for Canada. Likewise, it is important to mention that, unlike the results shown in Sobarzo (1992), the present version deals with the removal of both tariff and nontariff barriers (NTBs).

This chapter is organized as follows. Section II presents a brief review on trade policy in Mexico. Section III describes the characteristics of the model. Section IV comments on the main findings. Finally, Section V contains some concluding remarks as well as some comments on the limitations of the approach.

II. Trade Policy

In 1983, after the debt crisis, the Mexican government conducted extensive trade liberalization that has taken the economy from being one of the most protected in the 1970s to one of the most open by the 1990s.[1] Such measures were implemented in three stages.

In the first stage, from 1983 to 1985, the de la Madrid administration gradually opened the market to foreign participation by simplifying the tariff schedule, reducing the import licensing requirements,[2] and reducing the number of items with official prices.[3]

The second stage was marked by Mexico joining the GATT in 1986, which strengthened the trade liberalization process by freeing more imports from the import licensing requirements, by further reducing tariff levels, and by phasing out official prices. Indeed, by the end of 1987, the use of official prices was virtually eliminated; import tariffs were reduced, from a range of 0 to 100 percent in 1985, to a range of 0 to 20 percent by the end of December 1987 [USITC (1990)].

As a result of these measures, the Mexican economy moved in only three years from a regime in which almost all imports were subject to import licenses to a regime in which import permits were required in only a few selected sectors.

Finally, in the third stage, the government has attempted to consolidate these measures by liberalizing some sectors and reducing the level of tariffs even more. Thus, for instance, the trade-weighted average tariff level fell from 25 percent in 1985 to 10 percent in 1990. Likewise, whereas 35 percent of Mexican import value was subject to the licensing requirement in 1986, only 230 categories (out of nearly 12,000) were subject to this requirement in 1990.[4]

III. The Model
Overview of the Model

The structure of the model is outlined in Table 3.1. With some exceptions, notably the introduction of economies of scale, the assumptions of the model are very similar to those of conventional applied general equilibrium models. In view of this, we will provide only a basic overview of the model in this section and then proceed to discuss the modeling of economies of scale. The full set of model equations are shown in the Appendix.

The model is calibrated using a social accounting matrix (SAM) of the Mexican economy for 1985. The SAM separates the rest of the world in two regions: North America (NA) and rest of the world (ROW). It should be mentioned that the SAM (as well as the model) incorporates these two regions only in a reduced form manner; that is, they enter as suppliers of Mexican imports and as demanders for Mexican exports. As noted in Table 3.1, domestic and imported commodities are assumed to be imperfect substitutes based on the Armington assumption,[5] and Mexican exports face downward-sloping demand curves in NA and ROW (see the Appendix).

Producers combine Armington aggregates of domestic and imported intermediate inputs in fixed proportions; capital and labor are combined based on Cobb-Douglas value added functions. Finally, intermediates and net output are combined in fixed proportions.

Table 3.1. *General Characteristics of the Model*

1. <u>Level of Aggregation</u>. The model identifies 27 production sectors, each sector producing a single commodity. Of these 27 commodities, 21 are tradable while the remaining 6 commodities are non-traded.

2. <u>Dimensions</u>. There are two factors of production, capital and labor, which are mobile between sectors (in addition, capital is also mobile between countries). It is assumed that there is one representative consumer and that there are three regions: Mexico, North America (NA), which includes the U.S. and Canada, and the rest of the world (ROW). Only the Mexican economy is explicitly modeled. For other regions, we postulate separate import supplies from NA and ROW, as well as separate demands for Mexican exports from the two regions.

3. <u>Production</u>. All production activities combine intermediate inputs in fixed proportions but allow for some degree of substitution between domestic and foreign commodities. They also combine labor and capital by means of a Cobb-Douglas production function to generate value added which, in turn, combines in fixed proportions with intermediate inputs.

4. <u>Foreign Trade</u>. Each sector produces a share for domestic markets and exports the remaining share to NA and ROW. Exported commodities face downward sloping demand curves which depend, among other things, on a price elasticity of demand. On the import side the small country assumption is adopted, and domestic and foreign commodities are assumed to be imperfect substitutes (in the Armington manner). The numeraire is chosen by setting the consumer price index equal to one.

5. <u>Final Demand</u>. There is a single representative consumer that demands goods according to a Cobb-Douglas utility function. The same assumption is adopted for government and investment expenditures.

The income received by factors of production is divided between consumption, savings, and payment of direct taxes, using fixed expenditures shares. A single representative consumer is assumed. The consumer's preferences are assumed to obey homothetic separability [see Varian (1983)] between commodities. Therefore, a two-stage decision process is implied by utility maximization. In the first stage, represented by Cobb-Douglas preferences, the consumer allocates total consumption expenditure between commodities based on indexes of prices for all goods. In the second stage, represented by CES preferences for each good, the consumer allocates expenditures on each commodity between domestic goods, imports from NA, and imports from ROW. This latter decision is based on relative prices of goods obtained from different regions; only prices of goods within the sector and expenditures on these goods are needed to make this determination.

Similar behavior is assumed for government expenditure. Domestic and foreign savings determine the level of investment. Both factors of production, capital and labor, are perfectly mobile between sectors, and capital is also assumed to be mobile between countries.[6] The price of capital is thus fixed and given by the world rental rate. The aggregate supply of labor is assumed fixed so the wage adjusts to clear the labor market. It is important to mention that in order to incorporate the assumption of perfect mobility of capital between countries, it was necessary to modify the benchmark equilibrium, because any surplus (deficit) in the current account balance was interpreted as a reduction (increase) in the capital endowment of Mexicans.

Modeling Economies of Scale

In modeling economies of scale, we have followed the assumptions of the Harris (1984) model; that is, we have assumed that some firms, in some industrial activities, do not behave as pure competitors. Essentially, we have three types of industries: competitive, regulated, and imperfectly competitive. (Table 3.2 shows how each sector was classified.) Constant returns to scale are assumed in the competitive industries. In the regulated industry, the petroleum sector, we simply assume that both the quantity produced and the domestic price are fixed by the government. The quantity exported is equal to domestic production minus domestic demand. For imperfectly competitive sectors, costs, pricing behavior, and entry conditions are specified based upon Harris (1984). Firms' costs are the sum of fixed and variable costs, both of which entail hiring the services of labor and capital. In each case, an increase in the wage/rental ratio will induce firms to substitute capital for labor. Marginal cost is assumed to be independent of the firm's production level, so average cost is declining everywhere. Thus, for a given level of output, X, a firm's total costs are as follows:

$$C = F(w,r) + V(P,w,r)X \tag{3.1}$$

Table 3.2. *Elasticity Values Used to Calibrate the Mexican Model*

	σ	ß	δ
Agriculture	3.0	2.0	competitive
Mining	0.5	2.0	competitive
Petroleum	0.5	3.0	regulated
Food	1.125	2.0	0.85
Beverages	1.125	2.0	0.71
Tobacco	-	2.0	0.72
Textiles	1.125	2.0	0.78
Wearing apparel	1.125	3.0	0.84
Leather	1.125	3.0	0.82
Wood	1.125	3.0	0.89
Paper	0.5	3.0	0.62
Chemicals	0.5	3.0	0.68
Rubber	0.5	3.0	0.71
Non-metallic prod	0.5	3.0	0.75
Iron and Steel	0.5	3.0	0.83
Non ferrous met	0.5	3.0	0.75
Metallic prods.	0.5	3.0	0.83
Non elect. mach.	0.375	3.0	0.98
Elect. mach.	0.375	3.0	0.55
Transp. equip.	0.375	3.0	0.66
Other manufac.	0.375	6.0	0.85
Construction	-	2.0	competitive
Electricity	-	2.0	competitive
Commerce, Hotels	-	2.0	competitive
Transp. & Comm.	-	2.0	competitive
Financial serv.	-	2.0	competitive
Other services	-	2.0	competitive

σ = Armington elasticity of substitution between domestic goods, imports from NA (Canada and the United States), and ROW (the rest of the world, excluding North America).

ß = Export demand elasticity

δ = Inverse scale elasticity (the ratio of marginal to average cost).

where $F(\cdot)$ is fixed cost, which depends on the prices of labor and capital, and V is variable cost, which is a function of prices of intermediates, P, as well as prices of labor and capital. Average cost is equal to total cost divided by the level of output, X:

$$AC = F/X + V \qquad (3.2)$$

Thus, as the level of production increases, there is a gain in efficiency because average cost declines. As will be explained later, for each imperfectly competitive industry in the model, the degree of unexploited scale economies is measured by the inverse elasticity of scale, which is defined as the ratio of marginal to average costs.

Following Harris (1984), we assume two pricing behaviors. First, we assume a modified Cournot-Chamberlain equilibrium at the industry level, where firms set prices conditional on the elasticity of the firm's perceived demand curve, according to the Lerner condition[7]

$$(P - MC)/P = 1/\eta \qquad (3.3)$$

where the degree of deviation between price, P, and marginal cost, MC, is inversely related to the absolute value of the perceived elasticity of demand, η. For this rule to be valid, it is necessary that $\eta > 1$.

Assumed free entry and exit of firms ensures zero economic profits in all industries so that price equals average cost. Naturally, for this adjustment to take place it is necessary to assume that there are no barriers to entry of firms, other than fixed costs.[8]

Note that we are not assuming that all firms are selling perfect substitutes. Following Harris (1988), the basic economic idea is that an industry consists of some number of firms, each of which is producing similar goods but also has an identical cross–price elasticity of demand with the other firms in the commodity group. In the context of general equilibrium, firms are assumed to have local knowledge of the market elasticity of demand for the product group within which they sell, and the market elasticity is a weighted average of intermediate, final, and export demands. At the level of the firm, the assumption is that an individual firm views its own demand as proportional to market demand; that is, firms assume that their market share is constant.

The second pricing rule also follows Harris (1984) and constitutes an attempt to capture the existence of an oligopolistic market. This rule follows the Eastman and Stykolt model of protected oligopolies.[9] According to this model, domestic firms set prices in a collusive manner around a focal point price, which is determined as the international price plus the tariff; a removal of tariffs, therefore, leads to an immediate reduction of the domestic price. The extent to which the domestic price falls will be determined by the degree of collusion. At one extreme, if collusion is total, when a tariff is removed, the corresponding domestic price should fall in exactly the same proportion. The actual response of domestic prices then will be controlled by a parameter reflecting the degree of collusion, whose value will vary between zero and one. Later in the chapter we shall make some comments on the value of this parameter. It is important, however, to mention that for the purposes of the present model we considered North American prices as a reference point, rather than the prices of the rest of the world. The United States is, by and large, Mexico's main commercial partner and can be seen as a large economy compared to Mexico.

With imperfect competition in some sectors, the adjustment of the economy in response to trade liberalization is very different than adjustment in models that assume perfect competition in all sectors. Indeed, in the context of imperfect competition, a tariff reduction causes the firm's markup to fall and implies that some firms must leave the industry (because profits are negative), with the result that fewer firms serve a larger market at lower unit costs. Compared to perfectly competitive models, there is thus an additional efficiency gain.

Parameter Values

Three sets of parameter values are required to solve the model. They are elasticities of substitution between domestic output, imports from North America, and imports from the rest of the world (σ); export demand elasticities (β); and inverse scale elasticities (δ). Table 3.2 reports values for the three sets of elasticities. It is important to mention that the values of σ and β are best guesses.

The values of inverse scale elasticities were specified following calculations carried out by Hernandez (1985). He estimated what he calls *net scale economies* at the industry level, which measures the extent to which economies of scale are exploited (see Hernandez, Chapter VIII).[10]

IV. **Results**

The results presented in this section assume a complete elimination of barriers to trade within North America. Unlike the results shown in Sobarzo (1992), where only tariffs were removed, in the present version we have also dealt with NTBs. In doing that we used squared trade coverage ratios as measures of NTBs in the following manner. The trade coverage ratio, as given in Roland-Holst et al. (1992, p. 542), represented the price equivalent of the NTBs in the benchmark data set, but this price distortion was applied only to the portion of imports in each sector subject to some form of NTBs. We then assumed complete NTB liberalization, holding the share of imports covered by NTBs in each sector constant and letting the quota premium vary endogenously. Finally, we calibrated the model using these squared trade coverage

Table 3.3. *Values of NTB Measures Used in the Benchmark Equilibrium (percent)*

Agriculture	
Mining	
Petroleum	
Food	
Beverages	
Textiles	
Wearing apparel	
Leather	
Wood	
Paper	
Chemicals	
Rubber	
Non-metallic products	18.1
Iron and steel	
Non-ferrous metals	6.8
Metallic products	15.7
Non-electrical machinery	12.7
Electrical machinery	22.1
Transport equipment	29.8
Other manufactures	33.8

ratios with the purpose of taking the ad valorem price gaps to zero in the counterfactual policy experiment.[11] Note that even though we estimated these squared trade coverage ratios, we are not explicitly modeling NTBs; that is, we have not explicitly introduced quantity-rationing mechanisms into the model. Table 3.3 shows the NTB measures used in each sector.

It is also important to recall the closure rule adopted in our present version of the model. Labor is perfectly mobile between sectors, though in fixed aggregate supply, so that the wage becomes the variable that adjusts to clear the labor market. Capital, on the other hand, is assumed to be mobile not only between sectors but also between countries. Therefore, its price is fixed and given by the world rental rate. Remember that this last assumption means that any additional increase in the stock of capital will be capital endowed by foreigners, not Mexicans. Finally, to be consistent with this scenario, we assumed a variable trade balance and a fixed real exchange rate.

Turning to the analysis of results, Table 3.4 provides a summary of the main

Table 3.4. *Summary of Results (percent changes)*

GDP	9.9
Wage	21.7
Trade balance	-115.7
Welfare..	4.4

aggregate effects. GDP increases by 9.9 percent and the wage goes up by 21.7 percent. The Mexican economy clearly experiences a very strong adjustment. The balance of trade deteriorates markedly (115.7 percent). This deterioration is financed through capital inflows whose value is approximately $9,181 million. Welfare, measured as the equivalent variation, increases by 4.4 percent. Note that the increase in GDP is far higher than the increase in welfare. This difference is explained, as we already mentioned, by the fact that the income generated by capital inflows accrues to foreigners, not Mexicans.

Table 3.5 shows results for each sector. Looking at changes in gross domestic output, it can be appreciated that, with the exception of agriculture, all production activities expand, and such expansion is particularly strong in activities such as construction, nonelectrical machinery, iron and steel, mining transport equipment, and electrical machinery, among others.

The factor movements between sectors are described in columns 7 and 8 in Table 3.5. In particular, the numbers in column 8 suggest that if GDP were to increase as our results indicate, the economy would have to experience very large movements of labor between sectors. Because the price of capital is assumed to be fixed at the world rental price, its use, with the exception of agriculture, increases in all sectors. Here, given that we assumed a Cobb-Douglas production function between labor and capital, one would expect that some substitution of capital for labor might have taken place. If NAFTA results in a high rate of Mexican economic growth, this would likely result in high economic adjustment costs for Mexico, as it would imply a very strong reallocation of labor (as shown by the employment changes in Table 3.4). The feasibility of this reallocation in the short-to-medium run merits serious consideration, although this is beyond the scope of the present investigation.

The implications of North American trade liberalization for foreign trade is described in the third through sixth columns of results in Table 3.5. The behavior of exports to North America are shown in the third column, while exports to the rest of the world appear in the fourth column. Exports to North America go up in nearly all tradable sectors and, in particular, the increase is very strong in the wearing apparel, rubber, leather, tobacco, and textiles sectors. Services, on the other hand, experience a contraction in the level of exports to North America. This is surely explained by the fact that their relative

Table 3.5. *Effects of Trade Liberalization within North America on Mexico,*
by Sector (percent changes)

	P_i	XO_i	E_i^{na}	E_i^{rw}	M_i^{na}	M_i^{rw}	K_i	L_i
Agriculture	-2.1	-8.3	0.2	-4.0	224.7	-2.5	-4.6	-21.6
Mining	3.9	31.6	-8.3	-8.9	37.6	34.7	29.8	6.6
Petroleum	-0.1	5.7	-11.7	-	6.8	5.7	-	-
Food	-5.4	2.5	9.1	1.9	68.4	-1.9	6.2	-12.7
Beverages	-7.9	5.4	7.9	0.7	70.0	-3.7	10.6	-9.1
Tobacco	1.9	5.9	16.5	-3.8	-	-	11.3	-8.5
Textiles	-6.4	7.6	14.8	-0.2	14.3	-	14.7	-5.7
Wearing App.	-6.3	5.8	44.8	-1.4	21.1	-1.1	12.9	-7.2
Leather	-9.0	6.5	25.6	-	15.4	-	14.7	-5.7
Wood	-7.7	25.5	4.3	-	34.8	14.8	29.9	6.7
Paper	-5.0	6.7	7.7	4.9	26.1	5.7	12.4	-7.6
Chemicals	-4.6	10.1	7.9	1.1	14.8	7.7	15.0	-5.4
Rubber	-7.6	12.8	26.5	-0.6	16.4	8.5	19.5	-1.7
Non met. min	-7.6	30.7	4.1	-4.3	36.7	25.7	34.5	10.4
Iron & Steel	-6.3	38.9	9.9	2.9	58.1	36.4	45.7	19.7
Non Ferr. Met	-1.3	28.5	-0.1	-6.4	32.8	28.5	33.3	9.5
Metallic Prods.	-8.1	27.7	7.7	-1.9	31.9	22.6	35.4	11.2
Non Elec. Mach.	-6.9	48.2	3.0	-4.2	51.3	44.7	52.0	24.9
Electr. Mach.	-8.0	29.7	13.1	1.4	35.9	26.1	35.1	10.9
Transport Equip.	-9.6	30.4	9.0	7.3	39.7	26.7	33.7	9.8
Other Manuf.	-16.0	17.4	6.4	-4.0	25.1	8.1	19.6	-1.6
Construction	4.1	55.0	-	-	-	-	76.4	44.9
Electricity	4.6	9.8	-8.6	-	-	-	17.5	-3.4
Commerce	3.7	12.1	-7.2	-	-	-	14.0	-6.3
Transport	4.1	9.8	-8.2	-	-	-	14.6	-5.8
Financial Services	4.6	5.9	-8.7	-	-	-	10.6	-9.0
Other Services	8.7	2.7	-15.5	-	-	-	14.0	-6.3

Note: The variables shown are defined as follows: P_i = composite good price, XO_i = gross domestic output, E_i^{na} = exports to NA, E_i^{rw} = exports to ROW, M_i^{na} = imports from NA, M_i^{rw} = imports from ROW, K_i = capital, L_i = employment.

price goes up, because they do not experience efficiency gains from trade
liberalization associated with scale economies. This is shown by the output
price indexes in the first column of Table 3.5.

Exports to the rest of the world show a different pattern. Exports of food,
beverages, paper, iron and steel, chemicals, electrical machinery, and transport
equipment register modest increases. In the remaining sectors, exports to ROW
fall. This result suggest some trade diversion in favor of North America.

Insofar as imports are concerned, their behavior is described in the fifth and sixth columns of Table 3.5. Column 5 shows imports from North America, while column 6 refers to imports from the rest of the world. Very strong increases in Mexican imports from North America, particularly in the agriculture, food, and beverages sectors, are evident. With one or two exceptions, the remaining tradable sectors also registered strong increases. Imports from the rest of the world also increase, but to a lesser degree. Once again, these results indicate that some trade diversion towards imports from North America may take place, particularly in the case of commodities with a high Armington elasticity of substitution.

Finally, the first column shows the changes in prices of composite commodities, which are indexes of prices paid by consumers for domestic goods, imports from North America, and imports from the rest of the world. In approximately half of the sectors, prices go down, especially in the manufacturing sectors. Price of services, on the other hand, show increases.

In summary, adjustment of the Mexican economy to the removal of barriers to trade within North America, especially if scale economies are present, is driven in large part by the realization of scale economies and also by the assumption that the price of capital is fixed on world markets. The Mexican economy expands more easily under this latter assumption of perfectly elastic international supply of capital, and the assumed easy availability of foreign capital in turn facilitates the realization of scale economies in Mexico.

V. Concluding Remarks

The model of Mexico presented here has attempted to incorporate a form of imperfect competition into a fairly standard CGE model. The results of trade liberalization within North America, including both tariffs and NTBs, suggest that important gains from trade for Mexico are present. An important conclusion of the present study is that economies of scale matter for Mexico. Indeed, the results seem to suggest that, as a result of trade liberalization, a smaller number of firms will end up serving a larger market and making better use of existing factors of production. In particular, an important finding is that, if NAFTA results in substantial economic growth, adjustment costs faced by Mexican labor may be large, which poses questions of feasibility. Namely, can the Mexican labor market reallocate large number of workers within a reasonable period of time? Something similar can be said regarding capital inflows. Can Mexico make this capital inflow sustainable?

Undoubtedly the results depend very much both on parameter values as well as closure rules. In particular, it is possible that the degree of collusion may be a determining parameter. We assumed a value of 0.5 for all of the imperfectly competitive sectors. In doing that, we have followed Harris (1984). However, it must be pointed out that we have no empirical evidence for doing so. Moreover, we have no evidence at all that an equal value for all sectors is a reasonable assumption for the Mexican economy. It therefore remains to carry out some sensitivity analysis on this particular issue. The results presented here should therefore be taken cautiously.

Also, one has to bear in mind some of the limitations of this approach. First, although we incorporated tariff and nontariff barriers as tariff equivalent measures, one should remember that nontariff barriers are in fact quantity-rationing mechanisms and, therefore, the task of modeling these nontariff barriers as such lies in the future.

Second, some realism must be sacrificed in order to model scale economies in a very disaggregated framework, as we have done. Thus, for instance, while the assumption of free entry and exit of firms may be appropriate for some industries, it is clearly not so in those industries where high entry barriers exist. The automotive industry is perhaps the best example for which this assumption is inappropriate.[12] We hope, however, that this kind of model will provide some insights into the changes that the Mexican economy may go through in moving toward freer trade.

Appendix – Model Equations
Prices

- Prices of imports from North America (NA) in local currency:

$$PM_i^{na} = P_i^{na}(1 + t_i^{na})ER^{na} \tag{A3.1}$$

where P_i^{na} is the world price of commodity i in dollars imported from NA, t_i^{na} is the tariff rate on commodity i imported from NA, and ER^{na} is the exchange rate with NA, (price of one dollar in pesos).

- Prices of imports from the rest of the world (ROW) in local currency:

$$PM_i^{rw} = P_i^{rw}(1 + t_i^{rw})ER^{rw} \tag{A3.2}$$

where P_i^{rw} is the world price in foreign currency of commodity i imported from ROW, t_i^{rw} is the corresponding tariff rate, and ER^{rw} is the price of one unit of foreign currency in pesos.

- Prices of exports to NA:

$$PWE_i^{na} = PD_i/(1 + s_i^{na})ER^{na} \tag{A3.3}$$

where PWE_i^{na} is the selling price to NA (in dollars), PD_i is the domestic price of commodity i and s_i^{na} is the rate of subsidy (or export tax) on exports to NA.

- Price of exports to ROW

$$PWE_i^{rw} = PD_i/(1 + s_i^{rw})ER^{rw} \tag{A3.4}$$

where PWE_i^{rw} is the selling price to ROW (in foreign currency) and s_i^{rw} is the rate of subsidy (or tax) on exports to ROW.

- Price of the composite good:

$$P_i = [\alpha_i^\sigma PD_i^{1-\sigma} + \beta_i^\sigma PM_i^{na(1-\sigma)} + \tau_i^\sigma PM_i^{rw(1-\sigma)}]^{1/1-\sigma} \tag{A3.5}$$

where α_i, β_i, and τ_i are share parameters associated with commodities domestic, imported from NA, and imported from ROW, respectively, in the CES aggregator. The elasticity of substitution, σ_i, is defined as $1/1 - \rho_i$. In turn, the CES aggregator is defined as

$$Q_i = [\alpha_i QD_i^\rho + \beta_i QM_i^{na\rho} + \tau_i QM_i^{rw\rho}]^{1/\rho} \tag{A3.6}$$

- Price level:

$$P = \Sigma\Omega_i P_i \tag{A3.7}$$

- Net price equations (*PN*)

$$PN_i = PD_i(1 - td_i) - \Sigma a_{ij} P_j \tag{A3.8}$$

where td_i is the tax rate on the production of commodity i and a_{ij} is the input output coefficient.

Production

- Value-added functions:

$$X_j = \phi[\lambda_j L_j^\varepsilon + (1 - \lambda_j) K_j^\varepsilon]^{1/\varepsilon} \tag{A3.9}$$

where L_j and K_j are the quantities of labor and capital, respectively, used in sector j, ϕ is a scale parameter, and ε_j is defined as $(\gamma_j - 1)/\gamma_j$, where γ_j is the elasticity of substitution between capital and labor in sector j.

- Intermediate input demands:

$$II_{ij} = a_{ij} XO_j \tag{A3.10}$$

where XO_j is the gross domestic product of sector j.

- Functions for aggregation of inputs:

$$AI_j = \min(II_{ij}/a_{ij}) \tag{A3.11}$$

- Gross output functions:

$$XO_j = \min(AI_j, X_j/v_j) \tag{A3.12}$$

where v_j is a value-added coefficient indicating the value-added requirements per unit of production of commodity i in sector j.

Factor markets

- Derived industry demand for labor in sector j:

$$L_j = (1 - \lambda_j) \left[[\frac{\lambda_j \, r}{(1 - \lambda_j) w}]^{\varepsilon/(\varepsilon + 1)} + \lambda_j \right]^{1/\varepsilon} \cdot X_j/\phi_j \qquad (A3.13)$$

- Derived industry demand for capital in sector j

$$K_j = \lambda_j \left[[\frac{(1 - \lambda_j) w}{\lambda_j r}]^{\varepsilon/(\varepsilon + 1)} + (1 - \lambda_j) \right]^{1/\varepsilon} \cdot X_j/\phi_j \qquad (A3.14)$$

where r and w are the prices of capital and labor, respectively.

- Supply of labor:

$$L = \bar{L} \qquad (A3.15)$$

- Supply of capital:

$$r = \bar{r} \qquad (A3.16)$$

Income equations

- Net private income:

$$RP = (\sum L_i \cdot w + \sum K_i \cdot r)(1 - t_{dir}) \qquad (A3.17)$$

where t_{dir} is the income tax rate.

- Net government income:

$$\begin{aligned} RG = & (\sum L_i \cdot w + \sum K_i \cdot r) \cdot t_{dir} + \sum P_i^{na} \cdot M_i^{na} \cdot ER^{na} \cdot t_i^{na} \\ & + \sum P_i^{rw} \cdot M_i^{rw} \cdot ER^{rw} \cdot t_i^{rw} - \sum PD_i \cdot ER^{na} \cdot E_i^{na} \cdot s_i^{na} \\ & - \sum PD_i \cdot ER^{rw} \cdot E_i^{rw} \cdot s_i^{rw} + \sum PD_i \cdot td_i \cdot XO_i \end{aligned} \qquad (A3.18)$$

where M_i^{na} and M_i^{rw} refer to imports from NA and ROW, respectively, t_i^{na} and t_i^{rw} are the corresponding tariff rates, E_i^{na} and E_i^{rw} are exports of commodity i to NA and ROW, and s_i^{na} and s_i^{rw} are the subsidy (or tax) rates on exports to NA and ROW. Note that the fourth and fifth terms should have a positive sign if export taxes are greater than export subsidies.

Investment equations

- Savings-investment equality:

$$TINV = sp \cdot RP + sg \cdot RG + F^{na} \cdot ER^{na} + F^{rw} \cdot ER^{rw} \qquad (A3.19)$$

where *TINV* is total investment, *sp* and *sg* are the private and public income proportions devoted to savings, and F^{na} and F^{rw} are foreign savings from NA and ROW, respectively, expressed in foreign currency.

- Investment by destination sector:

$$Y_i = par_i \cdot TINV \qquad (A3.20)$$

where par_i is the share of sector i in total investment demand.

Consumption equations

- Private consumption of commodity i:

$$CP_i = parp_i \cdot (1-sp) \cdot RP/P_i \qquad (A3.21)$$

where $parp_i$ is the parameter associated with commodity i in the Cobb-Douglas utility function.

- Government consumption of commodity i:

$$CG_i = parg_i \cdot (1-sg) \cdot RG/P_i \qquad (A3.22)$$

where $parg_i$ is the parameter associated with commodity i in the Cobb-Douglas utility function.

Intermediate demand

- Intermediate demand:

$$V_i = \sum a_{ij} \cdot XO_j \qquad (A3.23)$$

External sector

- Export to NA demand functions:

$$E_i^{na} = E_0^{na}(\Pi_i/PWE_i^{na})^\eta \qquad (A3.24)$$

where Π_i is an "aggregate" world price reflecting an average of production costs in all countries, PWE_i has already been defined in equation A3.3, E_0^{na} is a constant term reflecting total world demand for commodity category i and the country's market share when $\Pi_i = PWE_i$, and η_i is the price elasticity of export demand for commodity i.

- Export to ROW demand functions:

$$E_i^{rw} = E_0^{rw}(\Pi_i/PWE_i^{rw})^\eta \qquad (A3.25)$$

where Π_i is an "aggregate" world price reflecting an average of production costs in all countries, PWE_i has already been defined in equation A3.4, E_0^{rw} is a constant term reflecting total world demand for commodity category i and the country's market share when $\Pi_i = PWE_i$, and η_i is the price elasticity of export demand for commodity i.

- Functions for imports from NA:

$$M_i^{na} = [(\beta_i \cdot PD_i)/(\alpha_i \cdot PM_i^{na})]^{\sigma-1} \cdot QD_i \qquad (A3.26)$$

where QD_i is the internal demand for domestically produced commodity i.

• Functions for imports from ROW:

$$M_i^{rw} = [(\tau_i \cdot PD_i)/(\alpha_i \cdot PM_i^{rw})]^{\sigma-1} \cdot QD_i \qquad (A3.27)$$

where QD_i is the internal demand for domestically produced commodity i.

Demand equations

• Demand for domestic commodities:

$$QD_i = RU_i(Y_i + CP_i + CG_i + V_i) \qquad (A3.28)$$

where RU_i is the ratio of domestic use to total demand for composite commodity i and is given by

$$RU_i = QD_i/Q_i = 1/f_i(1,QM_i^{na}/QD_i,QM_i^{rw}/QD_i) \qquad (A3.29)$$

where f_i is the CES aggregation trade function, as described by equation A3.6.

• Total demand for domestic commodities:

$$XD_i = QD_i + E_i^{na} + E_i^{rw} \qquad (A3.30)$$

Equilibrium conditions

• Equilibrium in the labor market:

$$\bar{L} = \Sigma L_i \qquad (A3.31)$$

• Equilibrium in the capital market:

$$K = \Sigma K_i \qquad (A3.32)$$

• Equilibrium in the commodity markets:

$$XO_i = XD_i \qquad (A3.33)$$

• External equilibrium with NA:

$$F^{na} = \Sigma P_i^{na} \cdot M_i^{na} - \Sigma PWE_i^{na} \qquad (A3.34)$$

• External equilibrium with ROW:

$$F^{rw} = \Sigma P_i^{rw} \cdot M_i^{rw} - \Sigma PWE_i^{rw} \qquad (A3.35)$$

Endnotes

1. In 1985, the government began a program to privatize its public firms. By the end of July 1990, the number of government-owned or -controlled entities had fallen from 1,155 in 1982 to 310 [USITC (1991)].

2. In this stage, the most significant measure was the removal of the import licensing requirement for a total of 2,000 categories in the Mexican tariff schedule.

3. Official prices were widely used by the Mexican government to combat dumping or subsidized import competition. Essentially, the government determines an "official" price that usually differs from the commercial value. In 1986, for instance, duties on approximately 1,000 items were calculated based on official prices.

4. These 230 controlled categories belong, for the most part, to a few sectors: agriculture, auto parts, pharmaceutical products, petrochemicals, apparel, wood, and wood products.

5. See Armington (1969).

6. This assumption was originally adopted by Harris (1984).

7. Notice that the model is not pure Cournot-type because we assume that demand is evenly shared by all firms in the industry.

8. It should be mentioned that before solving the model we defined two scenarios: benchmark equilibrium and base equilibrium. The benchmark equilibrium corresponds to the equilibrium under the historical data set. In this equilibrium firms earn positive or negative profits. However, in order to move to an equilibrium (base equilibrium) in which firms earn zero profits, markups had to be modified. The assumption here was that, in modifying the markups, an adjustment took place in prices, not in industrial structure. The latter is supposed to be more permanent than the former.

9. See Eastman and Stykolt (1960).

10. Estimates were based on the 1975 industrial census.

11. This procedure was suggested by Clint Shiells.

12. For a contrary view, see López-de-Silanes et al., this volume.

References

Armington, P.S. 1969. "A theory of demand for products distinguished by place of production." *International Monetary Fund Staff Papers* 16(March):59–78.

Eastman, H., and S. Stykolt. 1960. "A model for the study of protected oligopolies." *The Economic Journal* 70(June):336–47.

Harris, R. 1988. "A guide to the GET model," Department of Finance, Fiscal Policy and Economic Analysis Branch, Working Paper No. 88-10.

———. 1984. "Applied general equilibrium analysis of small open economies with scale economies and imperfect competition." *American Economic Review* 74(5):1016–32.

Hernandez, E. 1985. *La productividad y el desarrollo industrial en México.* Mexico, D.F.: Fondo de Cultura Económica.

Roland-Holst, D.W., K.A. Reinert, and C.R. Shiells. 1992. "North American trade liberalization and the role of nontariff barriers." In U.S. International Trade Commission, *Economy-wide modeling of the economic implications of a FTA with Mexico and NAFTA with Canada and Mexico.* USITC Publication 2508, May.

Sobarzo, H. 1992. "A general equilibrium analysis of the gains from trade for the Mexican economy of a North American free trade agreement." *World Economy* 5(1):83–100.

U.S. International Trade Commission. 1990. *Review of trade and investment liberalization measures by Mexico and prospects for future United States-Mexican relations, phase I.* Publication 2275, April.

U.S. International Trade Commission. 1991. *The likely impact on the United States of a free trade agreement with Mexico.* USITC Publication 2353, February.

Varian, Hal R. 1983. "Nonparametric tests of consumer behavior," *Review of Economic Studies* 50(January):99–110.

4

Some Applied General Equilibrium Estimates of the Impact of a North American Free Trade Agreement on Canada*

David J. Cox
University of Waterloo

I. Introduction

This chapter presents applied general equilibrium estimates of the impact on Canada of the proposed North American Free Trade Agreement (NAFTA) and outlines the model and data used. These results are an extension of research previously reported in a paper written with Richard Harris [Cox and Harris (1992)].

The inclusion of Mexico in a free trade area with Canada and the United States raises a number of issues from the Canadian perspective. Among these are the following: the impact of NAFTA on the volume and pattern of trade between Canada and Mexico, the impact of increased imports from Mexico on employment patterns and factor returns, the extent to which Canadian exports to Mexico will increase, and the potential diversion of Canadian exports to the U.S. market as U.S. tariffs on Mexican imports are removed. The volume of existing Canada-Mexico trade is relatively low. It was valued at 2.5 billion dollars in 1989, or 1 percent of Canadian trade. While the agreement presumably will increase trade, the magnitude of the effect is far from certain. At the same time, the United States is by far the largest trading partner of both Canada

* The paper reports some results from a joint research project undertaken with Richard Harris. The research underlying this paper was supported by the Fraser Institute and the Lily Foundation. This is a substantially revised version of the paper presented at the conference. I am grateful to the conference discussants for their comments. Any remaining errors are the responsibility of the author.

100

and Mexico, with each country sending over 65 percent of its exports to the United States. Under NAFTA, Canadian exporters will lose some of the competitive advantage they obtained vis-à-vis Mexico under the Canada-U.S. Free Trade Agreement (CAFTA). In quantitative terms, trade diversion effects could be substantial for Canada, which has potentially important implications for Canadian real income.

The analysis presented here is based on a static applied general equilibrium model of the Canadian economy. The model focuses explicitly on the industrial structure and conduct of the Canadian manufacturing industries and has been previously used to examine the impact of the Canada-U.S. Free Trade Agreement (CAFTA) on the Canadian economy; in this chapter, the model is extended to examine NAFTA.[1]

This chapter presents the results from three trade liberalization experiments. The first involves the impact of the ongoing CAFTA on the Canadian economy. CAFTA went into effect in January 1989 and is to be implemented in stages over a ten-year period; in this experiment I assume a full implementation. I next examine NAFTA. Using the CAFTA outcome as a benchmark, I ask what further impact NAFTA will have on the Canadian economy. Results from this experiment are reported at both the economywide level and at the sectoral level. The final experiment considers a scenario in which Canada does not ratify NAFTA, and the United States and Mexico sign a separate bilateral free trade agreement. Some commentators in Canada have referred to such an outcome as a hub-and-spoke (HASP) arrangement in which the United States, with two separate free trade agreements, is the hub and Canada and Mexico are the spokes.[2]

The organization of the chapter is as follows. Section II presents an overview of the model. Section III gives a detailed description of the model structure. Section IV describes the data used to calibrate the model. The fifth section presents the results from the CAFTA, NAFTA, and HASP experiments. In Section VI the sensitivity of the results from the NAFTA and HASP experiments with respect to some model parameters are discussed. The final section summarizes the main conclusions.

II. An Overview of the Model

The model is a general equilibrium model of the Canadian economy. In the model there are 19 industries, of which 14 produce internationally traded goods and the remaining 5 produce nontraded goods. The model is a less than complete regional general equilibrium model in that behavior in each of the foreign regions – the United States, Mexico, and the rest of the world (ROW) – is summarized by exogenous domestic prices and income and a set of export demand functions. Following Armington (1969), I adopt the assumption that the same physical commodities produced in each region are perceived by consumers and producers to be close but imperfect substitutes. As a result of these assumptions, Canada is viewed as an ''almost'' small open economy that faces perfectly elastic import supply functions from the foreign regions but in export markets faces a set of downward-sloping export demand functions.

There are two primary factors in the model: capital and labour. Each factor is assumed to be mobile between industries and firms. In addition, capital services are internationally mobile, at the exogenous world rental rate. Labour is internationally immobile, and its wage is determined in a competitive labour market. The resource endowment of the economy consists of a fixed supply of capital and labour. The aggregate income of the economy is derived from the ownership of the labour and capital endowment, possible economic profits accruing to firms in noncompetitive industries, and net government transfers. Government revenue is raised through the system of taxes, tariffs, and subsidies in place. All government revenue is transferred to the consumption sector in a lump-sum manner.

The industries in the model divide into two groups: the competitive constant returns to scale industries and the noncompetitive increasing returns to scale industries. There are nine competitive industries, which consist of the five nontraded-good industries and four traded-good industries. The noncompetitive industries consist of ten manufacturing industries that produce traded goods. Each noncompetitive industry is composed of an endogenously determined number of representative firms. The technology of each firm is characterized by decreasing average costs of production. Firms select their output price by choosing a markup on unit variable cost. Two hypotheses are used to characterize the pricing decision of the firm. The first hypothesis follows Negishi (1960–61) and is based on the notion of a perceived demand curve. Given its perceived demand curve, each firm selects the markup that maximizes profit. The other hypothesis is based on the collusive model of pricing advanced by Eastman-Stykolt (1960). Under this hypothesis, firms within an industry set the domestic price equal to the price of the competing foreign import good plus the domestic tariff. In the simulations of the model that I report, the actual price set is assumed to be a weighted average of the prices selected by the two hypotheses.

In the noncompetitive industries, freedom of entry and exit is assumed so that firms will enter and exit in response to existence of profits and losses. Long-run equilibrium at the industry level is characterized by the condition that all firms earn zero profits.

On the consumption side of the model, domestic final demand is generated by a single aggregate consumer who maximizes a utility function subject to the economy's budget constraint. For each commodity category, this process will yield a demand function for Canadian, U.S., Mexican, and ROW goods. Export demand for Canadian goods is generated in each of the foreign regions by an aggregate consumer with exogenous income. For each domestic traded-good industry, total demand for its product consists of domestic final demand, export demand from the foreign regions, and intermediate demand from other domestic industries.

A general equilibrium in the model is characterized by a situation in which all industries are in equilibrium, all product markets are clear, and in the labour market supply equals demand.

III. The Model

In this section the details of the model are presented. Some of the notation used in describing the model is listed in Table 4.1. In order to avoid excessive notation, the model will be outlined without reference to taxes, tariffs, or subsidies. In the empirical implementation of the model most of the relevant distortions are present.

Technology

In the competitive industries, technology is described by a constant-returns-to-scale, industry production function. The inputs of the production function include labour, capital, and the output of other industries (both do-

Table 4.1. *Notation*

Regional Superscripts:	c	Canada
	u	United States
	m	Mexico
	r	R.O.W.
Commodity Classes:	N:	index set for noncompetitive industries
	C:	index set for competitive industries
	T:	index set for traded goods industries
	L:	N U C
$p^c = (p_{ci})_{i \in L}$		Canadian commodity prices
$p^u = (p_{ui})_{i \in L}$		U.S. commodity prices
$p^m = (p_{mi})_{i \in L}$		Mexican commodity prices
$P^r = (p_{ri})_{i \in L}$		R.O.W. commodity prices
$w =$		domestic wage
$r =$		world rental on capital
$P =$		$(p_c, p_u, p_m, p_r, w, r)$ price system

mestic and imported). This technology is summarized by a unit cost function v^i. The functional form of v^i is Cobb-Douglas.

$$\log v^i (P) = \gamma_{oi} + \sum_{j \in L} \sigma_{ij} \log \Gamma_{ij} + \alpha_{iw} \log w + \alpha_{ir} \log r \qquad (4.1)$$

Γ_{ij} is the price index of a composite input used by industry i that includes both domestic and foreign varieties of good j. The functional form of Γ_{ij} is also Cobb-Douglas.

$$\begin{aligned} log\ \Gamma_{ij} = {}& log\ \gamma_{ij}^o + \beta_{ij}^c\ log\ p_{cj} + \beta_{ij}^u\ log\ p_{uj} \\ & + \beta_{ij}^M\ log\ p_{mj} + \beta_{ij}^r\ log\ p_{rj} \end{aligned} \qquad (4.2)$$

where the parameters $\{(\alpha_{ij}),\alpha_{iw},\alpha_{ir}\}$ *and* $\{\beta_{ij}^c),(\beta_{ij}^u),(\beta_{ij}^M),(\beta_{ij}^R)\}$ are the share parameters associated with the Cobb-Douglas functional forms.

Within each noncompetitive industry, each firm has an identical technology characterized by decreasing average costs of production. The total cost function of each representative firm consists of both variable and fixed costs. The fixed costs consist of labour and capital costs that represent the expenditure required to set up a plant. Fixed costs are given by the function

$$F_i(r,w) = r \cdot f_k^i + w \cdot f_L^i \qquad (4.3)$$

where f_K^i and f_L^i represent the amount of capital and of labour respectively, needed to set up a plant. Variable costs per unit of output are assumed to be independent of output. The total costs of the firm are

$$TC_i = F_i\ (r,w) + v^i(P)y_i \qquad (4.4)$$

where y_i is output per firm and v^i is now defined as variable unit cost and is assumed to have the same functional form as in the competitive industries. This specification of the total cost function leads to an average cost function that declines with the level of output and asymptotically approaches unit variable cost.

The input-output coefficients for domestic and imported intermediate goods are derived by Shepard's lemma applied to equations 4.1 and 4.2. The domestic Leontief matrix $A^c(P) = [\alpha_{ij}^c(P)]$ is defined by

$$\alpha_{ij}^c(P) = \frac{\alpha_{ij}\beta_{ij}v^i(P)}{p_{cj}} \qquad (4.5)$$

where a_{ij}^c is the demand for domestic good j per unit of output of good i. The Leontief matrices $A^u(P)$, $A^m(P)$, and $A^r(P)$ for imports from the United States, Mexico, and ROW are defined in a similar manner.

Final Demand

Final demand for each commodity category consists of domestic final demand and export demand by each of the foreign regions. Domestic final demand is assumed to be generated by a single consumer who maximizes an aggregate utility function. The functional form of the utility function is given by the log-linear form

$$\log U = \log \mu_o + \sum_{i \in L} \mu_i \log C_i \tag{4.6}$$

For each nontraded good, C_i represents the amount of the good consumed. For each of the traded goods, C_i is a CES aggregator

$$C_i = \left[\gamma_{ci} D_{ci}^{\rho_i} + \gamma_{ui} D_{ui}^{\rho_i} + \gamma_{mi} D_{mi}^{\rho_i} + \gamma_{ri} D_{ri}^{\rho_i} \right]^{1/\rho_i} \tag{4.7}$$

where D_{ci}, D_{ui}, D_{mi}, and D_{ri} are the consumption levels of domestic, U.S., Mexican, and ROW goods within each commodity category and $\sigma_{ci} = \dfrac{1}{1 - \rho_i}$ is the elasticity of substitution between all goods in category i. Use of the CES subaggregator embodies the Armington assumption that imported and domestic goods within each commodity category are viewed as imperfect substitutes by the consumer.

Given prices P for all commodities and income I, utility maximization leads to demand functions for all traded and nontraded goods. The demand for domestic traded good i is given by

$$D_{ci} = \frac{\mu_i \, I \gamma_{ci}^{\sigma_{ci}} \, p_{ci}^{-\sigma_{ci}}}{\gamma_{ci}^{\sigma_{ci}} \, p_{ci}^{1-\sigma_{ci}} + \gamma_{ui}^{\sigma_{ci}} \, p_{ui}^{1-\sigma_{ci}} + \gamma_{mi}^{\sigma_{ci}} \, p_{mi}^{1-\sigma_{ci}} + \gamma_{ri}^{\sigma_{ci}} \, p_{ri}^{(1-\sigma_{ci})}} \tag{4.8}$$

Final demand for goods from the other regions D_{ui}, D_{mi}, and D_{ri} have similar functional forms. Demand for nontraded good i is given by

$$D_{ci} = \frac{\mu_i \, I}{P_{ci}} \tag{4.9}$$

Final demand in each of the foreign regions is also generated by an aggregate consumer who, with exogenous income, maximizes a utility function subject to a budget constraint. As in the Canadian case, the utility functions of the foreign consumers have a nested form in which the top level is Cobb-Douglas and the bottom level is CES. Given the prices for goods from all regions, utility maximization in each foreign region will generate a demand function for Canadian, U.S., Mexico, and ROW goods. For example, in the United States utility maximization will yield a demand function E_{uci} for Canadian export good i of the form

$$E_{uci} = \frac{\mu_i^u \, I^u \, \gamma_{uci}^{\sigma_{ui}} \, p_{ci}^{-\sigma_{ui}}}{\gamma_{uci}^{\sigma_{ui}} \, p_{ci}^{1-\sigma_{ui}} + \gamma_{uui}^{\sigma_{ui}} \, p_{ui}^{1-\sigma_{ui}} + \gamma_{umi}^{\sigma_{ui}} \, p_{mi}^{1-\sigma_{ui}} + \gamma_{uri}^{\sigma_{ui}} \, p_{ri}^{1-\sigma_{ui}}} \tag{4.10}$$

U.S. demand for the goods from other regions will have a similar functional form, as will demand originating in Mexico and ROW.

Quasi Equilibrium

Before discussing firm behavior in the noncompetitive industries, I introduce the concept of a short-run quasi equilibrium. The short-run is a period in which the industrial structure in each of the noncompetitive industries is assumed to be fixed. The industrial structure variables include the markup on unit cost by firms $(m_i) = M$ and the number of firms $(Fm_i) = Fm$. Letting $S = (M, Fm)$ denote the vector of industry structure variables, a quasi equilibrium relative to a given S is a situation in which all commodity markets and the labour markets clear. A quasi equilibrium is a fictional device used to organize accounting within the model. It is closely related to, although not identical to, the Marshallian concept of a short-run equilibrium.

In a quasi equilibrium, domestic commodity prices are given by the equations

$$p_{ci} = m_i \, v^i \, (P) \quad i \varepsilon N$$

$$p_{ci} = v^i \, (P) \quad i \varepsilon C \tag{4.11}$$

Solving these equations will determine domestic commodity prices as a function of the wage rate, price-cost markups, and foreign commodity prices. Market clearing in domestic commodity markets requires that supply equals demand. In order to specify the equation of market clearing, I introduce the following notation: Let Z denote the vector of gross industry outputs, let $X(P,I,S)$ denote the vector of domestic final demand for all goods, and let the vector $E(P)$ represent the total export demand from all foreign regions, including zero demand for each of the nontraded goods. Using this notation, commodity market clearing is given by

$$Z = (I - A(P)^T)^{-1} \, (X \, (P,I,S) \, + \, E \, (P)) \tag{4.12}$$

Equilibrium in the labour market is given by

$$L = \sum_{i \varepsilon L} a_{iw}(P) \cdot Z_i \, + \, \sum_{i \varepsilon N} Fm_i \cdot f_L^i \tag{4.13}$$

where a_{iw} is the unit labour requirement in industry i.

Industry profits π_i in each noncompetitive industry are given by

$$\pi_i \, = \, Fm_i \left[(p_{ci} - v^i) \left(\frac{z_i}{Fm_i} \right) - F_i(r,w) \right] \tag{4.14}$$

where z_i is output per firm.

The aggregate income of the consumer is given by

$$I = wL \, + \, rK_D \, + \, \Psi \sum_{i \varepsilon N} \Pi_i \tag{4.15}$$

where L is the aggregate labour endowment and K_D is the domestic capital endowment. The last term represents the domestic share Ψ of total industry profits. The values of L, K_D, and Ψ are all assumed to be exogenous both in the short run and the long run.

Formally, a short-run quasi equilibrium relative to a given S is a wage $W(S)$, domestic commodity price vector $P^c(S)$, income $I(S)$, and vector of gross outputs $Z(S)$ that satisfies equations 4.11 through 4.15. Walras' Law implies that the balance of payments is in equilibrium. Balance-of-payments equilibrium refers to current account balance or the condition that the trade surplus be equal to the sum of rental payments on foreign-owned capital and economic profits accruing to foreign owners of domestic industry.

Firm Behavior in Noncompetitive Industries

Firms use a pricing rule in which price is set as a markup of price over unit variable cost. Two hypotheses are employed in describing the pricing behaviour of firms. Under the monopolistic pricing hypothesis (MPH), each firm perceives a demand curve for its product and on the basis of this chooses the markup of price over marginal cost that maximizes profit. The perceived demand curve is assumed to have the constant elasticity form

$$z_i = k_i \, p_{ci}^{-\varepsilon i} \tag{4.16}$$

The optimal price given by equation 4.16 is characterized by the Lerner rule

$$\frac{p_{ci} - v^i}{p_{ci}} = \frac{1}{\varepsilon_i} \tag{4.17}$$

The perceived demand elasticity ε_i is constructed by having each firm conduct a hypothetical comparative statics experiment in which it changes its price and then observes the change in its demand, assuming that industry demand is evenly shared by all firms in the industry. Consequently, the firm's perceived demand elasticity will be influenced by the underlying technology and preference parameters within the model. The formula for the perceived elasticity is given as a share-weighted average of the market elasticities of final, export, and intermediate demand. For industry i the elasticity is given by

$$\varepsilon_i = \varepsilon_i^c \cdot \frac{D_{ci}}{Z_i} + \varepsilon_i^u \cdot \frac{E_{uci}}{Z_i} + \varepsilon_i^m \cdot \frac{E_{mci}}{Z_i}$$
$$+ \varepsilon_i^r \frac{E_{rci}}{Z_i} + \sum_{j \in L} \frac{\alpha_{ji} Z_j}{Z_i} \varepsilon_{ij}^I \tag{4.18}$$

where ε_i^c is the domestic final demand elasticity, and $(\varepsilon_i^u, \varepsilon_i^m, \varepsilon_i^r)$ are the export demand elasticities in the United States, Mexico, and ROW; and ε_{ij}^I is the elasticity of demand for good i in industry j. These elasticities are in turn related to the parameters of the underlying utility and production functions.[3]

The other pricing hypothesis used is based on the Eastman-Stykolt (1960) model of a protected oligopoly in a small open economy. This is a collusive form of price setting in which domestic firms set their price equal to the focal point provided by the world price of the competing import good plus the domestic tariff. Given the three foreign regions in the model, the focal price could be provided by U.S., Mexican, or ROW imports. Based on the observation that U.S. producers are the leading foreign exporters to each of the manufacturing industries in the data set, it is assumed that the U.S. supply price plus the Canadian tariff on U.S. imports provides the relevant focal point:

$$p_{ci} = p_{ui} (1 + t_i^u) \qquad (4.19)$$

I refer to this form of pricing as the Eastman-Stykolt pricing hypothesis (ESH). Under this hypothesis, a cut in the Canadian tariff on U.S. imports provides a direct route by which domestic prices are lowered as a result of Canada-U.S. trade liberalization. Industrial organization studies of the Canadian manufacturing sector have given empirical support to this hypothesis.[4]

In the policy simulations of the model that I report, the actual price selected by the firm is taken to be an equally weighted average of the prices set according to the MPH and ESH. Although this mixed pricing rule is admittedly ad hoc, it is a tractable way of incorporating both sets of considerations.

Long-run Equilibrium

In a quasi equilibrium, economic profits in the noncompetitive industries will generally be nonzero because of the arbitrary number of firms and the markups used. In the long run, it is assumed that firms will freely enter and/or exit industries in which profits are nonzero. As a a result, long-run industry equilibrium is characterized by a zero-profit condition. In addition, it is assumed that the markups selected by firms will be consistent with the underlying pricing theory. For example, under the MPH, prices are set using the "true" demand elasticity calculated in equation 4.18.

Formally, a long-run equilibrium is a quasi equilibrium with these two additional properties: (1) firms earn zero profits in noncompetitive industries and (2) actual price-cost markups are determined by the appropriate pricing theory.

IV. Calibration

To make the model operational, numerical values must be assigned to all of the parameters. The starting point for the calibration of the model was the microconsistent data set assembled by Harris (1988) to examine CAFTA. This data set was constructed for the year 1981 and is based on an 88-industry version of the model. In order to calibrate the present model, the data set was aggregated to conform to the 19-industry classification. The decision to use a more aggregated model to analyze NAFTA was motivated by the difficulty of obtaining data on North American trade flows at the disaggregated level. In addition to aggregating the data, the 1981 trade flows between Canada, the United States, Mexico, and ROW were adjusted to reflect 1989 market shares in the North American market. This adjustment was done to partially reflect the substantial unilateral liberalization of trade that took place in Mexico in the late 1980s.

There are a number of parameters in the model where numerical values are of particular importance. Given the focus of the study on trade liberalization policies, an important set of parameters is the elasticities of substitution, which represent the consumer's willingness to substitute, within a product category, the products of the four regions. Another set of important parameters, given the presence of increasing returns to scale in production, are the scale elasticities of the cost functions used by firms withing the manufacturing industries. Values for these parameters are based on econometric estimates taken from the literature.

Values for some of the parameters used in the model are presented in Table 4.2. These values are treated as the central case specification. Sensitivity analysis is performed with respect to some of these parameters in Section IV of this chapter. The first column of the table reports the import price elasticities for Canada that were used to calibrate the consumption elasticities of substitution. The value of these import elasticities vary from -1.130 to -3.440. The consumption elasticities of substitution that are computed based on these estimates vary in magnitude from 1.010 to 4.802. In the second column of Table 4.2, the consumption elasticities of substitution for the U.S. consumer are presented. These elasticities vary in value from a low of 2.02 to a high of 3.714. In the absence of any estimates of these elasticities for Mexico and ROW, it is assumed that the U.S. parameter values also apply to these two regions.

Within the manufacturing industries an important parameter is the level of scale economies at the firm level. A common measure of the degree of unexploited scale economies is given by the inverse scale elasticity, which is defined as the ratio of marginal to average cost. As reported in Table 4.2, the inverse scale elasticities range in value from .816 to .941. The smaller is the scale elasticity, the larger is the degree of unexploited economies of scale.

The tariff barriers used in the model are presented in Table 4.3. They are expressed in ad valorem form and were derived from a number of sources of varying reliability. In most cases the trade barriers represent only tariff barriers with no allowances for quotas. They are representative of the tariff rates that were in existence in the mid- to late 1980s.

Once the elasticity parameters of the model are specified, the benchmark data set is interpreted as a quasi equilibrium of the model in which the observed number of firms and markups in the noncompetitive industries is given. The

Table 4.2. *Benchmark Equilibrium Data*

	Import Demand Elasticity	U.S. Elasticity of Substitution	Inverse Scale Elasticity
Food, Beer & Tobacco	-1.458	2.020	.816
Rubber & Plastic	-3.440	2.020	.939
Textiles & Leather	-1.402	3.426	.895
Woods & Paper	-2.150	2.822	.821
Steel & Metal Products	-1.378	2.534	.843
Transportation Equipment	-1.294	2.016	.896
Machines & Appliances	-1.421	3.624	.829
Non-metallic Minerals	-2.799	3.714	.893
Refineries	-2.070	2.020	.925
Chemicals, Misc. Mfg.	-2,053	3.016	.941
Agriculture	-1.940	2.020	
Forestry	-1.130	2.020	
Fishing	-2.220	2.020	
Mining	-2.244	2.020	

long-run equilibrium of the model is then solved by imposing the conditions that zero profits be earned in all industries and markups be selected optimally. It is from this position of long-run equilibrium that the policy exercises are conducted. The algorithm used to solve the long-run equilibrium of the model mimics the Marshallian process in which firms enter and exit in response to the existence of profits and losses. For a given industrial structure, a quasi equilibrium is solved using a numerical interpolation procedure.

V. Trade Liberalization Experiments
Canada-U.S. Free Trade Agreement (CAFTA)
The first trade liberalization experiment examines the impact of CAFTA on the Canadian economy. In this experiment Canada and the United States remove their tariffs against each other while maintaining their tariffs against Mexico and ROW. The results from the experiment are of independent interest; in addition, the CAFTA equilibrium serves as a benchmark for the NAFTA and HASP experiments.

The aggregate results from the CAFTA experiment are presented in Table 4.4. In general the results suggest that Canada benefits significantly from CAFTA. Gross domestic product (GDP) increases 4.5 percent as a result of

Table 4.3. *Ad Valorem Tariff Rates*

	Canada		U.S		Mexico
	Tariff on U.S. Exports	Tariff on Mexico Exports	Tariff on Canadian Exports	Tariff on Mexico Exports	Mexico Tariff on Canadian & U.S. Exports
Food, Bev. and Tobacco	5.7	5.4	5.1	2.6	13.27
Rubber and Plastic	9.4	8.3	4.5	0.2	15.73
Textile and Leather	15.8	15.1	9.8	7.7	16.86
Wood and Paper	3.8	8.6	1.2	1.7	10.37
Steel, Metal Products	5.3	8.0	3.0	2.5	12.57
Transportation Equip.	2.3	1.0	0.8	2.4	16.02
Mach. & Appliances	7.8	4.9	4.2	4.4	16.99
Non-metallic minerals	6.3	2.2	2.6	3.4	14.89
Refineries	0.5	0.0	0.6	0.1	4.40
Chemical, Misc. Mfg.	6.0	8.2	3.7	1.0	13.12
Agriculture	3.0	1.8	2.0	4.0	8.70
Forestry	0.0	0.0	0.2	0.0	9.30
Fishing	0.2	0.0	1.7	0.0	19.60
Mining	0.2	0.0	0.0	0.0	9.66

the agreement. The domestic wage increases by 5.5 percent. The aggregate consumer experiences a real income gain, as measured by the Hicks' equivalent variation as a percent of base national income, of 3 percent. The gain in real income is achieved despite a small decline in the economy's terms of trade.

A significant portion of the gain in welfare can be attributed to the rationalization that occurs within many of the manufacturing industries. Output per firm in the manufacturing sectors increases on average by 16 percent. This is a result, in many industries, of an increase in industry output and a reduction in the number of firms. The increase in output per firm leads to an average increase of 10 percent in labour productivity and 4.3 percent in total factor productivity. The volume of trade increases by 15 percent under CAFTA, and this is reflected in increases in both interindustry and intra-industry trade. The increase in the volume of Canada-U.S. trade is even greater – 25 percent. There is also a small increase (1 percent) in the volume of Canada-Mexico trade as a result of the agreement.

Table 4.4. *Impact on Canada of the Canada-U.S. Free Trade Agreement (CAFTA)*

Variable	Percentage Change
Real Income	3.085
Wage	5.629
Real GDP	4.566
Gross Output	7.803
Output per firm	16.294
Labor reallocation index	1.047
Labor productivity	9.961
Total Factor Productivity	4.279
Trade Volume (Aggregate)	14.769
Trade Volume (Can.-U.S.)	25.701
Trade Volume (Can.-Mexico)	1.090
Terms of Trade	-0.924

Notes: Real income is a measure if Canadian welfare using the Hicks' equivalent variation as a percentage of base national income. The output per firm index is a weighted average of output per firm in each of the manufacturing industries. The labor productivity index is a weighted average of labor productivity in each industry. Total factor productivity is measured by a geometric index of all inputs. The index of total factor productivity is a weighted average across all industries. The labor reallocation index is the percent of the labor force that moves between sectors. The terms of trade by an index of export prices divided by an index of import prices.

In summary, the results suggest that CAFTA will have a significant impact on Canadian real income and that this will be achieved through a rationalization of the Canadian manufacturing sector.

North American Free Trade Agreement (NAFTA)

This section reports the results of a NAFTA experiment in which Canada, the United States, and Mexico remove all tariffs on trilateral trade flows while maintaining in place their tariffs against ROW. The benchmark equilibrium for this experiment is the CAFTA equilibrium, which was reported in the previous section. In this experiment, it is asked what further benefits Canada might achieve by moving from the status quo position of CAFTA to NAFTA.

The aggregate effects of NAFTA are reported in the second column of Table 4.5. At the economywide level, NAFTA has very little impact. The increase in consumer real income generated by the agreement is a small .02 percent of national income. The increase in GDP is .8 percent, while the increase in the

Table 4.5. *Impact on Canada of the North American Free Trade Agreement (NAFTA) and a Hub-and-Spoke (HASP) Outcome (percentage changes)*

Variable	HASP	NAFTA
Real Income	0.002	0.017
Wage	0.000	0.121
Real GDP	-0.018	0.078
Gross Output	-0.026	0.121
Output per Firm	0.350	0.548
Labour Reallocation Index	0.000	0.053
Labour Productivity	0.012	0.125
Total Factor Productivity	-0.001	0.048
Trade Volume (Aggregate)	-0.001	0.003
Trade Volume (Can.-U.S.)	-0.049	-0.015
Trade Volume (Can.-Mex.)	-4.886	57.296
Terms of Trade	0.000	0.031

Note: See notes in Table 4.4 for definitions of variables.

wage rate is .12 percent. Unlike the CAFTA results, there are negligible increases in labour and total factor productivity. The industry rationalization effects that are associated with CAFTA do not materialize with NAFTA. In the manufacturing sector, output per firm increases on average by only .55 percent. The negligible impact NAFTA has on the allocation of resources is reflected in the small percentage of labour, .05 percent, that shifts intersectorally. There is virtually no change in Canada's overall trade volume, but the volume of trade with the United States falls by .2 percent, reflecting a small degree of diversion in trade in the U.S. market. In contrast, the volume of Canada-Mexico trade increases by a substantial 57 percent, although it must be remembered that this is relative to a small base level. The main theme of the results in this table is clearly the very small impact of NAFTA on the Canadian economy.

In Tables 4.6 and 4.7, sectoral results from the NAFTA experiment are

Table 4.6. *Industry Results: HASP (percentage changes)*

	Output	Employment	Markups	Number of Firms	Output per Firm
Food, Beer & Tobacco	.529	.476	-0.003	0.490	0.039
Rubber & Plastic	.051	-.593	-0.019	-9.772	0.030
Textiles & Leather	.017	-.061	-0.018	-0.013	0.030
Woods & Paper	-.024	-.093	-0.020	-0.066	0.042
Steel & Metal Products	.238	.161	-0.013	0.186	0.052
Transportation Equipment	.224	.141	-0.013	0.162	0.062
Machines & Appliances	.578	.578	-0.014	0.698	-0.119
Non-metallic Minerals	.060	-.016	-0.019	0.024	0.036
Refineries	.089	.027	-0.004	0.027	0.061
Chemicals, Misc. Mfg.	.053	-.330	-0.015	-4.352	4.606
Agriculture	.358	.257			
Forestry	-.044	-.110			
Fishing	.251	.180			
Mining	.123	.030			
Construction	.015	-.058			
Transportation	.036	-.027			
Communications	.028	-.027			
Utilities	.057	-.031			
Other Services	.024	-.041			

presented. Table 4.6 reports the percentage change in output, employment, price-cost markups, number of firms, and output per firm. Table 4.7 reports percentage changes in exports and imports by region.

Focusing first on Table 4.6, the results suggest that there is virtually no impact at the industry level. In all industries the change in output is less than 1 percent, and all industries, with the exceptions of woods & paper and forestry expand their output. In terms of employment, 11 industries, including all of the nontraded-good sectors, experience a fall in employment, although the fall is less than 1 percent in all cases. Of the industries that expand their output, rubber & plastic and machinery & appliances do the best, but the increases

Table 4.7. *Trade Results: NAFTA (percentage changes)*

	Exports			Imports		
	U.S.	Mexico	ROW	U.S.	Mexico	ROW
Food, Bev. & Tobacco	-.090	63.031	-.057	.189	7.289	.192
Rubber & Plastic	-.140	75.549	-.138	.155	15.682	.156
Textiles & Leather	-.414	183.327	-.212	.074	20.068	.074
Woods & Paper	-.199	66.704	-.166	.103	11.915	.103
Steel & Metal	-.195	62.810	-.136	.182	9.762	.183
Transportation Equipment	-.149	61.624	-.105	.129	1.662	.129
Machines & Appliances	-.603	162,206	-.278	.202	6.807	.206
Non-metallic	-.443	170.007	-.272	.132	2.818	.132
Refineries	-.023	17.007	-.023	.099	.099	.099
Chemicals, Misc. Mfg.	-.202	84,128	-.166	.118	13.331	.120
Agriculture	-.125	37.172	-.081	.417	2.550	.419
Forestry	-.211	40.746	-.223	.015	.000	.015
Fishing	-.202	95.055	-.204	.425	.425	.425
Mining	-.110	42.902	-.106	.133	.133	.133

are on the order of .5 percent. Turning to the industrial structure variables in the manufacturing sector, NAFTA has a slight procompetitive effect, resulting in a marginal decrease in price-cost markups. However, with the exception of rubber & plastic and chemicals & miscalleneous manufacturing, there is virtually no change in the number of firms in each industry and no impact on output per firm.

In Table 4.7, the impact of NAFTA on sectoral trade flows is presented. The table reveals a substantial increase in Canada-Mexico trade in all sectors. All sectors experience a very large increase in exports to Mexico, albeit from a very small base, with textiles & leather experiencing the largest gain, 183 percent. Clearly, Canadian producers benefit from improved access to the Mexican market. In the domestic market, imports from Mexico also increase in all industries, although to a lesser degree. Interestingly the sector that experiences the largest increase in Mexican imports is textiles & leather, with an increase of 20 percent. Overall, most industries experience an increase in net exports to Mexico.

A concern among Canadian producers is that NAFTA, by improving Mexican access to the U.S. market, will erode the competitive advantage of Canadian exporters to the U.S. The results of Table 4.7 suggest there is an element of truth to these fears, as exports to the U.S. decline in every industry. However, in quantitative terms the impact is trivial. In all industries the decline in exports to the United States is well under 1 percent. There is some displacement of Canadian exports to the United States by Mexican exports, but in general the impact is very small. The small decline in exports to the U.S is also matched by a small decline in exports to ROW by all industries.

The results from this trade experiment indicate that NAFTA will have little impact on the Canadian economy. At the aggregate level there is a favourable effect on GDP and real income, but the impact is small. The most notable feature of the results is the expansion in the volume of Canada-Mexico trade.

Hub-and-Spoke Model (HASP)

The last trade experiment is one in which the United States and Mexico sign a separate bilateral free trade agreement and Canada does not participate. I refer to such an arrangement as the hub-and-spoke model (HASP) in which the United States, with separate bilateral trade agreements, is the hub and Canada and Mexico are the spokes. In this section the results of a HASP outcome are presented under the assumption that the United States and Mexico completely remove their tariffs on bilateral trade. The benchmark equilibrium for this experiment is the CAFTA equilibrium. The question asked in this experiment is what economic impact a HASP arrangement would have on Canada relative to the status quo position of the CAFTA.

A summary of the aggregate results from the HASP experiment are presented in the first column of Table 4.5. Overall, the results suggest that a HASP arrangement will have very little impact on the Canadian economy. There is very little change in any of the aggregate statistics. There is a slight decline in GDP of .02 percent but virtually no change in aggregate real income. A HASP results in a very small reduction in the aggregate volume of trade. The volume of Canada-U.S. trade decreases by less than .05 percent, indicating that at the aggregate level a separate U.S.-Mexico FTA will result in very little diversion of Canada-U.S. trade. The impact on the volume of Canada-Mexico trade is more pronounced, with a decline of 5 percent.

Sectoral results from the HASP experiment are listed in Tables 4.8 and 4.9. Table 4.8 reports the percentage changes in output, employment, price-cost markups, number of firms, and output per firm caused by the HASP outcome. The conclusion that emerges from this table is the overall trivial effect the HASP outcome has at the industry level. Although output and employment are adversely affected in almost all industries, the impact is very small. Machinery & appliances suffers the largest loss in output, which is on the order of .2 percent; for all other industries the loss is less than .09 percent. In terms

Table 4.8. *Industry Results: HASP (percentage changes)*

	Output	Employment	Markups	Number of Firms	Output per Firm
Food, Beer & Tobacco	-.013	-.023	.000	-.025	.012
Rubber & Plastic	-.022	-.367	.000	-6.062	6.400
Textiles & Leather	-.041	-.040	.000	-.034	-.007
Woods & Paper	-.017	-.020	.000	-.025	.008
Steel & Metal Products	-.077	-.085	.000	-.095	.018
Transportation Equipment	-.087	-.088	.000	-.090	.003
Machines & Appliances	-.193	-.207	-.001	-.225	.033
Non-metallic Minerals	-.032	-.031	.000	-.025	-.007
Refineries	-.009	-.001	.000	-.001	-.008
Chemicals, Misc. Mfg.	-.026	-.210	.000	-2.759.	
Agriculture	-.013	-.013			
Forestry	-.016	-.016			
Fishing	-.014	-.014			
Mining	-.016	-.016			
Construction	.000	.000			
Transportation	-.011	-.011			
Communications	-.010	-.011			
Utilities	-.011	-.011			
Other Services	-.005	-.005			

of employment losses, rubber & plastic is the leading industry, but the loss is less than .4 percent. Within the manufacturing industries there is no change in the price-cost markups selected by firms, and with the exception of two industries, rubber & plastic and chemicals & miscellaneous manufacturing, there is virtually no impact on the number of firms or output per firm.

The impact of the HASP on the volume of trade by industry is reported in Table 4.9. The results in this table suggest that a separate U.S.-Mexico trade agreement will not significantly reduce Canadian exports to the United States. All industries suffer a decline in exports destined for the U.S., but in all cases the decline is very small. The industry suffering the largest loss in exports to

Table 4.9. *Trade Results: HASP (percentage changes)*

	Exports			Imports		
	U.S.	Mexico	ROW	U.S.	Mexico	ROW
Food, Bev. & Tobacco	-.033	-1.120	-.002	-.007	-.004	-.005
Rubber & Plastic	-.003	-2.554	-.002	-.032	-.029	-.031
Textiles & Leather	-.189	-2.319	-.003	-.023	-.020	-.022
Woods & Paper	-.027	-4.256	-.001	-.016	-.014	-.015
Steel & Metal	-.059	-10.187	.002	-.047	-.042	-.044
Transportation Equipment	-.047	-10.753	-.001	-.029	-.028	-.029
Machines & Appliances	-.319	-14.335	-.009	-.053	-.051	-.051
Non-metallic	.170	-3.175	.001	-.021	-.019	-.021
Refineries	-.001	-1.654	-.001	-.009	-.008	-.007
Chemicals, Misc. Mfg.	-.038	-12.266	-.001	-.023	-.019	-.021
Agriculture	-.043	-1.918	.000	-.011	-.010	-.012
Forestry	.000	-1.512	.000	-.016	.000	-.001
Fishing	.000	-5.153	.000	-.022	-.018	
Mining	.000	-0.954	.000	-.025	-.024	

the United States is machinery & appliances with a decline of .3 percent. Overall, Canadian industries do not suffer a significant loss of competitive advantage in the U.S. market. Canadian exports to Mexico are, however, adversely affected. Within the Mexican market, the reduction of tariffs on U.S. goods induces a substitution away from Canadian exports that affects all industries. Among the industries that suffer the biggest losses are steel & metal products, transportation equipment, and machinery & appliances, whose exports decline over 10 percent.

The conclusion that emerges from this trade experiment is that Canada will be little affected by nonparticipation in NAFTA.

VI. Sensitivity Analysis

This section considers the extent to which the results are sensitive to the numerical specification of the model. For the trade liberalization experiments, a key parameter is the elasticity that governs the willingness of the

Table 4.10. *Sensitivity Analysis: NAFTA*

Domestic Import Elasticities Scaling Parameters				
	1.0	2.0	2.5	3.0
Wage	.122	.122	.122	.122
Real Income	.017	.019	.019	.019
Can.-U.S. Trade Volume	-.015	-.010	-.008	-.007
Can.-Mex Trade Volume	57.296	58.119	58.426	58.581
Labour Productivity	.125	.124	.124	.123

U.S. Elasticity of Substitution Scaling Parameter				
	1.0	1.25	1.5	2.0
Wage	.122	.119	.056	.009
Real Income	.017	.017	.016	.015
Can.-U.S. Trade Volume	-.015	-.073	-.063	-.125
Can.-Mex. Trade Volume	57.296	57.002	56.6287	55.496
Labour Productivity	.125	.124	.086	.033

Mexican Elasticity of Substitution Scaling Parameters				
	1.0	1.25	1.5	2.0
Wage	.121	.182	.244	.702
Real Income	.017	.022	.034	.194
Can.-U.S. Trade Volume	-.015	-.019	-.004	.236
Can.-Mex. Trade Volume	57.296	79.166	105.639	176.026
Labour Productivity	.125	.168	.214	.789

consumer in each region to substitute, within a commodity class, the goods of all regions. In order to examine this issue for the NAFTA and HASP outcomes, I conducted a sensitivity analysis in which the consumer elasticities of substitution in Canada, the United States, and Mexico were separately varied.[5] The results from this investigation are reported in Table 4.10 for the NAFTA experiment and in Table 4.11 for the HASP experiment. The value of the scaling parameter in each experiment indicates the proportion by which the model parameter was scaled. The central case value of each model parameter corresponds to a scaling parameter value of 1.0.

Table 4.11. *Sensitivity Analysis: HASP*

Domestic Import Elasticities Scaling Parameters				
	1.0	2.0	2.5	3.0
Wage	.000	.000	.000	.000
Real Income	.002	.006	.005	.005
Can.-U.S. Trade Volume	-.049	-.047	-.047	-.047
Can.-Mex Trade Volume	-4.886	-4.909	-4.916	-4.919
Labour Productivity	.012	.013	.013	.013

U.S. Elasticity of Substitution Scaling Parameter				
	1.0	1.25	1.5	2.0
Wage	.000	.000	.000	.000
Real Income	.002	.001	-.003	.014
Can.-U.S. Trade Volume	-.049	-.072	-.104	-.202
Can.-Mex. Trade Volume	-4.886	-4.861	4.821	4.722
Labour Productivity	.012	.012	.011	.006

Mexican Elasticity of Substitution Scaling Parameters				
	1.0	1.25	1.5	2.0
Wage	.000	.000	.000	.000
Real Income	.002	.000	-.002	-.008
Can.-U.S. Trade Volume	-.049	-.059	-.061	-.081
Can.-Mex. Trade Volume	-4.886	-6.941	-9.294	-15.058
Labour Productivity	.012	.011	.011	.011

First, consider increases in the domestic elasticity of substitution that is achieved, through calibration, by an increase in the domestic demand elasticities. From Tables 4.10 and 4.11 it does not appear that variations in this parameter have much impact on either the NAFTA or HASP results. For the HASP experiment, this is not surprising because there is no reduction in the domestic tariff against Mexican goods. In the case of the NAFTA experiment, one might anticipate that the results would be sensitive because a greater degree of consumption substitutability would result in an increased demand for Mexican imports as the domestic tariff is removed. However, that is not the case. The volume of Canada-Mexico trade does increase as expected, but only marginally. There is little change in the other aggregate variables.

Given that over 70 percent of Canada's trade is with the United States, an important parameter for both the NAFTA and HASP experiments is the degree to which Mexican and Canadian goods are viewed as substitutes within the U.S. market. To the extent that Mexican and Canadian goods are close substitutes, one would anticipate that a removal of U.S. tariffs on Mexican imports would cause U.S. import demand to shift from Canadian to Mexican goods. Examining the HASP results, it is apparent that increasing the U.S. elasticity of substitution does negatively affect the volume of Canada-U.S. trade, although in absolute magnitude the impact is quite small. Higher values of the U.S. elasticity also lead to the HASP having a small negative impact on real income. For the NAFTA experiment, the impact is quite similar, with an increased elasticity value lending to a slight decrease in the volume of Canada-U.S. trade. The volume of Canada-Mexico trade also decreases slightly. The level of real income that results from NAFTA is little affected by the increased elasticity of substitution. Overall, the results from the NAFTA and HASP experiments are basically insensitive to changes in the U.S. elasticity of substitution.

Finally, consider increases in the Mexican elasticity of substitution. In the NAFTA experiment, this results in a very substantial increase in Canada-Mexico trade as Canada benefits vis-à-vis ROW from the cut in the Mexican tariff. A doubling of the elasticity of substitution results in the increase in the volume of Canada-Mexico trade moving from 57 percent to 176 percent. This increase in trade is also matched by an increase in real income that, though still small in absolute terms (.19 percent), represents a substantial increase from the base value of .017 percent. In the HASP experiment, increasing the Mexican elasticity of substitution results in a decreased in Canada-Mexico trade as the Mexican consumer shifts expenditure from Canadian goods to now-cheaper U.S. goods. With a doubling of the elasticity of substitution, the decrease in the volume of Canada-Mexico trade moves from -4.8 percent to -15 percent. The level of real income in Canada is also adversely affected to a small degree as the elasticity is increased.

VII. Conclusions

This chapter has provided some quantitative estimates of the impact on Canada of a number of North American trade liberalization initiatives. The analysis is based on a static applied general equilibrium model of the Canadian economy. The initiatives considered were the ongoing Canada-U.S. Free Trade Agreement, the proposed North American Free Trade Agreement, and a possible hub-and-spoke outcome with the U.S. and Mexico signing a separate free trade agreement.

The following conclusions emerge from this study. First, CAFTA leads to a significant increase in real income for the Canadian economy. The primary source of this welfare gain is a rationalization of the manufacturing sectors due to increased competition from U.S. producers and enhanced market access to the United States. Second, NAFTA would have little overall impact on the Canadian economy. The agreement generates a very small gain in real income. Canada would experience little in the way of diversion of exports from the U.S. market, while the volume of trade with Mexico would increase significantly. At the industry level there is very little change in output or employment, and in the manufacturing industries there is little change in the numbers of firms. Finally, if Canada does not ratify NAFTA and a HASP outcome is achieved instead, the results suggest that Canada will be little affected at either the aggregate or the industry level. Improved Mexican access to the U.S. market does not result in a significant diversion of Canadian exports to the United States. Overall, the results suggest that the effects of a NAFTA or a HASP outcome on Canada are likely to be indistinguishable.

As a final comment, the reader is cautioned that this analysis is based on a static model that does not take account of any effects NAFTA will have on income and productivity growth in Mexico. If such effects are significant, these results likely understate the impact of NAFTA on Canada. Integrating such growth effects into the analysis is clearly an important topic for future research.

Endnotes

1. The model is referred to as the General Equilibrium Trade (GET) model. A detailed technical description of the GET model is provided by Harris (1988).

2. See, for example, the discussion in Lipsey (1990) and Wonnacott (1990).

3. Expressions for the elasticities are derived explicitly in Harris (1988). See also Harris (1984).

4. Caves, Porter, and Spence (1980) provide an overview of oligopolistic pricing behavior in the Canadian manufacturing industries.

5. Other sensitivity experiments examining the impact of increases in Mexican productivity and real income as a result of NAFTA are presented in Cox and Harris (1992).

References

Armington, P.S. 1969."A theory of demand for products distinguished by place of production." *International Monetary Fund Staff Papers* 16:159–78.

Caves, R.E., M.E. Porter, and A.M. Spence, with J.T. Scott. 1980. *Competition in the open economy: A model applied to Canada.* Cambridge, MA: Harvard University Press.

Cox, D., and R. Harris. 1992. "North American free trade and its implications for Canada: Results from a CGE model of North American trade." *The World Economy* 15:31–44.

Eastman, H., and S. Stykolt. 1960. "A model for the study of protected oligopolies." *Economic Journal* 70:336–47.

Harris, R.G. 1984. "Applied general equilibrium analysis of small open economies with scale economies and imperfect competition." *American Economic Review* 74:1016–31.

———. 1988. "A guide to the GET model." Working Paper 88-10, Department of Finance, Ottawa, Canada.

Lipsey, R.G. 1990. *Canada at the U.S. Mexico free trade dance.* C.D. Howe Institute, Toronto.

Negishi, T. 1960–61. "Monopolistic competition and general equilibrium." *Review of Economics Studies* 28:196–01.

Wonnacott, R.J. 1990. *Canada and the U.S.-Mexico free trade negotiations.* C.D. Howe Institute, Toronto.

5

Properties of Applied General Equilibrium Trade Models with Monopolistic Competition and Foreign Direct Investment*

Drusilla K. Brown
Tufts University

I. Introduction

Applied general equilibrium (AGE) modeling has become the tool of choice in *ex ante* evaluation of international trade policy. However, economy-wide models frequently seem inscrutable to the outside observer and, in some cases, to the model designers themselves. It is sometimes difficult to untangle the economic mechanics underlying counterintuitive results.

For example, one of the more curious results from multicountry AGE models of a North American Free Trade Agreement (NAFTA) concerns the effect of economic integration on factor prices. Based on the Stolper-Samuelson Theorem, we might expect that the real return to at least one factor in each country will fall as a result of NAFTA. However, most of the general equilibrium models of NAFTA find that the returns to nearly all factors of production within North America rise. This is the case even for unskilled labor in the United States and capital in Mexico.

Analytical models generally provide an excellent guide to understanding AGE models in which goods markets are perfectly competitive.[1] Factor market imperfections, such as a rigid real wage, easily account for the nonnegative

* The paper reports some results from a joint research project undertaken with Richard Harris. The research underlying this paper was supported by the Fraser Institute and the Lily Foundation. This is a substantially revised version of the paper presented at the conference. I am grateful to the conference discussants for their comments. Any remaining errors are the responsibility of the author.

Mexican rental rate effects in the models of Bachrach and Mizrahi (1992) and Roland-Holst, Reinert, and Shiells (1992). National product differentiation, as in Hinojosa-Ojeda and Robinson (1991), and its associated term-of-trade effects played a role in maintaining the return to unskilled labor in the United States.

By comparison, analytical models with imperfectly competitive markets are rarely sufficiently general to satisfactorily explain results from the AGE models with increasing returns to scale, as in Brown, Deardorff, and Stern (1992a,b). Theoretical models with monopolistically competitive firms have been studied extensively. Some more notable contributions are Brown (1991), Harris (1984), Horstmann and Markusen (1986), Krugman (1980, 1981, 1991), Lancaster (1984), Markusen and Svensson (1985, 1986), and Markusen and Wigle (1989). However, simplifying assumptions such as (1) one country, (2) one sector, (3) one factor, (4) linear demands, (5) small country, or (6) constant elasticity demands limit the ability of the theoretical models to aid our understanding of the multicountry, multisector general equilibrium models.

Our purpose here is to draw on the existing literature dealing with the effects of trade policy on monopolistically competitive firms in order to elucidate some of the less transparent results of the Michigan Model's evaluation of NAFTA. The theoretical models will be used in combination with a simple numeric model that preserves the theoretical richness of the AGE models without the extensive sectoral detail.

II. The Michigan Model of NAFTA

The Michigan Model (see Brown, Deardorff, and Stern, 1992a) has been adapted to study North American economic integration. This is a model with 5 country groups, 23 tradable-goods sectors, 6 nontradable-goods sectors, and 2 intersectorally mobile primary inputs. Technology in most of the tradable sectors is increasing returns to scale, and the market structure is monopolistically competitive. Trade policy is introduced using tariffs and tariff equivalents of nontariff barriers, and international capital flows are permitted in some liberalization scenarios.

The model predicts that none of the concerns associated with economic integration are likely to emerge. Welfare rises in all three participating countries (Canada, the United States and Mexico), and the welfare losses by the rest of the world are minuscule. Canada's position in the U.S. market is not noticeably eroded by the addition of Mexico to the U.S.-Canada free trade agreement. Trade liberalization narrows the wage gap between U.S. and Mexican workers, perhaps stemming illegal immigration, but U.S. workers still gain from the agreement. Scale effects are positive in nearly all industries in all three countries, with the largest gains emerging in Mexico. Despite the fact that Mexico is a labor-abundant country, liberalization raises the return to

Table 5.1. *Changes in Economic Welfare Due to Formation of a North American Free Trade Area*

	United States		Canada		Mexico	
	Millions of US$	Percent GDP	Millions of US$	Percent GDP	Millions of US$	Percent GDP
1. NAFTA - Tariffs, NTBs	$ 6,449.1	0.1%	$3,508.4	0.7%	$1,977.2	1.6%
2. NAFTA - Tariffs, NTBs	13,226.6	0.3	3,662.9	0.7	6,298.5	5.0
3. U.S.- Mexico Tariffs, NTBs	3,664.5	0.1	78.2	0.0	1,922.7	1.5
4. U.S.-Mexico Tariffs, NTBs, FDI	10,654.1	0.2	234.2	0.0	6,255.3	4.9
5. U.S.-Canada	2,867.8	0.1	3,356.4	0.6	35.8	0.0

Note: Five experiments have been performed. These are:
1. Removal of tariffs on trade among the United States, Canada, and Mexico, plus a 25 percent expansion of U.S. import quotas imposed on Mexican exports of agriculture, food, textiles, and clothing.
2. Same as experiment (1) plus relaxation of Mexico's capital import controls that results in a 10 percent increase in the capital stock in Mexico.
3. Removal of tariffs on trade between the United States and Mexico, plus a 25 percent expansion of U.S. import quotas imposed on Mexico exports of agriculture, food, textiles, and clothing.
4. Same as experiment (3) plus relaxation of Mexico's capital import controls that results in a 10 percent increase in the capital stock in Mexico.
5. Removal of tariffs on trade between the United States and Canada. Source: Brown, Deardorff and Stern (1992a).

capital in Mexico relative to other countries in the model, attracting new foreign investment. The scale gains associated with a capital inflow into Mexico are so strong that the return to capital in Mexico actually rises relative to the return to capital in other countries. The fear that U.S. firms will relocate plants in Mexico seems largely unfounded. Adjustment costs associated with intersectoral factor reallocation in the United States will be very small, and pollution problems in Mexico should be somewhat mitigated by a free trade agreement [see Grossman and Krueger (1991)].

Several North American liberalization scenarios were evaluated using the Michigan Model. Detailed descriptions are provided in the footnote to Table 5.1. Experiments 1 and 2 consider the effect of trilateral tariff removal and some liberalization of nontariff barriers (NTBs). In experiment 1, capital is taken to be intersectorally mobile but not internationally mobile, whereas in experiment 2 some physical capital is assumed to flow into Mexico from outside North America. Experiments 3 and 4 are similar to 1 and 2, with the

Table 5.2. *Percent Changes in Real Return to Labor and Capital Due to Formation of a North American Free Trade Area*

	United States		Canada		Mexico	
	Wage	Rental Rate	Wage	Rental Rate	Wage	Rental Rate
1. NAFTA – Tariffs, NTBs	0.2%	0.2%	0.4%	0.4%	0.7%	0.6%
2. NAFTA – Tariffs, NTBs, FDI	0.2	0.2	0.5	0.5	9.3	3.3
3. U.S.-Mexico Tariffs, NTBs, FDI	0.0	0.1	-0.1	-0.1	0.7	0.6
4. U.S.-Mexico Tariffs, NTBs, FDI	0.1	0.1	0.1	0.1	9.3	3.3
5. U.S.-Canada Tariffs, NTBs, FDI	0.1	0.1	0.4	0.4	-0.1	-0.1

Note: Five experiments have been performed. See footnote to Table 5.1 for details.
Source: Brown, Deardorff, and Stern (1992a).

exception that liberalization occurs between the United States and Mexico only. Finally, experiment 5 evaluates tariff removal between the United States and Canada as provided for in the Canada-U.S. Free Trade Agreement (CAFTA).

The welfare effects, as measured by the equivalent variation, are reported in Table 5.1. Note, first, that an agreement is welfare improving for all participating countries in each liberalization scenario. The impact on Mexico is clearly largest, with welfare rising by as much as 5 percent of GNP with the adoption of NAFTA and increased capital inflows.

The impact of the agreement on the returns to capital and labor are detailed in Table 5.2. NAFTA has the expected effect of raising the wage-rent ratio in Mexico. Under trade liberalization scenario 1, wages in Mexico rise by 0.7 percent, and the return to capital rises by 0.6 percent. In addition, the U.S.-Mexican wage gap narrows. U.S. wages rise by only 0.2 percent. However, contrary to the Stolper-Samuelson Theorem, the return to the scarce factor in both countries rises.

In addition, the capital inflow into Mexico actually widens the rental rate gap between Mexico and the other countries of the model. For example, comparing experiments 1 and 2, in the absence of capital flows NAFTA raises the return to capital in Mexico by 0.6 percent, whereas in the presence of capital inflows the return to capital in Mexico rises by 3.3 percent. In comparison, in both experiments, the return to capital in the United States rises by only 0.2 percent.

Table 5.3. *Percent Change in Output per Firm, North American Free Trade: Tariffs, NTBs, and Foreign Direct Investment*

Sector		Mexico	United States	Canada
1	Agriculture	–	–	–
310	Food	1.99%	0.014%	0.01%
321	Textiles	1.42	0.56	0.58
322	Clothing	2.78	0.64	0.64
323	Leather Products	3.56	0.28	0.84
324	Footwear	3.22	0.35	1.29
331	Wood Products	1.89	0.17	0.67
332	Furniture, Fixtures	2.21	0.24	0.89
341	Paper Products	4.80	0.20	0.52
342	Printing, Publishing	5.39	0.12	0.16
35A	Chemicals	6.20	0.21	0.60
35B	Petroleum Products	12.51	0.05	0.59
355	Rubber Products	3.34	0.29	0.66
36A	Nonmetal Mineral Products	4.24	0.08	0.80
362	Glass Products	4.78	0.20	1.48
371	Iron, Steel	11.86	0.08	1.49
372	Nonferrous Metals	20.59	-0.42	2.66
381	Metal Products	11.11	0.03	1.85
382	Nonelectrical Machinery	9.84	0.11	0.92
383	Electrical Machinery	16.44	0.03	1.40
384	Transport Equipment	7.61	0.16	1.59
38A	Misc. Manufacturers	6.52	0.13	1.01
2	Mining, Quarrying	6.45	0.05	0.41

Note: Experiment 2. See footnote to Table 5.1 for details.
Source: Brown, Deardorff, and Stern (1992b).

The models with imperfect competition are especially designed to capture the scale effects of trade liberalization. In the Michigan Model, NAFTA raises firm output in nearly all industries in all three participating countries. The percentage changes in output per firm under liberalization scenario 2 are reported in Table 5.3. The scale gains are very small but still largely positive for the United States, generally less that 0.5 percent. Canada enjoys scale gains on the order of 1 to 2 percent. However, the scale gains in Mexico are quite strong, ranging from a low of 1.42 percent in the textile sector to 20.59 percent in nonferrous metals.

Some of these results could not possibly have emerged in a perfectly competitive homogeneous products setting and so must stem from the assumed market structure. The mechanics by which these results emerge, however, are not particularly transparent. In order to obtain a deeper understanding of the results presented above, a simple numeric monopolistic competition model is analyzed in the following section.

III. A Simple Numeric Model of Monopolistic Competition

The numeric model adopted here is nearly identical in structure to the multicountry, multisector version of the Michigan Model used to evaluate NAFTA. However, here the dimensions are reduced to two countries (H and F), two sectors (X_1 and X_2), and two factors of production (capital and labor). In addition, the model is not linearized before solution, as is the case with the Michigan Model.

The equations of the model along with variable and parameter definitions are listed in Table 5.4. A representative agent is taken to maximize a Cobb-Douglas utility function of the two composite goods, as given in equation 5.1. Each composite good is formed by aggregating over all of the domestically and foreign-produced varieties of each good using a CES aggregation function, as in equation 5.2. Here we allow for the possibility that consumers in each country may have a preference for varieties produced at home relative to those produced abroad. In most cases we will take $\gamma = 0.5$, implying that consumers are indifferent to the location of production. Utility maximization yields national demand for the output of each firm, as given by equation 5.3. The associated elasticity of demand is given by equation 5.4.

Monopolistically competitive firms use the elasticity of demand to calculate the optimal markup of price over marginal cost as in equation 5.5, but first elasticity of demand in each of the two markets must be aggregated to form a world market elasticity of demand for the firm. This is the case because we allow for arbitrage between national markets. In equation 5.5, each firm's perceived elasticity of demand is a sales-weighted average over the two national markets.

Although each firm receives the same price for domestic sales and export sales, the price paid by the foreign consumer is adjusted to reflect any ad valorem tariffs that apply. The landed price, then, is the world price adjusted for a tariff.

Technology is characterized by increasing returns to scale and is identical across the two countries. Increasing returns are accomplished assuming that firms must first make an initial investment, F, of capital and labor. Variable inputs are then employed in proportion to output. However, the capital-labor ratio for the variable inputs is the same as for fixed inputs so that technology is homogeneous. Both the fixed and variable input requirements are derived assuming a CES function of capital and labor. Cost minimization yields marginal cost given by equation 5.8 and firm demand for labor and capital given by equations 5.10 and 5.11, respectively. In both sectors, the elasticity of

Table 5.4. *Equations of the Model*

Utility Indicator

$$U_i = D_{i1}^{0.5} D_{i2}^{0.5} \qquad (5.1)$$

Product Aggregator

$$D_{ij} = \left[\gamma_{ij}^H n_{jH} (D_{ij}^H)^\rho + \gamma_{ij}^F n_{jF} (D_{ij}^F)^\rho \right]^{1/\rho} \qquad (5.2)$$

Product Demand

$$D_{ij}^r = \frac{0.5 \, E_i (\gamma_{ij}^r)^\sigma (P_{ij}^r)^{-\sigma}}{n_{jH} (\gamma_{ij}^H)^\sigma (P_{ij}^H)^{1-\sigma} + n_{jF} (\gamma_{ij}^F)^\sigma (P_{ij}^F)^{1-\sigma}} \qquad (5.3)$$

Elasticity of Demand by Market

$$\eta_{ij}^r = -\sigma + (\sigma-1) \frac{P_{ij}^r D_{ij}^r}{0.5 E_i} \qquad (5.4)$$

Aggregate Elasticity of Demand by Firm

$$\eta_{ij} = \eta_{Hj}^i \frac{D_{Hj}^i}{q_{ij}} + \eta_{Fj}^i \frac{D_{Fj}^i}{q_{ij}} \qquad (5.5)$$

Landed Price

$$P_{ij}^r = P_{wj}^r (1 + t_{ij}^r) \qquad (5.6)$$

Mark-up Pricing Rule

$$P_{wj}^i = \frac{MC_{ij}}{1 + \dfrac{1}{\eta_{ij}}} \qquad (5.7)$$

Marginal Cost

$$MC_{ij} = \left[(a_{ij}^L)^\gamma w_i^{1-\pi} + (a_{ij}^K)^\gamma v_i^{1-\pi} \right]^{1/(1-\pi)} \qquad (5.8)$$

Zero-Profits Condition

$$P_{wj}^i q_{ij} = w_i LD_{ij} + v_i KD_{ij} \qquad (5.9)$$

Labor Demand by Firm

$$LD_{ij} = \frac{(F + q_{ij})(a_{ij}^L)^\gamma w_i^{-\pi}}{\left[(a_{ij}^L)^\gamma w_i^{1-\pi} + (a_{ij}^K)^\gamma v_i^{1-\pi} \right]^{\pi/(\pi-1)}} \qquad (5.10)$$

Table 5.4. (cont.)

Capital Demand by Firm

$$KD_{ij} = \frac{(F + q_{ij})(a_{ij}^{K})^{\tau} v_i^{-\tau}}{\left[(a_{ij}^{L})^{\tau} w_i^{1-\tau} + (a_{ij}^{K})^{\tau} v_i^{1-\tau}\right]^{\mu(\tau-1)}} \qquad (5.11)$$

Labor Market Clearing Condition

$$L_i = n_{i1} LD_{i1} + n_{i2} LD_{i2} \qquad (5.12)$$

Capital Market Clearing Condition

$$K_i + \delta k_i = n_{i1} KD_{i1} + n_{i2} KD_{i2} \qquad (5.13)$$

Goods Market Clearing Condition

$$q_{ij} = D_{Hj}^{i} + D_{Fj}^{i} \qquad (5.14)$$

Home Country Income

$$E_H = w_H L_H + v_H K_H + \sum_{j=1}^{2} t_{Hj} n_{Fj} P_{wj}^{F} D_{Hj}^{F} \qquad (5.15)$$

VARIABLE DEFINITIONS

U_i Utility indicator for country i

D_{ij} Product aggregator for good j in country i

D_{ij}^{r} Demand in country i for good j produced by a representative firm in country r

η_{ij}^{r} Elasticity of demand in country i for good j produced by a representative firm in country r

η_{ij} Elasticity of demand for a representative firm in industry j in country i aggregated over the home and foreign markets

P_{wj}^{i} World price of good j produced in country i

P_{ij}^{r} Price of good j produced by country r paid by consumers in country i

MC_{ij} Marginal cost of a representative firm in industry j in country i

q_{ij} Firm output in industry j in country i

w_i Wage paid to labor in country i

v_i Return to capital in country i

LD_{ij} Labor demand by a representative firm in industry j in country i

KD_{ij} Capital demand by a representative firm in industry j in country i

n_{ij} Number of firms in industry j in country i

E_i Income in country i

Table 5.4. *(cont.)*

PARAMETER DEFINITIONS

γ_{ij}^r Demand parameter determing preference by counsumers in country i
     for good j produced in country r

σ Elasticity of substitution among different varieties of each good

t_{ij} Tariff imposed by country i on imports of good j

a_{ij}^L Production parameter determining capital or labor intensity

F Fixedinputrequirementofcapitalandlabor

δk_i Transfer of capital to country i

s Elasticity of substitution between capital and labor

substitution between capital and labor, s, is set equal to 2, though in some experiments s will be varied. Sector 1 is taken to be capital-intensive, and sector 2 is labor-intensive.

Factor market-clearing conditions are given by equations 5.11 and 5.12. In each case, factor demand summed over all firms must be equal to an exogenous supply. Labor supply in each country is assumed to be fixed, but we will allow for the possibility that capital flows from the foreign country to the home country, thus augmenting the capital stock in H and reducing the capital stock in F. Payments to foreign capital installed in H are remitted back to the residents of F.

Equilibrium in the goods markets simply requires that each firm produce enough to satisfy demand by both domestic and foreign consumers, as given by equation 5.14. The number of firms in each industry is determined by the zero-profits condition, as given by equation 5.9.

Finally, the model is closed with the income equation. Households in the home country receive payments to factors plus any tariff revenue, as in equation 5.15. Foreign income is taken to be the numeraire, but implicitly foreign income is composed of payments to factors installed both domestically and in country H.

The numerical model is written in the GAMS (General Algebraic Modeling System) and solved employing Rutherford's (1991) SLCP solver.

IV. Results

The model described above was employed to evaluate the effects of tariffs under various endowment and taste configurations. Results are reported in Tables 5.5–5.11.

Case I

We begin by considering the case in which countries H and F are completely identical in terms of factor endowments and preferences. Each country is endowed with 100 units each of capital and labor, consumers are indifferent to the national location of firms, and the elasticity of substitution among different varieties of each good, σ, is taken to be 3. Free trade equilibrium values for firm sales by market, world prices, number of firms, demand elasticity, firm output, and marginal cost are reported in the first two columns of Table 5.5. The other four columns of Table 5.5 report values for these variables under the assumption that country H is imposing a tariff on its imports of good 1 from F.

In several respects, the model produces the expected results. The tariff raises welfare for country H but lowers welfare for country F until the tariff reaches around 40 percent at which point home country welfare begins to decline with higher tariffs. Home firm sales of good 1 to the home market rise and imports fall. For example, with a tariff of 10 percent, home demand for good 1 produced by a representative home firm (H.X1 in Table 5.5) rises from 2.794 to 2.986, and home demand for good 1 produced by a representative foreign firm (F.X1) falls from 2.794 to 2.587. On the other hand, foreign demand for good 1 produced by a representative home firm falls from 2.794 to 2.598, but foreign demand for a representative foreign firm rises from 2.794 to 2.997. Home country terms of trade for good 1 improve by about 5 percent in the case of a 10 percent tariff. The tariff also has the normal Stolper-Samuelson effects on factor prices. An import tariff on the capital-intensive good lowers the wage-rent ratio at home, while the relative return to labor in F rises.

Perhaps a bit surprisingly, the effects of the tariff on sector 2 in H are identical to the effects in F. However, upon reflection, this is a fairly easy result to understand. If we substitute equations 5.3 and 5.4 into equation 5.5, we can find each firm's demand elasticity as a function of prices. That is

$$\eta_H = -\sigma + \frac{(\sigma - 1)P_H^{1-\sigma}}{n_H P_H^{1-\sigma} + n_F P_F^{1-\sigma}}$$

$$\eta_F = -\sigma + \frac{(\sigma - 1)P_F^{1-\sigma}}{n_H P_H^{1-\sigma} + n_F P_F^{1-\sigma}}$$

where the industry subscripts have been suppressed. Note that in the absence of any tariffs, home firms perceive a more elastic demand curve relative to foreign firms only if the relative price of home goods also rises – that is, if P_H/P_F goes up. This is, of course, the same condition under which total demand for a home country firm falls relative to a foreign firm. Therefore, in the absence of any tariff barriers, the firm that sells a relatively high quantity must also be on a *less* elastic part of the demand curve.

Turn now to the markup and zero profits conditions. We have that

$$\frac{q}{q + F} = \frac{MC}{ATC} = \frac{MC}{P} = \frac{MR}{P} = 1 + \frac{1}{\eta}$$

Table 5.5. Home Country Tariff on Imports of Good 1

Factor Endowments: KH = LH = KF = LF = 100
Demand Parameters: GAMMAH = GAMMAF = 0.5
SIGMAH = SIGMAF = 3

	tH.1=0		tH.1=10%		tH.1=30%		tH.1=40%		tH.1=50%	
	Home	Foreign	Home	Foreign	Home	Foreign	Home	Foreign	Home	Foreign
Utility	54.854	54.854	55.409	54.226	55.921	53.250	55.974	52.868	55.938	52.539
Product Demand										
H.X1	2.794	2.794	2.986	2.598	3.288	2.284	3.406	2.159	3.507	2.050
H.X2	2.794	2.794	2.858	2.732	2.953	2.640	2.988	2.606	3.018	2.578
F.X1	2.794	2.794	2.857	2.937	2.205	3.366	2.031	3.532	1.868	3.685
F.X2	2.794	2.794	2.858	2.732	2.953	2.640	2.988	2.606	3.018	2.578
World prices										
X1	2.459	2.459	2.535	2.417	2.671	2.347	2.731	2.318	2.788	2.293
X2	2.459	2.459	2.501	2.501	2.567	2.567	2.594	2.594	2.616	2.616
Number of firms										
X1	7.278	7.278	7.335	7.139	7.447	6.908	7.500	6.812	7.552	6.728
X2	7.278	7.278	7.222	7.416	7.115	7.639	7.065	7.730	7.017	7.810
Elasticity of demand by market										
H.X1	-2.863	-2.863	-2.855	-2.868	-2.843	-2.878	-2.838	-2.882	-2.833	-2.886
H.X2	-2.863	-2.863	-2.863	-2.868	-2.864	-2.864	-2.885	-2.865	-2.865	-2.865
F.X1	-2.863	-2.863	-2.868	-2.855	-2.880	-2.842	-2.885	-2.836	-2.890	-2.831
F.X2	-2.863	-2.863	-2.863	-2.863	-2.864	-2.864	-2.865	-2.865	-2.865	-2.865
Perceived elasticity										
X1	-2.863	-2.863	-2.861	-2.861	-2.857	-2.857	-2.855	-2.854	-2.852	-2.851
X2	-2.863	-2.863	-2.863	-2.863	-2.864	-2.864	-2.865	-2.865	-2.865	-2.865
Wage	1.000	1.000	1.015	1.022	1.039	1.057	1.049	1.071	1.057	1.084
Rent	1.000	1.000	1.032	0.978	1.090	0.943	1.116	0.929	1.141	0.916
Supply by a representative firm										
X1	5.588	5.588	5.584	5.584	5.572	5.571	5.565	5.562	5.557	5.553
X2	5.588	5.588	5.590	5.590	5.593	5.593	5.594	5.594	5.595	5.595
Marginal cost										
X1	1.600	1.600	1.649	1.572	1.736	1.525	1.775	1.506	1.811	1.489
X2	1.600	1.600	1.627	1.627	1.671	1.671	1.688	1.688	1.703	1.703

which implies that the firm with the higher sales must be on a *more* elastic portion of the demand curve.

These two conditions, of course, give us the result that in the absence of a tariff in sector 2, home firm sales, price, elasticity, and marginal cost must be equal to those of foreign firms. Equalizing marginal cost for the two different types of firms in sector 2 is accomplished by lowering w/v in country H while raising w/v in country F.

This unequivocal relationship between relative elasticity and quantity is relaxed in sector 1, where the home country is imposing a tariff. The bind that breaks is the relationship between elasticity and output. The tariff opens up a window in which a home (foreign) firm's quantity demanded can rise relative to a foreign (home) firm even though relative elasticity for the home (foreign) firm may be rising. But the tariff does not alter the relationship between elasticity and output that satisfies the zero-profits and profit-maximization conditions. Consequently, we can conclude that in sector 1, the firm with the higher quantity will also be on a relatively more elastic portion of the demand curve.

The question, then, is this: Which firms (H or F) end up with a relatively more elastic demand and a higher level of output? We might normally expect the tariff (Lancaster, 1984), by insulating domestic firms from foreign competition, to cause domestic firms to perceive a less elastic demand curve on their domestic sales. Similarly, the tariff inhibits the ability of foreign firms to compete in the home market (Horstmann and Markusen, 1986). Thus, we expect foreign firms to perceive a relatively more elastic demand curve. Indeed, the absolute value of the home elasticity for home goods does indeed fall from 2.863 to 2.855 in the case of a 10 percent tariff. In comparison, the absolute value of the home demand elasticity for foreign goods rises to 2.868.

The confounding factor, however, is that the tariff improves the home country's terms of trade. From equations 5.3 and 5.4 we can see that the absolute value of each firm's demand elasticity is negatively correlated with the price charged by competing firms. That is, each firm's demand curve becomes less elastic the higher the price of competing firms. The rise in the world price of the home good relative to the foreign good is associated with a more elastic foreign demand for home goods (2.868) as compared to the foreign demand for the foreign good (2.855).

One might expect that the direct effect of the tariff would dominate the secondary terms-of-trade effect, but that is not the case. When the tariff is set at 10 percent, both home and foreign firms each sell a total of 5.584. But at higher tariff levels, home firm output in sector 1 rises relative to foreign firm output, and its demand curve is concomitantly relatively more elastic.

It is worth noting at this point that the results in the previous paragraph will not hold generally. As will be seen below, there are situations in which the tariff is more anticompetitive for home firms than for foreign firms, as the theoretical literature leads us to expect.

However, one conclusion does seem to suggest itself throughout the results presented here. Protection is anticompetitive both at home and abroad. The tariff tends to make sector 1 less competitive for both foreign and domestic firms. That is, elasticity and firm output fall for both domestic and foreign producers in a tariffed industry even if the home country alone is imposing the tariff.

We saw this same result in the Michigan Model. As a consequence of the liberalization under NAFTA, firm output rose in nearly every sector in all three countries.

Curiously, the opposite occurs in sector 2. The demand curves for both the home and foreign firms become more elastic and firm output rises. This is presumably a consequence of the fact that the tariff in sector 1 shifts world demand toward sector 2. As the industry expands, the market is able to offer more variety, and competition intensifies.

Finally, we can also see that the tariff generates inefficient entry into sector 1 in country H, as is suggested by the analysis in Horstmann and Markusen (1986). The number of firms rises, and each sells less than before the tariff.

We turn now to consider the consequences of a home country tariff imposed on both goods 1 and 2. Results are reported in Table 5.6. The symmetry of this setting causes the tariff to impact sectors 1 and 2 identically. With the intersectorally distorting effect of the tariff now removed, the optimal tariff nearly doubles to around 75 percent.

Many of the same points above are evinced here as well, though there is one important difference. Above, as long as sector 2 was not subject to a tariff, it was necessary for the real return to labor to fall relative to foreign labor. However, with a uniform tariff, there is no change in relative factor prices within each country, though both home country capital and labor are better off than their foreign counterparts. The tariff-induced terms-of-trade gain for the home country feeds back onto factor prices, raising the value of the marginal product of both capital and labor.

To see this point, recall that in differentiated products models there are always three effects exerting competing influences on the return to each factor. Monopolistically competitive firms pay each factor according to

$$w = P_1\left(1 + \frac{1}{\eta_1}\right) MPL_1 = P_2\left(1 + \frac{1}{\eta_2}\right) MPL_2$$

$$r = P_2\left(1 + \frac{1}{\eta_2}\right) MPK_1 = P_2\left(1 + \frac{1}{\eta_2}\right) MPK_2$$

Table 5.6. Home Country Tariff on Imports of Goods 1 and 2

Factor Endowments: KH = LH = KF = LF = 100
Demand Parameters: GAMMAH = GAMMAF = 0.5
SIGMAH = SIGMAF = 3

	tH=0		tH=60%		tH=70%		tH=75%		tH=80%	
	Home	Foreign	Home	Foreign	Home	Foreign	Home	Foreign	Home	Foreign
Utility	54.854	54.854	58.522	49.034	58.606	48.402	58.619	48.110	58.616	47.833
Product Demand										
H.X1	2.794	2.794	3.948	1.610	4.066	1.484	4.120	1.426	4.171	1.372
H.X2	2.794	2.794	3.948	1.610	4.066	1.484	4.120	1.426	4.171	1.372
F.X1	2.794	2.794	2.081	3.476	1.987	3.562	1.942	3.603	1.899	3.642
F.X2	2.794	2.794	2.081	3.476	1.987	3.562	1.942	3.603	1.899	3.642
World prices										
X1	2.459	2.459	3.184	2.464	3.301	2.465	3.358	2.466	3.415	2.466
X2	2.459	2.459	3.184	2.464	3.301	2.465	3.358	2.466	3.415	2.466
Number of firms										
X1	7.278	7.278	7.303	7.304	7.310	7.311	7.313	7.314	7.316	7.317
X2	7.278	7.278	7.303	7.304	7.310	7.311	7.313	7.314	7.316	7.317
Elasticity of demand by market										
H.X1	-2.863	-2.863	-2.834	-2.897	-2.831	-2.902	-2.830	-2.904	-2.828	-2.906
H.X2	-2.863	-2.863	-2.834	-2.897	-2.831	-2.902	-2.830	-2.904	-2.828	-2.906
F.X1	-2.863	-2.863	-2.892	-2.829	-2.895	-2.824	-2.897	-2.822	-2.898	-2.820
F.X2	-2.863	-2.863	-2.892	-2.829	-2.895	-2.824	-2.897	-2.822	-2.898	-2.820
Perceived elasticity										
X1	-2.863	-2.863	-2.853	-2.852	-2.850	-2.850	-2.849	-2.848	-2.848	-2.847
X2	-2.863	-2.863	-2.853	-2.852	-2.850	-2.850	-2.849	-2.848	-2.848	-2.847
Wage	1.000	1.000	1.293	1.000	1.339	1.000	1.362	1.000	1.385	1.000
Rent	1.000	1.000	1.293	1.000	1.339	1.000	1.362	1.000	1.385	1.000
Supply by a representative firm										
X1	5.588	5.588	5.558	5.557	5.550	5.549	5.547	5.545	5.543	5.541
X2	5.588	5.588	5.558	5.557	5.550	5.549	5.547	5.545	5.543	5.541
Marginal cost										
X1	1.600	1.600	2.068	1.600	2.142	1.600	2.179	1.600	2.216	1.600
X2	1.600	1.600	2.068	1.600	2.142	1.600	2.179	1.600	2.216	1.600

where *MPL* and *MPK* are the marginal products of capital and labor, respectively. Normally Stolper-Samuelson effects will tend to push down the return to the factor *not* used intensively in the tariffed industry by reducing its marginal product. Opposing the Stolper-Samuelson effects is the positive terms-of-trade effect that pulls up the value of the marginal product on the world market relative to the price of imported goods. Finally, negative scale effects associated with protection push down the factor's real return measured in terms of the domestic good.

In the model with perfect symmetry, the Stolper-Samuelson effect is completely neutralized. Therefore, in the tariff-imposing home country, protection that raises the relative price of domestic output also raises the return to both factors in terms of the imported varieties. Improvement in the terms of trade is very likely the explanation as to why NAFTA raises the return to both capital and labor in the United States in several of the AGE models. U.S. tariffs against Mexico are currently very low, whereas Mexican tariffs significantly protect domestic firms. As a consequence, tariff removal resulted in an improvement in U.S. terms of trade, which tended to pull up the value of the marginal product of U.S. factors of production.

Factors in the foreign country are made worse off both due to the deterioration in the terms of trade and due to the anticompetitive effect of the tariff, which results in a loss of economies of scale. We can see more clearly the anticompetitive effect of the tariff in Table 5.7. Again, the two countries are identical with the exception that the home country imposes a tariff on import of both goods. However, σ, the elasticity of substitution among varieties, has been raised from 3 to 7.

In the last section of the table, we report the real return to each factor as measured by domestic output as given by

$$\frac{w}{P_1} = \left(1 + \frac{1}{\eta_1}\right) MPL_1 \quad \frac{w}{P_2} = \left(1 + \frac{1}{\eta_2}\right) MPL_2$$

$$\frac{r}{P_2} = \left(1 + \frac{1}{\eta_2}\right) MPK_1 \quad \frac{r}{P_2} = \left(1 + \frac{1}{\eta_2}\right) MPK_2$$

Here the anticompetitive effect of protection on each factor is apparent. The demand curves for foreign firms become less elastic the higher the home country's tariff. Consequently, firm output declines from 19.651 in the absence of a tariff to 18.358 when the home tariff is set at 40 percent. The loss in scale pushes down the return to foreign factors as measured in terms of the domestic good from 0.542 in the absence of a tariff to 0.537 when the tariff is set at 40 percent.

We have already seen in the case NAFTA that liberalization had very strong

Table 5.7. Home Country Tariff on Imports of Goods 1 and 2

Factor Endowments: KH = 100 LH = 100 KF=100 LF=100
Demand Parameters: GAMMAH = GAMMAF = 0.5
SIGMAH = SIGMAF = 9

	tH=0		tH=10%		tH=20%		tH=30%		tH=40%	
	Home	Foreign	Home	Foreign	Home	Foreign	Home	Foreign	Home	Foreign
Utility	30.778	30.778	31.287	30.105	31.386	29.600	31.235	29.227	30.960	28.951
Product Demand										
H.X1	9.826	9.826	12.000	7.507	13.581	5.587	14.647	4.114	15.336	3.031
H.X2	9.826	9.826	12.000	7.507	13.581	5.587	14.647	4.114	15.336	3.031
F.X1	9.826	9.826	7.881	11.626	6.138	13.028	4.714	14.042	3.612	14.747
F.X2	9.826	9.826	7.881	11.626	6.138	13.028	4.714	14.042	3.612	14.747
World Prices										
X1	1.844	1.844	1.938	1.846	2.033	1.850	2.127	1.856	2.219	1.861
X2	1.844	1.844	1.938	1.846	2.033	1.850	2.127	1.856	2.219	1.861
Number of Firms										
X1	2.759	2.759	2.777	2.777	2.819	2.820	2.872	2.873	2.925	2.926
X2	2.759	2.759	2.777	2.777	2.819	2.820	2.872	2.873	2.925	2.926
Elasticity of demand by market										
H.X1	-7.550	-7.550	-7.293	-7.836	-7.100	-8.091	-6.960	-8.300	-6.858	-8.462
H.X2	-7.550	-7.550	-7.293	-7.836	-7.100	-8.091	-6.960	-8.300	-6.858	-8.462
F.X1	-7.550	-7.550	-7.826	-7.283	-8.062	-7.071	-8.255	-6.915	-8.408	-6.804
F.X2	-7.550	-7.550	-7.826	-7.283	-8.062	-7.071	-8.255	-6.915	-8.408	-6.804
Perceived Elasticity										
X1	-7.550	-7.550	-7.502	-7.502	-7.389	-7.389	-7.254	-7.252	-7.122	-7.119
X2	-7.550	-7.550	-7.502	-7.502	-7.389	-7.389	-7.254	-7.252	-7.122	-7.119
Wage	1.000	1.000	1.050	1.000	1.099	1.000	1.146	1.000	1.192	1.000
Rent	1.000	1.000	1.050	1.000	1.099	1.000	1.146	1.000	1.192	1.000
Supply by a representative firm										
X1	19.651	19.651	19.507	19.507	19.168	19.166	18.761	18.756	18.367	18.358
X2	19.651	19.651	19.507	19.507	19.168	19.166	18.761	18.756	18.367	18.358
Marginal cost										
X1	1.600	1.600	1.680	1.600	1.758	1.600	1.834	1.600	1.908	1.600
X2	1.600	1.600	1.680	1.600	1.758	1.600	1.834	1.600	1.908	1.600
Real wage measured in terms of domestic good										
X1	0.542	0.542	0.542	0.542	0.540	0.540	0.539	0.539	0.537	0.537
X2	0.542	0.542	0.542	0.542	0.540	0.540	0.539	0.539	0.537	0.537
Real rent measured in terms of domestic good										
X1	0.542	0.542	0.542	0.542	0.540	0.540	0.539	0.539	0.537	0.537
X2	0.542	0.542	0.542	0.542	0.540	0.540	0.539	0.539	0.537	0.537

positive scale effects in Mexico and the return to both factors rose. The results seen in Table 5.7 strongly suggest that the scale gains in Mexico were sufficient to overcome the negative terms-of-trade and Stolper-Samuelson effects so that both factors in Mexico gain from the agreement.

In Table 5.8, we experiment with various combinations of home country tariffs. Not surprisingly, a uniform tariff across both industries yields the highest welfare. This result obviously depends on the symmetry of the two industries. Cross-sectoral differences in demand elasticity or elasticity of substitution between capital and labor could easily reverse this conclusion.

Case II

Our next objective is to explore the role of relative country size in determining the effect of a tariff. The configuration in Case I is maintained with the exception that the home country is now taken to be 50 percent larger than the foreign country. Results are reported in Table 5.9.

The optimal tariff is now about 85 percent, as compared to 75 percent when the countries were of equal size. This result obviously follows from the fact that the terms-of-trade gains from the home country tariff increase with its relative size. See, for example, that here a 70 percent tariff raises factor returns in the home country relative to the foreign country from unity to 1.393. In comparison, international relative factor returns rise to 1.339 when the two countries are of equal size, as can be seen in Table 5.6.

Case III

In light of the results obtained under Case II, it is interesting to consider the situation in which the tariff-imposing country is also relatively small. Table 5.10 contains results for the configuration in which the home country imposes a tariff, but the home country is only one-tenth the size of the foreign country.

Not surprisingly, the optimal tariff drops down to 55 percent, and terms-of-trade effects are considerably weakened. At the optimal tariff, the return to home country factors relative to foreign factors is only 7 percent higher.

However, the most striking result here is that relative scale effects of the tariff are now reversed. Notice that output per firm in the foreign country remains at 5.922 for all levels of the tariff, and perceived elasticity of the demand holds constant at 2.974. In contrast, home country firm output falls as the tariff rises. At the optimal tariff rate, home country firm output has fallen to 5.911 from 5.922 under free trade.

A consequence of reducing the size of the home country has been to diminish the role of the terms of trade in determining the demand elasticity, thus enhancing the importance of the tariff. However the influence of the terms of trade has not been completely eliminated. For if the tariff had been the only

Table 5.8. Home Country Tariff on Imports of Goods 1 and 2

Factor Endowments: KH = LH = KF = LF = 100
Demand Parameters: GAMMAH = GAMMAF = 0.5
SIGMAH = SIGMAF = 3

	tH1=80%, tH2=50% Home	Foreign	tH1=80% Home	tH2=60% Foreign	tH1=80% Home	tH2=70% Foreign	tH1=80% Home	tH2=80% Foreign	tH1=80% Home	tH2=90% Foreign
Utility	58.367	48.822	58.523	48.448	58.600	48.120	58.616	47.833	58.582	47.578
Product Demand										
H.X1	4.067	1.474	4.107	1.435	4.141	1.401	4.171	1.372	4.197	1.346
H.X2	3.906	1.660	4.008	1.551	4.095	1.456	4.171	1.372	4.237	1.298
F.X1	1.778	3.758	1.823	3.715	1.863	3.676	1.899	3.642	1.931	3.611
F.X2	2.287	3.281	2.150	3.409	2.021	3.529	1.899	3.642	1.784	3.748
World prices										
X1	3.279	2.400	3.329	2.424	3.374	2.446	3.415	2.466	3.452	2.484
X2	3.171	2.527	3.257	2.505	3.338	2.485	3.415	2.466	3.488	2.449
Number of firms										
X1	7.448	7.098	7.402	7.178	7.358	7.251	7.316	7.317	7.276	7.378
X2	7.164	7.512	7.216	7.441	7.267	7.376	7.316	7.317	7.363	7.264
Elasticity of demand by market										
H.X1	-2.827	-2.903	-2.827	-2.904	-2.828	-2.905	-2.828	-2.906	-2.829	-2.907
H.X2	-2.839	-2.895	-2.835	-2.899	-2.832	-2.903	-2.828	-2.906	-2.825	-2.909
F.X1	-2.900	-2.820	-2.899	-2.820	-2.899	-2.820	-2.898	-2.820	-2.898	-2.821
F.X2	-2.887	-2.834	-2.891	-2.829	-2.895	-2.825	-2.898	-2.820	-2.902	-2.816
Perceived elasticity										
X1	-2.847	-2.845	-2.847	-2.846	-2.847	-2.847	-2.848	-2.847	-2.848	-2.847
X2	-2.856	-2.856	-2.853	-2.853	-2.850	-2.850	-2.848	-2.847	-2.845	-2.844
Wage	1.283	1.033	1.319	1.021	1.353	1.010	1.385	1.000	1.415	0.991
Rent	1.335	0.967	1.353	0.979	1.370	0.990	1.385	1.000	1.398	1.009
Supply by a representative firm										
X1	5.541	5.536	5.542	5.538	5.542	5.540	5.543	5.541	5.543	5.542
X2	5.567	5.568	5.559	5.559	5.551	5.551	5.543	5.541	5.535	5.532
Marginal cost										
X1	2.127	1.557	2.160	1.572	2.189	1.587	2.216	1.600	2.240	1.612
X2	2.061	1.642	2.115	1.627	2.167	1.613	2.216	1.600	2.262	1.588

Table 5.9. Home Country Tariff on Imports of Goods 1 and 2

Factor Endowments: KH = LH = 150   KF = LF = 100
Demand Parameters: GAMMAH = GAMMAF = 0.5
                   SIGMAH = SIGMAF = 3

	tH=0		tH=70%		tH=80%		tH=85%		tH=90%	
	Home	Foreign	Home	Foreign	Home	Foreign	Home	Foreign	Home	Foreign
Utility	92.021	61.347	98.280	51.649	98.368	50.847	98.376	50.478	98.364	50.128
Product demand										
H.X1	3.400	2.267	4.470	1.178	4.555	1.088	4.594	1.047	4.631	1.008
H.X2	3.400	2.267	4.470	1.178	4.555	1.088	4.594	1.047	4.631	1.008
F.X1	3.400	2.267	2.452	3.173	2.347	3.269	2.297	3.314	2.249	3.357
F.X2	3.400	2.267	2.452	3.173	2.347	3.269	2.297	3.314	2.249	3.357
World prices										
X1	2.447	2.447	3.414	2.453	3.542	2.455	3.606	2.455	3.668	2.456
X2	2.447	2.447	3.414	2.453	3.542	2.455	3.606	2.455	3.668	2.456
Number of firms										
X1	10.817	7.211	10.842	7.246	10.847	7.254	10.849	7.258	10.852	7.262
X2	10.817	7.211	10.842	7.246	10.847	7.254	10.849	7.258	10.852	7.262
Elasticity of demand by market										
H.X1	-2.889	-2.889	-2.873	-2.920	-2.871	-2.923	-2.870	-2.925	-2.870	-2.926
H.X2	-2.889	-2.889	-2.873	-2.920	-2.871	-2.923	-2.870	-2.925	-2.870	-2.926
F.X1	-2.889	-2.889	-2.915	-2.844	-2.917	-2.840	-2.918	-2.837	-2.919	-2.835
F.X2	-2.889	-2.889	-2.915	-2.844	-2.917	-2.840	-2.918	-2.837	-2.919	-2.835
Perceived elasticity										
X1	-2.889	-2.889	-2.882	-2.875	-2.881	-2.872	-2.880	-2.870	-2.880	-2.869
X2	-2.889	-2.889	-2.882	-2.875	-2.881	-2.872	-2.880	-2.870	-2.880	-2.869
Wage	1.000	1.000	1.393	1.000	1.445	1.000	1.471	1.000	1.496	1.000
Rent	1.000	1.000	1.393	1.000	1.445	1.000	1.471	1.000	1.496	1.000
Supply by a representative firm										
X1	5.667	5.667	5.647	5.625	5.643	5.616	5.641	5.611	5.639	5.607
X2	5.667	5.667	5.647	5.625	5.643	5.616	5.641	5.611	5.639	5.607
Marginal cost										
X1	1.600	1.600	2.230	1.600	2.313	1.600	2.354	1.600	2.394	1.600
X2	1.600	1.600	2.230	1.600	2.313	1.600	2.354	1.600	2.394	1.600

Table 5.10. Home Country Tariff on Imports of Goods 1 and 2

Factor Endowments: KH = LH = 100 KF = LF = 1000
Demand Parameters: GAMMAH = GAMMAF = 0.5
SIGMAH = SIGMAF = 3

	tH = 0%		tH = 10%		tH = 50%		tH = 55%		tH = 60%	
	Home	Foreign	Home	Foreign	Home	Foreign	Home	Foreign	Home	Foreign
Utility	128.750	1287.498	129.729	1286.372	131.680	1280.962	131.698	1280.227	131.669	1279.488
Product Demand										
H.X1	0.538	5.384	0.684	5.238	1.364	4.549	1.454	4.457	1.544	4.365
H.X2	0.538	5.384	0.684	5.238	1.364	4.549	1.454	4.457	1.544	4.365
F.X1	0.538	5.384	0.529	5.393	0.483	5.439	0.477	5.445	0.471	5.451
F.X2	0.538	5.384	0.529	5.393	0.483	5.439	0.477	5.445	0.471	5.451
World prices										
X1	2.411	2.411	2.434	2.411	2.558	2.411	2.577	2.411	2.596	2.411
X2	2.411	2.411	2.434	2.411	2.558	2.411	2.577	2.411	2.596	2.411
Number of firms										
X1	7.005	70.051	7.005	70.051	7.012	70.052	7.013	70.052	7.015	70.053
X2	7.005	70.051	7.005	70.051	7.012	70.052	7.013	70.052	7.015	70.053
Elasticity of demand by market										
H.X1	-2.974	-2.974	-2.970	-2.975	-2.952	-2.977	-2.950	-2.977	-2.948	-2.977
H.X2	-2.974	-2.974	-2.970	-2.975	-2.952	-2.977	-2.950	-2.977	-2.948	-2.977
F.X1	-2.974	-2.974	-2.974	-2.974	-2.976	-2.974	-2.976	-2.974	-2.977	-2.974
F.X2	-2.974	-2.974	-2.974	-2.974	-2.976	-2.974	-2.976	-2.974	-2.977	-2.974
Perceived elasticity										
X1	-2.974	-2.974	-2.974	-2.974	-2.971	-2.974	-2.970	-2.974	-2.970	-2.974
X2	-2.974	-2.974	-2.974	-2.974	-2.971	-2.974	-2.970	-2.974	-2.970	-2.974
Wage	1.000	1.000	1.010	1.000	1.061	1.000	1.068	1.000	1.076	1.000
Rent	1.000	1.000	1.010	1.000	1.061	1.000	1.068	1.000	1.076	1.000
Supply by a representative firm										
X1	5.922	5.922	5.922	5.922	5.913	5.922	5.911	5.922	5.909	5.922
X2	5.922	5.922	5.922	5.922	5.913	5.922	5.911	5.922	5.909	5.922
Marginal cost										
X1	1.600	1.600	1.616	1.600	1.697	1.600	1.709	1.600	1.722	1.600
X2	1.600	1.600	1.616	1.600	1.697	1.600	1.709	1.600	1.722	1.600

force influencing foreign firm–perceived elasticity of demand, then the foreign demand curve would have become more elastic, and foreign firm output would have risen.

Once again, we have seen this result in the NAFTA models. Scale effects are largest in Mexico, the smallest economy with the highest pre-agreement protection.

Case IV

The rise in the return to a factor of production as a result of import protection clearly creates an incentive for that factor to migrate into the protected market. Conventional trade theory, using a homogeneous products model with constant returns to scale, tells us that import protection causes immigration of the scarce factor so that factor flows and goods flows are substitutes. [See Mundell (1957).] However, as we have seen above, in the differentiated products models, the returns to both the scarce and the abundant factors may rise with protection. As a consequence, the two countries may become less similar in endowments rather that more similar. Hence factor flows and goods trade may become complementary.[2]

This point is illustrated in Table 5.11. Here, we return again to the situation in which the two countries are identical, with the exception that the home country imposes a 20 percent import tariff on both goods. As expected, the tariff raises the return to labor and capital in the home country 10 percent above the return to capital and labor in the foreign country, as shown in the second column of results in Table 5.11.

We now allow the possibility of capital to migrate from country F to country H. The relocated capital is assumed to be owned by agents in country F, so the rental payments are remitted back to foreign country consumers. Capital flows from country F to country H of 10, 30, and 50 units are considered.

The capital flows, of course, increase the difference in factor endowments between the two countries. Before the tariff was imposed, the two countries had identical factor endowments. However, once 50 units of capital have moved from country F to H, country H becomes the capital-abundant country and specializes in the capital-intensive good.

This last point can be seen by considering the effect of the capital flows on the number of firms in each sector. In the absence of a tariff, there are 7.278 firms in each sector in each country. After the capital flow of 50 units, the number of sector 1 firms in H grows to 11.362, while the number of sector 2 firms falls to 6.839. The opposite occurs in country F. The number of sector 1 firms falls to 3.197, and the number of sector 2 firms rises to 7.728. Clearly, the effect of capital flows in this case is to increase intersectoral specialization.

Capital flows are welfare improving for the foreign country. For example, with no capital flows, welfare in the foreign country with the tariff is 52.427.

Table 5.11. Home Country Tariff on Imports of Goods 1 and 2

Factor Endowments: KH=100 LH=100 LH=100 KF=100 LH=100
Demand Parameters: GAMMAH = GAMMAF = 0.5
SIGMAH = SIGMAF = 3

	tH = 0 delta K = 0		tH = 20% delta K = 0		tH = 20% delta K = 10		tH = 20% delta K = 30		tH = 20% delta K = 50	
	Home	Foreign	Home	Foreign	Home	Foreign	Home	Foreign	Home	Foreign
Utility	54.854	54.854	56.940	52.427	56.787	52.582	56.512	52.870	56.278	53.132
Product Demand										
H.X1	2.794	2.794	3.285	2.298	3.243	2.341	3.161	2.424	3.080	2.507
H.X2	2.794	2.794	3.285	2.298	3.274	2.309	3.253	2.330	3.234	2.349
F.X1	2.794	2.794	2.527	3.056	2.484	3.098	2.400	3.180	2.317	3.260
F.X2	2.794	2.794	2.527	3.056	2.516	3.067	2.495	3.088	2.476	3.108
World Prices										
X1	2.459	2.459	2.705	2.460	2.688	2.449	2.658	2.428	2.629	2.409
X2	2.459	2.459	2.705	2.460	2.690	2.447	2.662	2.423	2.636	2.401
Number of Firms										
X1	7.278	7.278	7.282	7.282	8.098	6.465	9.730	4.832	11.362	3.197
X2	7.278	7.278	7.282	7.282	7.193	7.371	7.016	7.549	6.839	7.728
Elasticity of demand by market										
H.X1	-2.863	-2.863	-2.851	-2.876	-2.852	-2.874	-2.855	-2.871	-2.857	-2.868
H.X2	-2.863	-2.863	-2.851	-2.876	-2.850	-2.876	-2.850	-2.876	-2.850	-2.876
F.X1	-2.863	-2.863	-2.875	-2.850	-2.876	-2.848	-2.879	-2.846	-2.882	-2.843
F.X2	-2.863	-2.863	-2.875	-2.850	-2.875	-2.850	-2.874	-2.850	-2.874	-2.851
Perceived Elasticity										
X1	-2.863	-2.863	-2.861	-2.861	-2.861	-2.861	-2.862	-2.860	-2.862	-2.859
X2	-2.863	-2.863	-2.861	-2.861	-2.861	-2.861	-2.861	-2.861	-2.861	-2.861
Wage										
	1.000	1.000	1.100	1.000	1.094	0.995	1.082	0.985	1.072	0.976
	1.000	1.000	1.100	1.000	1.093	0.995	1.080	0.987	1.069	0.979
Supply by a representative firm										
X1	5.588	5.588	5.583	5.583	5.584	5.582	5.585	5.580	5.586	5.577
X2	5.588	5.588	5.583	5.583	5.583	5.583	5.583	5.583	5.583	5.583
Marginal Cost										
X1	1.600	1.600	1.759	1.600	1.749	1.593	1.729	1.579	1.711	1.566
X2	1.600	1.600	1.759	1.600	1.750	1.592	1.731	1.576	1.715	1.562

A small transfer of 10 units of capital raises welfare to 52.582, and foreign welfare rises to 52.870 with a capital flow of 30 units. This occurs, in part, because capital owners are able to earn a higher rate of return abroad than domestically.

The home country, however, is losing from the capital flows, even though world welfare rises. This is the case because home country terms of trade must deteriorate relative to the no-capital flow case. The remittance of factor payments by the home country must be balanced by a home country trade surplus. Thus, a fall in the price of home-produced varieties is necessary in order to induce foreign consumers to absorb relatively more home-produced goods.

The capital flows also tend to raise firm output in the industry in each country that uses that country's newly abundant factor intensively. That is, firm output in capital-intensive sector 1 in the home country rises from 5.583 with no capital flow to 5.584 with a capital flow of 10 units. Similarly, sector 2 firm output in the foreign country is also rising, with greater capital flows. The opposite is occurring in the sector that uses each country's newly scarce factor intensively. As a result, for a capital flow of 10 units, sector 1 firm output at home has risen but foreign firm output has fallen, while sector 2 firm output at home has fallen but foreign firm output has risen. The capital flow, then, by fostering greater specialization, generates scale gains for each country in the sector that uses its abundant factor intensively.

Equilibrium in the world capital markets will ultimately be restored when the return to capital in the two countries is once again equal. As can be seen from Table 5.11, capital flows into country H narrow the rental-rate gap generated by the tariff. The fall in home country prices associated with the capital inflow in turn lowers the return to capital in country H. For sufficiently large capital flows, the return to capital in H will fall to the level available in country F.

The complementarity between goods flows and capital flows was considerably stronger in the Michigan Model. In particular, we found that transferring capital from the rest of the world to Mexico actually raised the return to capital in Mexico relative to the rest of the world, although transferring labor to Mexico lowered the Mexican wage relative to the U.S. wage, as shown in Table 5.2. It seemed to be the case that the return to capital rose with the capital stock because of very strong positive scale effects on the Mexican economy that fed back onto the return to both capital and labor.

V. Conclusions

There are a few lessons concerning NAFTA that can be drawn from this exercise. First, it is fairly clear that the determination of scale effects associated with trade liberalization is complicated and difficult to anticipate. One might have expected that the relatively large tariff reductions in Mexico might actually exert an anticompetitive effect on U.S. firms. However, our results here indicate that a tariff imposed by one country tends to be anticompetitive for both domestic and foreign firms. In light of this result, U.S. scale gains in the Michigan Model are not surprising, even though current U.S. tariffs on Mexican exports are very low. In addition, the analysis of country size on the likely scale effects across countries creates a strong presumption that the small country will enjoy greater scale gains than larger countries. This result was born out in the large-scale NAFTA model.

Second, the results presented here help to understand why the U.S. real wage rate rose with trade liberalization, even though labor is the United States's relatively scarce factor. U.S. labor lost relative to capital but still gained absolutely. Mexican liberalization resulted in a terms-of-trade gain for the United States that pulled up the value of the marginal product of labor. This is the case, even though production in the United States overall became more labor-intensive and the marginal product of labor fell.

Finally, the multiple channels through which trade liberalization affects factors of production creates the possibility that factors and goods flows may be complements in a differentiated products model. However, results concerning international capital flows remain a bit of a mystery. In principle, it seems as if it might be possible to configure the model in such a way as to minimize the terms-of-trade losses associated with a capital inflow and maximize the scale gains associated with expanding country size. However, this task remains for the future.

Endnotes

1. For a discussion of the relationship between model structure and results, see Brown (1992).

2. For other examples in which trade and factor flows are complementary, see Markusen (1983).

References

Bachrach, C., and L. Mizrahi. 1992. "The economic impact of a free trade agreement between the United States and Mexico: A CGE analysis." Unpublished manuscript.

Brown, D.K. 1992. "The impact of a North American free trade area: Applied general equilibrium models." In *North American free trade: Assessing the impact*, edited by N. Lustig, B.P. Bosworth, and R.A. Lawrence. Washington, D.C. The Brookings Institution.

———. 1991. "Tariffs and capacity utilization of monopolistically competitive firms." *Journal of International Economics, 30*(3/4):371–81.

Brown, D.K., A.V. Deardorff, and R.M. Stern. 1992a. "A North American Free Trade Agreement: Analytical issues and a computational assessment." *The World Economy 15*(1):15–29.

———. 1992b. "Some conceptual issues in the modeling and computational analysis of the Canada-U.S. Free Trade Agreement." Unpublished manuscript, Tufts University.

Grossman, G., and A. Krueger. 1991. "Environmental impacts of a North American Free Trade Agreement." NBER Working Paper No. 3914.

Harris, R.G. 1984. "Applied general equilibrium analysis of small open economies with scale economies and imperfect competition." *American Economic Review* 74(5):1016–32.

Hinojosa-Ojeda, R., and S. Robinson. 1991. "Alternative scenarios of U.S.-Mexico integration: A computable general equilibrium approach." University of California, Berkeley, Department of Agricultural and Resource Economics Working Paper 609.

Horstmann, I.J., and J.R. Markusen. 1986. "Up the average cost curve: Inefficient entry and the new protectionism." *Journal of International Economics* 20(3/4):225–47.

Krugman, P. 1991. "Increasing returns and economic geography." *Journal of Political Economy,* 99(3):483–99.

———. 1981. "Intraindustry specialization and the gains from trade." *Journal of Political Economy, 89*(5):959–73.

———. 1980. "Scale economies, product differentiation, and the pattern of trade." *American Economic Review 70*(5):950–59.

Lancaster, K. 1984. "Protection and product differentiation." In *Monopolistic competition and international trade,* edited by H. Kierzkowski. Oxford: Clarendon Press.

Markusen, J.R. 1983. "Factor movements and commodity trade as complements." *Journal of International Economics 14*(3/4):341–56.

Markusen, J.R., and L.E.O. Svensson. 1985. "Trade in goods and factors with international differences in technology." *International Economic Review* 26(1):175–92.

———. 1986. "Factor endowments and trade with increasing returns: Generalizations and extensions." Unpublished manuscript, University of Stockholm and University of Western Ontario.

Markusen, J.R., and R.M. Wigle. 1989. "Nash equilibrium tariffs for the United States and Canada: The roles of country size, scale economies, and capital mobility." *Journal of Political Economy* 97(2):368–86.

Mundell, R.A. 1957. "International trade and factor mobility." *American Economic Review* 47(3):321–35.

Roland-Holst, D., K.A. Reinert, and Clinton R. Shiells. 1992. "North American trade liberalization and the role of nontariff barriers." Unpublished manuscript, Mills College.

Rutherford, T.F. 1991. "Extensions of GAMS for variational and complementarity problems with examples arising in economic equilibrium analysis." Unpublished manuscript, University of Western Ontario.

PART III

Sector-Focused Models

6

Agriculture in the Mexico–U.S. Free Trade Agreement: A General Equilibrium Analysis*

Santiago Levy
Boston University

Sweder van Wijnbergen
World Bank and CEPR

I. Introduction

Agriculture contributes less than 8 percent of Mexico's GDP. Nevertheless, when in June 1990 Presidents Salinas and Bush announced negotiations on a free trade agreement (FTA) between Mexico and the United States, it was clear that agriculture would be a major stumbling block. At stake is much more than the efficiency gains that liberalizing agriculture, particularly maize production, would bring to Mexico, substantial as we find them to be. Maize protection is Mexico's de facto rural employment and antipoverty program, so distributional concerns complicate the liberalization process. Further complications arise because, while high maize prices almost certainly contribute to, rather than alleviate, poverty, rapid liberalization would increase poverty during transition.

This paper focuses on the distributional effects of liberalizing maize in Mexico, the policies that can be put in place to alleviate them, and the incentive problems that would be caused by such policies. Our results, however, are of much wider interest than the FTA negotiations themselves. Agriculture has

* This paper was financed by the OECD Development Centre as part of their research project, "Developing Country Agriculture and International Economic Trends," and by the World Bank. Parts of this paper draw on Levy and van Wijnbergen (1992). We thank Ian Goldin and Hans Binswanger for helpful comments and discussions. The views expressed here do not necessarily coincide with those of the institutions with which we are affiliated.

been a major stumbling block in trade negotiations everywhere, having always been excluded from GATT negotiations until the recent Uruguay round, which almost collapsed because of it. In many cases the reasons are similar to the ones discussed in this paper.

Transitional problems like the ones analyzed in this paper are likely to arise in most major economic reforms. In particular, we focus on the implications for policy design of the absence of well-functioning capital markets, on the welfare costs of reforming only gradually, on the incentive problems created by trade adjustment policies, and on the redistributive aspects of policy reform in the presence of realistic limits on the array of intervention instruments available to the Government.

Maize is Mexico's key crop and main rural employer; it occupies the largest acreage, it is the most costly in terms of fiscal subsidies, and it is the most protected.[1] It is grown by subsistence farmers, mostly in rain-fed lands; it is also grown by medium- and large-scale farmers in rain-fed and irrigated lands. Because irrigated lands have higher yields, the latter groups, who are not among the poor, receive large inframarginal rents. Only 0.32 of every peso of subsidy reaches subsistence farmers [Levy and van Wijnbergen (1991)].

Tortillas, Mexico's main staple food, are mainly made from maize. The government subsidizes tortillas, but the subsidies fail to fully offset the effects of maize protection; thus the rural poor are *taxed* on their main consumption good. For landless workers and the 65 percent of maize producers whose land is so marginal that they are actually net maize buyers, this tax exceeds the subsidy they receive as producers.[2]

We show that liberalization lowers the value of rain-fed land, thus hurting the subset of the rural poor who own land by reducing the rents derived from this asset. This would lower the value of the main asset farmers can collateralize, reducing their access to credit at the very moment when such access is needed most. Liberalization also lowers the demand for rural labor. And because migration links rural and urban labor markets, liberalization of maize lowers wage rates across the board. The effects of liberalization thus spill over to the urban poor.

Lump-sum transfers are not a feasible option in Mexico, so other policies to protect the poor are needed. Moreover, Mexico's poor have limited access to capital markets, access that may in fact be reduced by the liberalization because it lowers land prices. Hence, these policies must not only focus on steady-state welfare but also on the transition period. And because the FTA is a permanent shock, these policies should also facilitate change towards other activities.

In section II we sketch an intertemporal model to trace the impact on households' welfare of Mexico–U.S. free trade in agriculture and of different adjustment policies. In section III we quantify the trade-offs between the speed of liberalization and the size of the efficiency gains; we also study the impact on labor and land markets. Section IV designs a program to facilitate adjustment towards free trade in maize that protects the rural poor during the transition. Political economy considerations that bear on the design of this program are addressed in section V. Section VI concludes.

II. Model Structure

Static Relationships

The economy is divided into an urban and a rural sector. The urban sector produces only a tradeable industrial good and a nontradeable services good. Each of these goods is produced with fixed intermediate inputs and a Cobb-Douglas technology for urban labor and sector-specific capital.

Land and rural labor produce five tradeable goods in the rural sector: maize, other basic grains, fruits and vegetables, other agricultural goods, and livestock. We distinguish between *rain-fed* (T1) and *irrigated* (T2) land, because yields and land/labor ratios for the same crop differ between types of land. We include tortillas as a pure consumption good. Tortillas are nontraded but, by assumption, perfectly elastically supplied at the zero-profit, tax/subsidy-inclusive price; their price depends only on the producer price of maize and any taxes or subsidies.

We distinguish six types of households, classified by ownership of factors of production. Four are in rural areas: landless rural workers, whose only asset is labor; subsistence farmers, who on average own two hectares of rain-fed land that they work themselves and participate in the rural labor market; rain-fed farmers, who own the remainder of the rain-fed land and half of the land used for livestock; and owners of irrigated land, who own the irrigated land and the other half of livestock land. Neither rain-fed nor irrigated farmers supply labor. Urban workers supply all urban labor, and urban capitalists own the urban capital stock.

Urban workers, landless rural workers, and subsistence farmers all have the same preferences, as do rain-fed and irrigated land owners and urban capitalists. The first group allocates a much larger share of expenditure to rural goods than the second, so changes in food prices have a much larger impact on the first group.[3]

Migration plays an important role in determining the incidence of changes in agricultural protection. Although migration to the United States has attracted most international attention, rural-urban migration inside Mexico is quantitatively more important. Mexico's rapid urban growth has been largely fueled by such migration and involves numbers in excess of any available estimate of the number of Mexican migrants currently in the United States [Garcia y Griego (1989)].

We therefore focus on internal migration and assume that migration flows keep the ratio of per capita utility differentials between landless rural workers (the most likely migrants) and urban workers (the most likely target group) constant. We use utility differentials rather than wage differences (as in the Harris-Todaro model) because urban transfers like the *tortivale* program also affect migration choices. We capture all such effects by focusing on total utility. With L^{ru} the stock of migrants from rural to urban areas, U_r and U_u per capita utility of a worker in the rural and urban areas, respectively, and the superscript 0 an initial equilibrium, we get

$$L^{ru} = k[(U_u/U_r)/(U_u^0/U_r^0)]^\eta - k; k > 0 \quad \eta \geq 0 \tag{6.1}$$

where η is the elasticity of migration to urban-rural utility differentials. Keeping utility differentials constant is achieved by setting η very high.

We distinguish *physical* land (the actual physical hectares of land allocated to a particular crop) from *effective* land (the amount actually usable). The relationship between them is

$$\tilde{T}_j = \tau_j \cdot T_j^{\phi j}; \tau_j > 0, \quad 0 < \phi_j < 1 \tag{6.2}$$

where $\sim$ denotes effective land; the subscript j refers to the four agricultural goods. Equation 6.2 is intended to capture incentives for crop rotation and other practices that preclude allocating all land to a single crop. Irrigated land is assumed to be better than rain-fed in that $\phi 1_j \leq \phi 2_j$ so that diminishing returns set in more slowly than in rain-fed lands. Hence, for the same price change, the supply response in irrigated lands is stronger.

Agricultural production functions exhibit constant returns to scale to labor and *effective* land; thus value added in maize, *m*, in rain-fed lands is

$$VA1_m = LR1_m^{1-\alpha 1m} \tilde{T}1_m^{\alpha 1m} = LR1_m^{1-\alpha 1m} \tau 1_m^{\alpha 1m} T1_m^{\phi 1m \alpha 1m} \tag{6.3}$$
$$= \rho 1_m LR1_m^{1-\alpha 1m} T1_m^{\lambda 1m}$$

$LR1_m$, $T1_m$ are rural labor and rain-fed lands allocated to maize; $\rho 1_m = \tau 1_m^{\alpha 1m}$ and $\lambda 1_m = \phi 1_m \cdot \alpha 1_m$. Similar functions apply to the other agricultural products in both types of land. Because $0 < \lambda < \alpha < 1$, there are diminishing returns to *physical* land for given labor intensity. Thus, for a wide range of prices, there need not be full specialization in agriculture.

Trade interventions are modeled as combinations of production and consumption taxes/subsidies. We also model direct lump-sum transfers to urban workers through the *tortivale* program. Such tortilla deliveries are inframarginal and thus equivalent to a direct income transfer. For given taxes and subsidies, domestic prices for tradeable goods follow world prices, as we assume domestic goods to be perfect substitutes for world goods and take world prices to be exogenous. But services are nontraded, so this market, like the markets for rural and urban labor and for rain-fed and irrigated land, is cleared by prices. Our model thus determines, via the excess demand functions in equation 6.4, factor prices and the real exchange rate:

$$LR^D(P) + L^{ru}(P) - LR^0 = 0 \qquad (6.4)$$
$$LU^D(P) - L^{ru}(P) - LU^0 = 0$$
$$T1^D(P) - T1 = 0$$
$$T2^D(P) - T2 = 0$$
$$qs_s(P) - qd_s(P) = 0$$

P contains the rural and urban wage rates, the rental rates on rain-fed and irrigated land, and the price of services (the real exchange rate). The vectors of goods' supply and demand are, respectively, qs and qd, the subscript s refers to services, and the superscript D denotes the market demand for a particular type of labor or land. LR^0 and LU^0 are the initial distribution of the total labor force so that in the base case $L^{ru} = 0$.

Intertemporal Relationships

At each period the economy is described by the excess demand functions in equation 6.4. But from one time period to the next, the economy changes as a result of exogenous and policy-induced changes. The exogenous changes are (1) growth of labor and population,[4] (2) Hicks-neutral technical change, (3) growth of the urban capital stock,[5] (4) government spending in nonagriculture items, and (5) the path of world prices. Importantly for our results, we assume that the rate of growth of productivity in rain-fed agriculture is lower than in irrigated agriculture. This reflects the fact that high-yielding varieties, pesticides, fertilizers, and other innovations are easier to implement in irrigated lands.

We model two policy-induced changes to alter the economy's growth path: trade policy and agriculture investments. Within trade policy, attention focuses on the sectors where liberalization occurs, on the date at which changes start, and on the speed at which they take place. Within agriculture investments, we focus on the size and time-profile of irrigation investments.

Investments in irrigation infrastructure change the endowments of irrigated and rain-fed land with a single-period gestation lag:

$$T1_t = T1_{t-1} - RI_{t-1}; T2_t = T2_{t-1} + RI_{t-1} \qquad (6.5)$$

RI is the number of hectares of rain-fed land transformed to irrigated land. Owners of rain-fed land (subsistence peasants and rain-fed farmers) are assumed to benefit from irrigation investments in proportion to the initial share of rain-fed land held by each group. The investments are paid for by the government. The real resource costs of irrigation are an increasing function of the stock of irrigated land, reflecting the fact that as these investments increase, lands of poorer-quality are encountered (due to greater distance from water resources, and so on). We capture this by

$$Q_t = q\left(\frac{\sum_{t=0}^{t-1} T2_i}{T2_0}\right)^\gamma; \quad q > 0; \gamma > 1 \tag{6.6}$$

where Q_t is an index of marginal costs of irrigation investments.

The rates of growth of labor in each period, gl_t, are exogenous, but migration responds to endogenously determined utility differentials, implying in turn that the urban and rural labor forces are determined endogenously by

$$LR_t = (LR_{t-1} - L_{t-1}^{ru})(1 + gl_{t-1}); \tag{6.7}$$
$$LU_t = (LU_{t-1} + L_{t-1}^{ru})(1 + gl_{t-1})$$

The Transition Path and the Steady State

We divide the future into a transition path and a steady state. The transition path lasts $T - 1$ years; the steady state obtains from period T onwards, going out to infinity. All policy-induced changes take place during the transition period. During this period, the rate of growth of labor also converges to that of the population. In the steady state, on the other hand, all households grow at the same rate, and the rate of growth of aggregate output, which equals the rate of growth of the capital stock, is given by the sum of labor and productivity growth.

Hence, by assumption, static and intertemporal relative prices remain unchanged over the interval $[T, \infty)$. This allows us to Hicks-aggregate the steady state path of the economy. It suffices to simply calculate period T values, because all future periods will be identical up to a uniform scale factor (growth rate) for all quantities. The aggregation process therefore only affects discount factors between $T - 1$ and T; these are larger than those between earlier periods because this "period" is replicated an infinite number of times (again, up to a uniform scale factor for all quantities).

Let the common and constant post-T growth rate be g and the real world interest rate be r^w. Define $\delta = 1/(1 + r^w)$ and $\delta_a = (1 + g)/(1 + r^w)$, where δ_a is the period-to-period growth-adjusted discount factor. Then the following expressions obtain for discount factors from year i back-to-period-1, $\delta(i)$:

$$\begin{aligned}
\delta(i) &= \delta^{i-1} && \text{for } i < T \tag{6.8} \\
&= \sum_{T}^{\infty} \delta^{i-1} = \frac{\delta^{T-1}}{1-\delta} && \text{for all } i > T \text{ combined}
\end{aligned}$$

Consider now the Net Present Value, NPV_y, of $\{y_t\}$, where $y_t = y_{t-1}(1 + g)$ for all $t > T$:

$$NPV_y = \sum_{1}^{\infty} y_t \cdot \delta^{t-1} = \sum_{1}^{T-1} y_t \cdot \delta^{t-1} + \delta^{T-1} \cdot \sum_{T}^{\infty} y_T \cdot (1+g)^{t-T}\delta^{t-T}$$

$$= \sum_{1}^{T-1} y_t \cdot \delta^{t-1} + \delta^{T-1} \sum_{T}^{\infty} y_T \cdot \delta_a^{t-T}$$

$$= \sum_{1}^{T-1} y_t \cdot \delta^{t-1} + \frac{\delta^{T-1}}{1-\delta_a} \cdot y_T$$

Thus the infinite horizon is captured by calculating period T only (out of all $[T,\infty)$ periods) but adjusting the period T discount factor to equal

$$\delta(T) = \frac{\delta^{T-1}}{1-\delta_a} \tag{6.10}$$

Budget Constraints and Welfare Measures

Only urban capitalists save and invest. Private investment is driven by the exogenously given growth of the capital stock. Private savings is a constant proportion of urban capitalists' income. This proportion is exogenous during the transition period but is endogenized in the steady state to satisfy their intertemporal budget constraint. Thus, if during the transition period they accumulated debt (assets), the steady-state savings rate is increased (decreased) so that the discounted value at time T of future savings over investment equals the value of the debt (assets) accumulated up through period $T-1$; see the Appendix for details.

Household's welfare is the present discounted value of the time-paths of utility $\{U_0^h \ldots U_{T-1}^h; U_T^h\}$. Let the rate of time-preference, ρ, be constant and equal for all households, and use a CRRA utility function to aggregate utility over time. If σ is the intertemporal elasticity of substitution, we calculate welfare of household h as

$$W_h = \sum_{1}^{\infty} \frac{u_h(c_t)}{(1+\rho)^t} = \sum_{1}^{T-1} u_h(c_t).\delta_{\text{pref}}^t$$

$$+ \frac{u_h(c_T)}{(1+\rho)^T} \sum_{T}^{\infty} \frac{(1+\sigma^{-1}.gc)^{t-T}}{(1+\rho)^{t-T}}$$

$$= \sum_{1}^{T-1} u_h(c_t).\delta_{\text{pref}}^t + \frac{u_h(c_T).\delta_{\text{pref}}^T}{1-\delta_{\text{prefA}}} \tag{6.11}$$

where $\delta_{\text{pref}} = \dfrac{1}{1+\rho}$ and $\delta_{\text{prefA}} = \dfrac{1+\sigma^{-1}.gc}{1+\rho}$

where gc is the steady-state rate of growth of per household consumption.

Because all private households satisfy their intertemporal budget constraint, the present discounted value (*PDV*) of the government deficit (surplus) equals the *PDV* of the trade deficit (surplus), *B*. We do not impose the condition that $B = 0$. Rather, we measure the difference between the *PDV* of the government deficit in the base path, denoted by B^0, and any *B* generated by an alternative path and interpret the difference as the change in resources generated by the policy change. For each path we calculate the lump-sum transfers (taxes) required so that each household in each period has the same current utility as in the base path. When the value of these income compensations are included as part of government's expenditures, as if in fact these compensations had been given, the difference between B^0 and *B* is the aggregate efficiency gain of any policy change.

III. The Impact of Free Trade in Maize

We study the implications of liberalizing maize by comparing a reference path for the economy that leaves maize and tortilla policies at their present levels with various alternatives where maize and tortilla prices are freed up; on the reference path there is no irrigation investment,[6] and U.S. protection of its fruits and vegetables (F&V) sector stays at its present level.[7]

Table 6.1 shows the efficiency gains and distributional impact of eliminating all taxes and subsidies to maize and tortillas. The efficiency gains measure the

Table 6.1. *Welfare and Efficiency Effects*

	Maize 1Y no CNA no F&V	Maize 5Y no CNA no F&V	Maize 1Y CNA no F&V	Maize 5Y CNA no F&V	Maize 5Y CNA F&V	Maize 6Y CNA early F&V
Subsistence Farmer[a]	0.967	0.971	1.007	1.011	1.013	1.015
Landless Rural Worker[a]	0.984	0.985	0.993	0.995	1.000	1.001
Rain-Fed Farmer[a]	0.943	0.949	0.996	1.001	1.000	1.003
Irrigated Farmer[a]	1.028	1.024	1.019	1.015	1.028	1.025
Urban Worker[a]	0.984	0.986	0.993	0.995	1.000	1.001
Urban Capitalist[a]	1.018	1.017	1.013	1.012	1.007	1.006
Efficiency Gains[b]	42.44	40.08	51.96	49.57	44.81	43.18
Cumulated Fiscal Gain[b]	23.17	21.94	18.04	16.76	13.64	12.50

[a] Measured as a percentage of the reference case.
[b] 1989 $ billions (U.S.); Mexico's GDP was $207 billion in 1989.

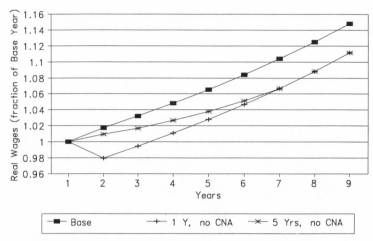

Figure 6.1. Rural Product Wages (no adjustment programs)

increase in national income assuming the government delivers lump-sum transfers (or levies) so that every household has always the same utility as in the reference path. The welfare changes measure the impact of various alternative adjustments but exclude the effects of such transfers.

In this section we only focus on the first two columns, where we evaluate the effects of liberalization *without* any adjustment policies. The first column shows the impact of an immediate elimination of all maize and tortilla taxes and subsidies; the second column shows the effects of a gradual change where maize moves linearly to world prices over five years (so that in the sixth year domestic and world prices are equal).

Instantaneous liberalization leads to very large efficiency gains. The *PDV* of these gains is $42.4 billion (U.S.). With a growth-adjusted discount rate of about 3 percent,[8] these efficiency gains translate into $1.22 billion (U.S.) of additional consumption *per annum*, or 0.6 percent of 1989 GDP. This is a very significant number for gains from removing taxes and subsidies to only two commodities: maize and tortillas. The efficiency gains of gradual liberalization are less, at $40.1 billion (U.S.), but actually not by very much. Distributing the adjustment over a five-year period reduces the net discounted value of the efficiency gains by only 5.5 percent. Thus, the efficiency costs of a more gradual approach do *not* seem large when compared to the benefits that maize liberalization eventually leads to.

But the aggregate efficiency gains have substantial distributional effects. To understand how different groups are affected by the policy change, first look at what happens to the prices of the factors of production. The more straightforward one is labor. As Figure 6.1 shows, rural product wages are adversely

Table 6.2. *Land Values and Land-Holdings (million pesos of 1989 per hectare)*

	Rain-fed Land	Irrigated Land	Land-holdings of Subsistence and Rain-fed farmers	Land-holdings of Irrigated farmers
Base Case	12.065	40.169	12.065	40.169
Case 1: 0 year adjustment, no CNA Program	9.231	40.800	9.231	40.800
Case 2: 5 year adjustment, no CNA program	9.443	40.725	9.443	40.725
Case 3: 0 year adjustment, with CNA program	9.180	40.668	11.499	40.668
case 4: 5 year adjustment, with CNA program	9.390	40.597	11.703	40.597
case 5: 5 year adjustment, with CNA program, access to US F&V market	9.608	42.175	12.030	42.175
case 6:as 5, but maize price cuts take last 6 years & start one year after CNA program	9.726	42.137	12.141	42.137

affected by the cut in maize prices. Although maize is less labor-intensive than fruits and vegetables, it is more labor-intensive than all other activities in agriculture; hence, rural product wages fall once maize prices go down.

Table 6.2 shows the discounted value of all current and future rental income for both types of land. Column 1 indicates that the value of rain-fed land drops by almost 25 percent under immediate liberalization, clearly a very significant capital loss. This is because most maize is grown in rain-fed lands, where substitution possibilities towards other crops are much more limited than on irrigated land. The value of irrigated land actually goes up. Because both substitution possibilities and labor-intensity are higher in irrigated lands, the positive effect of lower rural product wages offsets the negative impact of lower maize prices.

Contrasting the fall in land values with the reduction in rural product wages, it is clear that a larger part of the adjustment falls on land. The reason for this is that labor is more mobile than land. Labor can be reallocated within agriculture toward other crops with much more ease than rain-fed land, and in addition some of the impact on labor is shifted to urban workers through rural-to-urban migration.

Figure 6.2 shows the migration response. Note first that under the reference case, migration is substantial. Long-term productivity trends do not favor agriculture, particularly not rain-fed agriculture. This, together with the exhaustion of land on the extensive margin, makes it clear that even with current maize policies, future migration will be substantial. The model predicts a cu-

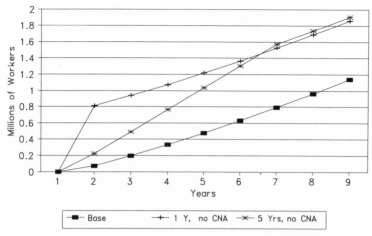

Figure 6.2. Cumulative Migration (no adjustment programs)

mulative migration of almost 1.2 million workers over the next decade. Such large migration suggests that maize protection as a rural employment policy is likely to fail increasingly or, alternatively, become much more expensive than it already is.

Immediate liberalization has a large impact on migration, adding 700,000 workers in a *single* year (Figure 6.2). Gradual liberalization also increases migration over the reference case but does so at a slower pace. However, after the adjustment is over, the cumulative amount of migration is the same.

Table 6.1 shows what these factor price developments imply for households' welfare. Rural landless workers lose out as rural wage rates fall. But their welfare drops less in percentage terms than rural product wages do, because they are also consumers of maize and profit from lower maize prices. As Figure 6.3 shows, the drop in the rural consumption wage is less than the fall in the rural product wage.

Subsistence farmers own rain-fed land and hire out as day laborers to other farmers; they are thus doubly hit as both the value of their land drops by 25 percent, and their labor income declines in line with the drop in rural wages (though they also benefit from lower consumer prices). The situation is more complex for rain-fed and irrigated farmers. They both lose because of lower maize prices, but they gain because of lower rural wages (because they are both net users of labor). These two factors are capitalized in land prices, and the balance is clear from Table 6.2: Rain-fed farmers lose substantially, whereas irrigated farmers experience a small gain. Note that under gradual liberalization, values of rain-fed land fall less than under liberalization, because protection-induced rents can be reaped for five additional years.

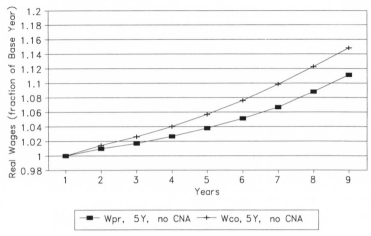

Figure 6.3. Consumption and Product Wages in Rural Areas

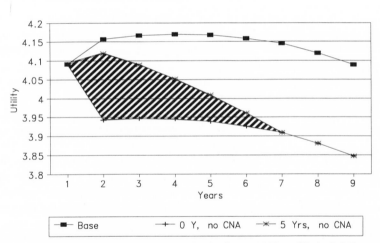

Figure 6.4. Cold Turkey versus Gradualism – Utility of Rain-fed Farmers

Figure 6.4 illustrates how this affects rain-fed farmers. The shaded area measures the differences in utility between immediate ("cold turkey") and gradual liberalization. The gradual path gives them additional rents during the transition (although at declining rates), but it produces no further gain once the transition is over.

Migration slows the drop in rural wages at the cost of increased downward pressure on urban wages. Figure 6.5 shows that despite lower consumer prices for maize, urban workers' real consumption wages fall relative to the base

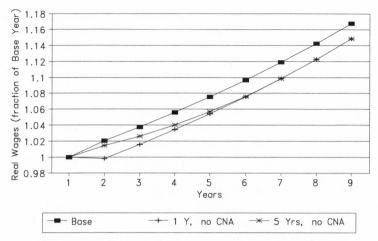

Figure 6.5. Urban Consumption Wages (no adjustment programs)

case. And with the marginal product of capital increasing as a result of higher urban employment, capitalists are better off.

To sum up: The efficiency gains of liberalization in the absence of adjustment policies are substantial but unevenly distributed. Immediate liberalization produces larger gains, but gradualism is not very costly; the aggregate efficiency gains foregone during the five-year transition are small. But the converse of this is that gradualism barely mitigates the welfare loss for the groups affected. Of course, prolonging the liberalization over more than five years further insulates the groups concerned from welfare losses but also further reduces the aggregate efficiency gains. The issue is therefore not only how quickly to liberalize but also what measures are taken during the transition to transfer some of the efficiency gains to the groups most affected by it. How this can be done is the subject of the next section.

IV. What Type of Trade Adjustment?

The inclusion of Mexican agriculture into the FTA is a permanent change. A poverty-minded adjustment program for such a change should therefore have two objectives – first, transfer income to those among the poor that are adversely affected, and second, facilitate their finding alternative sources of income. The major problem in the design of such a program is that the first objective usually conflicts with the second.[9]

A program designed to help *maize* producers would provide incentives to increase, or at least maintain, maize production, because benefits would decrease with lower output; such a program would discourage farmers from searching for alternative activities. Moreover, if the benefits were significant, the program would also provide incentives for rent-seeking and graft; the number of "registered" maize producers would soon exceed the rural population. This is particularly important in Mexico, where administrative capacity is weak, as are records of farm size and output. But more fundamentally, a program focused on transfering income to maize producers fails to alter underlying conditions in agriculture. For the adjustment program to be transitory, it must increase the productivity of the factors owned by the groups affected by the policy change so that after the program ends, these groups do not need further assistance. Section III indicates that in Mexico's case this translates into programs that can increase land values and stimulate the permanent demand for rural labor.

Table 6.2 indicates that at free trade prices, the average rental rate on irrigated land is four times that of rain-fed land. Thus, a program of investments in land improvements has a substantial potential for increasing land productivity.[10] Such a program is particularly promising because private irrigation investment has been discouraged by land tenure problems and explicit regulation, while public investment has been curtailed for budgetary reasons.[11] As a consequence, the return on such a program is likely to be high.

A public investment program focused on land improvements generates transitory demand for rural labor. By supporting the rural wage rate during the construction period, it eases the transition toward free trade for landless rural workers and subsistence farmers; by slowing down migration, it helps insulate urban workers from the policy change. And because irrigated land is about 2.4 times more labor-intensive than rain-fed (at the free trade crop composition), the program stimulates the *permanent* demand for rural labor. Thus, once the program is finished, it continues to provide employment opportunities in the rural areas.

But the program also helps to increase the value of the land owned by subsistence and rain-fed farmers. As some of their land is improved with irrigation and drainage, the capital loss suffered due to removal of protection is reduced. This, in turn, restores the value of their main collateral and enhances their access to credit. In addition, transforming land from rain-fed to irrigated lowers risks faced by farmers and augments crop choice. This facilitates a permanent adjustment away from maize cultivation.

Simulations 3 and 4 explore such a program. In both simulations we assume that a total of 1.1 million hectares of land are transformed from rain-fed to irrigation, with investments beginning in the second year and lasting a total of five years;[12] in simulation 3 maize and tortilla prices are liberalized immediately, while simulation 4 assumes a pari passu five-year adjustment path for price liberalization and irrigation investments.

Table 6.1 shows that the efficiency gains of maize liberalization accompanied by irrigation investments are over 20 percent higher than in the absence of irrigation (with slightly larger gains when liberalization is immediate). Moreover, the efficiency gains when gradual liberalization is accompanied by the irrigation program exceed by almost 17 percent the gains from immediate liberalization without adjustment program. Clearly, the potential gains from irrigation investments are large. This increased efficiency has two sources: the four-to-one difference in the level of productivity of irrigated versus rain-fed land and increase in the *average* rate of technical change in agriculture. Technical change is faster in irrigated land, and the program increases the share of total arable land that is irrigated.

Equally interesting are the distributive effects of the program. Column 4 of Table 6.1 indicates that the two groups directly dependent on the value of rain-fed land are both better off when gradual liberalization is accompanied by the irrigation program. The reason for this is shown in Table 6.2; although land prices are almost the same as in simulations 1 and 2 (the differences resulting from different behavior of wage rates), the value of the *land holdings* of these two groups is almost restored to the preliberalization levels, as these groups now hold a mix of rain-fed and irrigated land.

Figure 6.6 shows that rural wage rates are also higher when liberalization is accompanied by the irrigation program, generating benefits for landless rural workers and subsistence farmers and, by further slowing migration, for urban workers as well. As a consequence, the welfare of landless rural workers and urban workers is almost restored to the protection level (cf. Table 6.1). The converse of this tightening in the labor market is reflected in urban capitalists and irrigated farmers' welfare, which is correspondingly diminished (though still higher than under protection).

Figure 6.7 depicts the time-path of utility for rain-fed farmers for the five-year liberalization paths with and without the CNA program. With the CNA program, rain-fed farmers are initially worse off, reflecting the interaction between the rural labor market and the gestation period of irrigation investments. For them, the initial impact of the CNA program is a tightening of the rural labor market, with negative implications for second-period utility. It is only after the third year, when the irrigation works come on stream, that the benefits of land improvements outweigh the costs of higher rural wages. And though their welfare is higher than on the reference path, it takes five years for current-period utility to be higher. This interaction between the path of price declines, on the one hand, and the timing of irrigation investments, on the other, determines *when* the different groups receive the benefits of the adjustment program. All this is masked by the discounted value of utility, but such timing issues can be very important for the political economy aspects of the reform (as will be demonstrated in the next section).

The scenarios presented so far have ignored any change in U.S. protection towards Mexico's export crops. Simulation 5 considers a scenario in which

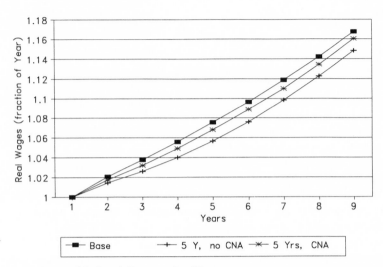

Figure 6.6. Rural Consumption Wages

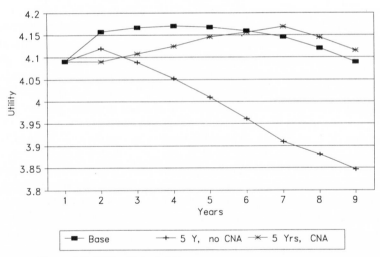

Figure 6.7. Utility Rain-fed Farmers

the gradual liberalization of the Mexican maize market is accompanied by a gradual liberalization over the same five-year period of the U.S. market for fruit and vegetables, the sector with the most significant agricultural trade barriers in the United States.[13] We assume that this simultaneous trade liberalization is accompanied by the same five-year CNA program considered before.

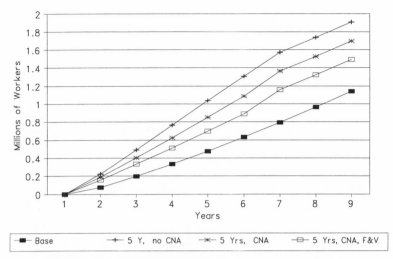

Figure 6.8. Cumulative Migration

Consider first the distributional effects of improved market access to the U.S. fruit and vegetable market. This policy combination generates a Pareto improvement vis-à-vis the reference case: The welfare of all households is at least equal to the protection situation, and for some there is a gain. Because fruits and vegetables is the most labor-intensive crop sector, a price increase shifts out the demand for rural labor, which translates into higher rural wages, reduced migration (Figure 6.8), and higher urban wages. Thus, the opening of the U.S. market has a positive distributional effect via higher wage rates. By reducing labor displacement, it facilitates the transition towards free trade in maize.

Irrigated farmers are more than compensated for the higher rural wages by higher prices for fruits and vegetables; their welfare increases (Table 6.1). But rain-fed farmers profit little from improved export prices for fruits and vegetables, and must also pay higher wages; thus, they constitute the only group in the rural areas that does not benefit directly from a comprehensive FTA.

Next, consider the effects of the U.S. liberalization on aggregate efficiency. Table 6.1 shows that the aggregate efficiency gains in simulation 5 are slightly lower than in 4, which has the same path for maize prices and irrigation investments. This seemingly paradoxical result follows from second-best effects. Because of the urban-rural wage differential, reallocating labor from rural to urban areas gives, *ceteris paribus*, efficiency gains. By slowing down migration, the gradual liberalization of the U.S. market diminishes the size of the gains from labor reallocation into urban areas.

Consider next the fiscal impact of the adjustment program. We focus on the

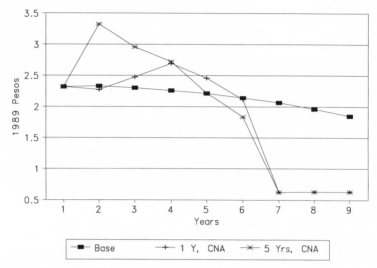

Figure 6.9. Fiscal Costs, Maize and Irrigation Interventions

tradeoff between fiscal savings from the reduction in maize and tortilla subsidies versus the fiscal cost of the CNA irrigation program. Figure 6.9 plots the fiscal impact of maize and tortilla subsidies: (1) the cost of maize production subsidies, (2) the revenue from tortilla taxes, (3) the cost of the *tortivale* program; and, for simulations 3 and 4, (4) the cost of irrigation investments.[14]

On the reference path the fiscal costs of maize interventions actually decline through time. This is because tortilla consumption, which under current policies is taxed, grows faster than subsidized maize production. When irrigation investments are undertaken, the fiscal position initially deteriorates but then improves after the fifth or sixth year. With gradual liberalization, this deterioration is initially quite sharp because only small savings are made each year on the costs of maize interventions. With immediate liberalization, the savings from maize interventions actually dominate the costs of irrigation investments in the first year, and the fiscal costs over the next four years are smaller than in the case of gradual liberalization. After the sixth year, when the irrigation program is complete, both alternatives generate lower costs than current policies.[15]

Table 6.1 indicates the net fiscal impact of each alternative: the net present value of the fiscal surplus in simulation 3 (4) is 3.5 percent (3.2 percent) higher than on the reference path. Current maize policies cost *more* than the adjustment programs proposed to ease the transition to free trade.

V. On the Pace of Adjustment

Much of the economic literature, and in fact Mexico's own experience, argues for fast-paced reforms. But in this case several points argue for

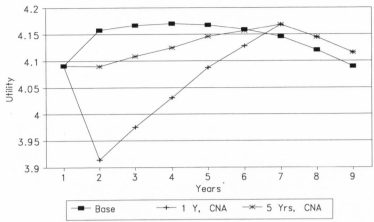

Figure 6.10. Utility Rain-fed Farmers – Adjustment Assistance and Timing

a more gradual approach, the first of which is the impact of speed of reform on labor markets and migration. As shown in Figure 6.2, if maize prices are liberalized instantaneously, roughly 700,000 workers are predicted to move almost straight away. This implies a migration of between 1 and 5 million people (average family size in rural areas is seven). This would put demands on urban infrastructure and labor markets that would be almost impossible to meet. A more gradual reform leads to the same migration but spreads it out over most of the coming decade, buying time to set up the infrastructure and training facilities needed to accommodate such a large group of migrants.

The second problem stems from the political dimensions of such a large reform effort. A reform that inflicts substantial losses on particular groups in society may be more difficult to implement, even if the majority benefits. In section IV we argued that a program focused on improving currently rain-fed land by irrigation and other productivity enhancements intervenes at the right margin; it makes subsistence and rain-fed farmers better off because the value of their land holdings recovers, and it also benefits landless rural workers through the labor market impact. But to fully restore land values to preliberalization levels requires at least five years because of technical and engineering constraints on construction. Immediate liberalization of maize, even if accompanied by the irrigation program, would therefore still impose substantial transitory losses; cf. Figure 6.10 for the case of rain-fed farmers. A gradual phasing-out of maize price supports mitigates this problem, although a *relative* decline (compared to the base case) is difficult to avoid for this group. But note that an absolute drop in utility is avoided if the CNA program is accompanied by gradual phasing-out of maize price supports.

A final argument concerns period-to-period losses. The rural poor have little access to capital markets to help them smooth consumption. Many live in

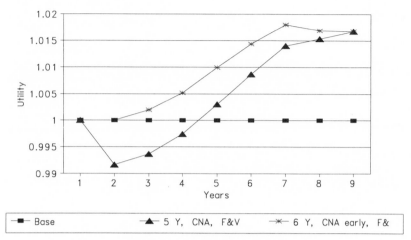

Figure 6.11. Utility Subsistence Farmers (fraction of base case)

extreme poverty and may have higher discount rates than assumed here, as survival is at stake. This implies that initial losses, even if the net change in discounted welfare is positive at the discount rate used here, may be particularly costly. But if the adjustment program was such that at *no point* during the transition was utility less than on the reference path, then the reforms would not hurt the rural poor for any discount rate. The government can then argue that they are being made better off, or at least not losing out, without asking them to wait five years before benefits materialize. Because it is administratively impossible for the government to reach the rural poor directly and because gradualism may avoid initial losses, this, too, calls for gradualism as a second-best solution. Simulation 6 explores these issues. We consider the same liberalization of the U.S. market for fruits and vegetables and the same irrigation program, but we assume that the liberalization of maize and tortilla prices is spread over *six* years. Further, we assume that the change in maize and tortilla prices begins one year *after* the irrigation program starts. This "irrigation first" scenario could be interpreted as a signal from the government to farmers of its intentions to help them adjust to free trade in maize; the government invests in productivity improvements *before* any sacrifice is asked for. This policy ensures that *all* households see their welfare increase vis-à-vis the reference path, though this comes at an efficiency cost. But this cost is not very large; total efficiency gains are only 4 percent smaller than the case where maize prices move pari passu with the irrigation program.

The pay-off to this efficiency cost is shown in Figures 6.11 and 6.12: Landless rural workers and subsistence farmers are better off at every point in time than under protection. And because spreading the maize pricing over a longer

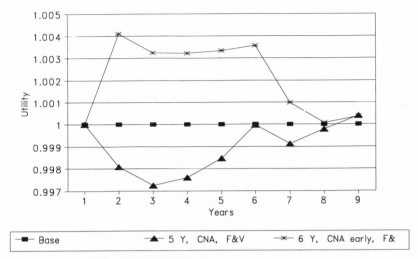

Figure 6.12. Utility Rural Workers

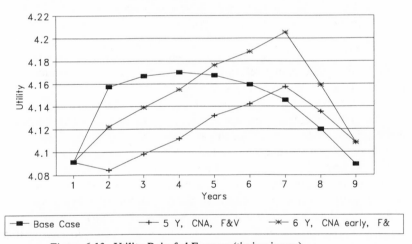

Figure 6.13. Utility Rain-fed Farmers (timing issues)

horizon also slows down migration, urban workers also have higher utility at each point in time. Thus, if price reforms and adjustment programs are timed carefully, *incorporating maize into the FTA can strengthen poverty alleviation efforts.*

Consider now farmers on rain-fed lands. Despite the timing changes in the irrigation and liberalization program, their utility is still less than the reference case for three years (Figure 6.13). As discussed, the CNA program tightens

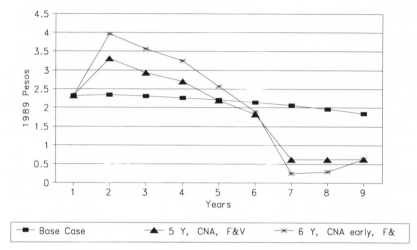

Figure 6.14. Fiscal Costs, Maize and Irrigation Interventions (timing issues)

the rural labor market. And although higher rural wages improve initial utility of subsistence farmers and landless workers, they also raise wage costs for rain-fed farmers. Thus, because the government can only help the first two groups via higher rural wages, it cannot simultaneously help rain-fed farmers in the initial phase of the reforms. This may call for other instruments to provide transitory support to this group (see below).

Figure 6.14 shows the fiscal impact of these timing changes. Initially, fiscal expenditures increase substantially because there are no savings from reduced maize subsidies while outlays for irrigation are made. But though it takes five years for the fiscal costs of interventions to fall below those under protection, Table 6.1 shows that in present-value terms this policy is still cheaper than continuing protection forever. The fiscal issue associated with the adjustment program is thus not one of overall costs but one of transitory financing.

But to label an issue as transitory is not to dismiss it as irrelevant. Fiscal authorities will want to ensure that if resources are commited to irrigation investments, maize prices will indeed be freed; adding the costs of irrigation investments to the costs of maize policies would put an undue burden on the fiscal accounts. At the same time, policymakers in charge of agriculture will want to ensure that if maize prices are freed, the resources required for irrigation investments will indeed be there; liberalizing agriculture in the absence of resources for adjustment would put an undue strain on the welfare of large numbers of the rural population. Thus the reform process needs a "commitment technology" to ensure that its two components – maize liberalization and the irrigation program – are carried out. Signing maize price liberalization as part of the FTA solves the first half of the commitment problem. But the second half still needs attention because there are legal impediments to multiyear commitments of fiscal expenditures in Mexico. What guarantees do the rural groups potentially affected by maize liberalization have that the irrigation program will be completed once the FTA negotiations are finished, even if the government moves first with its irrigation investments? What is optimal for the government to promise now may well not be optimal for it to deliver once the FTA has been signed.

The need for transitory financing for the adjustment program provides part of the solution. In particular, a multilateral organization could provide financing during the adjustment process to the FTA. Because the overall fiscal gains are positive in discounted-value terms, the loan can be paid back out of the savings made later in time. If such financing is made contingent not on the price reforms being carried out but on the irrigation programs promised, it would become expensive to renege. The credibility of the program is then increased by increasing the costs of failing to follow it through.

Recall also that liberalization reduces the value of the main collateral owned by subsistence and rain-fed farmers. These farmers will have better access to credit only if commercial banks are certain that the land improvements that will raise the value of the land available for collateral will indeed incur. A program of public credit guarantees could ensure farmers' access to credit. But, equally important in our context, by committing itself through credit guarantees, the government not only signals its intent to implement the adjustment program but also makes it more costly for itself to not implement it; after all, not following through on the irrigation program would reduce the value of the collateral for loans that carry a public guarantee. Again, increasing the expected cost of the guarantee scheme makes reneging on promises to implement the CNA program less attractive.

VI. Conclusions

Empirical evidence and theoretical analysis overwhelmingly support the view that liberalizing international trade leads to efficiency gains. Recent forays in the economics of imperfect competition have created some question marks by bringing in rent-shifting and second-best aspects but have not led to any strong presumption against this claim [Helpman and Krugman (1989)]. This paper fits the mold by demonstrating that the efficiency gains from liberalizing agricultural trade between the Unites States and Mexico are quite large.

But if the gains are so large, why has agriculture turned out to be so hard to open up? Our analysis raises points that are likely to feature in any satisfactory answer to this question. We show, in a realistic analysis of the consequences of including agriculture in the currently negotiated FTA between

Mexico and the United States, how efficiency gains fail to filter through to important groups in society. In particular, we show that in the absence of adjustment measures, all benefits accrue to the richer groups in both rural and urban areas. These effects are dramatically brought out early in the reform process by being capitalized in land values. This is surely a factor in the resistance by farmers against easing protection of agriculture.[16]

Standard trade theory counters these arguments by pointing out that aggregate efficiency gains imply that winners can compensate losers and still be better off themselves. This paper starts from the premise that instruments to effect such lump-sum transfers are not available. Compensations could also occur, although imperfectly, through indirect taxes and subsidies [Dixit and Norman (1980)], but this would require a degree of differentiation in the tax structure that would itself trigger substantial administrative and incentive problems. In more realistic circumstances, specific adjustment programs have to be designed to accompany a major trade reform.

Liberalizing maize in Mexico in the context of a permanent change like the FTA creates two incentive problems. First, it clearly hurts maize growers. But compensating farmers pro rata to their maize production would create an incentive to continue maize production, the opposite of what the reform is actually designed to achieve. Second, liberalizing maize has a substantial impact on rural labor markets and migration. Rural employment programs could be used to mitigate large labor dislocations and transfer income to workers. But such a program raises a key issue – how to get out of it as time goes by. If in current circumstances the government feels compelled to assist, those affected have every incentive *not* to adjust so as not to lose the transfers by changing the incentive structure the Government itself faces [Tornell (1991)]. Temporary adjustment programs need built in incentives for change.

We point out that to avoid these incentive problems, adjustment programs should focus not on offsetting the income loss associated with past activities, because that provides an incentive to continue them, but instead on improving the productivity of the assets owned by the groups harmed by the reforms. This solves both incentive problems. By not linking the program to past activities, there is no incentive to continue them, and once the assets of those affected are more productive, other opportunities will be easier to find, reducing pressure on the government to help out.

This paper argues the need for such a program in the context of opening up Mexican agriculture and designs one along the lines sketched before. In the specific circumstances of Mexican agriculture, this translates into investments that increase the productivity of rain-fed land via irrigation and other land improvements. We find that a program that transforms about 8 percent of the total stock of rain-fed land to irrigated restores the value of the land holdings of those affected by the liberalization. This restores the collateral value of land

and thus enhances subsistence and rain-fed farmers' access to credit precisely at the time when credit is most needed. In addition, the program helps owners of labor by generating rural employment during the construction period. More fundamentally, it increases the long-term demand for rural labor because irrigated land is substantially more labor-intensive than rain-fed. Thus, the program provides workers with alternatives once it ends; its transitory nature is thus credible.

Improving the value of assets that people own is like an investment program and thus takes time. In contexts where capital markets are imperfect, those affected may not be able to borrow against the value of future assets to smooth consumption over time. This is particularly important if those affected are, as in Mexico's case, amongst the poorest groups in society. We therefore argue for a gradual pace of reform. We first compute the efficiency gains of trade reforms under different liberalization speeds and find that gradualism is not too costly: spreading the liberalization over a five-year period lowers the present discounted value of the efficiency gains by only 5–6 percent. We next show that careful timing of both the liberalization and the adjustment program implies that the rural poor have always had higher utility along the adjustment path than under the protection path.

Embedding trade liberalization in a free trade agreement is a form of commitment technology to the reform process; thus arguments for cold turkey reforms on the grounds that this is the best form to show commitment to the reforms are less compelling in this case. But there is a different commitment problem, created by the time delays inherent in adjustment programs: How can the potential beneficiaries of adjustment programs be assured that those programs will be implemented once the trade liberalizations have been negotiated in the FTA? We argue that gradualism also contributes to solve this time-consistency problem. Because gradualism gives time to implement the productivity-enhancing programs, the beneficiaries do not have to give anything up before the benefits start coming in. Support by external organizations contingent on the adjustment programs can help in solving such commitment problems.

We hope the principles outlined in this paper for the design of adjustment programs will contribute to find efficient solutions to similar transitional problems. The analysis also suggests, however, that application of these principles requires careful analysis of the specifics of each case and of the mechanisms through which the different groups are affected. There may be general principles, but there are unlikely to be rigid rules applicable to each and every reform program.

Appendix: Model Structure, Data and Calibration

Model Structure

1. *Static Relations*

We begin with the static relationships of the model before turning to the intertemporal aspects. For ease of notation, we omit a time subindex for all variables (except where strictly necessary).

Goods, Factor Endowments, and Factor Ownership. The economy produces seven goods: maize, m; basic grains, g; vegetables, v; other agriculture, o; livestock, l; industry, i; and services, s. The first five goods are produced in the rural areas, the last two in the urban areas. Goods are produced by seven factors of production: rural labor, LR; urban labor, LU; rain-fed land, $T1$; irrigated land, $T2$; livestock land, $T3$; industry capital, KI; and services capital, KS.[17]

We distinguish between maize and tortillas, but we model tortilla production in a very stylized fashion. Tortillas are obtained from maize via a Leontief transformation that, for simplicity, requires no primary factors. Tortillas are assumed to be nontraded, with their price being a function only of the tax/subsidy-inclusive producer price of maize and any direct government taxes or subsidies to tortillas.

Factors of production are owned by six types of households: (1) landless rural workers, (2) subsistence farmers, who each own two hectares of rain-fed land and who allocate their labor between producing on their own land and participating in the rural labor market,[18] (3) rain-fed farmers, who own the remainder of the rain-fed land and half of the land devoted to livestock, and (4) irrigated farmers, who own all the irrigated land and the other half of livestock land. For both rain-fed and irrigated farmers, land ownership is the only source of income.

Urban households consist of workers, who own all urban labor, and capitalists, who own the capital stock in industry and services. There are H_h of each type of households ($h = 1,2,..,6$). Ownership shares are given by matrix $\mathbf{M} = \{m_{hj}\}$ where m_{hj} is household's h share of factor of production j.

Prices. World prices for traded goods, $\mathbf{pw}$[19] are exogenous. The price of services, the nontraded good, is ps. The vector of commodity goods prices is $\mathbf{p}_. = [\ \mathbf{pw}\ |\ ps]$. Modelling trade interventions as combinations of production and consumption subsidies and taxes, we write producer prices as

$$\mathbf{pp} = \mathbf{p}.*(1 + \mathbf{s}) \tag{A6.1}$$

where $\mathbf{s}$ is the vector of producer subsidies($+$)/taxes($-$), and .* denotes an element-by-element multiplication.

Consumer prices differ between rural and urban households, so we introduce separate vectors of consumer taxes($+$) or subsidies(-), $\mathbf{ct^r}$ and $\mathbf{ct^u}$, for rural and urban areas, respectively:

$$\mathbf{cp^r} = \mathbf{p}.*(1 + \mathbf{ct^r}) \tag{A6.2}$$

$$\mathbf{cp^u} = \mathbf{p}.*(1 + \mathbf{ct^u}) \tag{A6.3}$$

Urban and rural tortilla prices may also differ[20]. Because tortillas are only produced with maize, their price is

$$pt^r = a_{mt}*\mathbf{pp}_m*(1 - ts^r) = a_{mt}*\mathbf{pw}_m*(1 + \mathbf{s}_m)*(1 - ts^r) \tag{A6.4}$$

$$pt^u = a_{mt}*\mathbf{pp}_m*(1 - ts^u) = a_{mt}*\mathbf{pw}_m*(1 + \mathbf{s}_m)*(1 - ts^u) \tag{A6.5}$$

where a_{mt} is maize input per unit of tortillas and ts^r/ts^u are rural/urban tortilla subsidies. Note that as long as ts^r (ts^u) is less than $\mathbf{s}_m$, rural (urban) tortilla consumers pay a net tax, despite the fact that tortillas are "subsidized."

Intermediate input prices depend on production location (for example, maize sold as input into livestock in rural areas versus maize sold as input into industry in urban areas). Vectors $\mathbf{it^r}$ and $\mathbf{it^u}$ contain ad valorem taxes/subsidies on intermediate inputs for rural and urban areas respectively. Thus, the vectors $\mathbf{ip^r}$ and $\mathbf{ip^u}$ of intermediate prices to producers in rural and urban areas, respectively, are, in general, different.

Finally, we denote by w^r and w^u the rural and urban wage rates and by $r1$ and $r2$ the rental rates on rain-fed and irrigated lands, respectively.[21]

Technology. Intermediate inputs are used in in fixed proportions; primary inputs produce value added. Except for Hicks-neutral technical change, technology is constant through time. Matrix $\mathbf{A}$ contains intermediate input/output coefficients, with most elements exogenously given. However, we do allow substitution between maize and basic grains (mainly sorghum) as inputs into livestock. With a CES structure, the cost-minimizing I/O coefficients of maize and basic grains into livestock, a_{ml} and a_{gl}, are[22]

$$a_{ml} = \tau^\mu.(pa^*/ip^r_m)^\mu.a^* \tag{A6.6}$$

$$a_{gl} = (1 - \tau)^\mu.(pa^*/ip^r_g)^\mu.a^* \tag{A6.7}$$

Land Use. Land allocated to any given crop is subject to diminishing returns. To capture this, we make a difference between *effective* land, $\tilde{T}$, and *physical* land, T. The latter refers to the actual hectares allocated to a crop; the former, to the amount of land that is usable for producing that crop. The relationship between them is given by

$$\tilde{T} = \tau.T^{\phi} \qquad \tau > 0; 0 < \phi < 1 \qquad (A6.8)$$

so that as more (rain-fed or irrigated) physical land is applied to a crop, the amount of effective land grows less than proportionately. This captures incentives for crop rotation and other agricultural practices that result in crop diversification. Irrigated land is assumed to be better than rain-fed in the following way: $\phi 1 \leq \phi 2$; that is, as more irrigated land is allocated to a given crop, diminishing returns obtain more slowly than in rain-fed lands. Hence, for the same price change, the supply response in irrigated lands is stronger. As a result of yield differences, inframarginal rents accrue to owners of irrigated land in standard Ricardian fashion.

Value Added. Production functions are Cobb-Douglas, with constant returns to scale to labor and capital in the urban goods and to labor and *effective* land in the rural goods. So value added on maize cultivated in rain-fed lands is

$$VA1_m = LR1_m^{(1-\alpha 1m)} . \tilde{T}1_m^{\alpha 1m} = LR1_m^{(1-\alpha 1m)} . \tau 1_m^{\alpha 1m} T1_m^{\phi 1m.\alpha 1m} \qquad (A6.9)$$
$$= \rho 1_m . LR1_m^{(1-\alpha 1m)} . T1_m^{\lambda 1m}$$

where $LR1_m$, $T1_m$ are rural labor and rain-fed lands allocated to maize production, $\rho 1_m = \tau 1_m^{\alpha 1m}$ and $\lambda 1_m = \phi 1_m.\alpha 1_m$. Note that $0 < \lambda 1_m < \alpha 1_m < 1$, implying that equation A6.9 exhibits decreasing returns to scale between rural labor and *physical* land. As a result, although the number of agricultural goods exceeds the number of rural factors of production, there need not be full specialization.

Technical Change. Technical change is assumed to be Hicks-neutral in all sectors. A time-dependent constant premultiplies the Cobb-Douglas value-added function in all sectors. The rate of technical change in rain-fed land (equal to the rate of technical change in livestock) is less than in irrigated land. Rates of technical change in industry and services are assumed to be equal.

Goods Supply. Output vectors in rain-fed and irrigated lands are **q1** and **q2**, respectively. Output of livestock is denoted q3, while the output vector in the urban sector is **qu**. Hence, the vector of gross supplies is **qs** = [(**q1** + **q2**) | q3 | **qu**]. All sectors are perfectly competitive. Let **pn** be the vector of "net" or value-added prices, obtained by substracting from producer prices intermediate input costs. The derived demands for labor and land in agricultural production are (again using maize in rain-fed lands as an example)

$$T1_m = \{(1-\alpha 1_m)^{1-\alpha 1m} .\rho 1_m.pn_m.\lambda 1_m^{\alpha 1m} .w^{r\ (\alpha 1m-1)} \qquad (A6.10)$$
$$.r1^{-\alpha 1m}\}^{1/(\alpha 1m-\lambda 1m)}$$

$$LR1_m = \{(1-\alpha 1_m)^{(1-\lambda 1m)(\lambda 1m-\alpha 1m)} \lambda 1_m.^{-\lambda 1m} w^{r\ 1-\lambda 1m}$$
$$.r1^{\lambda 1m} (\rho 1_m.pn_m)^{-1}\}^{1/(\lambda 1m-\alpha 1m)}$$

Similar equations follow for other crops. In industry and services, capital is sector-specific, as is land in livestock, so only demands for rural labor in livestock, $LR3$, and for urban labor in industry, LU_i, and services, LU_s, are derived. Supply of goods follows from substituting optimal factor demands into the Cobb-Douglas production functions.

Household Incomes, Consumption and Savings. Production generates factor incomes: rural and urban wages, rents to rain-fed, irrigated, and livestock land; and quasi rents to capital in industry and services. **M**, the matrix of ownership shares, maps factor incomes **facinc** into household incomes.

In addition, households receive government transfers through the *tortivales* program, with a market value of **vt**. But because urban and rural tortilla prices differ, the market value of a given quantity of freely distributed tortillas to households of type h, $\mathbf{QT}_h$, depends on households' location. Thus, for example, for urban workers (the fifth household group) we have

$$\mathbf{vt}_5 = pt^u * \mathbf{QT}_5 \tag{A6.11}$$

The fiscal cost of the *tortivale* program, CT, is given by

$$CT = \sum_{h=1}^{6} a_{mt} * \mathbf{pp}_m . \mathbf{QT}_h > \sum_{h=1}^{6} \mathbf{vt}_h \tag{A6.12}$$

because the government has to purchase maize from producers at prices $\mathbf{pp}_m$ to make tortillas for the *tortivales*. But because tortillas are subsidized, the value of the transfer to households is less than the fiscal cost of the transfer to the government. The difference is an implicit subsidy to maize producers.

Collecting terms (and ignoring household's income taxes) we obtain **Y**, households' disposable income:

$$\mathbf{Y} = \mathbf{M} * \mathbf{facinc} + \mathbf{vt} \tag{A6.13}$$

Households save a constant proportion of their disposable income, φ_h, so savings for each household are

$$S_h = \varphi_h . \mathbf{Y}_h \tag{A6.14}$$

$(\mathbf{Y}_h - S_h)$ are consumption expenditures for households of type h. We assume a nested Cobb-Douglas/CES/CES utility function. The outer Cobb-Douglas nest allocates expenditures between three goods: industry, services, and a composite agricultural good. The next CES nest aggregates the five rural goods into a composite rural good. Finally, the last CES nest distributes maize consumption between raw maize and tortillas.[23] Solving the utility maximization problem for each household, we obtain consumption demands for tortillas, maize, and the remaining agricultural goods, as well as livestock, industry, and services. Demand for tortillas is then translated into maize demand given the input/output coefficient a_{mt}. This gives us the vector of total household consumption, **c**.

Given the homotheticity of preferences, we can construct an exact price index for each household, CPI_h, that depends on the location of the household (given differences in rural, cp^r, and urban, cp^u, consumer prices), as well as on the particular parameters of its utility function. Given these indices, we compute an index of the real consumption wage to rural and urban workers, Ω^r and Ω^u, respectively, as

$$\Omega^r = w^r/CPI_2 \tag{A6.15a}$$

$$\Omega^u = w^u/CPI_5 \tag{A6.15b}$$

where we use the preferences of landless rural workers and urban workers (household groups 2 and 5, respectively) for computing the relevant CPIs.

Investment and Total Demand. Private investment only takes place in industry and services. We take the rate of growth of the capital stock in industry and services in period t, gk_t, as exogenous. Let **invprop** be the vector of goods required to produce one unit of capital and assume that capital produced for industry and services has the same composition. The vector of private investment demands, **z**, is then given by

$$\mathbf{z}_t = (gk_t + gd_t).(KI_t + KS_t).\mathbf{invprop} \tag{A6.16}$$

where gd_t is the depreciation rate. Then total value of private investment is

$$I_t = \mathbf{p}_t.\mathbf{z}_t \tag{A6.17}$$

We only consider public investment in irrigation infrastructure. Let RI_t the number of hectares of rain-fed land that is transformed to irrigated in period t. Irrigation construction is assumed to require rural labor and intermediate inputs, given at the unit level by vector **inputirr** for goods and by *lrirr* for labor. The real resource costs of irrigation are assumed to be an increasing function of the stock of irrigated land, reflecting the fact that as these investments increase, lands of poorer quality are encountered (those with greater distance from water resources, steeper lands, and so on). We write

$$Q_t = q.\left(\sum_{t=0}^{t-1} T2_t / T2_0\right)^\gamma ; q > 0, \gamma > 1 \tag{A6.18}$$

where Q_t is an index of marginal costs applied to **inputirr** and *lrirr*, and $T2_0$ is the initial stock of irrigated land. Hence, the total demand for goods and labor required for irrigation investments is

$$\mathbf{g}_t = Q_t.RI_t.\mathbf{inputirr} \tag{A6.19a}$$

$$LRIRR_t = Q_t.RI_t.lrirr \tag{A6.19b}$$

Ignoring other components of government expenditures, the vector of total goods' demand is

$$qd = A^*qs + c + z + g \qquad (A6.20)$$

Migration. Let H_h be the total number of households of type h. Consumption quantities are divided by the total number of households of each type to obtain per capita consumptions. Substituting per capita consumptions into the utility function gives per household utility for each type of household, U_h.

Utility *functions* are identical, but parameters differ between urban workers, landless rural workers, and subsistence farmers, on the one hand, and rain-fed and irrigated land-owners and urban capitalists, on the other. The first group allocates a larger share of expenditure to rural goods compared to the second. Thus, changes in maize and tortilla prices have a larger impact on the first group. All members of the potential migrant population have the same utility function, so we can compare per-capita workers' utilities across locations.

Migration incentives result from rural-urban differences in consumption wages, Ω^r and Ω^u, and from differences in benefits derived from living in a given area (like the urban *tortivale* program). Letting L^{ru} be the stock of migrants that move from the rural to the urban areas, U_r and U_u the (per capita) utility of a worker in the rural and urban areas, respectively, and the superscript 0 an initial equilibrium, we write

$$L^{ru} = k[(U_u/U_r)/(U_u^0/U_r^0)]^\eta - k; \, k > 0, \, \eta \geq 0 \qquad (A6.21)$$

where k is a constant and η the elasticity of migration to urban-rural utility differentials. Note that $\eta = 0$ completely segments the urban and rural labor markets.

Excess Demands. At each period of time, total demands for land and labor are

$$T1^D(r1) = \Sigma \, T1_j \qquad (A6.22a)$$

$$T2^D(r2) = \Sigma \, T2_j \qquad \text{for } j = m,g,v,o. \qquad (A6.22b)$$

$$LR^D(w^r) = \Sigma \, LR1_j + \Sigma \, LR2_j + LR3 + \mathbf{LRIRR} \qquad (A6.22c)$$

$$LU^D(w^u) = LU_i + LU_s \qquad (A6.22d)$$

Note from equation A6.22c that rural labor demand includes the workers employed in constructing irrigation.

Given taxes and subsidies, domestic prices for tradeable goods follow from world prices, with net exports bringing tradeables supply and demand into balance. The same is not true of services. This market, jointly with the markets for rural and urban labor, and rain-fed and irrigated land, is cleared by prices.

Our model thus determines factor prices and the real exchange rate.[24] Let $\mathbf{P}$ contain these prices, that is, $\mathbf{P} = [w^r \mid w^u \mid r1 \mid r2 \mid ps]$. Excess demand functions to determine $\mathbf{P}$ are

$$LR^D(\mathbf{P}) + L^{ru}(\mathbf{P}) - LR^0 = 0 \qquad (A6.23a)$$

$$LU^D(\mathbf{P}) - L^{ru}(\mathbf{P}) - LU^0 = 0 \qquad (A6.23b)$$

$$T1^D(\mathbf{P}) - T1 = 0 \qquad (A6.23c)$$

$$T2^D(\mathbf{P}) - T2 = 0 \qquad (A6.23d)$$

$$qs_s(\mathbf{P}) - qd_s(\mathbf{P}) = 0 \qquad (A6.23e)$$

By construction, at the initial values for the exogenous variables $L^{ru} = 0$.

Given the value at time t for production and consumption taxes and subsidies, a solution to equation A6.23 provides allocations of rain-fed and irrigated land to each crop, a division of the total labor force between urban and rural areas as well as its allocation across goods, factor prices and the real exchange rate, and a utility level for each household.

2. *Intertemporal Relationships*

Accumulation Equations. At each period of time, the economy is described by the solution to equation A6.23. But from one period to the next, the economy changes as a result of exogenous and policy-induced changes. The exogenous changes are (1) growth of labor and population,[25] (2) Hicks-neutral technical change in urban and rural sectors, (3) growth of the capital stock in industry and services,[26] (4) government spending in nonagriculture items, and (5) the path of world prices. Policy-induced changes center on the path of taxes and subsidies, irrigation investments, and government transfer policies.

The endowments of land evolve if there are irrigation programs transforming rain-fed land into irrigated land:

$$T1_t = T1_{t-1} - RI_{t-1} \qquad (A6.24a)$$

$$T2_t = T2_{t-1} + RI_{t-1} \qquad (A6.24b)$$

Note that we assume a one-period gestation lag. All owners of rain-fed land (subsistence peasants and rain-fed farmers) are assumed to benefit from irrigation investments in proportion to the initial share of rain-fed land held by each group. The matrix of ownership shares, $\mathbf{M}_t$, is therefore updated at each period to reflect the fact that when irrigation investments take place, the increase in the endowments of irrigated land belongs to subsistence farmers and rain-fed farmers.

The number of households of each type also changes through time. Landless rural workers, subsistence farmers, and urban workers grow at the rate of growth of the labor force, gl_t, so that the urban and rural allocation of labor evolves according to

$$LR_t = (LR^{t-1} - L^{ru}_{t-1})(1 + gl_{t-1}) \qquad \text{(A6.25a)}$$

$$LU_t = (LU^{t-1} + L^{ru}_{t-1})(1 + gl_{t-1}) \qquad \text{(A6.25b)}$$

On the other hand, the number of rain-fed farmers, irrigated farmers, and urban capitalists grows according to

$$H_t = H_{t-1}(1 + gp_{t-1}) \qquad \text{(A6.26)}$$

where gp_t is the growth rate of population in period t. Finally, the capital stock in industry and services evolves according to

$$KI_t = KI_{t-1}.(1 + gk_{t-1}); \qquad \text{(A6.27a)}$$

$$KS_t = KS_{t-1}.(1 + gk_{t-1}) \qquad \text{(A6.27b)}$$

The Transition Path and the Steady-State. We take as starting point for our analysis a particular date ($t_0 = 1$ for convenience) and divide the future into a transition path and a steady state. The transition path lasts (at most) $T - 1 > t_0$ years; the steady state obtains in all periods from T onwards. All policy changes occur during the transition period. By assumption, static and intertemporal relative prices remain unchanged over the interval $[T,\infty)$. This allows us to Hicks-aggregate all of the steady-state path of the economy. It then suffices to simply calculate period T values, because all future periods will be identical up to a uniform scale factor (growth rate) for all quantities. The aggregation process therefore only affects the discount factors, which is much larger for the T period to account for the fact that this period is replicated (again, up to a uniform scale factor for all quantities) an infinite number of years.

Labeling the constant post-T growth rate g and the real interest rate r^w, this process works as follows. Define $\delta = 1/(1 + r^w)$ and $\delta_a = (1 + g)/(1 + r^w)$, where δ_a is the period-to-period growth-adjusted discount factor. Then the following obtains for the back-to-period-1 discount factors $\delta(i)$:

$$\delta(i) = \delta^{i-1} \qquad \text{for } i < T$$

$$= \sum_T^\infty \delta^{i-1} \qquad \text{for } i \geq T \qquad \text{(A6.28)}$$

$$= \frac{\delta^{T-1}}{1 - \delta}$$

Consider the net present value, NPV_y, of $\{y_t\}$, where $y_t = y_{t-1}(1 + g)$ for $t > T$:

$$
\begin{aligned}
NPV_y &= \sum_1^\infty y_t . \delta^{t-1} \\
&= \sum_1^{T-1} y_t . \delta^{t-1} + \delta^{T-1} . \sum_T^\infty y_T . (1 + g)^{t-T} \delta^{t-T} \\
&= \sum_1^{T-1} y_t . \delta^{t-1} + \delta^{T-1} . \sum_T^\infty y_T . \delta_a^{t-T} \\
&= \sum_1^{T-1} y_t . \delta^{t-1} + \frac{\delta^{T-1}}{1-\delta_a} . y_T
\end{aligned}
\tag{A6.29}
$$

Thus, the infinite horizon can be captured by calculating period T only (out of all $[T,\infty)$ periods) but adjusting the period T discount factor to equal

$$
\delta (T) = \frac{\delta^{T-1}}{1-\delta_a}
\tag{A6.30}
$$

Intertemporal Budget Constraints. With the exception of urban capitalists, we assume that private households do not save or invest. Thus, in each period their consumption equals their income. Because they satisfy their period-by-period budget constraint, they will automatically satisfy their intertemporal budget constraint.

Private investment by urban capitalists is given by equation A6.27, and private savings, all by urban capitalists, by equation A6.14. Their savings rate, φ_t, is assumed to be exogenously given during the transition period. Thus, urban capitalists are assumed to have access to the world capital market, where they can lend or borrow as required at the world real interest rate r^w. However, this convention cannot be maintained in the steady state. If the savings rate were mechanically extended through the steady-state period, there would be no guarantee that urban capitalists would remain within their budget constraint or, alternatively, exhaust all resources available to them. In both cases, welfare comparisons across different simulation experiments would be illegitimate.

To solve this problem, we endogenise the period T savings rate in such a way that, if maintained over the interval $[T,\infty)$, urban capitalists will exactly satisfy their intertemporal budget constraint. This means that over the interval $[1,\infty)$, the discounted value of their consumption expenditure equals the discounted value of their after-tax income net of investment expenditure. In particular, if during the transition period urban capitalists accumulated debt, the steady-state savings rate is increased, so the discounted value at time T of future savings over investment equals the current value of the debt accumulated up through period $T-1$. The converse holds if during the transition period urban capitalists accumulated assets.

Formally, this can be represented as follows. Define after-tax savings net of private investment, all in period i, as x_i and income net of taxes and investment expenditure as y_i. Then, $NPV_x(T)$ equals

$$
NPV_x(T) = \sum_T^\infty x_T \cdot \frac{(1 + g)^{t-T}}{(1 + r^w)^{t-T}}
$$

$$
= \frac{x_T}{1 - \delta_a}
$$

(A6.31)

Define debt accumulated through period $T-1$ as D_{T-1}. To satisfy the intertemporal budget constraint, x_T needs to satisfy

$$
\frac{x_T}{1 - \delta_a} = D_{T-1} \cdot (1 + r^w)
$$

$$
\Rightarrow \varphi_T \equiv \frac{x_T}{y_T}
$$

(A6.32)

$$
= \frac{D_{T-1}}{y_T} \cdot \frac{1 - \delta_a}{\delta}
$$

Welfare Measures. To make welfare comparisons across experiments, it is not enough just to make sure that all groups satisfy their intertemporal budget constraints. In many cases, the time-paths of period-by-period utility of a particular household across two simulations will cross, making period-by-period comparisons difficult. The solution is to calculate net discounted utility, or welfare, using the rate of time-preference to discount future welfare back to today. That procedure presents no problems for the interval $[1, T-1]$. However, one cannot simply copy the procedure followed for *NPV* measures in equations 6.9 or A6.29 for the interval $[T, \infty)$. The reason is that per household consumption grows at the rate gc,[27] but because of declining marginal utility, per household utility U_h will grow at a lower rate than gc. Because we use a constant relative risk aversion (CRRA) utility function to aggregate utility over time, the following relation between the two growth rates holds:

$$
\hat{U}_h = (1/\sigma)\hat{c}
$$

(A6.33)

where σ is the intertemporal substitution elasticity, and a hat ($\land$) over a variable denotes the rate of growth. This leads to the following expression for welfare, W_h, the net discounted utility for household h:

$$W_h = \sum_1^\infty \frac{u_h(c_t)}{(1 + \rho)^t}$$

$$= \sum_1^{T-1} u_h(c_t) \cdot \delta^t_{\text{pref}} + \frac{u_h(c_T)}{(1 + \rho)^T} \sum_T^\infty \frac{(1 + \sigma^{-1} \cdot gc)^{t-T}}{(1 + \rho)^{t-T}} \qquad (A6.34)$$

$$= \sum_1^{T-1} u_h(c_t) \cdot \delta^t_{\text{pref}} + \frac{u_h(c_T) \cdot \delta^T_{\text{pref}}}{1 - \delta_{\text{prefA}}}$$

$$\text{where} \quad \delta_{\text{pref}} = \frac{1}{1 + \rho} \text{ and } \delta_{\text{prefA}} = \frac{1 + \sigma^{-1} \cdot gc}{1 + \rho}$$

Data Sources

We constructed a Social Accounting Matrix (SAM) for 1989, the last year for which information was available for all the variables required for the model.

Our departure point was data provided by the Ministry of Agriculture (SARH) on value of gross output, physical output, and areas harvested (and thus yields) in rain-fed and irrigated lands in 1989 for 26 individual agricultural products. These products account for 68.3 percent of the value of output in agriculture in that year; unfortunately, no information was individually available for the other products that account for the remaining 31.7 percent of output, though we do have the totals for all the variables concerned. Table A6.1 lists the products for which information was available and maps them into the four agricultural sectors included in our model. We interpret the physical totals (in hectares) of harvested rain-fed and irrigated lands in 1989 as the endowments of these two factors of production. SARH also provided us with value of output in livestock industry as well as with cost data to divide, at the level of each of the five rural sectors, the value of total gross supply into wages, aggregate rents (but not its division between rain-fed and irrigated lands), and a seven-sector disaggregation of intermediate input costs.[28]

From the Sistema de Cuentas Nacionales de México, we obtain the 1989 totals for all the macroeconomic aggregates: national income, private investment, private consumption, direct taxes (on households and factors), indirect taxes, total government spending, private savings, and the trade balance, as well as gross value of demand and value added in industry and services. Data from Cuentas Nacionales was then combined with data from Banco de México. This allowed us to disaggregate the trade balance (at world prices) into the seven-sector aggregation used in our model. Subtracting sectoral net exports from sectoral gross demands gave us sectoral domestic demand, which we proceeded to divide between private consumption, private investment, and government demand using information from the 1985 I/O table but ensuring that the totals coincided with the 1989 National Accounts totals. With the

Table A6.1. *Agricultural Output, 1989*

Sector/product	GVS Rain-fed	GVS Irrigated	GVS Total*
I Maize	3,610	1,180	4,790
II Basic Grains	1,437	3,711	5,149
1.Rice	175	186	362
2.Wheat	119	1,585	1,704
3.Sorghum	805	904	1,710
4.Barley	155	41	196
5.Soy-Beans	89	885	974
6.Cartamo	57	89	146
7.Sesame Seed	35	19	54
III Key Products	2,363	1,609	3,972
1.Beans	455	292	748
2.Cotton	59	124	184
3.Sugar Cane	1,396	1,071	2,467
4.Coffee	264	0	264
5.Tabbaco	0	121	121
6.Cacao	149	0	149
7.Henequen	37	0	37
IV Fruits, Veg. And Rest	7,089	9,626	16,715
1.Chile	98	515	613
2.Strawberries	0	68	68
3.Sunflower	0.7	0.7	1.4
4.Tomatoes	0.1	1,393	1,502
5.Avocadoes	151	194	345
6.Alfalfa	12	2,251	2,263
7.Copra	131	59	190
8.Lemon	159	478	637
9.Apples	80	322	403
10.Oranges	343	147	490
11.Bananas	332	156	488
12.Rest	5,671	4,040	9,711

* Millions of 1989 pesos; totals may not match due to rounding errors; GVS = gross value of supply.
Source: Dirección General de Estadística, SARH.

information just described, we pieced together a consistent Social Accounting Matrix (SAM) for 1989.

The Sistema de Cuentas Nacionales also had data on the totals of employment in agriculture (including livestock), industry, and services. We interpret total agricultural employment as the initial rural labor force and total services and industry employment as the initial urban labor force. Employment figures are measured as number of workers. Data on the division of employment among the various crops (in each type of land) was unavailable; to remedy this situation, we proceed in three steps. First, we use technological information contained in Norton and Solis (1983) to construct approximate labor/land ratios in rain-fed and irrigated lands for our model's crop aggregation. Second, we use the SARH 1989 data on rain-fed and irrigated land allocated to each crop to calculate the employment implied by the observed land allocation. Third, because the total agricultural employment implied by these calculations fell short of the total employment registered in Cuentas Nacionales (by a factor of 27 percent), we augmented all labor/land ratios so that the calculated employment in fact matched the observed 1989 total. Note that because all labor/ land ratios were augmented by the same factor, *relative* labor intensities are equal to those implied in Norton and Solis (1983).

Our model requires information on the parameters for the land transformation functions [$\tau 1$, $\phi 1$] and [$\tau 2$, $\phi 2$]. Given our production technology, the price elasticity of supply for any crop (in any given type of land) is

$$e_S = 1/(\alpha - \alpha\phi) \tag{A6.35}$$

Given the shares of land in value added,[29] α, we selected values for ϕ in each type of land such that the aggregate supply elasticity (a production-weighted average of the supply elasticity in rain-fed and irrigated lands) matched, for the case of maize, estimated elasticities (see Levy and van Wijnbergen, 1991). Lack of previously estimated elasticities made this procedure impractical for other crops. In these cases, given the values for α, we simply choose values for ϕ such that (1) $\phi 1 \leq \phi 2$ and, (2) the associated division of output between rain-fed and irrigated lands matched the SARH data.

To obtain parameters for the utility functions, we used the 1984 Income-Expenditure Survey (IES) to compute expenditure shares for rural and urban households for each income decile. Unfortunately, however, our model's aggregation pattern was difficult to match with the IES expenditure classification. In particular, expenditures on food are *not* equal to expenditures on our composite rural good, because part of the output of rural goods is sold as input to industry, which in turn produces food (for example, wheat into bread). To remedy this situation, it would be necessary to disaggregate the industry sector into a food-producing sector and a rest-of-industry sector. Unfortunately, there were no 1989 data to carry this out. Hence, we arbitrarily reallocated the IES expenditure shares among the composite rural good, industry, and services. Such reallocation ensured that the households that could potentially migrate (subsistence farmers, landless rural workers, and urban workers) all had the same expenditure shares and substitution elasticities and that all nonmigrant households had equal shares and elasticities. As well, the aggregate consumption of each good resulting from the different household preferences and incomes matched the sectoral consumption totals registered in the SAM.

We turn to the tax and subsidy information. Elsewhere (Levy and van Wijnbergen, 1991) we calculated the implied urban and rural prices of maize for 1989 given that year's policy configuration. In addition, with the SARH and Banco de México data mentioned above, we calculated the production-weighted tariff for basic grains, the other sector of agriculture with significant protection in 1989. For industry, on the other hand, we assume an average tariff rate of 5 percent. VAT rates for industry and services, as well as direct tax rates on factors and households, were derived from our constructed SAM. For simplicity, we assumed that only urban capitalists pay direct income taxes.

Next, we discuss sources of data for the irrigation program. We obtained the complete portfolio of existing investment projects from the Comisión Nacional del Agua (CNA) for both development of new irrigation districts and rehabilitation of existing ones. The data included average costs, internal rate of return, and labor requirements per hectare renovated and/or irrigated for each project. All projects with an internal rate of return of 8 percent or more were ranked in order of increasing per unit cost of renovated/irrigated hectares. For this subset of projects, we computed average labor requirements for irrigation and obtained an estimate for *lrirr* in equation A6.19b. We also ran a simple OLS regression for equation A6.18 to obtain estimates of γ. The regression took this form:

$$\ln C_i = \ln q + \gamma \ln \sum_{i=1}^{n} RI_i + \varepsilon_i \qquad (A6.36)$$

where C_i is the average cost of renovating and/or irrigating RI_i hectares with project i and n is the total number of projects (ordered by increasing C_i). The regression had a very good fit, with (corrected) R^2 of 0.8630, and an estimated value for γ of 2.2118 (with a t-statistic of 36.895).

Finally, we assumed the following values for the other key parameters: (1) rate of time preference, 7 percent; (2) the intertemporal elasticity of substitution, 2; (3) the world rate of interest, 7 percent; and (4) the rate of growth population, 2 percent. In addition, we assumed that the initial rate of growth of the labor force is 3 percent and that it linearly converges to the rate of growth of population, 2 percent, over a ten-year period. Lastly, we assumed that the capital stock in industry and services and nonirrigation real government expenditures all grow at 4 percent.

Model Calibration
Calibration for 1989

We combine the various sources of information described above to compute an initial solution to the excess demand equations. The initial solution only computes a single-period equilibrium. For convenience we set world prices, **pw**, equal to unity, and choose units such that in the initial solution **p** = [**pw** | **ps**] is the unit vector. The numeraire is a bundle of domestic goods

Table A6.2. *Model Performance, Macro*

Variable	Observed Value	Calibrated Value	% Difference (absolute value)
Gross National Expenditure[a]	511.53	511.12	0.0008
1. Consumption	334.84	334.58	0.0007
2. Investment	117.81	117.82	0.0000
3. Government	54.45	54.47	0.0003
4. Trade Balance	4.41	4.24	0.0040
Gross National Income[a]	511.53	511.12	0.0008
1. Wages	131.96	136.30	0.0328
2. Rents	26.78	22.89	0.1699
3. Profits	304.97	303.56	0.0046
4. Indirect Taxes	47.79	48.36	0.0119
Employment[b]	21.88	21.88	0.0000
1. Rural	6.00	6.00	0.0000
2. Urban	15.88	15.88	0.0000

[a] Millions of millions of pesos of 1989.
[b] Millions of workers.

with the composition observed in 1989. By construction the real exchange rate is unity in the base solution.

Table A6.2 displays the difference between simulated and actual values for the main macroeconomic aggregates. Table A6.3 shows results at the sectoral level for agriculture. Three comments are relevant. First, the performance of the model at the macrolevel is quite satisfactory; the difference between estimated and actual values being in most cases smaller than 1 percent. Second, the model is able to reproduce almost exactly the pattern of output in agriculture, as well as the composition of the balance of trade. Note that for maize and vegetables in particular, the differences between actual and simulated values are almost negligible.

A third significant aspect of the base solution is that the *division* of the total output of each agricultural commodity between output obtained in rain-fed and irrigated lands mirrors the actual one. In addition, note that the estimated land allocations also match the actual ones, implying in turn that estimated yields are very close to observed yields. Unfortunately, as mentioned above, there are no original data against which the calculated allocations of labor to each crop can be contrasted, although the relative labor intensities calculated are similar to the data in Norton and Solis (1983).

Calibration for 1991

Significant changes occurred in agricultural policies between 1989 and 1991: (1) protection to maize was increased from 47 percent to 70 percent,

Table A6.3. *Model Performance, Sectoral*

Agricultural Sector	Observed Values	Calibrated Values	% Difference (absolute value)
I Maize			
GVS Rain-fed[a]	3,610	3,601	0.002
GVS Irrigated[a]	1,180	1,192	0.010
Rain-fed Land[b]	5,553	5,517	0.006
Irrigated Land[b]	915	902	0.014
Yields Rain-fed[c]	1.485	1.491	0.004
Yields Irrigated[c]	2.947	3.021	0.025
Net Exports[a]	-1083.7	-1077.7	0.005
II Basic Grains			
GVS Rain-fed	1,437	1,474	0.025
GVS Irrigated	3,711	3,713	0.000
Rain-fed Land	1,834	2,040	0.112
Irrigated Land	2,045	2,016	0.014
Yields Rain-fed	1.846	1.702	0.084
Yields Irrigated	3.925	3.983	0.014
Net Exports	-1754.1	-2165.4	0.234
III Key Products			
GVS Rain-fed	2,363	2,383	0.008
GVS Irrigated	1,609	1,584	0.015
Rain-fed Land	2,012	2,148	0.063
Irrigated Land	563	481	0.170
Yields Rain-fed	7.502	7.088	0.058
Yields Irrigated	20.190	23.242	0.151
Net Exports	1305.9	1469.4	0.125
IV Fr, Veg & Other			
GVS Rain-fed	7,089	7,069	0.002
GVS Irrigated	9,626	9,620	0.000
Rain-fed Land	3,865	3,557	0.086
Irrigated Land	1,393	1,515	0.080
Yields Rain-fed	5.906	6.399	0.083
Yields Irrigated	23.709	21.783	0.088
Net Exports	745.7	751.9	0.008

[a] Thousands of millions of pesos of 1989.
[b] Thousands of harvested hectares.
[c] Tons per hectare.

(2) tortilla subsidies were reduced substantially, particularly in urban areas, and (3) protection to other basic grains increased on average from 10 to 15 percent.

We recalibrated the model to reflect these changes. Starting from the 1989 base, the changes just mentioned were incorporated into the model, and the resulting equilibrium was considered as a benchmark 1991 equilibrium. This procedure has significant drawbacks in that the calculated 1991 equilibrium cannot at this point be contrasted with actual values. Nevertheless, we pursued this route because the changes are significant and because we believe this provides a more accurate estimate of the effects of the FTA.

We computed a ten-year reference path for the economy, where nine years are the adjustment period and, as described above, the tenth period summarizes the steady state. The reference path assumes that world prices are constant but incorporates Hicks-neutral technical change and the growth of capital, labor, population, and real government spending at the rates mentioned above. To focus on the effects of excluding/including maize in the FTA, the reference path incorporates a five-year liberalization of the basic grains sector, beginning in the second period. On the other hand, we assume that no investments in irrigation take place.

Endnotes

1. Import controls support a price 70 percent above the world price (allowing for transport costs and quality differentials); 42 percent of the total arable land is allocated to this crop, which employs one out of three rural workers. Subsidies to maize and tortillas cost about 1 billion (U.S.) in 1991.

2. In urban areas the tax is partly offset by deliveries of tortillas through the *tortivale* program. Under this program each urban family earning less than two minimum wages receives one kilo of tortillas per day free. This is less than daily family consumption, so the program is inframarginal.

3. Preferences are given by a nested Cobb-Douglas/CES/CES utility function. The outer nest CD allocates expenditures among a composite rural good, industry, and services. The next CES nest aggregates the five rural goods into a composite rural good. The last CES nest distributes maize consumption between raw maize and tortillas.

4. To reflect Mexico's demographic transition, the rate of growth of labor, 3 percent, is set higher than the rate of growth of population, 2 percent. During the transition period (see below) the rate of growth of labor slowly declines until in the steady state it equals that of population. Thus, households that own labor initially grow faster than households that own only land or capital.

5. In a fuller model of the impact of the FTA, investment rates in industry and services would clearly be endogenous. Here, however, we are interested in the effects of changes in agricultural liberalization only.

6. Also, on the reference path real government spending and the capital stock in industry and services grow at 4 percent annually. Productivity in the urban sector grows at 2 percent, and in rain-fed (irrigated) agriculture at 0.5 (1.5 percent).

7. We assume that protection to other agricultural sectors, basic grains in particular, is removed over a five-year horizon. This allows sharper focus on whether to include maize in the FTA and what kind of supporting policies is advisable. Because liberalization of grains is already incorporated in the base scenario, these results only provide measures of the efficiency gains (costs) from including (excluding) maize in the FTA.

8. We assume a (risk-adjusted) world real interest rate of 7 percent and long-term rates of technical progress and population growth such that steady-state growth is 4 percent. The growth-adjusted discount rate thus is 2.9 percent ($= (1.07/1.04 - 1)*100$), implying a growth-adjusted discount factor of 0.972.

9. Cf. Diamond (1982) for this point.

10. We refer to a program of "land improvements" to emphasize that it involves not only irrigation infrastructure but also investments in drainage, land leveling, ditch-clearing, and so on.

11. See Sanchez Ugarte (1991) for a description of water's regulatory regime in Mexico.

12. The program is assumed to irrigate 0.25 million hectares in each of the first three years, 0.20 in the fourth, and 0.15 in the fifth. This program is feasible given Mexico's previous experience in this area. We refer to the program as the "CNA program" because it would be implemented by the Comisión Nacional del Agua, Mexico's agency in charge of irrigation construction.

13. These barriers are equivalent to a 20 percent tariff [Feenstra and Rose (1991)]. But because the sector labeled here "fruits and vegetables" includes other crops (cf. the data appendix), the tariff is scaled back to 5 percent. Thus, prices faced by Mexican fruit and vegetable exporters increase by 1 percent during each of the five years of adjustment and then stay constant at the higher level.

14. Investment costs reflect the time-profile of the CNA program and the increased marginal costs of irrigating lower-quality lands. The last 150,000 hectares are, on average, 49 percent more expensive than the first 250,000.

15. The fiscal costs of intervention do not fall to zero because the costs of the *tortivale* program still have to be covered (though the *tortivale* program is cheaper because of the lower producer price of maize).

16. Krugman (1982) also links resistance to trade liberalization to factor price effects.

17. We separate land devoted to livestock from land devoted to agriculture because Mexican land tenure regulations preclude the use of agricultural land for livestock activities [see Heath (1990)].

18. Data on the distribution of ownership of land in Mexico are scarce. Various studies refer to the class of "subsistence farmers," who are of such small quantities of land that they must also participate in the labor market [see Masera (1990) and Salinas (1990)]. In this paper we *define* a "typical" subsistence farmer as one who owns two hectares of rain-fed land. Of course, in reality there is a continuum of ownership.

19. All price vectors are defined as row vectors, and all quantity vectors as column vectors. All vectors are in **bold**.

20. The government attempts to stop arbitrage on maize and tortillas via controls on maize distribution to tortilla mills and to other users of maize.

21. In what follows, the labels 1/2 on any variable refer to the rain-fed/irrigated distinction.

22. Let a^* be the exogenously given fixed quantity of feed per unit of livestock, given by

$$a^* = [\tau.a_{ml}^{\mu - 1/\mu} + (1-\tau).a_{gl}^{\mu - 1/\mu}]^{\mu/(1-\mu)} \quad \mu > 0,\ \mu \neq 1,\ \tau \,\varepsilon\, (0,1)$$

Given intermediate input prices, an exact price index for a^* is

$$pa^* = [\tau^\mu.ip_m'^{\,1-\mu} + (1 - \tau)^\mu.ip_g'^{\,1-\mu}]^{1/1-\mu}$$

Substituting pa^* in (A6.6) and (A6.7) gives matrix $\mathbf{A}(\mathbf{p})$.

23. Urban inhabitants consume maize mostly in the form of tortillas. In the rural areas the government purchases maize from producers at the price $\mathbf{pp}_m$ but sells maize flour to consumers at the price pt^r because there are fewer tortilla distribution outlets in rural areas. (This is why the *tortivale* program does not operate in rural areas.) Our model ignores the opportunity cost of time to rural households of making tortillas from maize flour but allows the maize to be consumed either as raw maize or as tortillas.

24. Recall that capital in industry and services (as well as land in livestock) are fixed. Thus, these factors just earn quasi rents.

25. To reflect Mexico's demographic transition, the rate of growth of labor, 3 percent, is set higher than the rate of growth of population, 2 percent. During the transition period (see below), the rate of growth of labor slowly declines until in the steady state it equals that of population. Thus, households that own labor initially grow faster than households that own only land or capital.

26. In a fuller model of the impact of the FTA, investment rates in industry and services would clearly be endogenous. Here, however, we are interested in the effects of changes in agricultural liberalization only.

27. Note that $gc < g$ because it is a *per household* measure. If gp is the rate of population growth, g, gc, and gp are linked as follows:

$$(1 + g) = (1 + gc).(1 + gp)$$

28. Unfortunately, these data did not permit disaggregation of intermediate input costs between rain-fed and irrigated lands, forcing us to assume the same input structure in each case.

29. As mentioned earlier, the SARH data did not divide total rents to land between rain-fed and irrigated. We carried out this division assuming that the share of rents accruing to rain-fed land was, in each crop, equal to the share of gross value of rain-fed output in total output.

References

Dixit, A.K., and V. Norman. 1980. *Theory of international trade.* London: Cambridge University Press.

Feenstra, R., and A. Rose. 1991. "Trade with Mexico and water use in California agriculture." Mimeo, University of California, Davis.

Garcia y Griego, M. 1989. "The Mexican labor supply, 1990–2010." In *Mexican migration to the United States: Origins, consequences and policy options,* edited by W. Cornelius. University of California; San Diego.

Harris, J.R., and M.P. Todaro. 1970. "Migration, unemployment, and development: A two-sector analysis." *American Economic Review.* 60(1):126–42.

Heath, J. 1990. "Enhancing the contribution of the land reform sector to Mexican agricultural development." Mimeo, World Bank, Washington, D.C.

Helpman, E., and P.R. Krugman. 1989. *Trade policy and market structure.* Cambridge, MA: MIT Press.

Levy, S. 1991. "Poverty alleviation in Mexico." PRE Working Paper no. 679, World Bank, Washington, D.C..

Levy, S., and S. van Wijnbergen. 1991. "Maize and the Mexico-United States Free Trade Agreement." Forthcoming, *El Trimestre Económico.*

———. 1992. "Transition problems in economic reform: Agriculture in the Mexico-US free trade agreement." Working Paper no. 967, World Bank, Washington, D.C.

Masera Cerutti, O. 1990. *Crisis y mecanización de la agricultura campesina.* El Colegio de Mexico, Mexico City.

Nathan Associates, Inc. 1989. *Comermax: A multimarket model of Mexico's agriculture.* Prepared for the Inter-American Development Bank, Washington, D.C., October.

Norton, R. and L. Solis. 1983. *The book of Chac: Programming studies for Mexican agriculture,* Baltimore: Johns Hopkins University Press.

Salinas de Gortari, R. 1990. "El campo mexicano ante el reto de la modernización." *Comercio Exterior* 40(9):816–29.

Sanchez Ugarte, F. 1991. "La utilización eficiente del agua y los derechos de propiedad." In *El efecto de la regulacion en algunos sectores de la economia mexicaná,* edited by F. Gil Diaz and A. Fernandez. Mexico City: Fondo de Cultura Económica.

Secretaria de Agricultura y Recursos Hidráulicos. 1984. *Anuario estadístico de la producción agricola nacional 1984.* Mexico City.

Tornell, A. 1991. "Time inconsistency of protectionist programs." *Quarterly Journal of Economics* 106:1 963–75.

7

Wage Changes in a U.S.–Mexico Free Trade Area: Migration Versus Stolper–Samuelson Effects*

Mary E. Burfisher
Economic Research Service,
U.S. Department of Agriculture

Sherman Robinson
Department of Agricultural and Resource Economics,
University of California, Berkeley

Karen E. Thierfelder
Economics Department,
U.S. Naval Academy

I. Introduction

A major issue concerning the establishment of a North American free trade agreement (NAFTA) is its impact on wages in Mexico and the United States. One argument is that the agreement will result in higher wages for unskilled labor in Mexico but lower wages for unskilled labor in the United States.[1] This view can be derived from the Stolper–Samuelson theorem, which links changes in wages and profits to the changes in product prices caused by trade liberalization.[2] Mexico is abundant in unskilled labor relative to the United States, and trade reform will increase Mexico's relative price of manufactured goods that it exports to the United States. According to the theorem, unskilled wages will fall in the United States and rise in Mexico as Mexican exports displace U.S. production of labor-intensive goods.[3]

There are a number of difficulties in applying the Stolper–Samuelson theorem to the case of NAFTA. First and foremost is that the two countries are linked by more than trade in commodities. In particular, there is a long history of labor migration between Mexico and the United States, and one would expect that such migration would be sensitive to wage changes brought about

* The authors would like to thank Roger Betancourt, Victoria Greenfield, Gene Mathia, and Clinton Shiells for helpful comments on earlier drafts. This work was partially supported under a cooperative agreement with USDA/ERS/ATAD. The opinions do not necessarily reflect the views of the authors' respective institutions.

195

by NAFTA. When using the Stolper–Samuelson theorem, one assumes that aggregate factor supplies are constant and that shifts in labor demand curves determine wage changes. However, the effects of trade liberalization on wages can be ambiguous when there is international labor mobility, which shifts the labor supply curve as well. One must account for the workers' migration decision.[4]

Second, Mexico currently strongly protects agriculture, especially the food corn sector, and agriculture uses rural labor relatively intensively. The Stolper–Samuelson effects are then more complex, with trade liberalization helping manufacturing, which uses unskilled labor intensively, and hurting agriculture, which uses rural labor intensively. As Mexico eliminates barriers to food corn imports, the rural wage should fall.[5] Given rural-urban migration within Mexico, the fall in rural wages will lead to an increase in the supply of labor to Mexican urban areas and to the manufacturing sectors. This will offset the increase in urban unskilled wages as the manufacturing sectors expand. There will also be an increase in migration pressure to the United States. The net wage changes in both the United States and Mexico will thus depend on a mix of Stolper–Samuelson and migration effects.

Finally, there are many existing distortions in both countries which will not be eliminated by NAFTA. For example, NAFTA does not affect trade barriers that Mexico and the United States maintain against other countries. In addition, there are other distortions, including existing taxes, subsidies, and intersectoral differences in wages and profit rates. All these complicate trade theory, requiring analysis of trade liberalization in a ''second-best'' environment.

In this paper, we examine the links between trade policy and wage changes in the United States and Mexico. We develop an analytical model to demonstrate the impact of both migration and changes in output prices on wages. We show that, in theory, migration and output price changes can have offsetting effects on wages. Furthermore, we identify the crucial elasticities that affect the labor demand and labor supply shifts.

The analytical results suggest that one needs an empirical model that allows for both Stolper–Samuelson and migration effects to assess the wage changes that will accompany NAFTA.[6] We use a computable general equilibrium (CGE) model that includes both the production links between factor prices and output prices and migration equations. When specifying migration, we assume that workers migrate between rural and urban areas in Mexico, as well as to the rural and urban labor markets in the United States, to maintain constant real wage differences. We discuss how our assumptions about migration, particularly the workers' migration decision, affect migration results in the model and ultimately the wage changes in each country. In the empirical model, we also explore the sensitivity of the wage changes to parameters by calculating various response elasticities.

In addition to migration, the empirical model captures other aspects of the U.S. and Mexican economies that violate the assumptions used to analyze the links between output prices and factor prices in neoclassical trade theory. There are a number of existing distortions, such as indirect taxes and sectoral wage differentials, that are incorporated in the model. We also assume Mexico and the United States have different production technologies, in the use of both intermediate inputs and primary factors.

Other aspects of the model qualify the results but do not violate the assumptions needed to use the Stolper–Samuelson theorem. For example, rather than assume goods are homogeneous, we maintain the Armington assumption that commodities are distinguished by country of origin. When the price of the imported variety changes, the price of the domestic good also changes, but by a lesser amount, depending on the elasticity of substitution. Consequently, the output and wage responses are weaker than in a model with homogeneous commodities.[7] We also capture the size differences between the two countries and Mexico's high trade dependence on the United States versus the United States' lower trade dependence on Mexico. These realistic features affect the magnitude of the links between output prices and factor prices.

The remainder of the paper is organized as follows. In section II, we present a simple general equilibrium model with migrating and nonmigrating factors to analyze the links to changes in factor prices. Except for dimensionality and substitution elasticities, this analytical model closely represents our empirical model. In section III, we describe our empirical model and compare our treatment of migration to the specification in other models. Our empirical model is a three-country, 11-sector, computable general equilibrium (CGE) model in which countries are linked through trade and labor migration flows. Because most of the migration anticipated under NAFTA will come from rural Mexico, we model farm sectors in detail, giving attention to the rural and unskilled labor markets and to the structure of agricultural programs.

In section IV, we present model simulations. The simulations are designed to explore the two mechanisms, price changes and migration, through which trade reform leads to wage changes.[8] In particular, we ask whether migration has a bigger impact on relative wages than do changes in relative output prices, the driving mechanism in the Stolper–Samuelson theorem. We find that migration generally has the dominant effect on wages under NAFTA. Finally, we create a distortion-free base run to provide a theoretically clean starting point to explore the Stolper–Samuelson effects in our empirical model. We then combine migration and a relative price change to analyze their impact in labor markets in the model with no distortions. This combination provides the best empirical representation of the theoretical model with migration and Stolper–Samuelson effects. We present conclusions in section V.

II. Analytical Model

Jones (1965) describes a simple general equilibrium model in which a representative country produces two goods with two factors. Assuming full-employment and zero-profit conditions, he analyzes the price linkages and quantity relationships important to trade theory. He demonstrates that changes in relative wages depend on changes in relative output prices and that changes in relative output depend on changes in both relative prices and the relative endowment. These results are summarized in equations 7.1 and 7.2.

$$(\hat{w} - \hat{r}) = (\hat{P}_1 - \hat{P}_2)\frac{1}{|\Theta|} \tag{7.1}$$

$$(\hat{X}_1 - \hat{X}_2) = \frac{1}{|\Lambda|}(\hat{L} - \hat{K}) + \frac{(\delta_L + \delta_K)}{|\Lambda||\Theta|}(\hat{P}_1 - \hat{P}_2) \tag{7.2}$$

where ^ indicates the percentage change in the variable and the other parameters are defined as follows:

w = the payment to labor

r = the payment to capital

X_1 = output of good 1

X_2 = output of good 2

P_1 = price of good 1

P_2 = price of good 2

L = aggregate labor supply

K = aggregate capital supply

Equation 7.1 links changes in factor returns to changes in output prices. Equation 7.2 links output changes to changes in both factor endowments and relative output prices.

Relative factor intensity, in the value sense, reflects the allocation of revenue to labor and capital in production. It is represented in the determinant of the matrix of factor payment shares by sector:

$$|\Theta| = \theta_{L1}\theta_{K2} - \theta_{L2}\theta_{K1} \tag{7.3}$$

where $\theta_{i,j}$ $i = L, K; j = 1, 2$ indicates the share of revenue from production of good j that is allocated to factor i. When $|\Theta| > 0$, good 1 is relatively labor-intensive in terms of the share of revenue allocated to labor.

Likewise, one can represent physical factor intensity in terms of the share of the endowments of labor and capital allocated to each sector. The determinant of the matrix of factor endowment shares is given by

$$|\Lambda| = \lambda_{L1}\lambda_{K2} - \lambda_{L2}\lambda_{K1} \tag{7.4}$$

where λ_{ij}, $i = L, K$; $j = 1, 2$ indicates the share of the endowment of resource i used in sector j. When $|\Theta| > 0$, good 1 is relatively labor-intensive.

Factor substitution in production allows producers to substitute away from the factor whose price increases. For example, as the relative wage increases, both sectors become relatively more capital-intensive. The following parameter represents the producer savings from switching to less labor-intensive production techniques when the relative wage increases and output does not change:

$$\delta_L = \lambda_{L1}\theta_{K1}\sigma_1 + \lambda_{L2}\theta_{K2}\sigma_2 \qquad (7.5)$$

Likewise, there are savings when producers switch to less capital-intensive production techniques when the relative payment to capital increases and output does not change:

$$\delta_K = \lambda_{K1}\theta_{L1}\sigma_1 + \lambda_{K2}\theta_{L2}\sigma_2 \qquad (7.6)$$

where σ_j is the production response to a relative factor price change in sector j and θ_{ij}, and λ_{ij} are defined above; δ_i $(i = L, K)$ is positive because all components are positive.

Both relative price changes and labor supply changes can affect relative factor returns. When the relative price changes, there are indirect links to wages due to output changes. The change in production generates a change in the demand for labor. For example, when output of the labor-intensive good expands, there is a net increase in labor demand.[9] When the relative endowment changes as well, there is a direct effect on wages as the supply of labor changes. One can summarize these labor demand and labor supply effects using Jones' equations. Substituting equation 7.1 into equation 7.2 and rearranging, one finds that

$$(\hat{w} - \hat{r}) = \left[(\hat{X}_1 - \hat{X}_2) - \frac{1}{|\Lambda|}(\hat{L} - \hat{K}) \right] \frac{|\Lambda|}{(\delta_L + \delta_K)} \qquad (7.7)$$

To incorporate the effects of changes in relative output prices on relative factor prices, one needs to know how responsive the relative output level is to a relative price change. Essentially, one must specify the shape of the production possibilities frontier (PPF) for goods 1 and 2. The output supply elasticity is defined as

$$\sigma_s = \frac{d(X_1/X_2)/(X_1/X_2)}{d(P_1/P_2)/(P_1/P_2)} \qquad (7.8)$$

In Jones' notation, the expression becomes

$$\sigma_s = \frac{(\hat{X}_1 - \hat{X}_2)}{(\hat{P}_1 - \hat{P}_2)} \qquad (7.9)$$

Using equations 7.1 and 7.2, which summarize technology in Jones' model, and assuming no endowment change, one can define the output supply elasticity as

$$\sigma_s = \frac{(\delta_L + \delta_K)}{|\Lambda|\,|\Theta|} \tag{7.10}$$

When there are no labor market distortions, which appear as exogenous wage differentials by sector, σ_s is positive because the sign of $|\Lambda|$ equals the sign of $|\Theta|$ and δ_L and δ_K are positive by definition.[10] Relative output increases as the relative price increases.

Substituting equation 7.10 into equation 7.7, one can describe both the price effect, which works through indirect links, and the migration effect on relative factor returns.[11]

When good 1 is relatively labor-intensive, $|\Lambda|$ positive. Using equation 7.11,

$$(\hat{w} - \hat{r}) = [\sigma_s(\hat{P}_1 - \hat{P}_2) - \frac{1}{|\Lambda|}(\hat{L} - \hat{K})]\frac{|\Lambda|}{(\delta_L + \delta_K)} \tag{7.11}$$

when the relative price of good 1 (the labor-intensive good) increases, the relative wage increases, as specified in the Stolper–Samuelson theorem. When the labor supply increases and prices are not held constant, there is downward pressure on wages. The wage change in response to an endowment change is independent of the relative factor intensity of good 1 and good 2.[12]

To compare the magnitude of the two changes, compare the coefficient on the percent change in prices to the coefficient on the percent change in the endowment. After simplifying, the coefficient on the relative price change reduces to

$$\frac{1}{|\Theta|} \tag{7.12}$$

When there is no endowment change, this coefficient describes the links between factor prices and output prices stated in the Stolper–Samuelson theorem. The more extreme the differences in factor intensities, the bigger the relative factor price change following a change in output prices. The coefficient on the relative endowment change reduces to

$$-\frac{1}{\delta_L + \delta_K} \tag{7.13}$$

This coefficient indicates the effect of a change in factor supply on relative factor prices when one allows the relative factor intensity in each sector to change. Because the relative output price, and therefore the relative factor intensities, can change, this version of an endowment change is more general than the endowment change described in the Rybczynski theorem. The coefficient in expression 7.13 reduces to zero when output prices are held constant.[13] In this special case, relative factor prices do not change, and one can derive the Rybczynski results.

A migration change essentially is an endowment change in Jones' specification. We assume workers migrate in response to relative wage differences. To determine migration levels, one must evaluate the labor market equilibrium in each country as well as the migration equation. The system of labor demand and labor supply equations by country, including migration between countries, is solved simultaneously. Labor demand in each country is a function of the output price and the relative wage. The vertical labor supply curve shifts when labor migrates. In theory, one might expect labor to migrate in response to wage differentials and move until wages are equal in both countries.[14] Studies of wages in the United States and Mexico, however, suggest that existing wage differentials will persist under trade liberalization.[15] We assume labor migrates to maintain a constant wage differential between the two countries.

To identify sources of the wage change in a simple general equilibrium model with migration, one can consider the forces affecting labor supply and demand independently. Labor demand shifts depend on changes in the relative output price – given factor intensities in production. For example, an increase in the output of the labor-intensive good means that labor demand will increase. The magnitude of the labor demand shift depends on the output elasticity to a relative price change and on the elasticity of labor demand to an output change. Given a fixed aggregate labor supply, the wage will increase following an increase in the price of the labor-intensive good.

When one allows labor to migrate and assumes workers migrate to maintain fixed wage differentials, labor moves into the country that experiences the wage increase under no migration. The increase in labor supply reduces the wage. Because the supply curve shifts, the wage elasticity of labor demand matters in determining wage changes in the home country. Migration occurs until the initial wage differential has been reestablished. When the labor demand curve is inelastic, a small amount of migration is needed to affect wages and restore the initial differential. More migration occurs when the labor demand curves in each country are more elastic.

As summarized in equation 7.11, wage changes become indeterminate when one allows migration in conjunction with price changes in the analytical two-country model. One needs to specify in more detail what motivates migrants. To determine the wage changes that will accompany NAFTA, one must use an empirical model that accounts for trade and migration flows. In an empirical model, the magnitude of the labor demand and labor supply changes will depend on the elasticities implicit in the observed base-year equilibrium. From the base data for each country, one can calculate empirically the output elasticity to a price change, the elasticity of labor demand to output changes, and the wage elasticity of labor demand by sector from data on the United States and Mexico.

III. Three-Country CGE Model
Core FTA-CGE Model

Our empirical model builds on earlier models of the U.S.–Mexico free trade area (FTA) by Hinojosa-Ojeda and Robinson (1992) and Robinson et al. (1993).[16] The FTA-CGE model is an 11-sector, three-country, computable general equilibrium model. The production and consumption behavior in the United States and Mexico is modeled in detail, and the two countries are linked through trade and migration flows. There are import demand and export supply equations to represent the interaction between the rest of the world and either the United States or Mexico. Table 7.1 presents aggregate data for the United States and Mexico, as well as the trade flows between them; the data are used to generate the benchmark or base solution of the FTA–CGE model.

Table 7.1. *Comparative Aggregate Data, United States and Mexico*

	Mexico	U.S.
GDP ($US billions, 1988)	175.0	4,485.7
Per Capita GNP ($US, 1988)	1,760	19,990
Trade flows (percent of GDP)		
Total exports	16.5	7.9
Exports to partner	10.1	0.4
Total imports	5.8	11.6
Imports from partner	4.3	0.9
Employment structure (percent)		
Rural labor	23.8	1.1
Urban unskilled labor	14.1	17.7
Urban skilled labor	37.1	48.5
White collar workers	25.0	32.7
Total	100.0	100.0
Population, ages 15-64 (millions)	49	162
Total population (millions)	84	246

Sources: Per capita GNP and population data refer to 1988 and come from World Bank, *World Development Report 1990*. Mexico's GDP is calculated using official exchange rates. Employment data are unpublished data from Dolores Nieto, Colegio de México. Trade and GDP data are from U.S. and Mexican social accounting matrices developed by the Economic Research Service, U.S. Department of Agriculture (USDA/ERS).

Mexico is a much smaller and poorer economy and has a higher share of trade in GDP than the United States. The United States market accounts for over 60 percent of Mexican exports, while Mexico buys only about 5 percent of total U.S. exports. As is typical of a developing country, rural labor is a large share of the Mexican labor force: 23.8 percent compared to 1.1 percent for the United States.

Table 7.2 shows the sectoral structure of GDP, employment, and trade for the two countries, as well as existing trade barriers. The model's 11 sectors include four farm and one food processing sector. The food corn sector refers to corn used for human consumption. In Mexico, this includes white corn, the small proportion of domestic yellow corn used for food, and No. 2 yellow corn imports from the U.S., which are assumed to enter food use. In the United States, the food corn sector refers to its world exports of No. 2 yellow corn. The program crops sector is composed of the other crops eligible for U.S. deficiency payments – feed corn, food grains, soybeans, and cotton. Other agriculture includes livestock, poultry, forestry and fishery, and other miscellaneous agriculture. The fruits and vegetables sector in Mexico includes beans, a major food crop.

The base year for Mexico is mostly 1988.[17] The United States uses a 1987 base year because of the severe contraction of agricultural output following the 1988 drought. Bilateral trade flows are from 1988. Because of the volatility in U.S. 1987–88 agricultural output, the model follows Adams and Higgs (1986) in the use of a "synthetic" base year for the United States, imposing 1988 U.S.–Mexican bilateral trade flows on a 1987 base U.S. economy.

The model is in the theoretical tradition of neoclassical, trade-focused, CGE models.[18] Each sector produces a composite commodity that can be transformed according to a constant elasticity of transformation (CET) function into a commodity sold on the domestic market or into an export. Output is produced according to a constant elasticity of substitution (CES) production function in primary factors and fixed input-output coefficients for intermediate inputs. The model simulates a market economy, with prices and quantities assumed to adjust to clear markets. All transactions in the circular flow of income are captured. Each country model traces the flow of income (starting with factor payments) from producers to households, government, and investors, and finally back to demand for goods in product markets.

Consumption, intermediate demand, government, and investment are the four components of domestic demand. Consumer demand is based on Cobb-Douglas utility functions, generating fixed expenditure shares. Households pay income taxes to the government and save a fixed proportion of their income. Intermediate demand is given by fixed input-output coefficients. Real government demand and real investment are fixed exogenously.

We use import demand equations based on the Almost Ideal Demand Sys-

Table 7.2. *Sectoral Structure of U.S. and Mexican Economies, Base Solution*

	GDP		Employment		Imports		Exports		Bilateral import barriers	
	Sectoral shares (percent) in:									
Commodity	U.S.	Mexico	U.S.	Mexico	U.S.	Mexico	U.S.	Mexico	U.S.	Mexico
Food corn	0.0	0.7	0.0	6.3	0.9	0.0	0.3	0.0	0.0	45.0
Program crops	0.5	1.1	0.4	5.3	2.9	0.0	3.3	0.1	0.0	12.9
Fruits/vegetables	0.2	1.1	0.4	3.5	0.1	0.6	0.4	3.0	13.2	12.5
Other agriculture	0.8	5.1	1.4	8.6	1.3	1.7	0.4	3.8	0.6	8.9
Food processing	1.7	6.2	1.5	2.5	5.2	2.2	2.9	3.6	3.8	8.2
Other light mfg.	4.5	5.5	5.1	2.7	4.3	15.0	7.0	6.0	4.7	8.1
Oil and refining	2.2	2.9	0.5	0.5	5.0	12.0	2.7	10.2	1.5	8.8
Intermediates	5.6	8.2	4.5	3.2	16.8	13.0	14.0	12.3	2.2	8.0
Consumer durables	1.9	2.5	1.7	0.8	14.5	28.3	10.0	18.7	1.8	12.0
Capital Goods	5.2	3.4	4.9	2.2	25.6	24.6	31.8	12.0	3.6	12.7
Services	77.4	63.3	79.6	64.4	23.5	2.6	27.5	30.3	0.0	0.0

Notes: Bilateral import barriers are the combined rate of trade-weighted tariffs and tariff equivalents of quotas on trade between Mexico and the United States. Percent composition columns sum to 100 percent, except for rounding error. Data are for 1987 for United States and 1988 for Mexico.

Sources: Burfisher, Thierfelder, and Hanson (1992).

tem (or AIDS).[19] The AIDS function is a flexible functional form that can generate arbitrary values of pairwise substitution elasticities at a given set of prices and also allows expenditure elasticities different from 1. It generates more realistic empirical price behavior than does the more common CES formulation.

The model includes six primary factors and associated factor markets: rural labor, urban unskilled labor, urban skilled labor, professional labor, capital, and agricultural land. Full employment for all labor categories is assumed and aggregate supplies are set exogenously. The model can incorporate different assumptions about factor mobility, including labor migration (discussed below). In the experiments reported here, we assume that agricultural land is immobile among crops but that all other factors are intersectorally mobile, including capital. Note, however, that labor markets are segmented. Rural labor does not work in the industrial sectors, and urban labor does not work in agriculture. These labor markets are linked through separate migration equations. The results should be seen as reflecting adjustment in the long-run, with capital able to leave the agricultural sectors.

Agricultural trade policies and domestic farm programs are modeled explicitly, including tariffs, import quotas, input subsidies to producers and processors, Mexico's tortilla subsidies to low-income households, and the U.S. deficiency payment program. Deficiency payments and the tariff-equivalents of quotas are determined endogenously and are not treated as fixed ad valorem wedges.

There are three key macrobalances in each country model: the government deficit, aggregate investment and savings, and the balance of trade. Government savings is the difference between revenue and spending, with real spending fixed exogenously but revenue depending on a variety of tax instruments. The government deficit is therefore determined endogenously. Real investment is set exogenously, and aggregate private savings is determined residually to achieve the nominal savings-investment balance.[20] The balance of trade for each country (and hence foreign savings) is set exogenously, valued in world prices.

Each country model solves for relative domestic prices and factor returns, which clear the factor and product markets, and for an equilibrium real exchange rate that brings aggregate export supply and import demand into balance, given the exogenous aggregate balance of trade in each country. The model determines two equilibrium real exchange rates, one each for the United States and Mexico, which are measured with respect to the rest of the world. The reported exchange rate is the price-level–deflated exchange rate; it is the nominal exchange rate deflated by a domestic price index. The cross rate (United States to Mexico) is implicitly determined by an arbitrage condition.

In this class of models, which include a nontraded domestic variety of each commodity, the real exchange rate is essentially the ratio of the prices of nontradable to tradable goods in each country.[21] Because commodities are valued in local currency (pesos in Mexico and dollars in the United States), prices within each country are normalized to a country-specific domestic price index.[22] The numeraire goods are aggregates of the nontraded goods in each country. This specification is convenient for a model in which the commodities are not homogeneous.

We do not specify production and consumption details for the rest of the world. Instead, we specify world demand and supply functions for traded goods, largely by assuming fixed world prices.[23] In effect, the model specifies sectoral export supply and import demand functions for each country and solves for a set of world prices that achieve equilibrium in world commodity markets. At the sectoral level, in each country, demanders differentiate goods by country of origin, and exporters differentiate goods by country of destination.

Four types of elasticity parameters are used in the model. The production specification requires sectoral elasticities of substitution among primary factors. The CET export supply functions require elasticities of transformation between goods sold on the home and export markets. The AIDS import demand functions require sectoral income elasticities and substitution elasticities for home goods and for goods from each import source. We have drawn on estimates and "guesstimates" from various studies, including Hinojosa-Ojeda and Robinson (1992); Hanson, Robinson, and Tokarick (1993); and Reinert and Shiells (1991).[24]

Migration

In the FTA–CGE model, we specify three migration flows: rural Mexican to rural U.S. labor markets, urban unskilled Mexican to urban unskilled U.S. labor markets, and internal migration within Mexico from rural to unskilled urban labor markets.[25] In equilibrium, international migration adjusts to maintain a specified ratio of real average wages, $wgdf_{mig}$, for linked labor markets in the two countries, measured in a common currency. Similarly, internal migration in Mexico maintains a specified ratio of average real wages between the rural and unskilled urban markets. The international migration equation is:

$$WF_{mig,mx} = wgdf_{mig} \cdot WF_{mig,us} \cdot \frac{EXR_{mx}}{EXR_{us}} \qquad (7.14)$$

where the index *mig* refers to the migration flow, $WF_{mig,k}$ is the real average wage, and EXR_k is the exchange rate. The domestic labor supply in each skill category in each country is adjusted by the migrant labor flow. In the internal migration equation for Mexico, rural and urban workers compare wages within Mexico, and there is no exchange rate effect.

Migration flows generated by the FTA–CGE model refer to changes in migration from a base of zero. They should be seen as additional migration flows due to the policy change, adding to current flows.[26] Current migration flows are substantial, both within Mexico and between Mexico and the United States.[27] In addition, the net migration flows generated by the model represent workers, or heads of households. In recent years, a substantial share of migrants have been family members. The model thus probably understates total increased migration due to a policy change, because family members will tend to migrate with workers.

Other empirical studies of U.S. trade with Mexico also include migration. For example, Levy and van Wijnbergen (1994) allow migration between rural and urban unskilled labor markets to maintain a fixed differential, as we do in our model. They model Mexico alone and do not account for migration to the United States. In addition, they use a utility based measure of real wage differences and account for transfer income and land rent in rural income. In this model, we assume only a wage comparison. In a larger version of this model, which includes 28 sectors and distinguishes irrigated from nonirrigated land, we also account for land rent in rural household income.[28] The correct differential in the migration equation depends on the workers' motivation. If workers migrate to remit income, utility measures based on personal consumption would not be appropriate. Instead, one would want a wage differential that incorporates exchange rate changes.

In a simple model of two goods and two factors, Hill and Mendez (1984) consider the effects of trade liberalization on the wage differential between the United States and Mexico. Using a migration elasticity, they then compute the amount of migration that would accompany the new wage differential. Our specification includes the migration effect and the price effect on wages simultaneously.

IV. Model Results

Scenarios

As summarized in Table 7.3, we specify five scenarios that are designed to explore wage and migration changes that accompany bilateral tariff and quota elimination between the United States and Mexico, but with no changes in domestic policies.[29] In the first three scenarios, we make alternative assumptions about labor migration to decompose the effects of relative price changes and migration on wages. In the scenario with full migration, we consider the sensitivity of migration to different model assumptions, focusing on the role of exchange rates and fixed wage differentials.

In scenarios 4 and 5, we explore the relationship between international mi-

Table 7.3.   *Description of Scenarios*

No.	Scenario	Description
1.	Free trade, no migration	Remove all bilateral tariffs and quotas.
2.	Free trade, internal Mexican migration	Scenario 1 plus allow rural-urban migration in Mexico.
3.	Free trade, international migration	Scenario 1 plus both rural-urban migration in Mexico, and labor migration between the U.S. and Mexico.
4a.	Stolper–Samuelson effects	Effects of a Mexican tariff in a distortion-free base model in which we remove factor payment differentials, sectoral differences in indirect and value added taxes, and bilateral tariffs and quotas. High transformation and substitution elasticities to minimize the effect of the Armington Assumption. No farm programs in either Mexico or the United States.
4b.	Stolper–Samuelson effects	Effects of a U.S. tariff in a distortion-free base model described in 4a.
5.	Stolper–Samuelson and migration	Migration and a U.S. tariff in a distortion-free base model described in 4a.

gration and Stolper–Samuelson effects in our empirical model. We remove distortions from the empirical model to create a theoretically clean base, consistent with the assumptions used in the Stolper–Samuelson theorem. In scenarios 4a and 4b, we look for Stolper–Samuelson wage effects following the introduction of various tariffs that cause relative output price changes in Mexico and the United States. In scenario 5, we introduce both a U.S. tariff and international migration into the distortion-free model, showing the dominance of migration effects on wages over Stolper–Samuelson effects under NAFTA.

Labor Migration and the Effects of NAFTA

In scenario 1, we consider bilateral trade liberalization between the United States and Mexico when there are no migration flows, in effect restricting rural labor to the farm sectors. To evaluate migration effects, we extend scenario 1 and allow internal migration within Mexico between rural and urban unskilled labor markets in scenario 2. Finally, in scenario 3 we allow both internal Mexican migration and international migration flows between the rural and urban unskilled labor markets in Mexico and the United States, in conjunction with bilateral trade liberalization.

We find that international migration reverses the effects of NAFTA on rural wages in the United States and Mexico (Table 7.4). With no migration, liberalization of the highly protected farm sectors causes Mexico's rural wage to decline over 5 percent, while the U.S. rural wage rises 0.8 percent, consistent with the Stolper–Samuelson theorem. Increasing the mobility of rural labor

Table 7.4. *Real Factor Returns under a U.S.-Mexico FTA, with and without Migration*

	No migration	Internal migration	Internal and international migration
Migration		--- 1,000 persons ---	
U.S. rural	0	0	20
U.S. urban unskilled	0	0	400
Mexican rural-urban	0	180	340
U.S. factor prices		--- Percent change from base ---	
Rural	0.8	0.9	-1.0
Urban unskilled	-0.1	-0.1	-1.0
Urban skilled	0.0	0.0	0.1
Professional	0.0	0.0	0.0
Agric. land	0.5	0.5	0.7
Capital	-0.1	-0.1	0.0
Mexican factor prices			
Rural	-5.3	-1.9	1.0
Urban unskilled	0.4	-1.9	1.0
Urban skilled	0.6	0.6	0.4
Professional	0.5	0.5	0.3
Agric. land	-6.6	-6.7	-7.6
Capital	0.2	0.3	0.2

diminishes the effects of falling Mexican farm prices on rural wages. When we assume labor can migrate between rural and urban areas in Mexico, Mexican rural wages decline by only 2 percent. As 180,000 workers migrate to urban areas, the decline in the labor supply partially offsets effect of a decline in labor demand on the rural wage. In Mexico's urban labor market, the migration effects dominate the labor demand changes. Urban unskilled wages in Mexico decline by 2 percent, despite the increase in labor demand as output expands under NAFTA. When we do not allow migration, Mexico's urban unskilled wages rise 0.4 percent, reflecting the increase in the demand for labor as the manufacturing sectors expand.

When we assume there is international migration, 360,000 rural Mexican workers (6 percent of the farm labor force) migrate to either urban Mexico or to the United States. This decline in the supply of rural workers causes Mexican rural wages to rise by 1 percent, dominating the agricultural price decline that works to reduce farm wages. In the United States, the increase in rural labor supply causes rural wages to fall by 1 percent, despite the upward pressure of rising farm prices on rural wages.

With international migration, the changes in the labor supply in Mexico's urban labor market depend on the net effect of labor entering from the rural areas and labor leaving to the U.S. urban areas. Under NAFTA, migration to the United States dominates and the Mexican urban labor supply declines. The decrease in labor supply and the increase in labor demand associated with output changes following NAFTA complement each other in terms of the effect on the urban wage in Mexico. The Mexican urban wage increases 1 percent, compared to an increase of 0.4 percent when only labor demand changes affect the wage in scenario 1.

In the United States, the urban wage declines further with international migration than in scenario 1, with no migration. With no migration, the decline in the demand for urban unskilled labor (following the price changes associated with NAFTA) reduces the urban unskilled wage by 0.1 percent. This Stolper–Samuelson effect is quite small. The increase in the supply of urban unskilled labor, in the scenario with migration, reduces the urban unskilled wage further. It declines by 1 percent in the United States – still small, but an order of magnitude larger than the Stolper–Samuelson effect.

Although the wage effects of NAFTA are dominated by migration flows, the effects of NAFTA on prices and factor demand are consistent with changes described in the Stolper–Samuelson theorem. The magnitude of these changes are summarized in Table 7.5. In Mexico, the most dramatic changes occur in the food corn sector, which has the highest initial protection, a tariff equivalent of 45 percent.

Aggregate effects of NAFTA are reported in Table 7.6. Unlike the case of factor prices, aggregate results of NAFTA are almost unchanged by varying the migration assumptions in scenarios 1–3. For the United States, there are no measurable aggregate efficiency gains from trade liberalization with Mexico in scenarios 1 and 2, and migration largely accounts for the small increases in GDP in scenario 3. In Mexico, real GDP increases slightly in all scenarios but is lowest in scenario 3, because labor migration to the United States reduces its labor endowment.

Bilateral trade increases significantly in all three NAFTA scenarios. For the United States, NAFTA is trade creating in all three scenarios, with imports rising from both Mexico and the rest of the world. For Mexico, NAFTA results in very small trade diversion as imports from the United States replace imports from the rest of the world.

Both countries' farm program expenditures fall under all three scenarios. In the United States, the decline in expenditure reflects a decline in the deficiency payment because farm prices rise with export growth to Mexico.[30] In Mexico, farm program expenditures fall because of the decline in farm output. Bilateral trade expansion occurs with virtually no effect on the international terms of trade.

Sectoral results are presented in Table 7.7. Bilateral export growth of both countries under NAFTA is highest in the farm sectors, reflecting the fact that both countries have provided relatively high trade protection to their agricul-

Table 7.5. *Price, Output, and Labor Demand Effects of an FTA with Internal and International Migration (Scenario 3)*

			Labor demand:	
	Output price	Output	rural	urban unskilled
United States	--- Percent change from base ---			
Food corn	3.1	6.7	10.2	na
Program crops	0.1	0.7	2.0	na
Fruit/vegetables	-0.1	0.4	1.6	na
Other agriculture	0.0	0.2	1.5	na
Food mfg.	0.1	0.1	na	2.2
Other light mfg.	0.1	0.1	na	2.2
Oil/gas	0.2	0.0	na	2.1
Intermediates	0.0	0.2	na	2.3
Consumer durables	0.0	0.2	na	2.2
Capital goods	0.0	0.1	na	2.2
Services	0.0	0.1	na	2.1
Mexico				
Food corn	-4.7	-13.1	-17.4	na
Program crops	-1.2	-5.5	-7.4	na
Fruit/vegetables	1.3	5.2	5.5	na
Other agriculture	0.2	0.0	-0.6	na
Food mfg.	0.1	-0.5	na	-1.9
Other light mfg.	0.3	0.6	na	-0.9
Oil/gas	1.7	0.0	na	-1.5
Intermediates	0.4	1.4	na	-0.1
Consumer durables	0.2	4.7	na	3.1
Capital goods	0.3	2.8	na	1.3
Services	0.2	-0.3	na	-1.7

Notes: Scenario 3 assumes removal of bilateral tariffs and quotas, as well as internal and international migration. NA denotes that the factor is not employed in that sector.

ture. Agricultural trade growth is accomplished mostly through changes in crop mix, with little change in total farm output in either Mexico or the United States. The net effect of labor migration for the agricultural sectors is to shift farm production from Mexico to the United States and to increase U.S. farm exports to Mexico.

Sensitivity of Migration Results to Model Specification

Because migration effects largely determine the wage changes following NAFTA, we explore the sensitivity of migration to our specification. We do sensitivity experiments against scenario 3, which includes bilateral trade liberalization and international migration.

Table 7.6. *Aggregate Effects of a U.S.-Mexico FTA, with and without Migration*

	Scenario 1: No migration	Scenario 2: Internal migration	Scenario 3: Internal and international migration
	--- Percent change from base ---		
Real GDP - U.S.	0.0	0.0	0.1
Real GDP - Mexico	0.5	0.6	0.3
Exchange rate - U.S.	0.0	0.0	0.0
Exchange rate - Mexico	2.1	2.2	2.0
U.S. exports to Mexico	8.4	8.7	8.6
U.S. exports to rest	0.0	0.0	0.2
U.S. imports from rest	0.1	0.1	0.2
Mexican exports to U.S.	5.0	5.0	5.1
Mexican exports to rest	4.7	5.0	4.6
Mexican imports from rest	-0.6	-0.6	-0.8
Farm program expenditure:			
U.S.	-0.7	-0.7	-0.5
Mexico	-1.5	-1.9	-2.6
Terms of trade:	--- Index, base = 1.0 ---		
U.S. to Mexico	1.01	1.01	1.01
U.S. to world	1.00	1.00	1.00
Mexico to U.S.	0.99	0.99	0.99
Mexico to world	0.99	0.99	0.99

Notes: The "real exchange rate" is the price-level–deflated exchange rate using the GDP deflator. A positive change represents a depreciation. Exports are valued at world prices (in U.S. dollars).

In the model, exchange rates can affect migration because we assume labor evaluates wages in a common currency. Totally differentiate the migration equation 7.14:

$$\hat{WF}_{MX} = wg\hat{d}f + \hat{WF}_{US} + e\hat{x}r_{MX} - e\hat{x}r_{US} \qquad (7.15)$$

where ^ designates percent change. It is possible that, while real wages measured in a common currency are equated, wages can grow at different rates measured in the domestic currency. One might even observe migrants moving from a labor market where real wages (in domestic prices) are rising to one in which they are falling. As the dollar appreciates relative to the peso, the peso value of the U.S. wage increases. If the exchange rate change is large enough, the U.S. wage in dollars might fall while its peso value rises.

The issue is in the specification of what motivates migrants. For example, if they are motivated by a desire to accumulate savings that they intend to repatriate, then migration will be sensitive to changes in the exchange rate. On

Table 7.7. *Sectoral Effects of an FTA on the United States and Mexico, with and without Migration*

	No migration		Internal migration		Internal and international migration	
	Output	Exports	Output	Exports	Output	Exports
	— percent change from base —					
United States						
Farm	0.2	44.5	0.2	47.9	0.4	51.3
Corn	4.9	128.4	5.2	134.9	6.7	141.8
Program crops	0.3	36.8	0.3	41.0	0.7	44.0
Fruit/vegetables	0.1	13.3	0.1	13.1	0.4	11.9
Other agric.	0.1	8.9	0.1	9.3	0.2	8.8
Food processing	-0.1	8.7	-0.1	9.0	0.1	8.5
Other light mfg.	0.0	7.4	0.0	7.6	0.1	7.1
Oil/gas	0.0	17.8	0.0	18.0	0.0	17.7
Intermediates	0.1	8.4	0.1	8.4	0.2	8.0
Consumer durables	0.0	9.5	0.0	9.5	0.2	9.3
Capital goods	0.1	9.5	0.1	9.5	0.1	9.2
Services	0.0	-2.4	0.0	-2.4	0.1	-2.6
Mexico						
Farm	0.1	10.2	-0.3	9.4	-1.1	8.8
Corn	-8.8	0.0	-10.8	0.0	-13.1	0.0
Program crops	-3.7	0.0	-4.5	0.0	-5.5	0.0
Fruit/vegetables	7.7	21.7	6.5	21.2	5.2	21.1
Other agric.	0.6	2.2	0.5	2.0	0.0	2.0
Food processing	0.1	7.7	0.0	7.6	-0.5	7.7
Other light mfg.	0.7	8.8	0.8	8.9	0.6	9.0
Oil/gas	0.0	4.3	0.0	4.3	0.0	4.5
Intermediates	1.5	4.0	1.6	4.1	1.4	4.2
Consumer durables	4.3	5.5	4.7	5.8	4.7	5.8
Capital goods	2.8	7.7	2.9	7.8	2.8	7.7
Services	-0.2	0.1	-0.1	0.2	-0.3	0.2

Notes: Real output and exports. Exports are to partner country (United States or Mexico).

the other hand, if workers care about the differences in the amounts of non-traded goods they can consume within each country, then migration will be insensitive to changes in the exchange rate.

To eliminate the exchange rate effects on the migration decision, we fix the exchange rate in the migration equation at the base-year level. Under bilateral trade liberalization, we find that urban unskilled migration from Mexico to the United States falls by half compared to scenario 3, in which the depreciating Mexican peso affects migration. In scenario 3, the decrease in the value of the peso makes dollar wages more attractive to potential migrants. Likewise, migration from rural Mexican to the rural labor market in the United States falls when the exchange rate does not affect the migration decision.

When we eliminate the exchange rate effects, both rural and urban unskilled wages fall in Mexico under NAFTA. In Mexico's rural labor market, migration effects no longer dominate the effects of relative price changes in Mexico. Migration will, however, substantially mitigate the downward pressure on wages – the rural wage declines by 0.5 percent as opposed to 5.3 percent in the scenario with NAFTA and no migration.

The labor supply change in Mexico's urban unskilled labor market is more complex. There is a decline in the labor outflow to the U.S. urban unskilled labor market; 195,000 workers leave, as opposed to 400,000 when exchange rates affect migration. While the workers entering from Mexico's rural labor market also declines (254,000 migrate from rural areas to the urban areas, as opposed to 340,000 migrants with exchange rate effects), the net result is an increase in the supply of urban unskilled labor. In contrast, there is a decrease in the labor supply when exchange rates are included in the migration decision. The increase in labor supply dominates the labor demand changes, and the urban unskilled wage declines by 0.5 percent in Mexico.

Migration effects still dominate in the United States but have less of an impact on wages, reflecting the decline in the migration flows. Rural and urban unskilled wages each fall by 0.5 percent in the United States when there is no exchange rate effect, as opposed to a decline of 1 percent each with an exchange rate effect.

When modeling migration, we assume the wage differentials between the United States and Mexico are held constant at their base-year levels. This treatment reflects a view that changes associated with NAFTA will not affect the wage differential in the migration equation; for example, we assume no changes in U.S. immigration restrictions. The results are certainly sensitive to this assumption. From equation 7.15, one can see that migration responds to changes in the wage differential parameter exactly the same as to changes in the exchange rate. For example, if Mexico grows more rapidly than the United States, the model will generate a large decrease in migration in order to maintain the wage differential. Over the long run, with increased Mexican growth, one expects to observe growth in wages, a narrowing of the wage differential between the two countries, and a reduction in migration pressure. We have not sought to capture this mix of effects in the model because these long-run trends are not directly related to NAFTA, and the FTA-CGE model has been used primarily to explore the impact of NAFTA.

Implied Elasticities

In our analytical work, we identify three elasticities that affect the magnitude of migration. Although we do not perform sensitivity tests around

Table 7.8. *Implied Elasticities in the FTA-CGE Model*

	United States	Mexico
Elasticity of labor demand with respect to the average wage:		
Rural labor	-0.88	-0.75
Urban unskilled labor	-1.87	-1.83
Output supply elasticity of corn with respect to output price	1.09	0.71
Elasticity of rural labor demand with respect to corn output	1.40	1.44

the elasticities, we can define the values implicit in our data on the U.S. and Mexican economies.[31] The differences in elasticities help to explain the patterns of migration changes we observe in the empirical model.

The labor demand elasticities indicate the amount of migration needed to maintain fixed wage differentials across the linked labor markets (Table 7.8). The more elastic the labor demand curve, the easier it is for the labor market to absorb labor without generating a large wage increase. For example, rural labor in Mexico can migrate either to the rural labor market in the United States or to the urban unskilled labor market in Mexico. The labor demand elasticity in Mexico's urban unskilled labor market is − 1.83, whereas the labor demand elasticity in the U.S. urban unskilled labor market is − 0.88. This difference in the labor demand elasticities helps to explain the ''domino effect'' we observe – rural workers in Mexico first go to the cities and then enter the U.S. urban unskilled labor market.

The output supply elasticity indicates the responsiveness of output to a relative price change. When output is very responsive to a relative price change, indicating curvature on the production possibilities frontier, there is potential for large migration flows. The output supply elasticity for corn, a sector which contracts under NAFTA, is 1.09. This slightly elastic supply curve and the dramatic price shock under NAFTA contribute to the large migration of workers out of Mexico's rural labor markets.

When output changes in response to a relative price change, the demand for labor also changes. For example, as the labor intensive good expands, the labor demand curve shifts to the right. If the labor demand curve is very responsive to output changes, one anticipates high levels of migration as there is initially pressure for wages to increase in that country. Focusing on corn, an important source of migration, we find that the elasticity of labor demand with respect to output is 1.44 in Mexico.

Stolper–Samuelson Effects in the 11-Sector Model

Our empirical results suggest that migration effects dominate the wage effects in equation 7.11 from the analytical model. However, one problem could be that a model of trade between the United States and Mexico violates the assumptions needed to develop the links between output prices and factor prices described in the Stolper–Samuelson theorem. The empirical model then becomes a poor test of the wage changes described in the analytical model. To better replicate the analytical model, we eliminate some of the distortions in the empirical model. We remove price distortions such as tariffs and quotas and remove sectoral differences in indirect and value added taxes. To minimize the impact of the Armington assumption, we increase the export transformation and import substitution elasticities. Other distortions that violate the assumptions of the Stolper–Samuelson theorem remain, including technology differences.

We introduce a relative price change in this stylized model by adding a 25 percent tariff on Mexican global corn imports, which raises Mexico's rural wage (Table 7.9). Because corn is relatively labor-intensive, this link between

Table 7.9. *Stolper–Samuelson Effects of Tariffs, with and without Migration, Percent Change from Base*

	Mexican 25% tariff on corn	U.S. 50% tariff on fruits and vegetables	U.S. tariff with migration
Mexico	--- Percent change from base ---		
Corn output	8.8	0.6	0.1
Fruit and vegetable output	-0.1	-16.8	-17.0
Corn imports	-85.2	-2.4	-0.5
Rural wage	2.3	-1.4	0.0
United States			
Corn output	-6.8	-0.3	0.0
Fruit/vegetable output	0.2	1.0	1.1
Fruit/vegetable imports	-1.2	-90.6	-90.1
Rural wage	-0.7	0.4	-0.1
	--- 1,000 persons ---		
Mexican-U.S. rural migration	0	0	4
Mexican-U.S. unskilled migration	0	0	47
Mexican rural-urban migration	0	0	54

Notes: Real output and exports. Trade is to partner country (United States or Mexico).

output prices and factor prices is consistent with the Stolper–Samuelson theorem. In the United States, conversely, corn output declines and rural wages fall.

A 50 percent tariff on U.S. global fruit and vegetable imports demonstrates a similar result: U.S. fruit and vegetable output rises, imports fall, and the U.S. rural wage rises. In Mexico, fruit and vegetable output falls dramatically, reflecting that Mexican exports to the United States account for a large share of Mexican production, and Mexican rural wages decline.

We next introduce migration into the scenario of a 50 percent tariff on U.S. fruit and vegetable imports. Because labor can now migrate out of Mexican agriculture, Mexican rural wages no longer fall when the United States imposes a tariff. In this scenario, 58,000 Mexican farm workers (about 1 percent of total farm labor) migrate out of Mexican agriculture, and 4,000 migrate to the United States. For the United States, we find that the effects of even a small labor migration flow dominate the Stolper–Samuelson effects of relative price changes. U.S. rural wages now decline with the introduction of a U.S. tariff.

In both countries, imports drop sharply following the imposition of a tariff, reflecting our assumption of very high elasticities of import substitution and export transformation in the distortion-free, non-Armington base. The result is much greater specialization than we would observe in the FTA-CGE model. This treatment biases the model in favor of Stolper–Samuelson effects and should be viewed as an outer-bound estimate of the response of trade to changes in relative prices. Yet, even with the dramatic (and empirically unlikely) changes in trade observed in the stylized model, the Stolper–Samuelson links to wages are found to be small, and migration flows are enough to reverse the price effects. An important policy implication is that, in the presence of migration, the U.S. adoption of a tariff can hurt both countries.

V. Conclusion

Much of the debate over potential wage changes arising from the creation of NAFTA reflects views about the links between output prices and factor prices as described in the Stolper–Samuelson theorem. The model underlying the theorem assumes no international factor mobility, which is obviously unrealistic for the U.S. and Mexico, where there is significant labor migration. We develop an analytic trade model that includes both relative-price and migration effects and show that the two effects on wages can work in opposite directions. Furthermore, migration effects can more than fully offset relative-price effects. When one accounts for migration, any assessment of the net change in wages arising from changes in trade policy becomes an empirical question.

To analyze the empirical importance of the two mechanisms, we use an 11-sector FTA-CGE model of the United States and Mexico, in which the two countries are linked by trade and migration flows. We find that Stolper–Samuelson effects occur but that they are very small and have perhaps been given too much emphasis in the debate over the wage effects of NAFTA. Furthermore, migration effects largely dominate indirect price effects, generating wage changes under NAFTA that are contrary to expectations based on the Stolper–Samuelson theorem alone. For example, with no migration, removing protection causes rural wages in Mexico to fall (and rural wages in the United States to rise), reflecting Mexico's current high levels of protection to agricultural sectors. These results are consistent with the Stolper–Samuelson theorem. When we allow migration, however, the wage effects are reversed. The decline in the rural labor supply in Mexico causes the rural wage to rise rather than fall. Conversely, in the United States, the rural wage falls, due to the increased rural labor migration from Mexico.

The analysis is more complex in the urban unskilled labor markets, where Mexican workers migrate both from rural areas to urban areas in Mexico and from urban areas in Mexico to urban areas in the United States. In this case, we find that including migration reinforces the relative-price effects of NAFTA on urban unskilled wages. In Mexico, there is a net decline in supply of, as well as an increase in demand for, urban unskilled labor; both effects create pressure for the Mexican urban unskilled wage to rise. On the U.S. side, increased migration under NAFTA leads to small wage declines for both rural and urban unskilled workers.

Because of the importance of migration in determining the wage effects of NAFTA, we explore the sensitivity of our empirical model to the specification of migration. The amount of migration is sensitive to the treatment of the exchange rate in the migration equation. If workers in Mexico make wage comparisons in a common currency (say, because they are at least partly motivated by a desire to remit income), then the amount of migration is sensitive to changes in the exchange rate. Under NAFTA, the model projects a real depreciation of the Mexican peso, which causes larger migration flows than would occur in a model in which migration is insensitive to changes in the exchange rate.

Finally, migration is very sensitive to the wage differential between the two countries. Given that Stolper-Samuelson effects are empirically very small and that technology is vastly different between the two countries, one would not expect to see any significant downward pressure on U.S. wages arising from changes in commodity trade and relative prices. Increased Mexican growth, however, would raise Mexican wages and lead to a significant decline in migration pressure. Our results support the view that both countries will gain from NAFTA if it succeeds in its primary goal of increasing Mexican growth.

Endnotes

1. See Leamer (1992) who argues, based on the Stolper-Samuelson theorem, that it is possible for wages to decline in the United States by $1,000 per year. He also assumes that Mexico

acquires U.S. technology and becomes much larger economically, comparable to Italy in the European Community.

2. The theorem starts from a trade model with two countries, two factors (labor and capital), and two commodities. When there are more than two factors and commodities (and more goods than factors), it is more difficult to predict how factor prices will change following a change in relative prices. See Jones and Sheinkman (1977) and Ethier (1984) for a discussion of multisectoral extensions of trade theorems.

3. An even stronger argument is provided by the factor-price-equalization theorem, which indicates that free trade in commodities can, under various strong assumptions, lead to equalization in factor prices in the trading countries, with U.S. wages falling to meet rising Mexican wages. The theorem requires the assumption that both countries have the same technology in all sectors, differing only in aggregate factor proportions. This assumption is certainly not met in the case of the United States and Mexico, where observed differences in production technology are enormous.

4. In the Heckscher-Ohlin model, trade in factors can be a substitute for trade in commodities. Both can have an identical effect on wages under certain assumptions such as unrestricted factor flows and incomplete specialization under free trade. The issue becomes more complex in U.S.-Mexico relations because technologies are very different and there are migration restrictions. One does not necessarily expect migration to have the same effect on wages as the labor demand changes described in the Stolper-Samuelson theorem.

5. Implicitly there is a change in Mexico's domestic policy as well. We assumed that the government removes its price guarantee, by which it supports farm incomes by paying more than the market price. The quota on corn helps to support domestic prices, reducing the payment the government must make to satisfy the price guarantees. For more analysis of changes in Mexico's domestic policies, see Burfisher, Robinson, and Thierfelder (1992).

6. Although NAFTA encompasses the United States, Mexico, and Canada, we focus on trade liberalization between the United States and Mexico only. Free trade with Mexico is the source of concern over wage changes in the United States.

7. The household consumes both imports and domestic goods that are aggregated into a composite consumption commodity using a constant elasticity of substitution equation. Likewise, there is a constant elasticity of transformation by which domestic output is converted into goods for either domestic consumption or export. Labor and capital are used to produce the domestic output.

8. In addition to Stolper-Samuelson and migration effects, terms-of-trade effects in the presence of economies of scale (for the United States, at least) have substantial effects on factor prices. See Brown (1994). We do not account for economies of scale in this paper.

9. Both sectors do become relatively more capital-intensive as the relative wage increases.

10. Jones (1971) describes conditions such that the sign of $|\lambda|$ does not equal the sign of $|\Theta|$. Essentially, $\sigma_s < 0$. See Thierfelder (1992) for a discussion of Jones' model with factor market distortions and an extension to include efficiency wage sectors that justify the presence of wage differentials.

11. One can show that equation 7.11 reduces to equation 7.1 when the endowment is constant.

12. See Jones (1965) for a discussion of technology changes and the impact on relative wages.

13. From equations 7.9 and 7.10, one can show that

$$\frac{1}{\delta_L + \delta_K} = \frac{(\hat{P}_1 - \hat{P}_2)}{(\hat{X}_1 - \hat{X}_2)}$$

Thus, the coefficient in expression 7.13 reduces to zero when relative output prices are held constant.

14. See Mundell (1957) for further discussion.

15. For example, Reynolds (1993) projects a wide gap between relative wages across the two countries regardless of forces that would promote convergence. Levy and van Wijnbergen (1994) assume that labor migrates within Mexico to maintain a fixed real income differential.

16. The latter provides a complete listing of the equations of the model. The FTA-CGE model is implemented using the GAMS software, which is described in Brooke, Kendrick, and Meeraus (1988).

17. The data base is documented in Burfisher, Thierfelder, and Hanson (1992). Unpublished data on Mexican employment were compiled by Dolores Nieto, Colegio de México.

18. Robinson (1989) and de Melo (1988) survey single-country, trade-focused, CGE models.

19. The AIDS specification in this model draws on work by Robinson, Soule, and Weyerbrock (1991).

20. Enterprise savings rates are assumed to adjust to achieve the necessary level of aggregate savings in each country.

21. See Devarajan, Lewis, and Robinson (1993) for a further discussion of the real exchange rate in CGE models.

22. This specification, by which we hold the domestic price index constant in the United States and Mexico, is used in other multi-country CGE models. See for example, Roland-Holst, Reinert, and Shiells (1994).

23. In two sectors, corn and program crops, we assume downward-sloping world demand curves for U.S. exports, and hence world prices are not fixed for these sectors.

24. In lieu of econometric estimation, one can do sensitivity analysis to check for the robustness of the model results using alternative elasticity parameters. See Burfisher, Robinson, and Thierfelder (1992) for a discussion of model sensitivity to the elasticities used in the food corn sector, a major source of migrating labor. See Burfisher (1992) for a discussion of model sensitivity to parameters in all sectors.

25. There is no internal migration between the urban and the rural labor market in the United States, but the two labor markets are implicitly linked, given the other migration flows.

26. Because NAFTA does not specify changes in migration laws, these numbers should be interpreted as changes in migration pressure; they indicate an increase in the potential for illegal immigration.

27. Various researchers have placed the net increase of undocumented Mexican immigrants in the U.S. to be around 100,000 a year during the 1980s. See Bean, Edmonston, and Passel (1990).

28. See Burfisher, Robinson, and Thierfelder (1992). We define real wages in terms of a single aggregate price index in each country. Levy and van Wijnbergen (1994) account for differences in consumption patterns across household groups.

29. See Robinson et al. (1993); Burfisher, Robinson, and Thierfelder (1992); and Burfisher (1992) for analysis of the economic effects and policy implications of NAFTA using the FTA-CGE model. In these papers, we consider a wide range of policy scenarios. For example, we consider changes in agricultural policies, particularly the elimination of Mexico's input subsidies to agriculture. We find substantially higher migration flows when Mexico eliminates domestic support in conjunction with NAFTA, as opposed to trade liberalization alone.

30. U.S. deficiency payments are modeled endogenously, with unit payments falling when producer prices rise. See Burfisher, Robinson, and Thierfelder (1992), Kilkenny (1991), and Kilkenny and Robinson (1990) for a discussion of how farm programs are modeled in the FTA-CGE model.

31. These elasticities, however, are from a general equilibrium model, not a partial equilibrium model in which only one variable changes. The numbers we report are effectively the ratios of two total derivatives.

References

Adams, P.D., and P.J. Higgs. 1986. "Calibration of computable general equilibrium models from synthetic benchmark equilibrium data sets." IMPACT Preliminary Working Paper no. OP-57, Melbourne, Australia.

Bean, F.D., B. Edmonston, and J.S. Passel, eds. 1990. *Undocumented migration to the United States: IRCA and the experiences of the 1980s.* Washington, D.C.: The Urban Institute Press.

Brooke, A., D. Kendrick, and A. Meeraus. 1988. *GAMS: A user's guide.* Redwood City, CA: The Scientific Press.

Brown, D. 1994. "Properties of computable general equilibrium trade models with monopolistic competition and foreign direct investment." In *Modeling trade policy: Applied general equilibrium assessments of North American free trade,* edited by Joseph F. Francois and Clinton R. Shiells. Cambridge, U.K.: Cambridge University Press.

Burfisher, M.E. 1992. "Agriculture in a U.S.-Mexico free trade agreement." Unpublished Ph.D. dissertation, Economics Department, University of Maryland.

Burfisher, M.E., Sherman Robinson, and Karen E. Thierfelder. 1992. "Agricultural policy in a U.S.-Mexico free trade agreement." *North American Review of Economics and Finance* 3(2):117–39.

Burfisher, M.E., Karen E. Thierfelder, and Kenneth Hanson. 1992. "Data base for a computable general equilibrium analysis of a U.S.–Mexico free trade agreement." Staff Paper, Economic Research Service, U.S. Department of Agriculture, Washington, D.C., Staff Report no. AGES-9225.

de Melo, J. 1988. "Computable general equilibrium models for trade policy analysis in developing countries: A survey." *Journal of Policy Modeling* 10:469–503.

Devarajan, S., J.D. Lewis, and S. Robinson. 1993. "External shocks, purchasing power parity, and the equilibrium real exchange rate." *World Bank Economic Review* 7(1):45–63.

Ethier, W. 1984. "Higher dimensional trade Theory." In *Handbook of international economics,* edited by R. Jones and P. Kenen, vol. 1. Amsterdam: North Holland Press.

Hanson, K., S. Robinson, and S. Tokarick. 1993. "United States adjustment in the 1990s: A CGE analysis of alternative trade strategies." *International Economic Journal* 7(2):1–23.

Hill, J.K., and J.A. Mendez. 1984. "The effects of commercial policy on international migration flows: The case of the United States and Mexico." *Journal of International Economics* 17:41–53.

Hinojosa-Ojeda, R., and S. Robinson. 1992. "Diversos escenarios de la integración de los Estados Unidos y México: Enfoque de equilibro general computable." *Economía Mexicana* 1(1):71–144. Also available in English as "Alternative scenarios of U.S.–Mexico integration: A computable general equilibrium analysis." Working Paper no. 609, Department of Agricultural and Resource Economics, University of California, Berkeley, 1991.

Jones, R.W. 1965. "The structure of simple general equilibrium models." *Journal of Political Economy* 73:557–72.

————. 1971. "Distortions in factor markets and the general equilibrium model of production." *Journal of Political Economy* 79(3):437–59.

Jones, R.W., and J.A. Scheinkman. 1977. "The relevance of the two-sector production model in trade theory." *Journal of Political Economy* 85(5):909–25.

Kilkenny, M. 1991. "Computable general equilibrium modeling of agricultural policies: Documentation of the 30-sector FPGE GAMS model of the United States." U.S. Department of Agriculture, Economic Research Service, Washington, D.C., Staff Report no. AGES 9125.

Kilkenny, M., and S. Robinson. 1990. "Computable general equilibrium analysis of agricultural liberalization: Factor mobility and macro closure." *Journal of Policy Modeling* 12:527–56.

Leamer, E.G. 1992. "Wage effects of a U.S.–Mexican free trade agreement." National Bureau of Economic Research, NBER Working Paper no. 3991.

Levy, S., and S. van Wijnbergen. 1994. "Transition problems in economic reform: Agriculture in the U.S.-Mexico free trade agreement." In *Modeling trade policy: Applied general equilibrium assessments of North American free trade*, edited by Joseph F. Francois and Clinton R. Shiells. Cambridge, U.K.: Cambridge University Press.

Mundell, R.A. 1957. "International trade and factor mobility." *American Economic Review* 47(3):321–35.

Reinert, K., and C.R. Shiells, 1991. "Trade substitution elasticities for analysis of a North American free trade area." U.S. International Trade Commission, Washington, D.C.

Reynolds, C. 1993. "Will a free trade area lead to wage convergence? Implications for Mexico and the United States." In *U.S.-Mexico Relations: Labor Market Interdependence*, edited by J. Bustamante, C. Reynolds, and R. Hinojosa-Ojeda. Stanford: Stanford University Press.

Robinson, S. 1989. "Multisectoral models." In *Handbook of Development Economics*, edited by Hollis Chenery and T.N. Srinivasan. Amsterdam: North-Holland.

Robinson, S., M.E. Burfisher, R. Hinojosa-Ojeda, and K.E. Thierfelder. 1993. "Agricultural policies and migration in a U.S.-Mexico free trade area: A computable general equilibrium analysis." *Journal of Policy Modeling*, forthcoming. A version that includes an appendix with a complete listing of the equations is available as Working Paper no. 617, Department of Agricultural and Resource Economics, University of California, Berkeley, 1992.

Robinson, S., M. Soule, and S. Weyerbrock. 1991. "Import demand functions, trade volume, and terms-of-trade effects in multi-country trade models." Unpublished manuscript, Department of Agricultural and Resource Economics, University of California, Berkeley.

Roland-Holst, D., K.A. Reinert, and C.R. Shiells. 1994. "North American trade liberalization and the role of nontariff barriers." In *Modeling trade policy: Applied general equilibrium assessments of North American free trade*, edited by Joseph F. Francois and Clinton R. Shiells. Cambridge, U.K.: Cambridge University Press.

Thierfelder, K.E. 1992. "Efficiency wages, trade theory, and policy implications: A computable general equilibrium analysis." Unpublished Ph.D. dissertation, University of Wisconsin.

World Bank. 1990. *World development report 1990*. Washington, D.C.

8

The Auto Industry and the North American Free Trade Agreement

Florencio López-de-Silanes
Harvard University and NBER

James R. Markusen
University of Colorado, Boulder, and NBER

Thomas F. Rutherford
University of Colorado, Boulder

I. Introduction

In December 1992, the heads of state of the United States, Canada, and Mexico signed a trade agreement that could significantly liberalize trade between these neighboring countries in North America. This chapter provides an analysis of the effects of the new agreement on one industry – the automotive sector. We focus on production, employment, and consumer welfare effects of the agreement as simulated in a calibrated general equilibrium model that accounts for production and trade in automotive parts, engines, and finished automobiles. The model distinguishes between the effects of the agreement on the "Big Three" North American firms and on foreign firms producing in North America. This distinction is quite important because the new agreement will introduce significant nontariff barriers (NTBs) in the form of content rules for firms selling in the expanded North American market. The model we have developed provides a framework in which we can evaluate the effects of these important new nontariff barriers that may become permanent features of the North American economic landscape.

The analytical framework employed in this chapter is based on two earlier papers [Hunter, Markusen, and Rutherford (1990) and López-de-Silanes, Markusen, and Rutherford, 1992)].[1] In this chapter, we have extended our previous modeling work in several areas. First, we now distinguish two primary factor inputs to production: labor, and capital. Second, our new model accounts for more aspects of intrafirm competition in the international auto market. Two

223

types of firms are distinguished, as in our earlier work, but this chapter accounts for production by foreign firms in North America. This distinction is quite crucial to tracing out the effects of the new agreement, particularly the extent to which the new North American content rules discourage Japanese and European auto producers from establishing production lines in the United States, Canada, and Mexico.

A third new feature in the present model is that we distinguish three types of automotive products: parts, engines, and finished cars. This disaggregation is essential in order to account for the effects of content rules that will affect trade in all of these products. Fourth, this chapter explicitly incorporates major nontariff barriers into the analysis. One of these, as just suggested, is minimum domestic-content regulations that stipulate the conditions under which an auto is considered North American–made and hence can be freely traded within North America. The other is the existing trade balance conditions in Mexico that require auto firms to export from Mexico if they wish to import into Mexico.

This chapter investigates the qualitative economic insights provided by three scenarios. First, we examine the effects of a free trade area (FTA) in which there are no domestic content provisions and in which Mexico's trade balance restrictions are eliminated. Second, we examine a free trade area in which there is a North American content provision (CR), replacing the current separate provisions in Mexico and between the United States and Canada that must be satisfied for cars to be freely traded within North America. We have tried to model this as closely as possible to the existing draft agreement. Third, we examine a scenario in which this domestic content requirement is maintained and, in addition, Mexico is allowed to maintain its trade balance restriction (CR/TB). In the draft agreement, Mexico is allowed to maintain this restriction in the short run, but it will be phased out in the long run. In all three scenarios, the three North American countries maintain their existing tariff barriers on non–North American imports.

Some of the principal results are as follows. (1) Under all three scenarios, we find that Mexico receives a significant, positive welfare benefit, while the United States, Canada, and the rest of the world (ROW) experience no change in welfare. (2) Results concerning employment in the auto sector are particularly interesting. The United States and Canada experience small employment gains in all three scenarios, while Mexico receives a significant loss (between 5 and 8 percent). Mexico gains employment in parts and in engine and assembly production by North American firms (the Big Three), but these gains are outweighed by losses in employment in engine and assembly production by foreign (Japanese and European) firms. Mexico loses its domestic content provision (parts and engines from the United States and Canada now qualify as "domestic"), relatively high tariffs on parts and cars are eliminated, and North

American integration results in a competitive disadvantage for foreign firms in general. (3) In North America as a whole, there is a small gain in total auto and engine production (about 1 percent) for North American firms under NAFTA. With the domestic content provision (scenario CR), the North American firms gain about 5 percent on autos and engines, while there are very large losses of production by foreign firms (25 percent for autos, 50 percent for engines). There is an overall decrease in North American auto and engine production, suggesting why the Big Three are strongly in favor of the domestic content requirement. The latter acts to the advantage of the North American firms in locating production most efficiently throughout North America and to the competitive disadvantage of the foreign firms with technologies that rely more heavily on imported engines and parts. (4) Employment in all three North American countries rises more (or falls less, in the case of Mexico) with the content restriction (scenario CR relative to scenario NAFTA), although foreign-owned plants experience large employment losses. (5) Allowing Mexico to maintain its trade balance restriction (scenario CR/TB) made little difference to the CR estimates. Mexico loses less employment under CR/TB relative to CR (and there is some switching of production between North American and foreign firms), but there is no welfare benefit to Mexico from the trade balance restriction (a tiny loss is calculated).

II. Model Specification

In this section, we will provide an overview of model structure, including the assumptions concerning technology, pricing behavior, ownership, the structure of final demand, and the important nontariff barriers to trade, including trade balance and domestic content provisions.

Trading Regions and Content Regions

The model consists of four regions: Canada (CAN), the United States (USA), Mexico (MEX), and the rest of the world (ROW). Each of these regions generates final demands that are modeled through the representative agent paradigm. The model is based on a conventional general equilibrium structure in which demand functions are uncompensated – income from factors of production and taxes are allocated to expenditures for final commodities. Income-expenditure balance in each region implies trade balance, net of remittances on foreign investments.

The model pays special attention to the structure of intraregional trade in autos and related goods (parts and engines). The majority of auto imports from ROW into North America come from Japan, whereas North American exports to ROW are spread among a larger number of countries. These exports are of very minor significance, so we do not feel that aggregation of the rest of the world plays an important role.

In this model, *content regions* refer to trade blocks within which domestic content provisions may apply. In the initial data, Mexico is a content region, and CAFTA (the Canadian-American free trade area) is a second content region. Content region NAFTA (the North American free trade area), adding Mexico to CAFTA, is created by counterfactual experiment, and various content rules can be examined for that region. Further discussion of content rules and content regions are postponed until the next section.

Produced Goods

There are two final goods and four produced goods in total in the model. A composite good called Y is an aggregate of all nonauto goods. Y amounts to about 97 percent of GDP in the North American economies. Autos are the second final good. Parts and engines are the remaining two produced goods and are inputs into auto production.

Primary Factors

There is one composite factor, which we will refer to as "labor," that is perfectly mobile across sectors within countries but perfectly immobile across countries. Capital inputs to the composite Y sector are perfect substitutes for capital inputs to auto parts production. The fixity of this capital stock, as is clear from basic trade theory, produces a rising marginal cost of labor supply to auto assembly and engine production. As the auto sector expands in a given region, it draws labor from the composite sector, raising the marginal product of labor in that sector and hence raising the wage of labor in the auto sector. The strength of this general equilibrium effect limits the expansion of the auto sector following trade liberalization and can be specified in the calibration procedure discussed later in the chapter. The magnitude of this effect is one of the major empirical unknowns of this chapter.

Autos and engines are produced with region-specific labor inputs and with capital endowments specific by region and firm to cars and engines. If the initial capital values are held fixed, we have in essence short-run experiments in which plant capacities are limited. The model allows for capital to be transformed between engines, autos, and regions, holding aggregate capital stocks constant within each firm. The elasticity of transformation is a choice parameter of the model. The higher the value of this elasticity, the easier it is, for example, to transform auto production capital in the United States into engine production capital in Mexico.

Firm Types

There are two types of auto firms in the model. The data on the Big Three firms are averaged, giving us three symmetric USA firms (referred to also as North American firms). All other firms are made symmetric by a similar averaging process, and these are referred to as ROW (or foreign) firms. Both types of firms have production in all three North American countries, and there is no explicit policy discrimination between types. The two types of firms are distinguished by their import and export behavior. USA firms do little importing or exporting outside of North America, and their cars have a high North American parts and engine content. ROW firms import a great deal into North America in addition to their local production and have a much lower North American content for their local production. Thus, a high North American content rule can *indirectly* discriminate against foreign firms, as we shall note later in the chapter.

Ownership

Auto firms own plants in different countries and thus coordinate their production, pricing, and sales decisions across their plants. Auto firms also own the engine plants, so engines are supplied to the auto firms at marginal cost. One engine is required per car. The parts sector is much more complex in reality, with the auto firms both producing parts and purchasing parts from literally hundreds of large and small independent suppliers. Our modeling decision is to treat parts producers as independently owned. The (large) auto producers are able to segment markets, so arbitrage conditions need not bind across markets. This assumption is consistent with our price data. The (small) parts producers are not able to segment markets.

The regional pattern of firm ownership (that is, the allocation of net capital returns) is exogenous, and the capital stock and ownership pattern remains constant through the analysis.

Technology, Pricing, and Entry/Exit in the Auto Industry

The nontariff barriers that we will examine in the following section create "shadow prices" on production and trade. Part of our solution for dealing with this problem is to distinguish between two types of marginal cost. First, there is the actual money cost of the inputs needed to produce a car, part, or engine. We will refer to these costs as *marginal costs of production*. Second, there are the additional costs associated with the shadow values of the trade balance and content rules. We will refer to marginal costs inclusive of these premia as *marginal costs of supply*. The difference between marginal costs of production and supply may be either positive or negative, depending on the nature of nontariff barriers. When, for example, a domestic content constraint is binding, the domestic marginal cost of supply for domestic parts will lie below the marginal cost of production, because purchasing a domestic part earns the firm a "credit" that can be used to import a foreign part.

Production in the auto industry is characterized by increasing returns to scale. Production cost for a type j (j = USA, ROW) firm in market i is given by a constant marginal cost of production (for a given price of labor and capital) times output plus a fixed cost (fc^j_i). The total cost for a type j firm production in region i is denoted C^j_i, with marginal costs of supply denoted mc^j_i.

$$C^j_i = mc^j_i * X^j_i + fc^j_i, \quad ac^j_i = \frac{C^j_i}{X^j_i} = mc^j_i + \frac{fc^j_i}{X^j_i} \tag{8.1}$$

where ac^j_i is average cost and X^j_i is output of a j-type firm in market i. Firm type j sets a markup m^j_i in market i, so pricing equations are written as follows:

$$p^j_{xi}(1 - m^j_i) = mc^j_i \tag{8.2}$$

where p^j_{xi} is the consumer price of type j autos in market i. All type j firms in a market are assumed to have the same price initially, but their products may or may not be perfect substitutes. Joint maximization by firm type j across markets further dictate that, if the firm ships to market i from market k, the firm sets the same market i markup m^j_i on that shipment. We assume free entry and exit of firms such that profits equal zero. This is made operational by assuming zero profits at the plant level. That is, no copy of an additional plant (one with the same output, shipments, prices, and markups as existing plants) can make positive profits. For a plant located in market k and shipping to some or all of the three North American countries, this condition is given by

$$\sum_i p^j_i \, m^j_i \, X^j_{ki} = fc^j_k, \quad i, k = (CAN, USA, MEX, ROW),$$
$$j = (USA, ROW) \tag{8.3}$$

An important problem in this class of models is the choice of imperfectly competitive behavior. The approach that we have chosen is basically a Cournot markup formula, in which firms view other firms outputs as constant, multiplied by a *conjecture parameter* that is calibrated to the benchmark market shares and thereafter held constant in the analysis. At the top level, or "nest," of the utility function, autos and the composite commodity are Cobb-Douglas substitutes. At the next level, autos are divided into aggregates of USA and ROW cars. In the lowest nest, there is a constant elasticity of substitution in demand (possibly infinite) between autos from two firms of the same type. Let σ_r be the elasticity of substitution in demand for autos of different firm types (r = USA, ROW). Let σ_f be the elasticity of substitution between cars produced by firms within the same type (for example, the elasticity of substitution between Fords and GM models). We assume that these elasticities are common across regions. Let θ^j_i denote the share of type j firms in total auto sales in market i. Let n^j_i denote the number of type j firms producing in market i.[2] The optimal Cournot markup (m^j_i) for a type j firm in market i is given by the formula[3]

Z. β^* is similarly drawn from data on the elasticity of scale in the other country and is used in forming Z_c^* as well as Z^*.)

Technology and Pricing in Engines

As noted above, technology is naturally restricted to one engine per car.[4] It is also true that engine trade is almost entirely intrafirm. Because firms within a given type (USA, ROW) are identical, we therefore have two types of engines; USA and ROW. USA engines are exclusively used in USA cars, and similarly for ROW cars and engines. Because engines sales are intrafirm, the relevant price is the marginal cost of *supply* (that is, trade balance and domestic content are included in the auto firms' assessments of the costs of different sources of supply). There are a number of difficulties incorporating scale economies in engine production into this overall production structure, one of which is the marginal-cost-pricing rule. In this version of the model, we have ignored scale economies in engine production and modeled engines as produced by capital and labor at constant cost.

The Structure of Final Demand

Final demand in each region arises from budget constrained utility maximization by a representative agent. There are therefore two aspects to the demand functions – sources of income and underlying preferences. Income derives both from primary factor earnings and tax revenue. The representative consumer in each region is endowed with labor and three types of capital. The first type of capital serves as input to automotive parts and nonautomotive production. The second and third types of capital are capital stocks associated with USA and ROW automotive firms, used in the production of engines and finished autos. Income also includes tariff revenue from parts, engines, and auto trade.

Representative consumers demand two final goods: finished autos and nonautomotive output. As noted above, the demand for autos incorporates differentiation between autos from different firm types. The top-level nesting between autos and other goods implies that a constant fraction of income is spent on these two aggregates.

Domestic Content and Trade Balance Premia

There are two classes of nontariff barriers that are central in the North American auto industry. First, there are (currently) *domestic content requirements* within Mexico and CAFTA, both of which are likely to be replaced by a single regional content provision within NAFTA. Secondly, there are *trade balance requirements* for firms producing in Mexico that may or may not be retained in NAFTA. There are therefore four types of nontariff barriers that are relevant to our analysis: the existing domestic content provisions in Mexico and in CAFTA, the existing trade balance provision in Mexico, and the content provision in NAFTA.

In our model, we interpret domestic or regional content ratios for autos as the sum of the value of parts and engines (at tariff-inclusive prices) from within the content region divided by the sum of the value of all parts and engines (at tariff-inclusive prices) used in the autos. Let VZ_{ki}^j and VE_{ki}^j denote the value of parts and engines, respectively, shipped by type j firms from country k to country i. Let TZ_{ki} and TE_{ki} denote the tariff rates on parts and engine trade, respectively, from country k to country i. Let c denote content regions ($c =$ MEX, CAFTA initially). Let VA_{ci}^j denote the value added in engine and auto assembly by firm j in region i that is included in the domestic content calculation for region c.[5] Finally, let α_c donate the minimum statutory regional content for firms producing in region c. Minimum domestic content restrictions are then represented by

$$\frac{VA_{ci}^j + \sum_{k \varepsilon c} VZ_{ki}^j (1 + TZ_{ki}) + \sum_{k \varepsilon c} VE_{ki}^j (1 + TE_{ki})}{VA_{ci}^j + \sum_{k} VZ_{ki}^j (1 + TZ_{ki}) + \sum_{k} VE_{ki}^j (1 + TE_{ki})} \geq \alpha_c \qquad (8.11)$$

for firms $j =$ USA,ROW; regions $i =$ CAN,MEX, and USA; and for content regions $c =$ CAFTA, MEX, and NAFTA. Under NAFTA, domestic content will include the labor of value added in auto assembly as well as parts and engines inputs, whereas under the existing CAFTA and MEX rules, $VA_{ci}^j = 0$.

Value-added, parts and engines used in country i and produced within the content region appear in both the numerator and denominator of equation 8.11. Equation 8.11 is a constraint in the general programming problem giving an auto firm's optimization problem. This constraint has an associated Lagrangean multiplier that is specific to firm type j operating in region $i \in c$.[6]

We denote the supply price of parts in region k by p_{zk}, and we denote by $\hat{p}_{zki}^j$ the supply price (inclusive of tariffs and content premia) to type j auto firms in region i ($i \in c$) of parts produced in region k ($k = i$ included as a special case). These prices are given by $(1 + TZ_{ki})p_{zk}$ plus the shadow content premia times the derivative of equation 8.11 with respect to the part in question. The effect of the content rule is to reduce the supply price or ''user cost'' of parts from within the content region because they effectively loosen the constraint. On the other hand, parts from outside the content region have their supply prices raised by the premia associated with the content rule expressed in equation 8.11.

The same pricing relationships hold for engines. However, unlike parts, which are all differentiated, engines are homogeneous within a firm type. Engines may be produced by a single firm in more than one country, so in equilibrium their marginal costs of supply (inclusive of tariffs and premia) are equated across countries between which engines are shipped. We let p_{ek}^j denote the marginal cost of production of an engine in region k by a type j firm. Supply prices (user costs) in region i, $\hat{p}_{ei}^j$ incorporate both tariffs and applicable domestic content premia in the source and destination regions.

Now we turn to the trade balance constraint that in this model applies only to Mexico and may or may not be retained in NAFTA. We model the trade balance constraint as requiring that the value of auto, parts, and engine imports into Mexico by auto firms divided by their exports of autos and engines (auto firms do not export parts) be less than or equal to a certain number, denoted β. We assume that tariffs are not counted in assessing the value of imports into a trade-balance region. Let VX_{ki}^j denote the value of auto trade by firm j from country k to country i. The trade balance constraint is given by

$$\frac{\sum_i \left[VX_{iM}^j + VZ_{iM}^j + VE_{iM}^j \right]}{\sum_k \left[VX_{Mk}^j + VE_{Mk}^j \right]} \leq \beta \; i,k \neq MEX \qquad (8.12)$$

where subscript M refers to Mexico. The inequality in expression 8.12 constitutes a second constraint on the firm's programming problems. This constraint has a Lagrangean multiplier that affects the (firm specific) shadow price attached to imports into Mexico as well as to exports of cars and engines from Mexico.

The overall intrafirm pricing relationships are complex, depending on which pairs of countries are in common content regions and whether trade balance restrictions apply in the importing or exporting country. Initial estimates of domestic content and trade balance premia are incorporated into the calibration program discussed in the following section.

IV. Calibration

The preceding sections have characterized equilibrium structure. We now summarize the steps involved in parameterizing the general equilibrium model. Calibration employs the model equilibrium conditions to transform a minimal set of input data describing the benchmark period (1989) into a consistent set of transaction values for that period. The calculations begin by determining market structure parameters that are consistent with free entry monopolistic competition in the markets for finished autos. Having determined markups consistent with given consumer prices, market shares, and free-entry monopolistic competition, we then calibrate producer prices for parts and engines, taking care to account for the role of distortionary tariff and nontariff barriers operating in the benchmark period. Finally, we calibrate value added and nonautomotive demands to be consistent with income-expenditure balance in each region. This section documents these calculations and provides an overview of the numerical values that emerge from this procedure.

Benchmark Data

All input data for the model are displayed in Tables 8.1–8.3. Table 8.1 presents aggregate macroeconomic statistics such as GDP, price elasticities of labor supply, and labor shares of value added for engines, autos, parts, and other goods. It also contains benchmark auto prices and assumed values for economies of scale at benchmark production. Scale economy estimates are based on engineering studies and are specified for both parts and finished auto production. For reasons of data limitations, the scale economy data are assumed to differ by region but not by firm within each region. Consumer price indices for autos are specified both by region and by firm. These inputs are subsequently combined to calibrate auto sector costs, as described below.

The entries in Table 8.2 summarize trade barriers that operate in the bench-

Table 8.1. *Input Data – Aggregate Statistics*

1. Macro Economic Parameters

	GDP	ELS
CAN	543.63	0.2
USA	5166.09	0.2
MEX	211.97	0.2
ROW	17495.40	0.2

GDP   Gross domestic product
ELS   Elasticity of labor supply to auto firms.

2. Labor Shares of Value-Added

	CAN	USA	MEX	ROW
Engines	75	88	57	75
Autos	50	55	28	43
Parts	40	50	30	40

3. Consumer auto price indices

	US	ROW
CAN	1.15	1.3
USA	1.0	1.2
MEX	1.4	1.5
ROW	1.0	1.1

4. Elasticities of scale

	AUTOS		PARTS
	US	ROW	PARTS
CAN	1.15	1.15	1.2
USA	1.1	1.1	1.1
MEX	1.7	1.7	1.5
ROW	1.1	1.1	1.1

Table 8.2. *Benchmark Data – Tariff and Nontariff Rates of Protection*

5. Domestic content premia - benchmark period (%)

	US	ROW
MEX	2	4
USA		6
CAN		6

6. Trade balance premia - benchmark period (%)

	US	ROW
MEX	14	17

7. Bilateral protection in benchmark (tariff rates)

CARS

	CAN	USA	MEX	ROW
CAN			0.20	0.125
USA			0.20	0.125
MEX	0.095	0.038		0.125
ROW	0.095	0.038	0.20	

PARTS

	CAN	USA	MEX	ROW
CAN			0.13	0.065
USA			0.13	0.065
MEX	0.092	0.040		0.065
ROW	0.092	0.034	0.13	

ENGINES

	CAN	USA	MEX	ROW
CAN			0.10	0.075
USA			0.10	0.075
MEX	0.092	0.031		0.075
ROW	0.092	0.031	0.10	

mark period. Tariff rates are specified on a bilateral basis for finished autos, parts, and engines. These rates reflect the existing CAFTA agreement under which all auto sector products move duty free between the United States and Canada. Existing nontariff barriers are portrayed in two tables that indicate the distortionary effect of Mexico's trade balance rules applying to auto firms and both Mexican and CAFTA content rules. These barriers are more complicated than ad valorem tariffs, but for purposes of calibration they are described as tariff equivalent levels of distortion. Our benchmark equilibrium adopts trade balance premia equal to 14 percent and 17 percent, respectively, for USA and ROW firms operating in Mexico. The domestic content premia in Mexico are assumed to be 2 percent and 4 percent, respectively, for USA and ROW firms. ROW firms producing in the United States and Canada are subject to domestic content premia that are assumed equal to a 6 percent tariff wedge on imported parts and engines. We emphasize that we use ad valorem equivalents of the nontariff barriers in order to reconstruct marginal cost indices in the benchmark period, but the counterfactual calculations authentically represent these policy instruments so that the tariff-equivalent rates of protection adjust endogenously.

The final set of numeric inputs (Table 8.3) describe intra- and international flows of autos, parts, and engines. In the model's benchmark equilibrium, there is also international trade in nonautomotive goods, but these values are set to values consistent with regional trade balance (that is, nonautomotive trade flows are specified as residuals).

Calibration of Auto Sector Costs and Conjectures

The calibration of market structure parameters begins with estimates of the elasticity of scale for auto assembly (ε), which we get from engineering data combined with output data. The scale elasticity is defined as the ratio of average to marginal cost. When we combine these estimates with an assumption of zero profits in the benchmark year, we have the following square system of nonlinear equations:[7]

$$\varepsilon_i^j \equiv \frac{ac_i^j}{mc_i^j} = 1 + \frac{fc_i^j}{mc_i^j * \bar{X}_i^j}$$

$$\bar{p}_{xi}^j \left(1 - m_i^j\right) = mc_i^j \qquad (8.13)$$

$$\sum_i m_i^j \bar{p}_{xi}^j \bar{X}_{ki}^j = fc_k^j$$

For the multiplant firms ($j = $ USA, ROW), this system of equations gives us 24 equations in 24 unknowns ($i = $ CAN,USA,MEX,ROW). ε_i^j together with benchmark prices and trade quantities are taken as given, and our preliminary calibration program then solves this system for the 24 unknowns m_i^j, mc_i^j, and fc_i^j. The benchmark markup rates are then combined with market shares and assumed firm level product differentiation with $\sigma_f = \sigma_r = 4$ to determine the conjectural variation parameters:

$$\Omega_i^j = \frac{4 \, m_i^j}{1 + 3\dfrac{\theta_i^j}{n_i^j}} \qquad (8.14)$$

In these assignments we use $n^{US} = 3$ and $n^{ROW} = 6$ for all regions j. The results of this calculation are displayed in Table 8.4.

The calibrated marginal costs permit us to then express the value of auto trade at factor cost:

$$\overline{VX}_{ik}^j = X_{ik}^j \, mc_i^j \qquad (8.15)$$

The values of engine and parts trade at factor cost are exogenous inputs, so we can then compute the implied export ratio for firms operating in Mexico. The benchmark value of β is determined by equation 8.12.

Table 8.3. *Benchmark Data – Auto Sector Trade Flows*

PARTS - US Firms

	USA	MEX	CAN	ROW
USA	60.769	1.213	8.486	6.715
MEX	0.372	0.816	0.054	
CAN	5.267	0.134	2.307	
ROW				28.417

PARTS - ROW Firms

	USA	MEX	CAN	ROW
USA	7.438		1.158	
MEX		0.874		
CAN	1.124		0.406	
ROW	11.584	0.534	1.041	184.265

ENGINES - US Firms

	USA	MEX	CAN	ROW
USA	8.691		0.185	0.170
MEX	0.572	0.470	0.242	
CAN			1.709	
ROW				3.979

ENGINES - ROW Firms

	USA	MEX	CAN	ROW
USA	1.176		0.229	
MEX		0.389		0.556
ROW			0.387	35.446

AUTOS - US FIRMS

	USA	MEX	CAN	ROW
USA	123.180			4.562
MEX	1.531	4.341	0.113	
CAN	10.176		10.081	
ROW				74.030

AUTOS - ROW FIRMS

	USA	MEX	CAN	ROW
USA	25.980			
MEX	0.457	2.894		0.290
CAN	2.583		1.779	
ROW	36.589		3.650	326.162

*   Units: billions of dollars, invoice value net of tariff

Given β, we then can calibrate "transport costs" for autos based on the zero-profit condition for active trade links.[8] This calculation takes into account the Lagrange multipliers associated with trade balance constraints applying in the source and destination countries.

Calibration of Auto Sector NTB Premia and Marginal Costs

We next consider the trade balance restrictions. Given input data specifying trade values and noting that domestic value added does not apply in either the MEX or CAFTA content regions, we can use equation 8.11 to cal-

Table 8.4. *Calibrated Market Structure Parameters*

PX0	BENCHMARK MARGINAL COST OF AUTOS			
	USA	MEX	CAN	ROW
US	0.909	0.730	0.955	0.909
ROW	1.091	0.812	1.130	1.001
MK0	BENCHMARK RATES OF MARKUP RATE ON MARGINAL COST			
	USA	MEX	CAN	ROW
US	0.091	0.479	0.170	0.091
ROW	0.091	0.459	0.130	0.090
OMEGA	CALIBRATED CONJECTURAL VARIATIONS			
	USA	MEX	CAN	ROW
US	0.387	2.154	0.727	0.794
ROW	1.102	5.160	1.564	0.629

ibrate values for α_{MEX} and α_{CAFTA}. We employ estimates of the content premia for imports into content regions MEX and CAFTA from outside those regions, expressed in tariff-equivalent form, to infer benchmark values for the content premia applied to equation 8.11 for each firm type in each content region (Mexico and CAFTA).

Having determined consistent benchmark values for α_c, β, and the content premia, we then infer values for the marginal costs of engines. Recall that two such costs are relevant – the marginal cost of production (at factor cost) and the marginal cost of supply (incorporating tariffs and premia arising from the two types of nontariff barriers). We begin by normalizing the marginal costs of engine production in ROW to unity for both firm types. We may then infer the value of production and supply prices in any region i and firm j for which VE_{iR}^j is positive. The marginal cost of supply may then be related to the marginal cost of production by taking into account any content premia which may apply. Referring to Table 8.3, we see from the trade pattern for engines that this determines the supply prices for U.S. engines in USA and the price of foreign engines in MEX.

We next calibrate supply prices for regions that import engines from regions in which supply prices have already been calibrated. The algebraic relations are somewhat more complicated than earlier, because we need to take account of the effect of trade balance and domestic content premia that apply in both the importing and exporting country. We continue making assignments in this fashion, inverting the zero-profit conditions for engine trade activities that are operated in the benchmark period and thereby inferring either the import price from the export market price or vice versa. This step in the calibration process is certainly the most delicate, because we need to simultaneously apply price wedges that arise from bilateral tariffs, MEX trade balance premia, and both

Table 8.5. *Calibrated Trade Balance Ratios, Content Ratios, and Engine Prices*

BETA	BENCHMARK VALUE RATIO OF IMPORTS TO EXPORTS (IN MEXICO)			
US	0.669			
ROW	0.459			

ALPHA	BENCHMARK INTRA-REGION VALUE CONTENT RATIO	
	MEX	CAFTA
US .USA		0.990
US .MEX	0.458	
US .CAN		0.960
ROW.USA		0.448
ROW.MEX	0.677	
ROW.CAN		0.535

PE0	SUPPLY PRICE OF ENGINES - NET OF TRADE BALANCE PREMIA			
	USA	MEX	CAN	ROW
US	0.930	0.992	0.991	1.000
ROW	1.221	1.003	1.221	1.000

PETILDA	DEMAND PRICE OF ENGINES - GROSS OF NTB PREMIA			
	USA	MEX	CAN	ROW
US	0.930	0.969	0.991	1.000
ROW	1.131	0.984	1.158	1.000

MEX and CAFTA content premia. The output from this procedure is displayed in Table 8.5.

Closure of Income Expenditure Balance = Trade Balance

Having computed marginal costs of engine production and supply, we have fully characterized the benchmark equilibrium financial flows within the auto sector. A summary of these equilibrium values is given in Table 8.6, which indicates the relative importance of factor costs, transport costs, tariff barriers, trade balance premia, and domestic content premia for the auto and engine trade links that are active in the benchmark period. We see, for example, from the top panel in Table 8.6 that trade balance premia for U.S. firms operating in Mexico provided an effective subsidy of 7.518 percent on shipments from MEX to USA. Also, for engines shipped by ROW firms into Canada, the CAFTA content premia are assumed to have the same effect as a 5.365 percent tariff.

The final step in the calibration process is to infer values for net trade in nonautomotive goods that are consistent with trade balance. We make this inference by setting consumption levels for the nonautomotive aggregate in order that the value of regional expenditure (for autos and other goods) in each region is equal to the value of nonautomotive output, parts production, tariff

Table 8.6. *Cost Components for Autos and Engines*

```
XCOST    COMPONENTS OF DELIVERED MARGINAL COST FOR AUTOS

US FIRMS
             COST         TX          TC         MUBI
USA.USA    100.000
USA.ROW    100.000      12.500     -12.500
MEX.USA     80.295       3.051      24.172      -7.518
MEX.MEX    100.000
CAN.USA    105.057                  -5.057
CAN.CAN    100.000
ROW.ROW    100.000

ROW FIRMS
             COST         TX          TC         MUBI
USA.USA    100.000
MEX.USA     74.434       2.828      28.550      -5.812
MEX.MEX    100.000
MEX.ROW     81.104      10.138      15.091      -6.333
CAN.CAN    100.000
ROW.USA     91.775       3.487       4.737
ROW.CAN     88.566       8.414       3.020
ROW.ROW    100.000

          COST     DIRECT PRODUCTION COSTS
          TX       TARIFF COSTS
          TC       TRANSPORT COST
          MUBI     TRADE BALANCE PREMIA


ECOST    COMPONENTS OF DELIVERED MARGINAL COST FOR ENGINES

US FIRMS

             COST         TE          MUC        MUBI
USA.USA    100.000
USA.ROW     93.023       6.977
MEX.USA    106.682       3.307                  -9.989
MEX.MEX    100.000                  -2.367
MEX.CAN    100.164       9.215                  -9.379
CAN.CAN    100.000
ROW.ROW    100.000

ROW FIRMS
             COST         TE          MUC        MUBI

USA.USA    100.000                  -7.380
USA.CAN    100.000                  -5.218
MEX.MEX    100.000                  -1.911
MEX.ROW    100.310       7.523                  -7.833
ROW.CAN     81.883       7.533       5.365
ROW.ROW    100.000


COST     DIRECT PRODUCTION COSTS
MUBI     TRADE BALANCE PREMIA
TE       TARIFF
MUC      CONTENT PREMIA
```

Table 8.7. *Features of the Benchmark Equilibrium*

INPSHR	SUMMARY REPORT OF AUTO SECTOR INPUTS (%)		
	PARTS	ENGINES	VA
US .USA	57.197	7.869	34.933
US .MEX	58.090	10.504	31.406
US .CAN	56.092	11.037	32.871
US .ROW	52.851	6.184	40.965
ROW.USA	72.778	3.843	23.379
ROW.MEX	53.294	12.906	33.800
ROW.CAN	54.625	13.517	31.857
ROW.ROW	50.231	9.814	39.955

MACRO	SUMMARY REPORT OF REGIONAL AGGREGATE VALUES					
	Y	X	E	Z	T	RKX
USA	5166.090	144.471	10.351	85.779	1.971	22.479
MEX	211.970	7.325	2.229	2.116	0.245	2.666
CAN	543.630	24.266	1.709	9.238	0.277	4.391
ROW	17495.400	434.136	39.812	225.841	1.039	109.213

Y	NON-AUTOMOTIVE PRODUCTION
X	VALUE OF AUTO PRODUCTION AT MARGINAL COST
X	VALUE OF ENGINE PRODUCTION AT MARGINAL COST
Z	VALUE OF PARTS PPRODUUCTION AT MARGINAL COST
T	VALUE OF TARIFF REVENUE
KX	RETURN TO AUTO SECTOR CAPITAL

revenues, capital earnings in the auto sector, and labor earnings in the auto sector (Table 8.7).

A necessary (but not sufficient) test of the internal consistency of the benchmark calculation involves the replication of the benchmark equilibrium. That is, we use the function parameters computed through the foregoing sequence and then check that, given benchmark policy parameters, all of the market clearance conditions, zero-profit conditions, and side constraints are satisfied. In this replication, we find that the benchmark equilibrium is accurately satisfied to the sixth digit.

V. Simulation Results

As noted in the Introduction, we calculate three scenarios. NAFTA refers to a free trade area between Canada, the United States, and Mexico, with no content or trade balance provisions. CR refers to the same free trade area but with a minimum North American content provision of 62 percent on parts, engines, and labor. CR/TB adds the existing trade balance restriction in Mexico. In the draft agreement, Mexico is allowed to retain this provision in the short run, but it will be dropped in the long run. In all scenarios, each country retains its existing external tariffs.

Table 8.8 gives estimates of welfare changes for the three scenarios. The effects of North American free trade in the auto sector has essentially zero

Table 8.8. *Welfare Changes*

a) Hicksian-equivalent variation (%)			
	FTA	CR	CR/TB
USA	0	-0.008	-0.01
MEX	0.489	0.499	0.494
CAN	-0.007	-0.009	-0.009
ROW	0.001	0.002	0.002
b) % EV as fraction of auto demand			
	FTA	CR	CR/TB
USA	0	-0.207	-0.238
MEX	10.534	10.753	10.645
CAN	-0.214	-0.275	-0.277
ROW	0.022	0.096	0.074

effect on Canada, the United States, and ROW. Mexico, however, experiences a welfare gain of 0.5 percent, significant for the size of the sector (about 3 percent of Mexican GDP) and the low level of initial protection in the United States. The content region scenario (CR) has a very slight additional effect on welfare, while adding the trade balance restriction has a tiny negative additional effect on Mexico and the United States. Note that ROW is not made worse off under any scenario. The basic conclusion of Table 8.8 is that free trade in the auto sector is basically a Mexican issue. Mexico clearly benefits from the agreement in aggregate welfare terms, while no other country is significantly harmed.

When we disaggregate the sector into autos, parts, and engines and look at production and employment effects, we get a much richer and more complex story. Table 8.9 gives the employment effects (percent changes) for the three scenarios. In the first block of Table 8.9, we see that the United States and Canada are both estimated to capture small overall employment gains in each of the three scenarios. Looking down Table 8.9, we see the United States gains employment in engines (North American firms) and parts and in the assembly of North American autos under CR and CR/TB. The United States loses employment in assembly and engine production by foreign firms. Canada gains employment in engine production by North American firms, in assembly by foreign firms, and in parts production under CR and CR/TB. Canada loses employment in auto assembly by North American firms. Canadian employment benefits from the content restrictions, although it opposed a high content restriction in the negotiation.

Table 8.9 shows that Mexico loses employment under all three scenarios, but it loses less under CR than under NAFTA and less under CR/TB than under CR. Mexico's losses are in engine production by both types of firms and in auto assembly by foreign firms except in the scenario CR/TB. The loss

Table 8.9. *Employment*

a) All firms - parts, engines and assembly

	FTA	CR	CR/TB
USA	0.097	1.05	1.033
MEX	-8.461	-7.839	-5.704
CAN	0.837	2.009	1.991
ROW	-0.129	-0.491	-0.63

b) North-American firms - engines

	FTA	CR	CR/TB
USA	2.352	6.921	7.017
MEX	-31.045	-30.702	-35.671
CAN	14.253	15.264	15.31
ROW	-0.44	-5.382	-4.698

c) Foreign firms - engines

	FTA	CR	CR/TB
USA	-16.815	-44.717	-45.793
MEX	-70.766	-70.794	-56.525
CAN	0	0	0
ROW	2.502	4.26	3.947

d) North-American firms - auto assembly

	FTA	CR	CR/TB
USA	-0.209	4.909	5.006
MEX	96.83	97.838	81.673
CAN	-9.299	-8.489	-8.45
ROW	-3.983	-9.842	-9.158

e) Foreign firms - auto assembly

	FTA	CR	CR/TB
USA	-0.47	-34.008	-35.305
MEX	-28.219	-28.166	7.19
CAN	28.049	29.463	29.499
ROW	-0.102	1.975	1.664

f) Parts production

	FTA	CR	CR/TB
USA	0.379	2.263	2.304
MEX	15.432	16.946	13.405
CAN	-0.865	0.624	0.522
ROW	-0.415	-2.236	-2.338

of engine production is consistent with a widely held view that much of the investment in engine production in Mexico was due to the content and trade balance restrictions. Mexico gains employment in parts production and in assembly by North American firms.

There is an interesting contrast between Canada and Mexico in Table 8.9 with respect to auto assembly. Canada loses employment in assembly by North

American firms and gains employment in assembly by foreign firms. The pattern is the opposite in Mexico. We calculated detailed price and profitability changes for both types of firms in all countries, breaking down an impact effect on profits into changes in the prices of labor, capital, engines, and parts. Results show that foreign firms are disadvantaged in all three North American countries under NAFTA and CR, but the impact is less severe in Canada than in the United States and Mexico. In particular, the changes in shadow prices (marginal costs of supply) due to trade liberalization makes engines much cheaper in Canada *relative* to engines in Mexico for the foreign firms. The foreign firms also find labor and capital becoming relatively more expensive in Mexico relative to Canada. The big difference between these effects and those for the North American firms lies in the parts sector. For both types of firms, North American–made parts (particularly from the United States and Canada) become cheaper in Mexico than in Canada. But the U.S. and Canadian parts are a greater share of the value of output for North American firms than for foreign firms (which use Mexican or ROW parts). Thus, the elimination of the Mexican content region or its expansion to include the United States and Canada is of significant benefit (on the parts inputs) to North American firms and of far less benefit to foreign firms. Mexico becomes a relatively less attractive location for the foreign firms, and Canada becomes a second best location for producing for the North American market (in others words, Canada is not becoming more attractive in an absolute sense).

A final result to note from Table 8.9 is a very small decrease in employment in ROW. Looking down Table 8.9, we see that foreign firms increase production of engines and autos in ROW, but North American firms decrease production of engines and autos in ROW by a larger amount.

Table 8.10 shows corresponding production changes. These numbers track those for employment very closely, and there is very little additional insight gained from them. We will leave it to the reader to examine these figures.

Table 8.11 gives price changes. Once again, big numbers are only found in Mexico. Consumer prices for both types of cars fall in Mexico, giving it a consumer surplus gain. The fall in parts prices in Mexico (due to the elimination or expansion of the content region) also contributes to increased efficiency in auto production. Recall also that both autos and parts are increasing-returns industries, implying that any expansion in output generates an excess of price over marginal cost. With zero profits (in excess of the return to capital), this return is fully captured by the country of production in terms of high wages due to increased productivity (lower average cost), except for a portion captured by foreign owners of capital. Thus, the increased production of and lower prices for autos and parts in Mexico reflect the capture of scale economies and a real wage effect in addition to the consumer surplus effect.[9]

The results shown in Tables 8.9–8.11 assume an elasticity of transformation

Table 8.10. *Auto Sector Production*

a) Parts

	FTA	CR	CR/TB
USA	0.339	2.192	2.235
MEX	20.48	22.188	21.254
CAN	-0.616	1.009	0.906
ROW	-0.448	-2.248	-2.373

b) North-American firms - engines

	FTA	CR	CR/TB
USA	2.308	6.801	6.895
MEX	-23.465	-28.125	-32.268
CAN	13.986	14.986	15.029
ROW	-.0462	-5.317	-4.658

c) Foreign firms - engines

	FTA	CR	CR/TB
USA	-16.637	-44.401	-45.471
MEX	-68.604	-68.707	-53.578
CAN	0	0	0
ROW	2.476	4.024	3.710

d) North-American firms - autos

	FTA	CR	CR/TB
USA	-0.266	4.549	4.64
MEX	95.427	96.357	85.038
CAN	-8.771	-7.97	-7.936
ROW	-3.85	-9.475	-8.844

e) Foreign firms - autos

	FTA	CR	CR/TB
USA	-0.404	-34.755	-35.986
MEX	-23.73	-23.979	12.774
CAN	26.949	25.676	25.702
ROW	-0.026	1.566	1.252

between auto sector capital in autos and engines and between difference countries of 10. Panels d and e of Table 8.11 indicate that this apparently high value still results in significant departures for equality of rates of return across countries. North American firms experience an increase in the return to capital in the United States and Mexico but a fall in Canada. Foreign firms experience an increase in the return to capital in Canada but a fall in the United States and Mexico. The lack of an infinite elasticity of transformation has the effect of dampening some of the changes, in particular choking off the expansion of U.S. firms in Mexico and the contraction (expansion) of foreign firms in Mexico (Canada).

Table 8.12 shows the value of total North American changes in auto and engine production by the two types of firms individually and in total (that is, the sum of the changes in the three North American countries). This table shows more clearly how each type of agreement acts to the relative advantage of the North American firms and to the disadvantage of the foreign firms. In

Table 8.11. *Prices*

a) Consumer prices for North American cars

	FTA	CR	CR/TB
USA	-0.069	-0.211	-0.204
MEX	-9.092	-9.134	-6.499
CAN	0.289	0.275	0.281
ROW	-0.024	0.027	0.025

b) Consumer prices for Foreign cars

	FTA	CR	CR/TB
USA	-0.037	0.896	0.913
MEX	-4.507	-4.422	-0.549
CAN	-0.488	-0.145	-0.149
ROW	-0.036	0.22	0.209

c) Supply prices for parts

	FTA	CR	CR/TB
USA	-0.068	-0.276	-0.279
MEX	-7.532	-8.147	-7.053
CAN	0.26	0.006	0.026
ROW	0.026	0.221	0.22

d) Return to capital - North American firms

	FTA	CR	CR/TB
USA	0.053	0.637	0.653
MEX	6.993	7.198	6.678
CAN	-0.77	-0.54	-0.53
ROW	-0.295	-0.73	-0.658

e) Return to capital - Foreign firms

	FTA	CR	CR/TB
USA	-0.219	-3.776	-3.948
MEX	-2.625	-1.942	1.981
CAN	2.135	2.582	2.585
ROW	-0.184	0.688	0.658

the first panel (NAFTA), both firm types increase output of autos, but there is a large decrease in the value of engine production by the foreign firms. Overall, the value of North American auto production increases by 1 percent, while the value of engine production falls by 5.4 percent [as we noted earlier, this does not necessarily imply that the total number of engines produced decreases, because there is a rearrangement of production among countries with different marginal costs (prices) and different content shares]. The second panel of Table 8.12 (CR) shows that the introduction of the content provision has a very significant, beneficial effect on the U.S. firms. It also now has a very significant negative effect on auto production as well as engine production by foreign firms. Total effects are negative for both autos and engines. These results are consistent with the desire of the U.S. firms (and their unionized workers!) to have the domestic content restrictions. The third panel of Table 8.12 gives relatively similar results for CR/TB.

NAFTA, particularly with the content restrictions, favors the North Amer-

Table 8.12. *North American Auto Production (% change)*

NAFTA			
	NA Firms	Foreign Firms	Total
Autos	1.023	1.007	1.020
Engines	0.911	-37.849	-5.463
CR			
	NA Firms	Foreign Firms	Total
Autos	5.110	-25.834	-1.256
Engines	4.517	-54.532	-5.195
CR/TB			
	NA Firms	Foreign Firms	Total
Autos	4.963	-23.545	-0.901
Engines	4.262	-48.501	-4.415

ican firms and disadvantages the foreign firms for reasons noted above. The North American firms rely heavily on North American–made parts and engines. Liberalization within North America then allows these firms to capture significant gains from rationalization. The foreign firms either do not rely as heavily on North American parts and engines, or in the case of foreign firms in Mexico, source their engines and parts primarily in Mexico. The foreign firms thus do not receive the same opportunities from rationalization that liberalization provides to the North American firms. A failure to receive the same advantage becomes a competitive disadvantage, and foreign firms contract their overall North American operations.

VI. Summary and Conclusions

The Introduction and the preceding section summarize many of the key features of the model and the counterfactual simulations. We will therefore touch on only a few highlights here. The model advances our earlier work in several ways. First, assembly, parts, and engines are all treated separately. Second, there is a more sophisticated treatment of ownership, with foreign firms producing in North America in addition to exporting to it. Third, there are two primary factors of production, capital and labor. Capital is mobile within the multinational firms in that it can move between engines and assembly within the firm and among plants in different countries. A second type of capital is mobile between parts production (modeled with independent firms) and the numeraire competitive good. Fourth, principal nontariff barriers are modeled, including the domestic content provisions in Mexico and in CAFTA (the Canadian-U.S. free trade area) and trade balance restrictions in Mexico.

As in our earlier work, scale economies in auto and parts production are explicitly modeled, as is imperfect competition and multinational price/output coordination in the auto industry.

Three scenarios are modeled: NAFTA, which is a free trade area with no content or trade balance restrictions; CR, which is NAFTA plus North American content restrictions; and CR/TB, which is CR plus the existing trade balance restriction in Mexico. In terms of welfare, we find that free trade is basically a Mexican issue, with Mexico receiving significant benefits in all scenarios, and the United States, Canada, and ROW experiencing a zero net welfare change. The trade balance does not benefit Mexico.

Perhaps the most surprising results, at least relative to some popular expectations, lie in the employment and welfare numbers. We estimate that Mexico loses auto sector employment in all three scenarios, while the United States and Canada gain slightly. This is clearly due to the elimination (NAFTA) or expansion of the Mexican content region (CR) that has been supporting Mexican production and employment. Mexico has significant losses in auto and engine production by foreign firms that outweigh expansion by U.S. firms and by parts producers. The United States experiences a loss in production and employment by foreign firms that is slightly outweighed by expansion of North American firms and parts producers. Results for Canada are something of the mirror image of those for Mexico, with increased output and employment by foreign firms, contraction by North American firms, and essentially zero change in parts production.

Overall, all three scenarios benefit North American firms at the expense of foreign firms. The North American firms rely heavily on North American inputs, and the ability to rationalize production within North America leads to a significant increase in competitiveness for the North American firms. The foreign firms tend to rely more on imported parts and engines, or in the case of production in Mexico, source their parts and engines from within Mexico. Thus, liberalization within North America benefits the foreign firms much less. The most striking results are with CR (NAFTA plus the content restriction), in which the North American firms increase their total North American production of engines and autos about 5 percent, while the foreign firms contract auto production by 25 percent and engine production by about 50 percent.

In the CR scenario, total North American production of autos and engines decreases, entirely due to the downscaling of foreign firms, while parts production in all three countries increases relative to NAFTA. This result is intuitive: The content rules force the substitution of North American for imported parts and raises the costs of (foreign) autos. Although this benefits the North American firms and increases total employment in the U.S. and Canadian auto sectors (and Mexico loses less employment) relative to NAFTA, there is no benefit to the United States and Canada in terms of welfare (a tiny loss is calculated due to the imposition of the content rule). As we see so often in international trade, benefits to a particular industry do not automatically translate into welfare benefits. The results are also consistent with lobbying by U.S. firms and the UAW for the content rule; the losers are the foreign firms and the (largely nonunionized) workers in those firms.

Appendix: Markup Equations with Differentiated Firms and Firm Types

The following features of the auto market as represented in the model are determinants of the nature of competition: (1) autos produced by different firm types are distinct (imperfect substitutes in demand), (2) autos produced by individual firms within a single type of firm may be perfect or imperfect substitutes, and (3) demand for the aggregate of autos (from all firms) is price-responsive with a constant elasticity form. In this Appendix, we derive formulae that characterize Cournot competition within such an environment.

Within each region, utility functions are Cobb-Douglas, so demand for the aggregate of autos from all firm types has the form

$$A(p_A) = \bar{A} p_A^{-\mu}$$

where p_A is the price index for the composite of all autos, $\bar{A}$ is the reference demand for autos at $p_A = 1$, and μ is the Marshallian price elasticity of demand. (The regional subscript r is suppressed in this and the following equations in order to simplify notation.) The auto aggregate is a constant elasticity substitution composite of autos from all firm types written.

$$A = \left(\sum_\tau \alpha_\tau^{1/\sigma} S_\tau^{\frac{\sigma-1}{\sigma}} \right)^{\frac{\sigma}{\sigma-1}} = \phi(S)$$

in which τ indexes firm types, S_τ is an aggregate of autos supplied to the regional market by type τ firms, and σ is the elasticity of substitution between autos from different firm types. Letting $f \in \tau$ denote firms that are of type τ, we have

$$S_\tau = \left(\sum_{f \in \tau} q_f^{\frac{\eta-1}{\eta}} \right)^{\frac{\eta}{\eta-1}} = \Psi(q)$$

and we have a price index for the composite demand defined by

$$p_A = \min \sum_\tau p_\tau \frac{S_\tau}{A}$$

s.t. $\phi\left(\dfrac{S}{A}\right) = 1$

Likewise, the price index for supply from type τ firms is

$$p_\tau = \min \sum_{f \in \tau} \pi_f \frac{q_f}{S_\tau}$$

s.t. $\Psi\left(\dfrac{q}{S_\tau}\right) = 1$

The aggregate and type τ cost functions have associated demand functions:

$$S_\tau(p_\tau, p_A, A) = \alpha_\tau \left(\frac{p_A}{p_\tau}\right)^\sigma A$$

and

$$q_f(\pi_f, p_\tau, S_\tau) = \left(\frac{p_\tau}{\pi_f}\right)^\eta S_\tau \text{ for } f \in \tau$$

both of which can be inverted to express price as a function of the quantity supplied.

Let firm f be type τ. It chooses a supply quantity q_f to maximize profit:

$$\Pi_f(q) = \pi_f q - C_f(q)$$

where $C_f(q)$ is the total cost function for firm f. Marginal cost can be regarded as constant at fixed factor prices, so we have the familiar optimality condition equating marginal cost and marginal revenue:

$$\frac{\partial \pi_f}{\partial q} q + \pi_f = c_f$$

This can be rewritten to express marginal cost in terms of the sale price and an optimal Cournot markup, $c_f = \pi_f(1 - \tilde{m}_f)$ where:

$$\tilde{m}_f = -\frac{1}{e_f} = -\frac{\partial \pi_f}{\partial q_f} \frac{q_f}{\pi_f}$$

and e_f is the firm f perceived elasticity of demand.

The derivation of e_f depends on the producers' anticipation of other producers' response to a change in q_f (in the Cournot framework, firms compete in quantities). To compute e_f, we begin with the inverse demand function, π_f (q_f, p_τ, S_τ). Applying the chain rule:

$$\frac{\partial \pi_f}{\partial q_f} = \frac{\partial}{\partial q_f}\left\{\left(\frac{S_\tau}{q_f}\right)^{1/\eta} p_\tau\right\} = -\frac{1}{\eta}\frac{\pi_f}{q_f} + \frac{1}{\eta}\frac{\pi_f}{S_\tau}\frac{\partial S_\tau}{\partial q_f} + \frac{\pi_f}{p_\tau}\frac{\partial p_\tau}{\partial q_f}$$

Under Cournot conjectures, the term $\dfrac{\partial S_\tau}{\partial q_f}$ is computed holding q_j fixed for $j \neq f$:

$$\frac{\partial S_\tau}{\partial q_f} = \left(\frac{S_\tau}{q_f}\right)^{1/\eta}$$

and the term $\dfrac{\partial p_\tau}{\partial q_f}$ is computed by applying the chain rule a second time:

$$\frac{\partial p_\tau}{\partial q_f} = \frac{\partial p_\tau}{\partial S_\tau}\frac{\partial S_\tau}{\partial q_f}$$

Combining, we have

$$\frac{\partial \pi_f}{\partial q_f}\frac{q_f}{\pi_f} = -\frac{1}{\eta} + \frac{1}{\eta}\frac{q_f}{S_\tau}\left(\frac{S_\tau}{q_f}\right)^{1/\eta} + \frac{q_f}{p_\tau}\left(\frac{S_\tau}{q_f}\right)^{1/\eta}\frac{\partial p_\tau}{\partial S_\tau}$$

Making the substitution $\left(\dfrac{q_f}{S_\tau}\right)^{-1/\eta} = \dfrac{\pi_f}{p_\tau}$, we have

$$\frac{1}{e_f} = -\frac{1}{\eta} + \frac{1}{\eta}\frac{\pi_f q_f}{p_\tau S_\tau} + \left(\frac{\partial p_\tau}{\partial S_\tau}\frac{S_\tau}{p_\tau}\right)\frac{\pi_f q_f}{p_\tau S_\tau}$$

Applying the same calculations at the next level and invoking the Cournot conjecture, we have

$$\frac{\partial p_\tau}{\partial S_\tau}\frac{S_\tau}{p_\tau} = -\frac{1}{\sigma} + \left(\frac{1}{\sigma} - \frac{1}{\mu}\right)\theta_\tau$$

where θ_τ is the market share of type τ firms and

$$-\frac{1}{e_f} = \frac{1}{\eta} + \left(\frac{1}{\sigma} - \frac{1}{\eta}\right)\frac{1}{N_f} + \left(\frac{1}{\mu} - \frac{1}{\sigma}\right)\frac{\theta_\tau}{N_f}$$

Endnotes

1. Neither of the earlier papers was primarily intended as an attempt to estimate the effects of NAFTA. Hunter, Markusen, and Rutherford (1990) was primarily concerned with estimating the impact of multinational price and output coordination on trade liberalization scenarios and on the effects of market segmentation (free trade for producers versus free trade for consumers). López-de-Silanes, Markusen, and Rutherford (1992) adds a parts sector and focuses primarily on

the question of optimal trade policy for imported intermediate inputs (parts imports into Mexico) when those parts are used in an increasing-returns final-goods industry (autos) and when the imported intermediates are complementary for domestic intermediate produced with increasing returns to scale.

2. In the markup formulae, we use the number of firms *producing* in a given market as a proxy for the number of firms *selling* in a given market.

3. See the Appendix for the derivation of this markup equation.

4. There is a caveat. In our benchmark calibration, the technology for auto production is not constant across countries, and, specifically, the value share of engines in auto cost is different in the United States and Mexico. For this reason, even though engines enter as a fixed-coefficient input to auto production within each region, the worldwide engine production and auto production need not move one for one because production effects change the share of various regions in aggregate supply.

5. NAFTA is likely to include some portion of value added in auto assembly along with domestic parts and engines inputs in the calculation of domestic content, whereas in the existing content regions (CAFTA and MEX), only parts and engines are relevant.

6. The shadow prices associated with content region c need not be equilibrated for all regions $i \in c$. That is to say, the extent to which a 62 percent North American content provision affects input choice need not have the same degree of distortion in Mexico as in Canada.

7. In this and the following equations, variables which appear with an overline represent benchmark equilibrium values employed in the calibration.

8. For simplicity in the present analysis, we fix at zero any bilateral (auto or engine) trade links that are inactive in the benchmark period. In the counterfactual scenarios we do, however, accommodate "corner solutions" in situations where changes in relative prices cause one or more trade links to become inactive.

9. We do not have good data on firm ownership. We assume that the capital stocks in autos and engines in each country are owned in proportion to the size of that capital stock in the total capital stock of the firm type. Thus, if the capital in autos and engines owned by North American firms in Mexico is 10 percent of all auto and engine capital owned by North American firms initially, Mexico (that is, the representative Mexican consumer) is assumed to receive 10 percent of the return to capital owned by North American firms in all countries. This assumption has the effect (desirable or not) of smoothing the effects of changes in the return to capital in different countries on the incomes of those countries. For example, the large return to capital owned by North American firms in Mexico shown in panel d of Table 8.11 is largely captured in U.S. income, not in Mexican income.

References

Brown, D.K. 1989. "Market structure, the exchange rate and pricing behavior by firms: Some evidence from computable general equilibrium trade models." *Weltwirtschaftliches Archiv* 125:441–63.

Brown, D.K., and R.M. Stern. 1989. "Computational analysis of the U.S.-Canada free trade agreement: The role of product differentiation and market structure." In *Trade policies for international competitiveness*, edited by Robert Feenstra. Chicago: University of Chicago Press.

Dixit, A.K. 1988. "Optimal trade and industrial policies for the U.S. automobile industry." In *Empirical methods for international economics*, edited by Robert Feenstra. Cambridge: MIT Press.

Eaton, J., and G. Grossman. 1986. "Optimal trade and industrial policy under oligopoly." *Quarterly Journal of Economics* 101:383–406.

Harris, R.G. 1984. "Applied general equilibrium analysis of small open economies with scale economies and imperfect competition." *American Economic Review* 74:1016–32.

Harris, R.G., and D. Cox. 1984. *Trade, industrial policy, and canadian manufacturing.* Toronto: University of Toronto Press.

Harrison, G., T. Rutherford, and I. Wooton. 1989. "The economic impact of the european." *AEA Papers and Proceedings* 79(2):288–94.

Horstmann, I.J., and J.R. Markusen. 1986. "Up the average cost curve: Inefficient entry and the new protectionism." *Journal of International Economics* 11:531–51.

Hunter, L., J.R., Markusen, and T.F. Rutherford. 1990. "Trade liberalization in a multinational dominated industry." University of Colorado and NBER working paper.

Kehoe, T., and J. Serra-Puche. 1983. "A computational general equilibrium model with endogenous unemployment: An analysis of the 1980 fiscal reform in Mexico." *Journal of Public Economics* 22:1–26.

López-de-Silanes, F. 1989. "The automotive industry in Mexico: A model of its regulations." ITAM Thesis, Mexico City.

López-de-Silanes, F., J.R. Markusen, and T.F. Rutherford. 1992. "Complementarity and increasing returns in imported intermediate inputs." University of Colorado and NBER working paper.

Markusen, J.R. 1984. "Multinationals, multi-plants economies, and the gains from trade." *Journal of International Economics* 16. Rreprinted in *International trade: Selected readings*, edited by Jagdish Bhagwati. Cambridge: MIT Press.

Markusen, J.R., and A.J. Venables. 1988. "Trade policy with increasing returns and imperfect competition: Contradictory results from competing assumptions." *Journal of International Economics* 24, 299–316. Reprinted in *Imperfect competition in international trade*, edited by Gene Grossman. Cambridge: MIT Press, 1992.

Markusen, J.R., and R.M. Wigle. 1989. "Nash equilibrium tariffs for the United States and Canada: The roles of country size, scale economies, and capital mobility." *Journal of Political Economy* 97:368–86.

Norman, V. 1989. "EFTA and the internal european market." *Economic Policy* 9:429–65.

_____. 1990. "Assessing trade and welfare effects of trade liberalization." *European Economic Review* 34:725–51.

Rutherford, T.F. 1989. "General equilibrium modelling with MPSGE." University of Western Ontario, manuscript.

Smith, A., and A.J. Venables. 1988. "Completing the internal market in the European Community: Some industry simulations." *European Economic Review* 32:1501–25.

Venables, A.J. 1985. "Trade and trade policy with imperfect competition: The case of identical products and free entry." *Journal of International Economics* 19:1–19.

_____. 1990a. "The economic integration of oligopolistic markets." *European Economic Review* 34:753–73.

_____. 1990b. "International capacity choice and national market games." *Journal of International Economics*, 29: 23–42.

Wigle, R.M. 1988. "General equilibrium evaluation of Canada-U.S. trade liberalization in a global context." *Canadian Journal of Economics* 21:539–64.

Data Sources Used for Model Parameterization

Altschuler, A. et al. 1985. "The future of the automobile: The report of MIT's international automobile program." Cambridge: MIT Press.

AMDA (Asociación Mexicana de Distribuidores de Automobiles). *Cifras del sector automotor en México.* Several issues.

AMIA (Asociación Mexicana de la Industria Automotriz). *La industria automotriz de México en cifras. Several issues.*

Automotive News, various issues.

Automotive News, Market Data Book Issue. Several years.

Auto Parts O.E.M., Studies in Canadian Export Opportunities in the U.S. Market. External Affairs Canada.

Banco de México. *Indicadores Económicos*, several issues.

Berry, S., V. Grilli, V. and F. López-de-Silanes. 1992. *The automobile industry and the U.S.-Mexico free trade agreement*. Cambridge: MIT Press.

Bozz-Allen and Hamilton e Infotec. 1987. "Industria de autopartes." Bancomext and SECOFI. study, Mexico.

Estadística Industrial Annual y Mensual, Dirección General de Estadística. Secretaria de Programación y Presupuesto, Mexico, D.F. Various years.

Helpman, E., and P.R. Krugman. 1985. *Market structure and foreign trade: Increasing returns, imperfect competition, and the international economy*. Cambridge, MA: MIT Press.

INEGI (Instituto Nacional de Geografía y Estadística). Several publications and data bases.

Japan Automobile Manufacturers Association, INC. Several issues.

López-de-Silanes, F. 1991. "Automobiles: Mexican perspective." In *U.S.-Mexican Industrial Integration: The road to free trade*, edited by Sidney Weintraub. Westview Press, Inc.

López-de-Silanes, F. 1989. "The Automobile Industry in Mexico: A Model of its Regulations." Instituto Tecnológico Autónomo de México. Economics Thesis. Mexico City, Mexico.

Motor Vehicle Manufacturers' Association of Canada. Several issues.

Motor Vehicle Manufacturers Association of the U.S., Inc. Several issues.

SECOFI (Secretaria de Comercio y Fomento Industrial). International Trade Data Base.

Statistics Canada. "Canadian Economic Observer." Canada.

———. International Trade Division. Several Issues.

———. "National Income and Expenditure Accounts," System of National Accounts. Various volumes.

———. *Annual survey of manufactures*. Several volumes.

U.S. Department of Commerce, *Census of Manufactures*. Several volumes.

———. *General imports and exports*. Bureau of the Census. Various issues.

U.S. International Trade Commission. 1985. *The internationalization of the automobile industry and its effects on the U.S. automobile industry*. Reports to Congress. USITC publication 1712.

———. Survey of Current Business, Economics and Statistics Administration & Bureau of Economic Analysis. Various issues.

U.S. International Trade Commission. 1987. *U.S. global competitiveness: The U.S. automotive parts industry*. Reports to Congress. USITC publication 2037.

Motor Vehicles Manufacturers Association of the U.S. *World motor vehicles data*. Various volumes.

WARDS' Automotive Annual. Various volumes.

9

Trade Liberalization in Quota-Restricted Items: The United States and Mexico in Textiles and Steel*

Irene Trela
University of Western Ontario

John Whalley
University of Western Ontario and
National Bureau of Economic Research

I. Introduction

This paper uses numerical general equilibrium modeling[1] to analyze the possible consequences of bilateral free trade between the United States and Mexico in two key sectors – textiles[2] and steel. These sectors are especially important to possible bilateral negotiations because of the voluntary export restraints (VERs) and other barriers that restrict bilateral trade. Changes in these arrangements will likely be one of the more central Mexican bilateral negotiating demands, certainly as far as trade in manufactures are concerned. Because of the quotas involved, however, such liberalization must also be seen in the context of the wider system of global trade restraints in these sectors involving third countries, a theme our paper emphasizes.

Our model results clearly show that liberalization in both of these sectors is jointly advantageous for the United States and Mexico, with the specifics of the liberalization package important for the configuration of gains. These effects are not that large, but Mexico is the larger gainer, reflecting both the

* This paper was presented at the Conference on Modeling North American Free Trade held in Washington, D.C., on June 27, 1991. A shorter version (without the technical structure of the models presented in the appendix) was published in *The World Economy*. We are grateful to Cecilia Siac and Len Waverman for help and encouragement and to the Fraser Institute, the Centre for International Studies at the University of Toronto, El Colegio de México, and the Donner Canadian Foundation for support. Earlier versions of these two models were developed under a grant from the Social Sciences and Humanities Research Council, Ottawa.

much smaller size of Mexico's economy relative to the United States' and the more significant U.S. barriers in these sectors. Our results also suggest that liberalization will have adverse effects on third countries. Gains to the United States not only reflect conventional trade liberalization gains on the production and consumption side but also reflect reduced rent transfers to quota-restricted third countries due to lowered domestic United States market prices from bilateral liberalization with Mexico. These reduced rent transfers to third countries thus amplify bilateral incentives for U.S.-Mexican trade liberalization but occur at the expense of third countries. A further set of calculations analyzes possible consequences of a trilateral free trade arrangement involving the United States, Mexico, and Canada. Results seem to imply that the additional effects of a trilateral arrangement beyond a bilateral arrangement are small.

We analyze various bilateral liberalization options in textiles and steel using two existing applied general equilibrium models of global trade in those sectors that we have developed in earlier work for purposes unrelated to U.S.-Mexican trade liberalization [see Trela and Whalley (1990) and Clarete et al. (1991)]. Each is what we term a targeted general equilibrium model, capturing detail within the sector but having full general equilibrium closure for the rest of the economy. We have made a series of modifications to each to apply them to U.S.-Mexican trade issues. The resulting textile and apparel model covers four regions: two major developed country importers, the United States and Canada; Mexico; and a 33-country aggregate of the remaining Multi-Fibre Arrangement (MFA) exporting countries, which we label as the rest of the agreement countries (ROA). The model covers five goods: four textile and apparel items and one composite other good (residual GDP).

The steel model covers the United States, Canada, Mexico, and the rest of the Voluntary Restraint Agreement countries (ROA). Unlike the textiles model, it also factors in adjustment costs in its trade policy analysis, reflecting the original model design. Three industries (goods) are identified: a steel-producing industry, a steel-consuming industry, and an all-other-goods industry representing residual GDP.

We use these two models to evaluate a number of potential policy changes reflecting different possible forms that freer U.S.-Mexican trade in textiles and steel could take. These include both the complete elimination of tariffs and bilateral quotas and the elimination of tariffs but only relaxation (not elimination) of quotas. A further set of calculations analyzes the possible consequences of a trilateral free trade arrangement involving the United States, Mexico, and Canada. Results are reported on the impacts on welfare, production, trade, and rent transfers, and the themes emerging are those emphasized above.

II. U.S.-Mexican Trade in Textiles and Steel

Table 9.1 sets out trade flows and barriers for U.S.-Mexican textiles and steel trade.[3] The U.S. is Mexico's largest market for steel exports, ac-

Table 9.1. *Trade Flows and Barriers Between the U.S. and Mexico in Textiles and Apparel and Steel*

TRADE	TEXTILES AND APPAREL	STEEL
U.S. exports:		
1989 total (million dollars)	5787	2950[1]
Change, 1985-89 (annual percent)	20	47[1]
U.S. imports:		
1989 total (million dollars)	30153	9750
Change, 1985-89 (annual percent)	11	3
U.S. exports to Mexico:		
1989 total (million dollars)	704	427[1]
Change, 1985-89 (annual percent)	25	33[1]
U.S. exports from Mexico:		
1989 total (million dollars)	755	252
Change, 1985-89 (annual percent)	19	24
Mexico's exports:		
1989 total (million dollars)	830[1]	720[1]
U.S. as percent of total	91[1]	43[1]
Mexico's imports:		
1989 total (million dollars)	1100[1]	771[1]
U.S. as percent of total	64[1]	65[1]
BARRIERS		
Average tariffs, 1990:		
U.S. (percent)	6[2]	4
Mexico (percent)	12-20	10
Nontariff barriers:		
U.S.	Quantitative restraints	Quantitative Restraints[4]
Mexico	Import-licensing requirement[3]	None

[1] Estimated.
[2] Represents the estimated effective rate of duty on U.S. imports from Mexico in 1989.
[3] Mexico requires import licenses for six textile mill products.
[4] Scheduled to expire March 1992.
Source: USITC (1991), Table 4.1.

counting for just under one-half of exports in 1989. Levels are limited by a voluntary restraint agreement (VRA) (scheduled to expire in March 1992), although these are expected to rise.[4] As a supplier of steel to the United States, Mexico is small, accounting for 2.6 percent of all U.S. steel imports, or 0.4 percent of U.S. domestic consumption in 1989. While the U.S. imports steel from Mexico, Mexico remains one of the more important foreign markets for U.S. steel, accounting for 15 percent of all such exports in 1989. U.S. steel exports to Mexico have grown significantly in recent years, increasing by 33 percent annually over the 1985 to 1989 period. U.S. tariffs on steel and steel products currently range from 0.5 percent to 11.6 percent, and Mexico's duties currently range from 10 to 15 percent, having been reduced from 50 percent in the early 1980s.

U.S. trade with Mexico in textiles has also grown rapidly in recent years, with an average annual growth of 19 percent in U.S. imports and 25 percent in U.S. exports between 1985 and 1989. U.S. imports from Mexico mainly comprise reexports of garments assembled using U.S. components in the maquiladora zone. Apparel imports accounted for almost 75 percent of total U.S. imports of textiles from Mexico in 1989, and almost 90 percent of these apparel imports were dutiable under HTS item number 9802.00.80.[5]

In part, this growth in trade in these products reflects trade and other policy changes in Mexico since 1985. Mexico has been undergoing major, modernizing economic reform that has stressed the opening to trade and investment and a reduction in state intervention. Mexico has also entered into a series of trade understandings with the United States, one being the 1987 Framework Understanding, now considered a landmark in U.S.-Mexican bilateral relations, and another being the 1989 Consultative Understanding Regarding Trade and Investment.

The 1987 Framework Understanding included an "Immediate Action Agenda" that called for bilateral negotiations on several contentious subjects, including textiles and steel. These negotiations concluded with the signing of two sectoral accords – the Steel Agreement[6] (signed on December 29, 1987) and the Textile Agreement (signed on February 13, 1988 and retroactive to January 1988).

The 1987 Steel Agreement modified the 1985 steel agreement between the United States and Mexico[7], and the United States agreed to a one-time 12.4 percent increase in Mexico's steel quotas for 1988. In addition, the agreement introduced quotas on steel wire products and changed the basis for calculating adjustments in Mexico's export ceilings. In turn, Mexico agreed to lower its tariffs on steel imports from 38 to 20 percent ad valorem and eliminate all official steel import reference prices.

In 1989, the United States further liberalized quotas on imports of steel from Mexico under a Steel Trade Liberalization Program begun in September. This increased Mexico's quota under the U.S. VRA program begun in 1984[8] and achieved agreement with Mexico to eliminate trade distorting practices in steel.[9]

Since 1985, Mexico has also significantly liberalized access restrictions affecting its own market for textiles, removing almost all major nontariff trade barriers, including its restrictive import-licensing requirements, and sharply reducing tariffs, which currently range from 5 to 10 percent ad valorem.

The United States has also liberalized quotas on imports of Mexican textiles over the same period. Under a four-year Textile Agreement, negotiated under

Table 9.2. *Quota Utilization Rates for U.S. Imports of Textiles and Apparel and Steel from Mexico*

		Quota Utilization Rate
Textiles and Apparel	1981-83	35
	1985-87	61
Steel	1986	98
	1987	87
	1988	71

Data for textiles and apparel is from Erzan et al. (1990); 1986 data for steel is provided by staff at the USITC, while data for later years is from USITC (1989b), Table I-1 and I-2.

the auspices of the MFA, U.S. quotas on imports of Mexican textiles were raised, reserving a portion of the increased quotas (ranging from 50 to 90 percent) for a "special regime" created for articles assembled in Mexico from U.S.-made and -cut fabrics. U.S. duties on imports of textiles average around 15 percent, but, because of the preponderance of U.S. components in garments from Mexico, the effective trade-weighted rate is only 6 percent.

The agreement was further liberalized in an amendment effective January 1990. The amendment eliminated quotas on 52 types of Mexican textiles and increased quotas on the remaining categories. This amendment also further liberalized access for products made from U.S.-made and -cut fabric and added additional flexibility provisions in many product areas, allowing producers more rapid adjustments to changing fashion trends. Textile experts predicted at the time that as a result of the new agreement, Mexican textile and clothing exports to the United States could double over the next two years.[10]

As a consequence, and following Mexico's accession to GATT in 1986, trade between the United States and Mexico has become increasingly more important. Negotiation of a wider U.S.-Mexican FTA is the mechanism now being considered for a further broadening of bilateral trade between the two countries. Establishing freer trade in textiles and steel would be a central Mexican objective within such negotiations as far as manufactured trade is concerned.

What the implications are of a possible bilateral elimination of U.S. textile and steel quotas against Mexico depends in part on one's prognosis of the extent to which quotas in either of these areas are still binding, an issue which has been the source of controversy for some time. Data reported in Erzan et al. (1990) and USITC (1989b), reproduced here as Table 9.2, emphasizes how sharply drawn this debate is. Average quota utilization rates are reported for Mexico, averaged separately over two series of product categories, one covering textiles and the other covering steel. These utilization rates are generally below 100 percent but, at the same time, are also volatile over time. They also differ across individual textile and apparel and steel product categories. For example, in 1988, quota utilization rates for steel product categories by Mexico ranged from 42 percent in semifinished steel to 97 percent in steel wire and wire products.[11] A similar dispersion of quota utilization rates can be seen across individual textile and apparel product categories.

Although this data is far from conclusive as to the degree of restrictiveness of quotas in these two areas, there are also reasons why binding quotas can seem to be nonbinding and hence imply difficulties of interpretation of this data. Quotas assigned to firms within Mexico may not be fully utilized due to the unwillingness of firms to reassign or reallocate unused quotas for fear of losing their quota allocation in future years. Furthermore, categorywide quotas may not be filled due to aggregate quota limitations and, therefore, not appear to be binding at the subaggregate level while be binding at the aggregate level. Moreover, carryovers from one year to the next mean that quotas that appear to be nonbinding in any given year may be binding if one looks at a period covering more than one year. Whether or not quotas are binding has important implications for our modeling results that follow, and it is important to emphasize that in our model we assume bilateral quotas in these two sectors to be fully binding.[12]

III. Two Sectoral General Equilibrium Models for Analyzing the Effects of Liberalized Trade in Textiles and Steel in U.S.-Mexican Bilateral Trade

To assess more fully what the effects of liberalized trade in textiles and steel in U.S.-Mexican bilateral trade could be, we have used two existing applied general equilibrium models. These are conventional constant-returns-to-scale competitive trade models built for purposes quite different from their use here. They depart from earlier models in explicitly embodying bilateral quota restrictions, with rents accruing to exporters. We have further adapted each of them beyond their original design [see Trela and Whalley (1990) for the textile model and Clarete et al. (1991) for the steel model] for our analysis of present U.S.-Mexican sectoral trade issues.

It is perhaps worth emphasizing at the outset that, as with all such exercises, there are many ways in which the models we use are incomplete for the purposes at hand. The data used relate to the mid- to late 1980s, before the recent sharp growth in U.S.-Mexican trade and before the liberalizations of 1988 and 1990. Estimates of the ad valorem protective effects of these trade restraints are not only scarce but are also not up to date and do not capture the recent changes. Hence, when we use the model to evaluate the possible effects of U.S.-Mexico free trade, our results are relative to the 1986 situation and not relative to the partial liberalization that has already occurred in 1988 and 1990.

Also, we have to use our model under assumptions about the direction of trade; in the case of the steel model, we assume that trade flows are unambiguously from Mexico to the United States, both before and after liberalization. The relevant barriers in this exercise become U.S. barriers against Mexican steel products, not Mexican barriers against U.S. products, even though in practice such barriers exist and trade does flow from the United States to Mexico in these products.

Emphasizing these weaknesses hopefully clarifies why we focus on the broad themes of our model results and why we make no claims as to point estimates of impacts. We use our models to analyze various trade scenarios including bilateral free trade, a possible trilateral free trade agreement between the U.S., Mexico, and Canada; and multilateral free trade. We are looking for qualitative insights (are effects positive or negative, which effects seem big and which small) more than for the generation of precise quantitative estimates or forecasts.

The Textile and Apparel Model

Our general equilibrium textile and apparel model consists of four regions: two major developed country importers, the United States and Canada, and two exporting regions, Mexico and a 33-country aggregate of the remaining supplying MFA countries, which we label as the rest of the agreement countries (ROA). There are four textile and apparel product categories[13] and one composite other good (residual GDP).[14]

Production in each country involves nested constant elasticity of transformation (CET) production possibilities frontiers involving the four textile and apparel products and the composite other good (residual GDP). Consumer demands reflect utility-maximizing behaviour, with a single demand side agent assumed in each country. Nested constant elasticity of substitution (CES) functions are used.

In the model, productive potential in all regions (the CET functions) reflect the actual size of regions in terms of GDP. The United States and Canada are treated as net importers of textiles and apparel (and exporters of the other good), while all other regions are modeled as exporters of textiles and apparel (and importers of the other good). Trade in textiles and apparel among exporting regions is assumed away; otherwise, differences in supply prices in the model between these regions would be arbitraged away. Interdeveloped country trade is quota (although not tariff) free. Thus, the model captures trade diversion effects between developed countries due to their joint bilateral quotas on exports by developing regions, and domestic prices in the two developed countries therefore depend on the quota policies of both developed countries. An algebraic statement of the model is given in Appendix A.

Importantly, the model treats goods as homogeneous across regions, rather than as heterogeneous (the Armington assumption), as is commonly done in other applied general equilibrium trade models [see the discussion of the Armington assumption in Shoven and Whalley (1984)]. This assumption is used because it greatly reduces the dimensionality of the equilibrium problem that needs to be solved relative to an Armington-type approach and also minimizes difficulties in separating out trade data by region, especially if efforts to incorporate product quality differences across regions are to be made. Also, the need to deal with cross-hauling (regions both importing and exporting the same product), which in part motivates the use of the Armington assumption in other models, does not arise here in the same way because two-way trade between developed and developing countries in textiles and apparel is small. In addition, the Armington assumption is well known for the strong and often artificial terms-of-trade effects it induces in numerical results [Brown (1987)].

The Steel Model

The steel model is similar in several respects to the textile and apparel model except for one important structural difference – it also incorporates adjustment costs in trade policy evaluation [see Clarete et. al. (1991)]. The time period for the analysis is 40 years, the assumed length of the working life for relocating labour; the period is assumed to be characterized by zero growth. The model specifies four regions: one major importing region, the United States; and three exporting regions, Canada, Mexico, and a 20-country aggregate of the remaining VRA countries, which we label as the rest of the agreement countries (ROA).[15] The United States is modeled as large relative to imports from other regions and thus is large in its demand for exports from these regions. As a result, relative prices of traded goods are endogenously determined in the model.

The industries and commodities identified are a steel-producing industry (industry/commodity 1), a steel-consuming industry (industry/commodity 2),[16] and an all-other-goods industry (industry/commodity 3). All three produced commodities can be used as intermediate inputs, but only the latter two correspond to identifiable final demand consumer goods. The resource endowment of the U.S. economy comprises two factors of production – capital and labour. As with the textile model, we do not differentiate between commodities on the basis of origin (products are homogeneous between countries).

Adjustment costs appear in the model, reflecting its original design.[17] In the model, these costs arise from any movement of labour between industries and are reflected in a transactions services requirement per unit factor moved. This services requirement, which can be interpreted as wages foregone during the unemployment period for labour, drives a wedge between the buying price of labour in expanding industries and the selling price of labour in contracting industries. It also dampens the quantitative effects of trade policy shocks because it serves to partially inhibit the movement of labour to other industries.

Production in the home country (the United States) combines a fixed-coefficient Leontief system for intermediate inputs and value-added CES production functions that use capital and labour as inputs. The demand side of the U.S. economy is represented by a single representative consumer who is assumed to have a CES utility function. Other regions produce commodities that are identical to U.S. products and trade with the United States by both importing and exporting. Commodities 1 and 2 are importables in the United States, and commodity 3 is the exportable. In equilibrium, non-U.S. countries meet desired net trades by the United States, but because the desired trades of exporting regions reflect their size relative to the United States, world prices of tradeables are endogenously determined. Foreign demand is derived from CES utility-maximizing behaviour, while foreign production in each country is represented by a CET production possibilities frontier involving the three produced commodities (as in the textile and apparel model). Details of these functions and how they are used in the model are given in Appendix A.

Implementing the Modeling Approaches

To determine parameter values for the demand, production, and transformation functions in the two models, we use calibration procedures similar to those used in other applied general equilibrium models [see Mansur and Whalley (1984)]. For each model, the requirement placed on these parameter values is that they be capable of replicating the benchmark data set as an equilibrium solution to the model, given extraneous estimates of elasticities of substitution. To calibrate the textile and apparel model, we use a multicountry microconsistent equilibrium data set we have constructed for 1986. For the steel model, we use a 1986 multicountry microconsistent equilibrium data set capitalized to reflect an assumed 40-year stationary state, which, in turn, provides a 40-year time horizon for labour reallocation decisions. We discount the stream of incomes and expenditures in our 1986 data set over the 40-year time horizon using a discount rate of 5 percent. In using this procedure, we make the strong assumption that there is no growth within the period.

Different basic data sources have been used in constructing these data sets, and various incompatibilities between primary sources have had to be dealt with. Data problems are also encountered in estimating the supply prices that are central to the model analyses because they affect the estimates of rent transfer per unit export in the base data. Details on how these and other data issues have been tackled, together with data sources and detail on calibration procedures and elasticity parameters used are given in Appendix B.[18]

For each model we perform a series of counterfactual calculations around the base-year data. In equilibrium in each model, all markets clear, and external sector balance conditions for each country hold. Export quotas have the effect of segmenting national from global markets so that in the presence of these quotas, separate market-clearing prices for each quota restricted product are determined. In counterfactual equilibria (where both U.S. quota and tariff restrictions on Mexican trade are removed), producer prices in Mexico increase, stimulating both production and exports, while consumption increases and production falls in the United States. Detrimental terms-of-trade effects occur for third countries. Comparing counterfactual and benchmark equilibria thus provides the basis for policy evaluation in each model.

IV. Results

We have used the two models described in the earlier sections of this paper to analyze the two sectoral components of a possible U.S.-Mexico bilateral free trade arrangement, covering the areas of textiles and steel. We concentrate on welfare and other related effects, including impacts on trade flows, production, and rent transfers.

Table 9.3 reports results from the central case variants of the two models. We report the welfare effects for each of the two separate sectoral initiatives. In the case of the textile and apparel model, we use the annual data embedded in the model structure; in the case of the steel model, we use data reflecting the 40-year time horizon that the model contains to capture the accompanying adjustment process.

In both of these cases, gains occur for the United States and Mexico, while losses occur for Canada and ROA. Gains to Mexico suggest that conventional trade liberalization effects on the production and consumption side, reflecting improved access more than offset losses from foregone rent transfers as U.S. quotas and tariffs against Mexico are removed. Canada loses for reasons emphasized in the Introduction to our paper. It loses market share in the United States through the increased entry of products from Mexico into the United States. Gains occur for the United States from lowered prices, but with reductions in U.S. prices, losses occur for ROA due to the lowered value of transferred quota rents. Additionally, in the steel model, lowered prices stimulate demand for steel by U.S. steel-consuming industries. U.S. suppliers respond to the price reduction by lowering production, and this is accompanied by a reduction in employment in the industry.

The reduction of U.S. steel prices has a number of implications for U.S. steel-consuming industries. Most significantly, the lowered cost of using steel decreases production costs for domestic steel-consuming industries and expands their ability to compete with foreign suppliers. Lower production costs translate into increased production and employment in the U.S. steel-consuming industries. An employment gain in this industry therefore partially offsets the employment loss in the U.S. steel-producing industry as U.S. tariffs and

Table 9.3. *Welfare Effects of Bilateral U.S.-Mexico Sectoral Free Trade in Textiles and Apparel and Steel*[1]

	Hicksian Equivalent Variations ($ billion 1986)		As a % of GDP[2]		As a % of domestic use of product[2]	
	Textiles and Apparel (one year)	Steel (over 40 years)	Textiles and Apparel (one year)	Steel (over 40 years)	Textiles and Apparel (one year)	Steel (over 40 years)
U.S.	0.5	3.2	0.01	0.006	0.4	0.2
Mexico	2.1	25.9	1.2	1.6	38.0	154.2
Canada	-0.001	-0.9	0	-0.01	-0.01	-0.8
ROA	-0.5	-4.7	-0.03	-0.004	-0.4	-0.1

[1] This involves the sectoral removal of both U.S. bilateral quotas and tariffs on imports of textiles and apparel and steel from Mexico.
[2] In the case of steel, the values of GDP and domestic use of product represent discounted present values over 40 years.

quotas on imports of steel from Mexico are removed. Efficiency gains from labour reallocation, however, are partially offset by adjustment costs because these costs involve real resource use.[19]

Although these effects are qualitatively in the direction one might expect a priori, they are nonetheless small when expressed as a fraction of GDP. In columns 3 and 4 of Table 9.3, the reported fractions of GDP involved are extremely small, with the sole exception of Mexico, which gains approximately 1 percent of GDP through bilateral liberalization in textiles and apparel, with an approximate equal amount in steel. If the gains involved are expressed as a fraction of domestic use of product in the restricted sector (consumption plus intermediate use), estimated effects are somewhat larger. In the case of Mexico, these are 38 percent of domestic use of textiles and apparel and 154 percent of domestic use of domestic steel.

In Table 9.4, we report the welfare effects of alternative variants of the bilateral sectoral deals considered in Table 9.3. Case 1 reports results from Table 9.3, whereas Case 2 examines only the sectoral removal of U.S. quotas, leaving tariffs in place. In Case 2, the benefits to the U.S. are larger than under Case 1 because of their more advantageous terms of trade as a result of not also eliminating their tariffs. Smaller gains result for Mexico because their market access is reduced by U.S. tariffs. The adverse consequences for Canada are about the same as under Case 1.

Case 3 in Table 9.4 looks at a sectoral removal of U.S. tariffs only on imports of textiles and apparel and steel from Mexico, leaving quotas in place, whereas Case 4 examines a sectoral doubling of U.S. quotas against Mexico relative to the base data, leaving tariffs in place. Welfare effects in both cases are small relative to the effects in Case 1, suggesting that the net effects reported in Case 1 are largely due to U.S. liberalization of quotas against Mexico.

Table 9.5 reports the welfare effects of a trilateral U.S.-Mexico-Canada sectoral free trade arrangement. Comparing these results to those of Table 9.3, a trilateral arrangement in textiles and apparel and steel leaves results by region largely unchanged compared to Table 9.3. Slightly larger gains occur for the U.S. in the textile and apparel case due to a larger positive terms-of-trade effect and corresponding lowered value of transferred quota rents to ROA. Mexico is slightly worse off in the textile and apparel case because of reduced access to the U.S. market. Although there is a reduction in rent transfers from the U.S. to ROA, these are more than offset by increased rent transfers from Canada, and thus the adverse consequences for ROA are slightly smaller in the textile and apparel case. Despite improved access in the U.S. market, Canada is worse off in the textile and apparel case compared to Table 9.3 because of increased rent transfers to ROA. Results for steel yield slightly smaller gains to both the U.S. and Mexico compared to Table 9.3 because of a smaller decline in Canadian access of steel products to the U.S. market. Overall, how-

Table 9.4. *Welfare Effects of Variants of Bilateral Sectoral Arrangements in Textiles and Apparel and Steel*
[$ billion (U.S.), 1986]

	Case 1		Case 2		Case 3		Case 4	
	Textiles and Apparel (one year)	Steel (over 40 years)	Textiles and Apparel (one year)	Steel (over 40 years)	Textiles and Apparel (one year)	Steel (over 40 years)	Textiles and Apparel (one year)	Steel (over 40 years)
U.S.	0.5	3.2	1.3	7.0	-0.1	-0.2	0	1.6
Mexico	2.1	25.9	1.0	21.8	0.1	0.1	0	1.3
Canada	-0.001	-0.9	-0.001	-0.8	-0.001	0	-0.001	-0.3
ROA	-0.5	-4.7	-0.4	-4.6	-0.01	0	0	-1.4

Case 1: As in Table 9.3.
Case 2: Sectoral removal of U.S. quotas only on imports of textiles and apparel and steel from Mexico.
Case 3: Sectoral removal of U.S. tariffs only on imports of textiles and apparel and steel from Mexico.
Case 4: Sectoral doubling of U.S. quotas on imports of textiles and apparel and steel from Mexico, leaving tariffs in place.

Table 9.5. *Welfare Effects of Trilateral U.S.-Mexico-Canada Sectoral Free Trade*

	Hicksian Equivalent Variations ($ billion 1986)		As a % of GDP		As a % of domestic use of product	
	Textiles and Apparel (one year)	Steel (over 40 years)	Textiles and Apparel (one year)	Steel (over 40 years)	Textiles and Apparel (one year)	Steel (over 40 years)
U.S.	0.6	2.7	0.01	0.005	0.5	0.2
Mexico	2.0	25.6	1.1	1.6	36.7	152.1
Canada	-0.05	-0.01	-0.01	-0.0002	-0.5	-0.01
ROA	-0.4	-5.0	-0.03	-0.004	-0.4	-0.1

Note: In the textiles and apparel model, trilateral free trade involves both the United States and Canada removing both bilateral quotas and tariffs on imports from Mexico, as well as tariffs between each other. In the steel model, however, only U.S. bilateral quotas and tariffs are removed because Canada is treated as an exporter in the model.

Table 9.6. *Trade, Production, and Rent Transfer Effects of Bilateral Sectoral Free Trade*

	Textiles and Apparel		Steel
	Textiles	Apparel	
% change in U.S. imports from:			
Mexico	n.a.	3775.7	3416.7
Canada	-36.3	-100.0	-38.1
ROA	0	0	0
% change in production in:			
U.S.	-0.1	-5.0	-10.7
Mexico	5.2	115.7	94.1
Canada	-0.1	0.1[1]	-4.1
ROA	-0.2	-0.6	-0.002
% change in rent transfers from U.S. to:			
Mexico	-100		-100
ROA	-9.4		-43.2

n.a.: not applicable.

[1] In this particular case, the price in Canada increases in the counterfactual, which is the reason why production in Canada increases rather than falls as in the United States. This effect is so small as to not affect results, but it occurs because the textile and apparel model is formulated in such a way that if, in the counterfactual equilibrium, there is no bilateral trade between the United States and Canada in a sector (textiles or apparel), then the arbitrage condition linking prices in that sector between the two countries will no longer hold.

ever, results from the two models seem to imply that the additional effects of a trilateral arrangement compared to a bilateral arrangement are small.

Table 9.6 reports trade, production, and rent transfer effects of bilateral sectoral free trade in textiles and apparel and steel. Trade effects for Mexico are large, but because the base for the changes are so small, the changes in trade flows in dollar terms are modest. Increased U.S. imports from Mexico come at the expense of decreased imports from Canada; diversion from ROA is negligible because their share in the U.S. market is protected by their bilateral quota agreement with the U.S. Production effects of bilateral sectoral free trade again yields large percentage changes in production in Mexico and smaller changes in textiles and apparel and steel in the U.S., Canada, and ROA. Rent transfers to Mexico disappear in this case, but there are also significant reductions in rent transfers to ROA, reflecting terms-of-trade effects and corresponding quantity effects, which are produced when U.S. tariffs and quotas against Mexico are removed.

Table 9.7 reports sensitivity analyses for the bilateral sectoral free trade results in Table 9.3. These focus on Hicksian equivalent variations in billions

Table 9.7. *Sensitivity Analysis for Bilateral Sectoral Free Trade Results in Table 9.3 (Hicksian equivalent variations in billions of 1986 U.S. dollars)*

	Textiles and apparel						Steel				
	Case 1	Case 2	Case 3	Case 4	Case 5	Case 6	Case 7	Case 8	Case 9	Case 10[1]	Case 11[1]
U.S.	0.2	0.8	0.5	0.4	0.6	0.4	2.7	4.3	3.2	3.2	3.2
Mexico	1.5	2.6	2.0	1.9	2.0	2.1	1.75	35.2	21.8	25.9	25.9
Canada	-0.001	-0.001	-0.002	-0.001	-0.002	-0.001	-0.7	-1.0	-0.9	-0.9	-0.9
ROA	-0.3	-0.7	-0.6	-0.5	-0.6	-0.4	-3.8	-6.0	-4.5	-4.7	-4.7

Case 1: As in Table 9.3, but with transformation elasticities in production in Mexico and ROA set equal to 0.5.
Case 2: As in Table 9.3, but with transformation elasticities in production in Mexico and ROA set equal to 1.5.
Case 3: As in Table 9.3, but with transformation elasticities in production in the United States and Canada set equal to 0.5.

Case 4: As in Table 9.3, but with substitution elasticities in consumption in Mexico and ROA set equal to 0.5.
Case 5: As in Table 9.3, but with substitution elasticities in consumption in the United States and Canada set equal to 0.5.

Case 6: As in Table 9.3, but with substitution elasticities in consumption in the United States and Canada set equal to 1.5.

Case 7: As in Table 9.3, but with transformation elasticities in production in Mexico, Canada, and ROA set equal to 0.5.

Case 8: As in Table 9.3, but with transformation elasticities in production in Mexico, Canada, and ROA set equal to 1.5.

Case 9: As in Table 9.3, but with substitution elasticities in consumption in Mexico, Canada and ROA set equal to 0.5.
Case 10: As in Table 9.3, but with substitution elasticities in consumption in the United States set equal to 0.5.
Case 11: As in Table 9.3, but with substitution elasticities in consumption in the United States set equal to 1.5.

[1] Results are the same as in Table 9.3 because the United States uses steel in intermediate demand only, except in the results for Mexico, which indicate a slightly higher degree of sensitivity. Overall, however, the qualitative behaviour of the model is largely unaffected.

of 1986 U.S. dollars for the two cases of textiles and steel. Relatively little sensitivity occurs with changes in transformation and substitution elasticities in the case of textiles and apparel, and also in the case of steel. Finally, in Table 9.8 we have made further analyses where we initially double the quotas against Mexico before moving to sectoral free trade. This is because our 1986 data does not already incorporate the effective doubling of U.S. quotas against Mexico in steel, textiles, and apparel which would occur even without NAFTA. As can be seen from the results, the estimated effects by region are largely unchanged compared to Table 9.3, suggesting that the potential gains to the United States and Mexico from a widespread sectoral free trade arrangement will nonetheless be there even if the increases in quota rents in the intervening years are taken into account.

V. Conclusion

In this paper, we use numerical general equilibrium modeling to investigate the possible impacts of various bilateral free trade arrangements involving the United States and Mexico in the two key sectors of textiles and steel. We focus on these sectors because of the importance of quota restrictions and other barriers that limit trade and because changes in these arrangements will likely be one of the central Mexican negotiating objectives in a bilateral Mexico-U.S. negotiation, certainly as far as trade in manufactures is concerned. The models we use are based on earlier modeling efforts in which we have been involved [see Trela and Whalley (1990) and Clarete et al. (1991)]. We make a series of adaptations in each to apply them to U.S.-Mexican free trade issues. The models are standard competitive general equilibrium models but also incorporate the range of quota restrictions implied by MFA textile restrictions and voluntary export restraints under the U.S. Steel Restraint Program.

A series of interesting themes emerge. Results seem to show clearly that liberalization in both of these sectors is jointly advantageous for the United States and Mexico but importantly will also have adverse effects for third countries. The majority of the gains accrue to Mexico, but gains for the United States also reflect the operation of quota restraints against third countries. The effect of liberalization in the United States in these sectors is not only to yield conventional trade liberalization gains on the production and consumption side but also to reduce transfers to quota-restricted third countries (under bilateral liberalization) due to lowered domestic U.S. prices. These reductions in rent transfers to third countries typically amplify the bilateral incentives to engage in trade liberalization between the United States and Mexico because these occur at the expense of third countries. These third-country effects also apply to Canada. Our results for textiles and apparel suggest that although a trilateral FTA would improve Canada's access in the U.S. market, this effect would be

Table 9.8. *Incremental Welfare Effects of Bilateral U.S.-Mexico Sectoral Free Trade Following an Initial Doubling of U.S. Quotas Against Mexico*

	Hicksian Equivalent Variations ($ billion 1986)		As a % of GDP[1]		As a % of domestic use of product[1]	
	Textiles and Apparel (one year)	Steel (over 40 years)	Textiles and Apparel (one year)	Steel (over 40 years)	Textiles and Apparel (one year)	Steel (over 40 years)
U.S.	0.5	1.6	0.01	0.003	0.4	0.1
Mexico	2.1	24.6	1.2	1.5	30.9	76.8
Canada	0	-0.6	0	-0.009	0.	-0.5
ROA	-0.5	-3.1	-0.03	-0.003	-0.4	-0.05

[1] The values of GDP and domestic use of product incorporate the initial doubling of U.S. quotas against Mexico.

more than offset by increased rent transfers to ROA from Canada, and thus the adverse consequences for Canada would be greater.

Results also indicate that the precise form of liberalization is also important. Liberalization of tariffs on textiles and apparel by the United States against Mexican imports with no relaxation of quotas has the effect of increasing rent transfers to Mexico and tends to have adverse consequences for the United States. Thus, the interplay between tariff and quota liberalization will also be important in these sectors, and negotiating objectives will likely be framed not only in terms of incremental moves towards freer trade but also in terms of the manipulation of particular policy instruments.

Appendix A: Structure of the Two General Equilibrium Models Used

The Steel Model

Level of Aggregation in the Model

The industries and commodities we identify in the model are a steel-producing industry (industry/commodity 1), a steel-consuming industry (industry/commodity 2),[1] and an all-other-goods industry (industry/commodity 3).

Production. Production in the home country (the United States) combines a fixed-coefficient Leontief system for intermediate inputs and value added with CES production functions that generate value added from capital and labour. For industry j, the production function is given by

$$Q_j = \min\left[\min\left(\frac{x_{1j}}{a_{1j}}, \frac{x_{2j}}{a_{2j}}, \frac{x_{3j}}{a_{3j}},\right), VA_j \right] \quad j = 1,...3 \qquad (A9.1)$$

where Q_j is the output of good j, a_{ij} ($i = 1,..3$) are the fixed intermediate input requirements per unit of output, x_{ij} are the intermediate inputs, and VA_j is value added. The latter is produced from capital and labour according to a CES production function

$$VA_j = \gamma_j \left[\alpha_j K_j^{\frac{\rho_j^{-1}}{\rho_j}} + (1 - \alpha_j)L_j^{\frac{\rho_j^{-1}}{\rho_j}} \right]^{\frac{\rho_j}{\rho_j^{-1}}}, \quad j = 1,...3 \qquad (A9.2)$$

where γ_j is a constant defining units of measurement, α_j is a share parameter, K_j and L_j are capital and labour, and ρ_i is the elasticity of substitution between factor inputs.

Partially mobile labour between industries is accommodated within the model by assuming that there are adjustment costs associated with any inter-industry transfer of labour. These costs are reflected in a labour services requirement per unit labour moved, which can be thought of as a period of unemployment that any interindustry relocation of labour requires. As a result, in the model labour becomes quasi-fixed, and wages fail to equalize across industries. Three industry-specific wage rates therefore need to be considered,

---

[1] This industry represents other nonsteel manufacturing industries.

but at the same time there are bounds on these wage rates given by the size of adjustment costs. These, in turn, reflect the labour service requirements for moving labour between any pair of industries.

Because the model is used to evaluate adjustment costs relative to an initial (or prechange) equilibrium, unlike in the traditional Arrow-Debreu equilibrium model, the initial allocation of labour by industry becomes a parameter of the equilibrium system. We define the total economywide labour endowment as

$$\bar{L}^s = \sum_{j=1}^{3} \bar{L}_j^s$$

where $\bar{L}_j^s$ is the initial allocation of labour in industry j. At any set of prices, industry j may use more than, less than, or the same amount of labour that is initially located in the sector. We therefore need to define three types of industries when characterizing an equilibrium for the model

$$U = \{\text{industry } j | L_j = \bar{L}_j^s\};$$
$$E = \{\text{industry } j | L_j > \bar{L}_j^s\}; \qquad\qquad \text{(A9.3)}$$
$$C = \{\text{industry } j | L_j < \bar{L}_j^s\} \; \forall_j$$

where U, E, and C refer to unchanged, expanding, and contracting industries, respectively.

In characterizing an equilibrium, we define L_j, the labour actually used in industry j in terms of proportional scalars of the initial allocation of labour in each industry. Denoting β as a vector of sector-specific labour demand scalars,

$$L_j = \beta_j \bar{L}_j^s \quad j = 1,...3 \qquad\qquad \text{(A9.4)}$$

where $\bar{L}_j^s$ is the amount of labour initially allocated to industry j and $\beta_j \geq 0$, $\forall_j$. As we show below, β is a vector of endogenous variables that determine whether industry j is expanding, contracting, or unchanging relative to its initially allocated labour, which in the case of the model we use is the allocation of labour that prevailed prior to the change in U.S. steel policies. The β vector is calculated as part of the general equilibrium solution to the model.

Using these values of L_j, specific wage rates for each industry can be derived. However, adjustment costs associated with moving labour between industries establishes bounds on these wage rates. We assume that λ units of labour services are required to move one unit of labour from one industry to another, where $0 < \lambda < 1$. Firms in expanding industries will demand labour until the value marginal product of labour equals the upper-bound cost of hiring labour, which we denote as $\bar{w}$. Labour initially allocated to contracting industries will move to expanding industries until the value marginal product of labour remaining in the contracting industries equals $\hat{w}$, the wage received by sellers of labour, taking into account adjustment costs. Because of the bounds on the two wage rates established by adjustment costs, $\hat{w} = \hat{w}(1 - \lambda)$. A value marginal product of labour in any industry of less than $\hat{w}$ provides incentives for labour to leave the industry. In unchanged industries, the wage rate lies between $\bar{w}$ and $\hat{w}$, because labour is best off by remaining in the industry.

Wage rates by industry, reflecting these bounds, are thus given as follows:

$$
w_j = \begin{cases} \bar{w} \ \forall_j \in E; \\ \min\,(\bar{w},\,\max\,(w_j,\,\hat{w})) \ \forall_j \in U; \\ \hat{w} \ \forall_j \in C; \end{cases} \tag{A9.5}
$$

and the rental price of capital in expanding and contracting industries can then be derived by residual.

The number of workers moving between industries is estimated as the sum of employment changes in contracting industries. The assumption that λ units of labour services are required to move one unit of labour from one sector to another implies that once-and-for-all adjustment costs are given by

$$
T = \sum_{j \in C} - \bar{L}_j^s - L_j)\lambda\hat{w} \tag{A9.6}
$$

Consumption. The demand side of the domestic economy in the model is represented by a single representative consumer who is assumed to have a CES utility function, that is,

$$
U = \left[\sum_{j=1}^{3} \beta_j X_j^{\frac{\theta-1}{\theta}} \right]^{\frac{\theta}{\theta-1}} \tag{A9.7}
$$

where X_j is the quantity of the jth good consumed, β_j are share parameters, and θ is the elasticity of substitution.

This single agent is endowed with all the capital and labour used in the domestic economy that, along with any government transfers (tariff revenues, transferred quota rents to the restrained countries), yields the consumer's income. The budget constraint for the single agent can be written as

$$
\sum_{j=1}^{3} P_j^{us} X_j = \sum_{j=1}^{3} w_j \bar{L}_j^s + r\bar{K}^s + (T - R) \tag{A9.8}
$$

where T is tariff revenue collected and R is quota rents transferred to the quota restrained countries.

Maximizing (A9.7) subject to (A9.8) yields the demand functions

$$X_j = \frac{I\beta_j^\theta}{P_j^\theta \left[\sum_{i=1}^{3} P_i^{1-\theta}\beta_i^\theta \right]} \quad j = 1,...3 \qquad (A9.9)$$

where

$$I = \sum_{j=1}^{3} w_j \bar{L}_j^s + r\bar{K}^s + (T-R) \qquad (A9.10)$$

External Sector. An external sector is specified in our model to capture U.S. trade activity. This sector is aggregated into three regions – Mexico (region 2), a 22-country aggregate of the remaining VRA countries (region 3), and Canada (region 4), a non-VRA country – each of which produces commodities that are identical to U.S. products and trades with the United States by both importing and exporting so that, in equilibrium, it meets desired net trades by the United States. Because these regions are small relative to the United States in the model, world prices of tradeables are endogenously determined. Commodities are treated as importables if net imports by the US are positive and as exportables if net imports are negative; commodities 2 and 3 are importables and commodity 3 is an exportable in the model.

Consumer demand in each region is derived from a CES utility function identical to the one in the United States (see equation A9.7), while production is represented by a constant elasticity of transformation production possibilities frontier involving the three producer commodities

$$F_k = \gamma_k \left[\sum_{j=1}^{3} b_{jk} Y_{jk}^{\frac{c-1}{c}} \right]^{\frac{c}{c-1}} \quad k = 2,...,4 \qquad (A9.11)$$

where Y_{jk} is output of good j in region k, b_{jk} are share parameters, γ_k is a scale factor, and c is the elasticity of output transformation.

Each region's trade with the United States in the three commodities is given by the difference between production and consumption in the region, that is,

$$M_{3k} = X_{3k} - Y_{3k} \quad k = 2,...4 \qquad (A9.12)$$

$$E_{jk} = Y_{jk} - X_{jk} \quad j = 1,2, k = 2,...4 \qquad (A9.13)$$

where M_{jk} are imports of good j by region k from the United States and E_{jk} are exports by region k to the United States.

The model incorporates an external sector balance condition for each region that requires the value of imports to equal the value of exports evaluated at international prices.

$$P_3^{us}M_{3k} = \sum_{j=1}^{2} P_j^{us} \frac{E_{jk}}{1 + t_{jk}} \quad k = 2,...4 \tag{A9.14}$$

where t_{jk} is the tariff rate on imports of commodity j from region k.

Exports of commodity 1 by regions 2 and 3 to the United States also have to satisfy the constraints implied by the U.S. VRAs.

$$E_{1k} \leq \bar{B}_{1k} \quad k = 2,3 \tag{A9.15}$$

where $\bar{B}_{1k}$ are the quotas on imports of commodity 1 by the United States from region k.

Equilibrium. A general equilibrium in this model is thus given by goods prices $P_j(j = 1,...3)$, the wage rate in expanding sectors $\bar{w}$, the labour demand scalars $\beta_j(j = 1,...3)$, tariff revenues T, and quota rents R, all denoted by a vector $(P_j^*, \bar{w}^*, \beta_j^*, T^*, R^*), j = 1,...,3$, such that

1. Demands equal supplies in the labour market

$$\sum_{j=1}^{3} L_j = \bar{L}^s - \sum_{j \in C} (\bar{L}_j^s - L_j)\lambda \tag{A9.16}$$

2. Bounds on industry-specific wage rates hold

$$w_j = \bar{w}^* \; \forall_j \in E; \tag{A9.17}$$
$$w_j = \min(\bar{w}^*, \max(w_j, \hat{w})) \; \forall_j \in U;$$
$$w_j = \hat{w} \; \forall_j \in C$$

3. Quotas are binding

$$E_{1k} \leq \bar{B}_{1k}, \quad k = 2,3 \tag{A9.18}$$

4. Quota rents received by restrained regions equals that transferred to them by the United States

$$R_k^* = P_1^k \bar{B}_{1k} q_k \quad k = 2,3 \tag{A9.19}$$

where q_k is the quota premia rate on U.S. imports of commodity 1 from region k and P_1^k is the consumer price in region k for commodity 1

5. Tariff revenues collected on imports equal revenues disbursed on the demand side of the economy

$$T^* = \sum_{j=1}^{2} \frac{P_j^{US}}{1 + t_j} (X_j - Q_j)t_j \tag{A9.20}$$

The model is solved using MPS/GE [Rutherford (1989)].

The Textile and Apparel Model
Level of Aggregation in the Model
The four textile and apparel products in the model involve two aggregate categories of restricted textiles and apparel and two comparable aggregate categories of unrestricted textiles and apparel.

Production. Each of four regions in the model is assumed to have a nested constant elasticity of transformation production possibilities frontier involving the four textile and apparel products[2] and one composite other good,

$$\bar{F}^j = \left[a^j A^{j\,\frac{\sigma_1^j - 1}{\sigma_1^j}} + (1 - a^j)T^{j\,\frac{\sigma_1^j - 1}{\sigma_1^j}} \right]^{\frac{\sigma_1^j - 1}{\sigma_1^j}}, \quad j = 1,...4 \qquad (A9.21)$$

where

$$T^j = \delta^j \left[\sum_{j=1}^{4} b_i^j C_i^{j\,\frac{\sigma_2^j - 1}{\sigma_2^j}} \right]^{\frac{\sigma_2^j}{\sigma_2^j - 1}}, \quad j = 1,...4 \qquad (A9.22)$$

and

$$C_i^j = \lambda_i^j \left[d_i^j X_i^{j\,\frac{\sigma_{3i}^j - 1}{\sigma_{3i}^j}} + (1 - d_k^j)X_\ell^{j\,\frac{\sigma_{3i}^j - 1}{\sigma_{3i}^j}} \right]^{\frac{\sigma_{3i}^j}{\sigma_{3i}^j - 1}}, \qquad (A9.23)$$

$$i = 1,...,2;\ \ell = i + 2;\ j = 1,...,4$$

This treatment implies that in production in each region j, there is first substitution between aggregate categories of restricted textiles and apparel (X_i^j) and comparable aggregate categories of unrestricted textiles and apparel (X_ℓ^j), yielding composites of the categories (C_i^j), then between the composites (C_i^j), yielding a composite textile and apparel category (T^j); and finally between the composite (T^j) and other goods (A^j). σ_1^j, σ_2^j, and σ_{3i}^j are substitution elasticity parameters for region j in this three-level nesting structure, and a^j, b_i^j, and d_i^j are share parameters, with $\Sigma b_i^j = 1$. δ^j and λ_i^j are constants that define units for the composites appearing in the nesting hierarchy. The nesting hierarchy used in each region's production is shown in Figure A9.1.

The composite other good is assumed to be freely traded. We use this as a

---

[2] The index i runs from 1,...2 for the restricted products and for the unrestricted products from 3,...4.

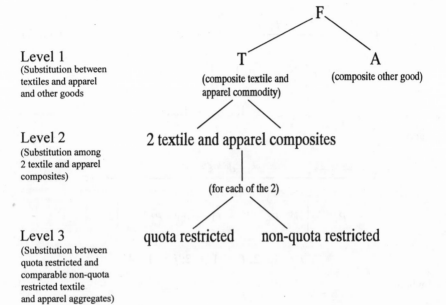

Level 1
(Substitution between textiles and apparel and other goods

Level 2
(Substitution among 2 textile and apparel composites)

Level 3
(Substitution between quota restricted and comparable non-quota restricted textile and apparel aggregates)

Figure A9.1. Nesting Structure Used to Represent Production in Each Region

numeraire and set its price equal to unity in all regions. Hence, assuming profit-maximizing behaviour, producers in each region choose quantities X_i^j for each of the four product categories to maximize

$$\sum_{i=1}^{4} P_{Xi}^j X_i^j + A^j \quad j = 1,...4 \tag{A9.24}$$

subject to equations A9.21, A.22 and A9.23, where P_{Xi}^j are the prices prevailing in region j for the four textile and apparel aggregates X_i^j.

This yields output supply functions

$$T^j = \frac{\bar{F}^j}{\left[a^j D^{j-\frac{\sigma_1^j-1}{\sigma_1^j}} + (1 - a^j) \right]^{\frac{\sigma_1^j}{\sigma_1^j-1}}}, \quad j = 1,...4 \tag{A9.25}$$

$$A^j = \left[\frac{\bar{F}^{-\frac{\sigma_1^j-1}{\sigma_1^j}} - (1 - a^j)T^{j-\frac{\sigma_1^j-1}{\sigma_1^j}}}{a^j} \right]^{\frac{\sigma_1^j}{\sigma_1^j-1}}, \quad j = 1,...4 \tag{A9.26}$$

$$C_i^j = \cfrac{b_i^{j\sigma_2^j} T^j}{P_{Ci}^{j\,\sigma_2^j} \delta^j \left[\sum_{\ell=1}^4 b_\ell^{j\sigma_2^j} P_{C\ell}^{j\,1-\sigma_2^j} \right]^{\frac{\sigma_2^j}{\sigma_2^j - 1}}}, \qquad (A9.27)$$

$$i = 1,...4; j = 1,...,4$$

and

$$X_i^j = \cfrac{d_i^{j\sigma_{3i}^j} C_i^j}{P_{Xi}^{j\,\sigma_{3i}^j} \lambda_i^j \left[d_i^{j\sigma_{3i}^j} P_{Xi}^{j\,1-\sigma_{3i}^j} + (1 - d_i^j)^{\sigma_{3i}^j} P_{X\ell}^{j\,1-\sigma_{3i}^j} \right]^{\frac{\sigma_{3i}^j}{\sigma_{3i}^j - 1}}}, \qquad (A9.28)$$

$$i = 1,...2; \ell = 1 + 2; j = 1,...4$$

where

$$D = \left(\frac{P_T^j a^j}{1 - a^j} \right)^{\sigma_1}, \quad j = 1,...4 \qquad (A9.29)$$

P_T^j is the producer price in region j for the composite textile and apparel product T^j,

$$P_T^j = \cfrac{\left[\sum_{i=1}^4 b_i^{j\sigma_2^j} P_{Ci}^{j\,1-\sigma_2^j} \right]^{\frac{1}{1-\sigma_2^j}}}{\delta^j}, \quad j = 1,...4 \qquad (A9.30)$$

and P_{Ci}^j are the producer prices in region j for the two textile and apparel composites C_i^j,

$$P_{Ci}^j = \cfrac{\left[d_i^{j\sigma_{3i}^j} P_{Xi}^{j\,1-\sigma_{3i}^j} + (1 - d_i^j)^{\sigma_{3i}^j} P_{X\ell}^{j\,1-\sigma_{3i}^j} \right]^{\frac{1}{1-\sigma_{3i}^j}}}{\lambda_i^j}, \qquad (A9.31)$$

$$i = 1,...2; \ell = i + 2; j = 1,...4$$

Consumption. Consumer demands are generated from utility-maximizing behaviour, with a single demand-side agent assumed in each region. Each agents' utility function is of nested CES form, with a structure similar to that on the production side, that is,

$$U^j = \left[\hat{a}^j \hat{A}^{j \frac{\hat{\sigma}^j_1 - 1}{\hat{\sigma}^j_1}} + (1 - \hat{a}^j)\hat{T}^{j \frac{\hat{\sigma}^j_1 - 1}{\hat{\sigma}^j_1}} \right]^{\frac{\hat{\sigma}^j_1}{\hat{\sigma}^j_1 - 1}}, \quad j = 1,...4 \qquad (A9.32)$$

$$\hat{T}^j = \left[\sum_{i=1}^{4} \hat{b}^j_i \hat{C}^{j \frac{\hat{\sigma}^j_2 - 1}{\hat{\sigma}^j_2 - 1}}_i \right]^{\frac{\hat{\sigma}^j_2}{\hat{\sigma}^j_2 - 1}}, \quad j = 1,...4 \qquad (A9.33)$$

$$\hat{C}^j_k = \left[\hat{d}^j_i \hat{X}^{j \frac{\hat{\sigma}^j_{3i}}{\hat{\sigma}^j_{3i}}}_i + (1 - \hat{d}^j_i)\hat{X}^{j \frac{\hat{\sigma}^j_{3i} - 1}{\hat{\sigma}^j_{3i} - 1}}_\ell \right]^{\frac{\hat{\sigma}^j_{3i}}{\hat{\sigma}^j_{3i} - 1}}, \qquad (A9.34)$$

$$i = 1,...2; \ \ell = i + 2; j = 1,...4$$

where $\hat{\sigma}^j_1$, $\hat{\sigma}^j_2$, and $\hat{\sigma}^j_{3i}$ are elasticity parameters in region j, and $\hat{a}^j$ $\hat{d}^j$, and $\hat{b}^j_i$ are share parameters, with $\Sigma \hat{b}^j_i = 1$.

The budget constraint for the single agent in each region is

$$\sum_{i=1}^{4} P^j_{X_i} \hat{X}^j_i + \hat{A}^j = \sum_{i=1}^{4} P^j_{X_i} X^j_i + A^j + R^j + Q^j, \quad j = 1,...4 \qquad (A9.35)$$

where R^j are tariff revenues collected in region j and Q^j is the value of quota premia received on exports by region j, reflecting transfers of quota rents from developed countries.[3] Tariff rates t^j_i apply to imports of product category i by developed country j.

Maximizing equation (A9.32) subject to equations A9.33, A9.34, and A9.35, yields the demand functions

$$\hat{T}^j = \frac{I^j}{Z^j + \hat{P}^j_T}, \quad j = 1,...4 \qquad (A9.36)$$

$$\hat{A}^j = I^j - \hat{P}^j_T \hat{T}^j, \quad j = 1,...4 \qquad (A9.37)$$

$$\hat{C}^j_i = \frac{\hat{b}^{j \hat{\sigma}^j_2}_i (I^j - \hat{A}^j)}{\hat{P}^{j \hat{\sigma}^j_2}_{C_i} \left[\sum_{\ell=1}^{2} \hat{b}^{j \hat{\sigma}^j_2}_\ell \hat{P}^{j 1 - \hat{\sigma}^j_2}_{C\ell} \right]}, \quad i = 1,...2; j = 1,...4 \qquad (A9.38)$$

and

---

[3] In our model, revenue and quota rents are separately identified, because for the developed country's importers tariff revenues are positive and quota rents are zero, and for the exporting regions the opposite is true.

$$\hat{X}_i^j = \frac{\hat{a}_i^{j\hat{\sigma}_{3_i}}\left(\hat{P}^j - \hat{A}^j - \sum_{m \neq i} \hat{P}_{Cm}^j \hat{C}_m^j\right)}{\hat{P}_{X_i}^{j\hat{\sigma}_{3_i}}\left[\hat{a}_i^{j\hat{\sigma}_{3_i}} P_{X_i}^{j\,1-\hat{\sigma}_{3_i}} + (1-\hat{a}_i^j)^{\hat{\sigma}_{3_i}} P_{X\ell}^{j\,1-\hat{\sigma}_{3_i}}\right]}, \tag{A9.39}$$

$$i = 1,...2;\ \ell = i + 2;\ m = 1,...2;\ j = 1,...4$$

where

$$\hat{P}^j = \sum_{i=1}^{4} P_{X_i}^j X_i^j + A^j + R^j + Q^j,\quad j = 1,...4 \tag{A9.40}$$

$$\hat{Z}^j = \left(\frac{\hat{P}_T^j \hat{a}_i^j}{1-\hat{a}_i^j}\right)^{\hat{\sigma}_i},\quad j = 1,...4 \tag{A9.41}$$

$\hat{P}_T^j$ is the consumer price in region j for the composite textile and apparel product $\hat{T}^j$,

$$\hat{P}_T^j = \left[\sum_{i=1}^{7} \hat{b}_i^{j\hat{\sigma}_2} \hat{P}_{Ci}^{j\,1-\hat{\sigma}_2}\right]^{\frac{1}{1-\hat{\sigma}_2}},\quad j = 1,...4 \tag{A9.42}$$

and $\hat{P}_{Ci}^j$ are the consumer prices in region j for the four textile and apparel composites $\hat{C}_{Ci}^j$,

$$\hat{P}_{Ci}^j = \left[\hat{a}_i^{j\hat{\sigma}_{3_i}} P_{X_i}^{j\,1-\hat{\sigma}_{3_i}} + (1-\hat{a}_i^j)^{\hat{\sigma}_{3_i}} P_{X\ell}^{j\,1-\hat{\sigma}_{3_i}}\right]^{\frac{1}{1-\hat{\sigma}_{3_i}}}, \tag{A9.43}$$

$$i = 1,...2,\ \ell = i + 2;\ j = 1,...4$$

Trade. Each region's trade in the four product categories and in the composite other good is given by the difference between production and consumption. Thus, for each of the four product categories, imports under product category i by developed country k from region j, M_i^{kj}, summed over supplying regions minus exports under product category i by k to developed country n, E_i^{kn}, summed over developed countries, are given by

$$\sum_{j=1}^{4} M_i^{kj} - \sum_{n=1}^{2} E_i^{kn} = \hat{X}_i^k - X_i^k,\quad i = 1,...4;\ k = 1,...2 \tag{A9.44}$$

and exports by developing region j to developed country k, $E_i^{jk}\ (= M_i^{kj})$, summed over developed countries, are

$$\sum_{k=1}^{2} E_i^{jk} = X_i^j - \hat{X}_i^j,\quad i = 1,...4;\ j = 3,...4 \tag{A9.45}$$

Exports by developed country k to developing region j of the E_A^{kj}, summed over developing regions, equal the difference between production and consumption in the developed country, that is,

$$\sum_{j=3}^{4} E_A^{ki} = A^k - \hat{A}^k, \quad k = 1,...2 \tag{A9.46}$$

and imports by developing region j from developed country k, M_A^{jk} ($= E_A^{kj}$), summed over developed countries, equal desired imports by country j, that is,

$$\sum_{k=1}^{2} M_A^{jk} = \hat{A}^j - A^j, \quad j = 3,...4 \tag{A9.47}$$

In equilibrium, net trades in all products sum to zero across all countries.

Imports of the four textile and apparel products by the developed countries also have to satisfy the constraints implied by their bilateral quotas:

$$M_i^{kj} \leq \bar{B}_i^{kj}, \quad i = 1,...2; j = 3,...4; k = 1,...2 \tag{A9.48}$$

where $\bar{B}_i^{kj}$ are the quotas on imports of product category i by developed country k from developing region j. These bilateral quotas have the effect of segmenting national markets in restricted exporting regions such that different domestic prices will apply for each of the two restricted product categories. In applying the model, we calibrate it to a data set in which developed country quotas are assumed to be binding, and then examine alternative counterfactual situations in which quotas are removed.

Equilibrium. Equilibrium in the model is given by a set of regional prices for the four product categories relative to the price of the composite other good, and revenue and quota rents for each region ($P_{X_i}^{*j}$, R^{*j}, Q^{*j}) such that

1. Markets clear for the four product categories

$$\sum_{j=1}^{4} \hat{X}_i^j = \sum_{j=1}^{4} X_i^j, \quad i = 1,...4 \tag{A9.49}$$

2. Markets clear for the composite other good

$$\sum_{j=1}^{4} \hat{A}^j = \sum_{j=1}^{4} A^j \tag{A9.50}$$

3. The government budget is balanced in each developed country (that is, tariff revenues collected on imports equal revenues disbursed on the demand side of the economy).

$$R^{*j} = \sum_{j=1}^{4} t_i^j P_{X_i}^j \max(0, \hat{X}_i^j - X_i^j), \quad j = 1,...2 \tag{A9.51}$$

4. Quotas are binding

$$M_i^{kj} \leq \bar{B}_i^{kj}, \quad i = 1,...4; j = 3,...4; k = 1,...2 \tag{A9.52}$$

5. Income from quota rents assumed when evaluating demands equals that transferred by the developed countries to each exporting region

$$Q^{*j} = \sum_{k=1}^{2} \sum_{i=1}^{4} q_i^{ki} P_{X_i} \bar{B}_i^{kj}, \quad j = 3,...4 \tag{A9.53}$$

where q_i^{kj} is the quota premia rate on imports of product category i by developed country k from region j.

The model is solved using MPS/GE [Rutherford (1989)].

Appendix B: Data, Model Parameterization, and Elasticity Parameter Values

The Steel Model

To determine parameter values for the demand, production, and transformation functions in this model, we use calibration procedures similar to those used in other applied general equilibrium models [see Mansur and Whalley (1984)]. We employ a 1986 multicountry microconsistent equilibrium data set capitalized to reflect a 40-year stationary state and provide a 40-year time horizon for labour reallocation decisions. We discount the stream of incomes and expenditures in our 1986 data set over the 40-year time horizon using a discount rate of 5 percent. In using this procedure, we make the strong assumption that there is no growth within the period.

A number of data sources are used in assembling this data set. Data on labour income, value added, and value of production in U.S. steel-producing and steel-consuming industries are taken from United Nations (1989). The value of production of other goods in the United States is calculated by subtracting the value of production of steel-producing and steel-consuming products from GDP in the United States Data on GDP in the United States and labour income in the other goods industry in the United States is from United Nations (1990).

For the composition of inputs used in the U.S. steel-producing industry, we use input-output data from U.S. Department of Commerce (1984). All three commodities produced in the United States are used as intermediate inputs in production by the U.S. steel-producing industry. In the model, only steel and other goods are taken to be intermediate inputs in the U.S. steel-consuming industry.

The cost of steel used in producing steel-consuming products in the U.S. is given as the residual between value of production plus imports of steel and the cost of steel used in the steel-producing industry. The cost of other goods required to produce steel-consuming products in the United States is given by residual.

Data on the value of production of steel-producing products in Mexico and Canada are taken from United Nations (1989) as is data for value of production of steel-consuming products in Canada. Data on the value of production of steel-consuming products in Mexico is taken from UNIDO (1987a). Data on the value of production of steel-producing and steel-consuming products in

ROA is not readily available, so we use a GDP-weighted average of the shares of iron and steel and other manufacturing gross output in GDP in the countries comprising ROA for which data is readily available and assume that they reflect the shares of iron and steel and other manufacturing gross output in GDP in ROA. GDP in ROA is estimated as the sum of the GDPs in all the countries comprising ROA. Data on GDP by country is from United Nations (1989), while data on gross output is from United Nations (1990). The value of production of other goods in ROA is given by subtracting the value of production of steel-producing and steel-consuming products from GDP in ROA.

Data on the value of net U.S. imports of steel-consuming products by country of origin are from the U.S. Department of Commerce (1988), while data on U.S. imports of steel-producing products by country of origin is from USITC (1989a). External sector balance conditions are used to calculate the value of trade in all other goods in each country. For each model product in each country, the value of consumption is determined as the residual between value of production and net trade.

To analyze counterfactual equilibria in which adjustment costs occur with this data, we also need to specify what it would cost in the United States to move one worker from one industry to another. We assume that all workers laid off due to an elimination of VRAs on steel would, on average, be out of work for the same period, and we use Bale's (1976) estimate of 31 weeks as the duration of unemployment for import-impacted workers. We assume that labour time (unemployment) is the only component of adjustment costs. Thus, workers compare the discounted present value of the income differential from relocation to once-and-for-all adjustment costs in making their decisions to move between industries.

The unit cost of production (supply price) of the steel-producing commodity in Canada and the unit cost of production of the steel-consuming commodity in Mexico, ROA, and Canada can be approximated by the U.S. price minus the tariff. Data on the tariff rate on the steel-producing commodity is taken from Tarr and Morkre (1984), whereas the tariff rate on the steel-consuming commodity is approximated by the average tariff rate on manufactures, taken from Schott (1989).

Problems, however, arise when we try to estimate supply prices of the steel-producing commodity in quota-restrained regions, which in the model include Mexico and ROA. These are important because they will determine the assumed severity of trade barriers in the United States. However, quota price data is currently not available, so data on unit costs of production of the steel-producing commodity are needed to calculate supply prices in the quota-restrained regions in the model. To estimate the unit cost of production of the steel-producing commodity in ROA, we take a trade-weighted average of the unit costs of production across all the countries comprising ROA. This data, however, is only readily available for a few of the countries comprising ROA, including Japan, Germany, United Kingdom, France, South Korea, and Brazil. If we adopt a units convention that defines physical units for all goods as those amounts that, in equilibrium, sell in the United States for $1, then supply prices of these countries can be calculated as the ratio of the exporting country's relative unit costs compared to the United States. Data on unit costs of production are from USITC (1989b).

We use an indirect method of estimating unit costs of production in the other countries comprising ROA. We assume that the unit costs can be approximated by the ratio of the exporting country's relative wage rate in the steel-producing industry compared to the United States. We apply a further correction for the relative efficiency of labour and product quality across countries by also multiplying by each country's relative value of gross output per worker in the steel-producing industry compared to the United States. Value of gross output per worker is given by dividing wages per employee by wages in value added and then dividing by value added in gross output. Data on wages per employee, value added in gross output, and wages in value added in the steel-producing industry in each country are from UNIDO (1985). The supply price of the steel-producing commodity in Mexico is calculated in a similar manner.

We also need to specify substitution elasticities that appear in the transformation, production, and utility functions in the model. The substitution elasticity in production for the steel-producing commodity in the United States is taken from Heckman (1978) as reported in Tarr (1989). For production of the steel-consuming commodity in the United States, the substitution elasticity is approximated by the arithmetic average of elasticities for individual manufacturing industries, reported separately in Piggott and Whalley (1985). The elasticity in production for the all-other-goods commodity in the United States is approximated by the arithmetic average of elasticities for agriculture, mining, other consumer goods, and traded services, reported separately in Tarr (1989). An elasticity value of unity is used for the output transformation functions in Mexico, ROA, and Canada. We assume a Cobb-Douglas specification for the preference functions in all countries in the model, which is equivalent to setting these elasticities to unity. Because of the potentially crucial nature of these elasticity values for model behavior, we use these values as our central set of values around which sensitivity analyses are later performed.

Once constructed, the benchmark equilibrium data set is used to generate parameter values for the transformation, production, and demand equations of our model. The requirement placed on these parameter values is that they be capable of replicating the benchmark data set as an equilibrium solution to the model, given extraneous estimates of elasticities of substitution.

The calibration procedures used involve first the decomposition of the

benchmark transactions data represented in value terms into separate obser-
vations on equilibrium prices and quantities. As noted above, a units convention is adopted that defines physical units for all commodities as those amounts
that in equilibrium sell in the United States for a price of $1. The assumption
that marginal revenue products of factors are equalized in all uses in the benchmark equilibrium permits a similar physical concept to also be used for all
factors, defining a unit of labour to be that receiving a dollar of income in the
prechange equilibrium. Once elasticity values have been selected, share parameters for the demand, production, and transformation functions in the
model can be determined from the price and quantity data and the assumption
of agent optimization in each country [see Mansur and Whalley (1984)].

The Textile and Apparel Model

We calibrate the textile and apparel model to a multicountry microconsistent equilibrium data set we have constructed for 1986, which we aug-
ment by values of elasticities of transformation and substitution. A number of
data sources are used in assembling this data set. Data on the value of imports,
by MFA product category and country of origin, are from the U.S. Department
of Commerce (1987a, 1987b, 1987c) and Canadian Department of External
Affairs (unpublished data, 1987).[4] The major problem we had with this data
in our earlier work [see Trela and Whalley (1990)] was that it was difficult to
make comparisons across countries because of the different textile and apparel
categories used in administering quotas in each country or region. Because no
such cross-country data set existed, we constructed an as-close-as-possible 14-
good cross-country data set to produce trade data under the different aggregated MFA quota categories used in the model.[5] Applying the model to U.S.-
Mexican trade issues, however, has made solving for an equilibrium in the
model more difficult due to the large dimensionality of the problem. To solve
this problem, we have reduced the dimensionality of the model by aggregating
the 14 textile and apparel products in the model into four aggregate categories.
For the same reason, we have also aggregated the number of supplying developing countries in the model into two regions – Mexico and a 33-country

---

[4] In using this data, we assume that all bilateral quotas were fully binding in the year in
question.

[5] In order to capture trade diversion effects between developed countries due to their
joint bilateral quotas on exports by developing countries, we had to allocate interdeveloped country trade between quota-restricted and unrestricted products. Otherwise,
based on the level of aggregation used in our model, all interdeveloped country trade
would be in unrestricted products, and trade diversion effects would not be property
captured by the model. We assumed that for each developed country the distribution
between quota-restricted and unrestricted products in interdeveloped country trade was
the same as the distribution of the developed country's trade with the developing
countries in these products.

aggregate of the remaining supplying MFA countries, which we label as the rest of the agreement countries (ROA). Below we report on a number of data sources used in constructing the data set for use in calibrating this model.

Data on the value of production in the United States for textiles and apparel in separate aggregate categories are taken from the U.S. Department of Commerce (1987d), whereas data for Canada, Mexico, and the developing countries comprising the ROA are from the United Nations (1986).[6] The value of production of other goods in all regions in the model is given by subtracting the value of production of textiles and apparel from GDP in each region. GDP in ROA is estimated as the sum of the GDPs in all the countries comprising ROA. Data on GDP by country are from the World Bank (1986). External sector balance conditions are then used to calculate the value of trade in other goods in each region. For each model product in each region, the value of consumption is determined as the residual between value of production and trade.

Unit costs of production of the four textile and apparel aggregates in ROA are calculated in two steps, based on data used in the earlier model. First, in aggregating the 33 MFA countries that comprise ROA, new quota prices are calculated by taking production-weighted averages of quota prices in those countries. Second, in aggregating the 14 textile and apparel categories we used in the earlier model into the four textile and apparel categories we use in the new aggregated model, new quota prices are calculated by taking production-weighted averages of quota prices using the earlier data that fall within the categories used in the new model.

The data we used in estimating supply prices in the earlier model, however, was not free of problems. While the unit costs of unrestricted quota products could be approximated by the U.S. price minus the tariff, the problem with data arose when we tried to estimate supply prices of restricted quota products. These are central to any calculation of the impacts of developed country textile and apparel quotas, because they affect estimates of rent transfer per unit export.

Although quotas are freely traded in several exporting countries, comprehensive quota price data is only readily available for Hong Kong, and only limited quota price data is available for Taiwan. Hence, quota price data in a range of countries could not be used. Also, quotas are not necessarily allocated to the most efficient producers within countries, and so even if actual costs of current producers are known, the minimum potential unit cost for each textile and apparel product in the various countries remains unknown. In the earlier

---

[6] We were unable to obtain production data for some of the developing countries. In these cases trade data, along with estimates of mill consumption to export ratios obtained from FAO (1985) were used to calculate the value of production of each of the two aggregate textile and apparel product categories in each country.

model we therefore used an indirect method of estimating supply prices of quota restricted items in developing countries closely related to that used by Hamilton (1988).

We took a simple average of Hong Kong quota prices in 1983 and the first five months of 1984 for each of 15 apparel product categories exported by Hong Kong to the United States, based on calculations made by Hamilton (1986) and assumed them to reflect the quota prices for the 15 categories in 1984. This price data is given in Table 9.9. Hong Kong quota prices of the other MFA apparel products exported to the U.S. were calculated on the basis of an average of the quota prices given in Table 9.9. In aggregating the MFA apparel products in the U.S. into the six restricted apparel product categories we used in the earlier model, new quota prices were calculated by taking trade-weighted averages of quota prices using the Hamilton data that fall within the categories used in the model.

Quota prices for textile products from Hong Kong would appear to be significantly lower than for apparel, as quota restrictions are less severe. Because no data were available, we assumed quota prices on textile products to be one-half the average of quota prices for apparel products given in Table 9.9.[7]

The calculated quota prices in the earlier model, expressed as export tax equivalents, were then converted into import tariff equivalents[8] and used, along with data on tariff rates on U.S. imports of textiles and apparel obtained from GATT (1984), to calculate unit production costs in Hong Kong of each of the seven restricted product categories used in the model.

Our method of calculating production costs of quota-restricted items in other supplying countries in the earlier model was to assume that for each product category, the unit cost could be approximated by the unit cost in Hong Kong multiplied by the ratio of the supplying country's relative wage rate in textiles and apparel compared to Hong Kong. We applied a further correction for the relative efficiency of labour and product quality across countries by also multiplying by each country's relative value of gross output per worker in textiles and apparel compared to Hong Kong. This made a large difference to estimated supply prices.[9] Value of gross output per worker is given by dividing wages per employee by wages in value added and then dividing by value added in gross output. Data on wages per employee, value added in gross output, and

---

[7] This is consistent with Cline (1987), who assumes that the tariff equivalent of textile quotas has averaged 15 percent increment beyond tariff protection since 1981 and some 25 percent on apparel.

[8] U.S. export tax equivalents are converted into import tariff equivalents by multiplying by the ratio of f.o.b. and c.i.f. values of clothing imported from Hong Kong. (The f.o.b./c.i.f. ratio is approximately 0.39.) See Hamilton (1986).

[9] Hamilton (1988) analyzes these differences between Hong Kong, Taiwan, and South Korea and concludes they are small and can be ignored. Here, with 34 supplying countries, these factors become considerably more important.

Table 9.9. *Hong Kong Quota Prices[1] for Selected Apparel Items Exported to the U.S. from Hamilton (1986)*

Category Description	Number	1984[2]
Men's cotton jacket	333/334	19
Ladies' cotton jacket	335	27
Cotton Knit shirt and blouse	338/339	50
Men's cotton woven shirt	340	38
Ladies cotton woven shirt	341	36
Ladies cotton woven skirt	342	37
Cotton knit sweater	345	59[4]
Men's cotton pant	347	50
Ladies cotton pant	348	63
Ladies wool knit blouse	438	19
Wool knit sweater	445/446	120
Men's MMF jacket[3]	663/634	23[4]
Ladies' MMF shirt[3]	635	15[4]
MMF Knit shirt and blouse[3]	638/639	27
Men's MMF woven shirt[3]	640	64[4]
Ladies' MMF woven blouse[3]	641	58[5]
Ladies' MMF pant	648	!![5]
Average[6]		42

n.a.: not available
[1] As a percent of export price.
[2] Average over the period January 1983 to May 1984.
[3] MMF = man-made fibres.
[4] January to May 1984 only.
[5] January to December 1983 only.
[6] From the proportion of total rent to total export value inclusive of total rent.

wages in value added for textiles and apparel are from UNIDO (1985). The resulting average supply prices of quota-restricted products by country, both adjusted and unadjusted for differences in labour productivity and product quality, for 1984 are presented in Table 9.10. As can be seen, the correction for labour productivity and product quality makes a very large difference to these estimates, as large as a factor of ten in some cases. The value of quota rents received by each of the developing countries is calculated by using the supply prices of quota-restricted products by country and the trade data by model product category by country.

The modified model also requires elasticity values for transformation surfaces and preferences in each country. For the bottom level of nesting, assumed values of -0.50 and 5.0 are used for all pairwise nests between comparable restricted and unrestricted commodities and in all countries. Given that there are no literature estimates to guide the choice of these values, we justify our specification as follows. An assumption of smooth substitutability in production between comparable restricted and unrestricted commodities would not be appropriate, because there would be no effect of the quotas. Therefore, a

Table 9.10. *Calculated Average Supply Prices of Quota Restricted Textiles and Apparel by Country, 1984 (all prices are expressed relative to U.S. supply prices of unity)*

Exporting Country	Adjusted for differences in labour productivity and product quality 1984	Unadjusted for differences in labour productivity and product quality 1984
Bangladesh	0.31	0.04
Brazil	0.25	0.25
Bulgaria	0.55	0.31
China	0.46	0.09
Columbia	0.39	0.26
Czechoslovakia	0.56	0.31
Costa Rica	0.51	0.44
Dominican Republic	0.56	0.26
Egypt	0.49	0.13
Guatemala	0.49	0.25
Haiti	0.46	0.11
Hong Kong	0.56	0.56
Hungary	0.44	0.17
India	0.46	0.07
Indonesia	0.42	0.07
Korea	0.41	0.32
Macau	0.49	0.50
Malaysia	0.38	0.16
Mauritius	0.42	0.13
Mexico	0.49	0.52
Nepal	0.46	0.04
Pakistan	0.46	0.09
Panama	0.56	0.39
Peru	0.49	0.25
Philippines	0.51	0.10
Poland	0.55	0.31
Romania	0.49	0.55
Singapore	0.52	0.45
Sri Lanka	0.46	0.10
Taiwan	0.49	0.49
Thailand	0.49	0.16
Turkey	0.27	0.30
Uruguay	0.52	0.53
Yugoslavia	0.48	0.38

Source: Based on data from Hamilton (1986) and methods described in the text.

low elasticity value is used for all regions, implying a limited ability to substitute products on the supply side. In contrast, a high degree of substitutability is assumed on the demand side of the model. This has some claim to plausibility because from the consumers, point of view the relative difference in product characteristics is small.

For both the developed and developing regions, we assume a Cobb-Douglas specification for both transformation and preference functions at the top two levels, which is equivalent to setting all these elasticities to unity. Because of the potentially crucial nature of these elasticity values for model behavior, we use these as our central set of elasticity values around which sensitivity analyses are performed. The calibration procedures used to generate the parameter values for the model involve first decomposing the data represented in value terms into separate price and quantity data. This is done through a units convention that defines physical units for all commodities as those amounts that in equilibrium sell in the United States for $1. Hence, domestic prices in developing regions for quota-restricted items are less than $1, and domestic prices in Canada are less than, greater than, or equal to $1, depending upon the direction of trade. Once elasticity values have been selected, share parameters for the CES and CET functions in the model are given from the price and quantity data and the assumption of agent optimization in each country [see Mansur and Whalley (1984)].

Endnotes

1. See also Hirojosa-Ojeda and Robinson (1991) for further numerical general equilibrium analysis of U.S.-Mexico trade liberalization.

2. In the paper we will use the terms *textiles* and *textiles and apparel* interchangeably.

3. See also the more general discussion of U.S.-Mexico trade issues in Reifman (1991).

4. During the September 1984 to 1989 period, Mexico agreed to limit its exports to 0.49 percent of U.S. apparent consumption (AC). Under a renewal agreement, Mexico is limited to 0.95 percent of AC in the initial period (October 1989 to December 1990) and 1.1 percent in the remainder (through March 1992).

5. Under HTS item 9802.00.80, formerly known as TSUS item 807.00, imported articles assembled wholly or partly with U.S. fabricated components are assessed duty only on the value added abroad.

6. The first sectoral accord actually covered both steel (the Steel Agreement) and alcoholic beverages (the Alcoholic Beverages Agreement).

7. Under the 1985 agreement (which became effective in February but was retroactive to September 1984), Mexico (along with six other major steel-exporting countries) agreed to limit its steel shipments to a specified share of the U.S. market for a five-year period (for more information on these shares, see note 4).

8. For more information on Mexico's export quotas under the new agreement, see note 4.

9. Mexico currently has a requirement for procurement of Mexican-made materials for Mexican government projects and by parastatal firms.

10. See USITC (1990a), p. 2-6, footnote 49.

11. USITC (1989b), Table I-2.

12. We note that Hong Kong's quota utilization rates in apparel are less than 100 percent, but quota rights are traded at positive prices.

13. The four textile and apparel products categories in the model involve two aggregate categories of restricted textiles and apparel and two comparable aggregate categories of unrestricted textiles and apparel. This approach of dividing textile and apparel aggregates into restricted and unrestricted categories is employed because despite the MFA, significant volumes of trade in textiles and apparel take place in unrestricted quota categories. Consequently, when we aggregate the MFA categories into two aggregate categories of textiles and apparel used in the model, we find for several of the supplying countries many of the quota categories in the aggregates for which the country has no quotas and other categories for which it does. We deal with this problem in the model by further dividing the textile and apparel aggregates into restricted and unrestricted quota categories. Also, we make an assumption of qualitative differences between comparable restricted and unrestricted categories. Otherwise, if products in unrestricted categories are treated

as perfect substitutes for restricted quota products, then in a competitive model countries would substitute costlessly into MFA products not subject to quota.

14. This structure differs from that of our earlier model [Trela and Whalley (1990)], which consists of three major developed country importers, the United States, Canada and the EEC; 34 developing country exporters, 14 specific textile and apparel product categories; and one composite other good (residual GDP); the 14-commodity level of aggregation reflects the constraints implied by generating as close as comparable cross-country data sets as possible to cover trade under the different MFA quota categories used by the United States, Canada, and the EEC. The structural difference reflects the difficulty in solving the earlier model for the analysis of U.S.-Mexican trade policy issues due to the large dimensionality of the problem. To solve this problem, we reduced the dimensionality by aggregating the number of countries in the model into four trading regions (with the EEC not included) and the number of textile and apparel product categories to four.

15. The earlier version of the model specified only two regions: the United States and the rest of the world (ROW), the latter representing an aggregate of 20 VRA countries and Canada (the largest non-VRA supplier). To apply this model to the analysis of U.S.-Mexican trade policy issues, both Mexico and Canada are separated from the 21-country aggregate and treated individually in the model.

16. This industry represents other nonsteel manufacturing industries.

17. The original steel model was developed for the purpose of evaluating the pitfalls in modeling labour-adjustment costs from trade policy shocks.

18. Because we do not use the Armington assumption of product heterogeneity by country, we are unfortunately not able to utilize the detailed product category estimates of elasticities of trade substitution for analysis of North American free trade options produced by Reinert and Shiells (1991).

19. Because adjustment costs are endogenously determined in the steel model, welfare effects reported in Table 9.3 are net of adjustment costs.

References

Bale, M.D. 1976. "Estimates of trade-displacement costs for U.S. workers." *Journal of International Economics* 6:245–50.

Brown, D.K. 1987. "Tariffs, the terms of trade, and national product differentiation." *Journal of Policy Modelling* 9:503–26.

Canada, Department of Finance. 1990. "Canada and a Mexico-United States trade agreement." Working paper, Ottawa.

Clarete, R.L., I. Trela, and J. Whalley. 1991. "Pitfalls in evaluating labour adjustment costs from trade shocks: Illustrations for a removal of U.S. trade restraints on steel using an applied general model with transactions costs." Centre for the Study of International Economic Relations, University of Western Ontario, London, Canada.

Cline, W.R. 1987. *The future of world trade in textiles and apparel.* Washington, D.C.: Institute for International Economics.

Erzan, R., J. Goto, and P. Holmes. 1990. "Effects of the Multi-Fibre Arrangement on developing countries' trade: An empirical investigation." In *Textiles trade and the developing countries: Eliminating the Multi-Fibre Arrangement in the 1990s,* edited by Carl B. Hamilton. Washington, D.C.: World Bank.

Food and Agricultural Organization of the United Nations (FAO). 1985. *World apparel fibre consumption survey.*

General Agreement on Tariffs and Trade (GATT). 1984. *Textiles and clothing in the world economy.* Background study prepared by the GATT Secretariat to assist work undertaken by the contracting parties in pursuance of the decision on textiles and clothing taken at the November 1982 ministerial meeting, Geneva, Switzerland.

Hamilton, C. 1986. "An assessment of voluntary restraints on Hong Kong exports to Europe and USA." *Economica* 53.

_____. 1988. "Restrictiveness and international transmission of the 'New' protectionism." In *Issues in U.S.-EC trade relations*, edited by R. Baldwin, C. Hamilton, and A. Sapir. National Bureau of Economic Research and University of Chicago Press.

Heckman, J. 1978. "An analysis of the changing pattern of iron and steel production in the twentieth century." *American Economic Review* 68:123–33.

Hinojosa-Ojeda, R., and S. Robinson. 1991. "Alternative scenarios of U.S.-Mexico integration: A computable general equilibrium approach." Working Paper no. 609, Department of Agricultural and Resource Economics, Division of Agriculture and Natural Resources, University of California.

Mansur, A., and J. Whalley. 1984. "Numerical specification of applied general equilibrium models: Estimation, calibration and data." In *Applied general equilibrium analysis*, edited by H. Scarf and J. Shoven. Cambridge: Cambridge University Press.

Piggott, J., and J. Whalley. 1985. *UK tax policy and applied general equilibrium analysis*. Cambridge: Cambridge University Press.

Reifman, A. 1991. *A North American free trade area? A brief review of the major issues*. Report No. 91-418 RCO. Washington, D.C.: Congressional Research Service.

Reinert, K.A., and C.R. Shiells. 1991. "Trade substitution elasticities for analysis of a North American free trade area." U.S. International Trade Commission and U.S. Department of Labor, Washington, D.C.

Rutherford, T. 1989. "General equilibrium modelling with MPS/GE." Department of Economics, University of Western Ontario, London, Canada.

Schott, J.J., ed. 1989. *Free trade areas and US trade policy*. Washington, D.C.: Institute for International Economics.

Shoven, J., and J. Whalley. 1984. "Applied general equilibrium models of taxation and international trade." *Journal of Economic Literature* 22:1007–51.

Tarr, D.T. 1989. *A general equilibrium analysis of the welfare and employment effects of U.S. quotas in textiles, autos and steel*. Bureau of Economics Staff Report to the Federal Trade Commission, Washington, D.C.

Tarr, D.T., and M.E. Morkre. 1984. *Aggregate costs to the United States of tariffs and quotas on imports: General tariff cuts and removal of quotas on automobiles, steel, sugar, and textiles*. Bureau of Economics Staff Report to the Federal Trade Commission, Washington, D.C.

Trela, I., and J. Whalley. 1990. "Global effects of developed country trade restrictions on textiles and apparel." *Economic Journal* 100:1190–1205.

United Nations. 1986. *Industrial statistics yearbook 1984*, vol. 1: General industrial statistics. New York.

_____. 1989. *Industrial statistics yearbook 1987*, vol. 1: General industrial statistics. New York.

_____. 1990. *National accounts statistics: Main aggregates and detailed tables, 1987*. New York.

United Nations Industrial Development Organization (UNIDO). 1985. *Handbook of industrial statistics 1984*. New York.

_____. 1987a. *Industry and development: Global report 1987*. Vienna.

_____. 1987a. *U.S. general imports of cotton manufactures* . TQ 2730, Washington, D.C.

_____. 1987b. *U.S. general imports of wool manufacture*. TQ 2740, Washington, D.C.

_____. 1987c. *U.S. general imports of man-made fiber manufactures*. TQ 2760, Washington, D.C.

_____. 1987d. *U.S. industrial outlook*. Washington, D.C.

_____. 1988. *United States trade: Performance in 1987.* Washington, D.C.

U.S. Department of Commerce. 1984. *Survey of current business.* Washington, D.C.

U.S. International Trade Commission (USITC). 1989a. "Monthly report on the status of the steel industry." USITC Publication 2162, Washington, D.C.

_____. 1989b. "The western U.S. steel market: Analysis of market conditions and assessment of the effects of voluntary restraint agreements on steel-producing and steel-consuming industries." USITC Publication 2165, Washington, D.C.

_____. 1990a. "Review of trade and investment liberalization measures by Mexico and prospects for future United States–Mexican relations: Phase I." USITC Publication 2275, Washington, D.C.

_____. 1990b. "Review of trade and investment liberalization measures by Mexico and prospects for future United States–Mexican relations: Phase II." USITC Publication 2326, Washington, D.C.

_____. 1990c. "Monthly report on the status of the steel industry." USITC Publication 2332, Washington, D.C.

_____. 1991. "The likely impact on the United States of a free trade agreement with Mexico." USITC Publication 2353, Washington, D.C.

World Bank. 1986. *World development report 1986.* New York: Oxford University Press.

PART IV

Dynamic Models

10

A Dynamic Dual Model of the North American Free Trade Agreement

Leslie Young
University of Texas, Austin

José Romero
El Colegio de México

I. Introduction

This paper develops a multiperiod, general equilibrium model of the Mexican economy to estimate the effects of NAFTA. The model assumes a small open economy that takes as given the world interest rate and prices of each traded industry (all except construction). The domestic interest rate is equal to the world rate plus a "risk-premium." For each traded good, the domestic price is equal to the world price plus a tariff percentage. In line with the classification in the "Sistema de Cuentas Nacionales de México," the model considers three capital goods industries (machines, buildings and vehicles) and nine consumption/intermediate goods activities (see Table 10.1).

The model has several features that make it particularly suitable for an analysis of the impact of NAFTA on the Mexican economy. Its construction involves the econometric estimation of 24 separate models (one unit cost function for the output and one unit cost function for physical capital in each industry).

An important feature of our model is that the dynamics of the response of the Mexican economy to changes in relative prices are based on intertemporal optimization by firms. This is especially important for simulations of trade liberalization, because expected future alterations in trade policies will have consequences for decisions in the present.

In the model, production takes place in two stages. In stage I, the representative firm in each sector produces two aggregates: (a) capital, using machines,

301

Table 10.1. *Industries*

1) **AGR**: agriculture, livestock, forestry, hunting and fisheries.
2) **MIN**: coal, iron minerals, non-ferrous metals minerals, stones, and other non-metallic minerals.
3) **OIL**: oil and gas extraction, oil refining, and basic petrochemicals.
4) **FOO**: processed food, beverages, and tobacco.
5) **TEX**: textiles, apparel, and leather products.
6) **CHE**: basic chemicals, fertilizers, resins, medicines, cleaning products, and other chemicals.
7) **MET**: iron and steel, non-ferrous metals, and metallic products.
8) **MAC**: electric and non-electric machinery.
9) **VEH**: automobile vehicles and parts, and other transportation equipment.
10) **BUI**: construction.
11) **SER**: electricity, retail, transport and communications, financial services, other services.
12) **MIS**: wood products, paper, rubber, non-metallic minerals products, and other industries.

Classification format: INEGI, "Sistema de Cuentas Nacionales de México."

buildings, and vehicles, and (b) materials, using various intermediate goods. In each period, the appropriate mix of capital goods used to produce the aggregate capital is that which minimizes the cost of production given that period's prices of the three capital goods. In a similar fashion, the appropriate mix of intermediate goods used to produce the materials is that which minimizes the cost of production given the nine intermediate goods prices. In stage II, the firm produces a single "product" using labor, capital, and materials. The product of each industry has different uses; it can be used as an intermediate good for the same or a different industry, it can be used to satisfy final demand, and sometimes it can be combined in different proportions to produce specific capital goods.

All producers seek to maximize profits. The choice variables in each period are labor, intermediate goods, and the level of investment. Labor and intermediate goods are selected to minimize costs, whereas the level of investment is selected such that producers reach their optimal capital intensity in the long-run (long-run profit maximization). The time required to reach the optimal intensity depends on the adjustment costs facing the economy to produce the nontraded capital goods (construction) needed for investment in each period.

The model assumes full employment and an exogenous annual rate of population growth of 2 percent. The amount of employment in 1989 was 22.4 million workers. At an annual rate of growth of the labor force of 2 percent, that figure is expected to reach 27.9 million by 2003. We find that, at the current real interest rate of 15 percent, the long-run effect of NAFTA is a 3.1 percent increase in Mexican gross domestic product (GDP) at world prices.

Table 10.2. *Average Ad Valorem Tariffs*

Sector:	Tariff:
1) AGR	13.38 %
2) MIN	9.75 %
3) OIL	9.36 %
4) FOO	14.00 %
5) TEX	16.15 %
6) CHE	11.22 %
7) MET	12.99 %
8) MAC	13.37 %
9) VEH	16.00 %
10) BUI (non tradable)	0.00 %
11) SER	0.00 %
12) MIS	11.90 %

Source: SECOFI, Secretaría de Comercio y Fomento Industrial.

The gains are significantly greater if NAFTA reduces real interest rates. If these fall to 12 percent, then gross domestic product increases by 11.9 percent in the long run.

Our estimates of the benefits from NAFTA are higher than estimates from existing static models. The reason could be as follows. The recent economic liberalization of Mexico has already led to a substantial reduction in tariffs. Because existing nominal rates of protection are quite low (see Table 10.2), removing these distortions leads only to minor gains in a model where both consumption and production losses from tariffs are essentially proportional to nominal rates of protection. In our model, the consumption losses from tariffs are likewise quite small (on the order of 0.25 percent of GDP). However, compared to partial equilibrium approaches, the rich structure of intersectoral flows in our model captures more of the distortionary impact of the existing tariff structure on the value added in various sectors. We therefore obtain higher estimates of the production losses arising from intersectoral discrepancies in *effective rates of protection* [Corden (1966, 1975)]. At the same time, the dynamic structue of our model allows us to capture effects missed by static AGE models. As explained in section XII, the high real interest rates prevailing in Mexico imply that tariffs on capital goods lead to particularly severe intersectoral discrepancies in effective rates of protection. Our model also captures additional gains from NAFTA from improved efficiency in input use within sectors and in the intertemporal allocation of resources within and across sectors.

Table 10.3. *Industry's Share of the Labor Force*

YEAR	AGR	MIN	OIL	FOO	TEX	CHE	MET	MAC	VEH	BUI	SER	MIS	Total
1970	34.4%	1.2%	0.6%	3.5%	2.7%	1.1%	1.4%	1.1%	0.6%	6.3%	44.2%	3.1%	100%
1971	34.5%	1.2%	0.5%	3.5%	2.7%	1.1%	1.2%	1.1%	0.6%	5.9%	44.6%	3.0%	100%
1972	33.0%	1.2%	0.5%	3.4%	2.7%	1.1%	1.2%	1.2%	0.6%	6.5%	45.5%	3.0%	100%
1973	32.8%	1.2%	0.5%	3.4%	2.7%	1.1%	1.2%	1.4%	0.7%	7.0%	45.3%	2.9%	100%
1974	30.6%	1.3%	0.5%	3.5%	2.7%	1.1%	1.3%	1.3%	0.7%	7.3%	46.8%	3.0%	100%
1975	30.3%	1.2%	0.5%	3.4%	2.5%	1.1%	1.3%	1.3%	0.7%	7.5%	47.5%	2.8%	100%
1976	28.6%	1.2%	0.5%	3.3%	2.4%	1.1%	1.3%	1.3%	0.7%	7.7%	48.9%	2.9%	100%
1977	30.0%	1.2%	0.5%	3.2%	2.4%	1.1%	1.2%	1.2%	0.6%	7.1%	48.6%	2.8%	100%
1978	28.9%	1.2%	0.5%	3.2%	2.3%	1.1%	1.3%	1.2%	0.7%	7.9%	49.0%	2.8%	100%
1979	26.7%	1.2%	0.5%	3.2%	2.4%	1.1%	1.3%	1.3%	0.7%	8.4%	50.3%	2.9%	100%
1980	25.9%	1.3%	0.6%	3.1%	2.4%	1.1%	1.3%	1.3%	0.7%	8.9%	50.5%	2.9%	100%
1981	27.0%	1.0%	0.4%	2.9%	2.1%	1.0%	1.1%	1.2%	0.9%	10.4%	49.4%	2.6%	100%
1982	26.2%	1.1%	0.1%	3.0%	2.1%	1.0%	1.1%	1.1%	0.8%	10.2%	50.8%	2.6%	100%
1983	27.9%	1.1%	0.4%	3.0%	2.0%	1.1%	1.0%	0.9%	0.7%	8.4%	51.2%	2.4%	100%
1984	27.5%	1.1%	0.5%	3.0%	1.9%	1.1%	1.0%	0.9%	0.7%	8.8%	51.1%	2.4%	100%
1985	27.6%	1.2%	0.5%	3.0%	1.9%	1.0%	1.0%	0.9%	0.8%	8.9%	50.8%	2.5%	100%
1986	27.3%	1.2%	0.5%	3.1%	1.9%	1.1%	0.9%	0.9%	0.7%	8.7%	51.2%	2.5%	100%
1987	27.6%	1.2%	0.5%	3.0%	1.9%	1.1%	0.9%	0.9%	0.7%	8.7%	50.9%	2.5%	100%
1988	27.6%	1.3%	0.5%	3.0%	1.8%	1.1%	0.9%	0.9%	0.8%	8.6%	51.0%	2.5%	100%
1989	26.8%	1.2%	0.5%	3.0%	1.8%	1.1%	0.9%	0.9%	0.8%	9.5%	50.9%	2.6%	100%

Source: INEGI, "Sistema de Cuentas Nacionales de México."

The experiments assume that each industry's share of the labor force can deviate from its current share by 30 percent either way. This assumption corresponds to the recent history of Mexico (see Table 10.3). Earlier models assumed perfect labor mobility yet estimated much smaller gains from NAFTA. In general, we found that when the gains from NAFTA are greater, the greater the deviations allowed in the structure of employment. Thus, the benefits from NAFTA to Mexico would be substantially enhanced by government policies that facilitate labor mobility, such as an expansion of educational opportunities.

The model predicts the effects of NAFTA, across the 12 sectors, in variables such as production, employment, capital stock, wages, rentals, and so on. As a point of reference for the simulations that follow, in Table 10.4 we present the observed values of those variables in 1989 (the last year for which the information is available).

II. The Dual Approach to Policy Modeling

The key innovation in our modeling technique is the consistent use of duality in a dynamic open economy model that extends the model of Young

Table 10.4. *Values in 1989*

Industry	GDP	Employment	Capital	Wage	Rentals
	(world prices)				
AGR:	33.229	5,999.24	* 29.722	1.16	978.42
MIN:	7.271	271.54	12.394	5.63	405.23
OIL:	12.917	111.50	137.191	21.42	45.60
FOO:	26.119	673.69	14.157	7.60	1,456.72
TEX:	10.847	408.59	3.617	8.28	1,914.14
CHE:	11.361	244.12	17.148	14.04	620.13
MET:	9.773	201.98	16.751	15.22	560.01
MAC:	7.469	207.46	7.721	13.94	733.15
VEH:	8.236	179.77	9.875	16.03	628.96
BUI:	25.097	2,133.20	2.137	5.35	2,873.03
SER:	316.164	11,398.67	169.459	6.83	1,097.82
MIS:	22.754	580.35	16.105	9.90	1,158.77
Total:	491.307	22,410.11	436.277		

GDP: Gross Domestic Product, billions of 1980 pesos.
Capital: Capital stock, hundred billions of 1980 pesos.
* Estimated.
Employment: Thousands of persons.
Wage: Millions of current pesos.
Rentals: Millions of current pesos per each hundred million units of capital.
Source: INEGI, "Sistema de Cuentas Nacionales de México."
Source: Banco de México, Acervos de Formación de Capital, Gerencia de Información Económica.
Source: SECOFI, Secretaría de Comercio y Fomento Industrial.

and Romero (1990). The monograph of Dixit and Norman (1980) established the dual approach as the standard method of presenting *theoretical* issues in international economics because of the clarity and economy that results when the first-order conditions for consumer and producer choice are impounded in the dual functions specifying their behavior. Duality also facilitates clarity and economy in *empirical* modeling of international issues. The dual approach to estimating a sector's production function and determining its factor demands via the cost function is well-known [see Bachrach and Mizrahi (1992)]. We go further by stating *all* the equilibrium conditions of the model in terms of the estimated cost functions. Because these cost functions incorporate the optimal intraperiod input choices of firms, this obviates the first-order conditions for these choices. In calculating the steady growth path of the economy, we also bypass the first-order conditions for output and investment by exploiting the intertemporal relationship between the price of capital and the stream of future rents from the capital. In calculating the transition to steady growth, we can again bypass the first-order conditions for output and investment by using the Second Fundamental Theorem of Welfare Economics and the maximization procedures built into the Brooke et al. (1988) computational package to duplicate market outcomes.

These techniques mean that our dynamic general equilibrium model does not require explicit computation of *any* first-order conditions. This sharply reduces the number of equations, yielding a compact, yet transparent, model that is readily computable.

III. Estimation of the Unit Cost Functions

For each sector, we have price indices both for the broad categories of labor, capital, and materials and for the outputs of each of the 12 sectors, including individual intermediate and capital goods. Labor and materials are used up in one period, but capital goods depreciate over time while receiving a rental from the profits of that sector. Of course, there is no way to impute rentals separately to the individual capital goods: machines m, buildings b (which includes all construction) and vehicles v. Nor do we have individual depreciation rates for these goods.

Given the form in which the data is available (see Tables 10.11–10.21 in Appendix A), it is natural to view production as taking place in two stages. In stage I, the representative sector i firm produces (a) a composite capital good K_i using machines, buildings, and vehicles and (b) a composite intermediate good M_i using various intermediate goods. In stage II, the firm produces good i using K_i, M_i, and labor L_i. The time t mix of capital goods m,b,v used to produce K_i is that minimizing the cost of production, given the time t prices p_{mt}, p_{bt}, p_{vt} of the three capital goods. The depreciation rate d_i of K_i comes directly from the data. The time t rental r_{it} on a unit of K_i equals the time t profits in sector i, divided by the amount of K_i that equals the time t value of sector i capital, divided by its price p_{iKt}. Thus

$$r_{it} = \frac{(\text{time } t \text{ profits} \cdot p_{iKt})}{(\text{time } t \text{ value of capital})} \tag{10.1}$$

All production functions are assumed to exhibit constant returns to scale. The unit cost function for K_i is assumed to be a translog function $C_{iK} (p_m, p_b, p_v)$ of the prices of the individual capital goods.

Because time series data for the composition of each intermediate good are not available, we couldn't estimate its unit cost function econometrically. We assumed that M_i is produced by a Cobb-Douglas production function so that its unit cost is a Cobb-Douglas function of the vector $p = (p_1,..,p_n)$ of intermediate goods prices:

$$C_{iM}(p) = f_i \, p_1^{s_{i1}} \, p_2^{s_{i2}} \cdots p_n^{s_{in}} \tag{10.2}$$

where s_{ij} is the share of intermediate good j in the total cost of the intermediate goods used in the production of good i. These shares are obtained from the input-output matrix. The constant f_i is chosen so that the price that emerges from equation 10.2 equals the price index of the composite intermediate good q_i in the base year (1980 = 1). Finally, the stage II production function of sector i is estimated indirectly from its unit cost function $C_i(w_i, r_i, q_i)$, which is assumed to be a translog function of the wage w_i, the rental r_i, and the price q_i of M_i.

IV. Input Demands

The unit cost function for good i as a function of the sector i wage and rental rate and the prices of individual intermediate goods can be obtained by substituting the unit cost function for intermediates estimated in stage Ib for the intermediate-goods price q_i into the cost function $C_i(w_i, r_i, q_i)$ estimated in stage II:

$$c_i(w_i, r_i, p) = C_i[w_i, r_i, C_{iM}(p)]$$

By the Shephard-Samuelson relations, the sector i demand for labor a_{iL}, the composite capital good a_{iK}, and the individual intermediate goods is obtained by differentiating c_i with respect to the corresponding price (or rental in the case of the capital). The demand A_{ik} for capital good k $(= m,b,v)$ per unit of the composite capital good K_i is obtained by differentiating C_{iK} with respect to p_{ik}. Thus, the sector i demand for capital good k per unit of output is

$$a_{ik}(w_i, r_i, p) \equiv a_{iK}(w_i, r_i, p) \, A_{ik}(p_m, p_b, p_v).$$

V. Stochastic Specification of the Cost Functions

To estimate the unit cost functions, we choose the transcendental logarithmic (or *translog*) function. Assuming constant returns to scale, exogenous factor prices w_i, r_i, and q_i, and imposing symmetry on the second-order partial derivatives, the translog cost function is given by

$$\ln c_i = a_{i0} + a_{iL}\ln w_i + a_{iK}\ln r_i + a_{iM}\ln q_i + \frac{1}{2}b_{iLL}(\ln w_i)^2$$

$$+ b_{iLK}(\ln w_i)(\ln r_i) + b_{iLM}(\ln w_i)(\ln q_i) + \frac{1}{2}b_{iKK}(\ln r_i)^2 \tag{10.3}$$

$$+ b_{iKM}(\ln r_i)(\ln q_i) + \frac{1}{2}b_{iMM}(\ln q_i)^2$$

Differentiating equation 10.3 with respect to the logs of the prices gives the cost share equations

$$s_{iL} = a_{iL} + b_{iLL} \ln w_i + b_{iLK} \ln r_i + b_{iLM} \ln q_i$$
$$s_{iK} = a_{iK} + b_{iLK} \ln w_i + b_{iKK} \ln r_i + b_{iKM} \ln q_i \qquad (10.4)$$
$$s_{iM} = a_{iM} + b_{iLM} \ln w_i + b_{iKM} \ln r_i + b_{iMM} \ln q_i$$

Because the shares must sum to unity, we have

$$s_{iL} + s_{iK} + s_{iM} = 1$$

and the bs sum to zero in each column (and row). Imposing the rowwise constraints on the bs in the three share equations gives the system

$$s_{iL} = a_{iL} + b_{iLL} \ln(w_i/q_i) + b_{iLK} \ln(r_i/q_i) \qquad (10.5)$$
$$s_{iK} = a_{iK} + b_{iLK} \ln(w_i/q_i) + b_{iKK} \ln(r_i/q_i)$$

To formulate an econometric model of the unit cost function, we add stochastic components to the system of equations for the cost shares (10.5):

$$s_{iL} = a_{iL} + b_{iLL} \ln(w_i/q_i) + b_{iLK} \ln(r_i/q_i) + \varepsilon_{iL} \qquad (10.6)$$
$$s_{iK} = a_{iK} + b_{iLK} \ln(w_i/q_i) + b_{iKK} \ln(r_i/q_i) + \varepsilon_{iK}$$

where ε_{iL} and ε_{iK} are unobservable random disturbances for the cost shares of the industry i. Because the cost shares for all inputs sum to unity for each industry, the random disturbances corresponding to the cost shares are not distributed independently. Therefore, the estimation method used was Zellner's (1962) Seemingly Unrelated Regressions (SUR) method, which computes estimates of the system of equations 10.6 using joint GLS. The translog unit cost functions for physical capital were estimated using the same procedure. The estimation results are presented in Table 10.5 and 10.6.

VI. Steady Growth

All models with a finite horizon T encounter the problem of modeling investment in capital goods that would not be fully depreciated until after year T. Our approach is to suppose that the time T capital stock and investment rates are at the levels corresponding to a *steady growth path*, where goods prices are steady but every sector's output, labor force, and capital stock expand at a fixed rate g so that factor returns and capital goods prices are steady also.

The steady growth rental r_i on a unit of capital in sector i satisfies

$$p_i = c_i(w_i, r_i, p) \quad i = 1,..,12 \qquad (10.7)$$

In equilibrium, the price of new sector i capital equals the unit cost of capital $c_{iK}(p_m, p_b, p_v)$; it also equals the present value of the rentals from that unit, future

Table 10.5. *Unit Cost Functions for Mexican Industries (parameter estimates, t-ratios in parentheses)*

Parameter	AGR	MIN	OIL	FOO	TEX	CHE	MET	MAC	VEH	CON	SER	MIS
a_{iL}	0.6166	0.4643	0.0040	0.2059	0.4283	0.1891	0.2483	0.3788	0.2084	0.5642	0.8246	0.3349
	(11.32)	(9.50)	(0.14)	(16.40)	(11.21)	(7.48)	(13.54)	(11.94)	(10.72)	(35.16)	(12.15)	(14.54)
a_{iK}	0.4809	0.3267	0.9421	0.1617	0.0911	0.2640	0.2485	0.0898	0.1685	0.1574	0.1907	0.1448
	(7.99)	(6.93)	(9.25)	(30.32)	(1.19)	(22.13)	(14.19)	(2.81)	(9.83)	(8.85)	(4.02)	(7.69)
b_{iLL}	0.1072	0.1222	0.0099	0.0513	0.1016	0.0678	0.1086	0.1361	0.0613	0.1088	0.2085	0.0941
	(7.82)	(4.93)	(1.07)	(10.03)	(8.93)	(6.16)	(10.15)	(6.30)	(5.97)	(20.20)	(7.93)	(8.74)
b_{iLK}	-0.0160	-0.0631	-0.0598	-0.0351	-0.0463	-0.0715	-0.0990	-0.1631	-0.0653	0.0041	-0.1170	-0.1106
	(-1.06)	(-2.49)	(-4.67)	(-16.62)	(-2.09)	(-13.50)	(-6.13)	(-6.51)	(-6.05)	(0.70)	(-6.44)	(-11.35)
b_{iKK}	0.0351	0.101	0.2775	0.1109	0.1281	0.1035	0.1895	0.2337	0.1085	0.0194	0.1465	0.1937
	(1.54)	(3.32)	(5.93)	(23.45)	(2.80)	(22.09)	(5.93)	(6.78)	(3.69)	(2.01)	(4.91)	(15.21)

Table 10.6. *Unit Cost Functions for Capital Goods in the Mexican Industries (parameter estimates, t-ratios in parentheses)*

Parameter	AGR	MIN	OIL	FOO	TEX	CHE	MET	MAC	VEH	CON	SER	MIS
a_{iL}	0.3453	0.4042	0.6868	0.3571	0.1774	0.2672	0.3441	0.3254	0.3251	0.1104	0.5330	0.2827
	(89.11)	(32.17)	(16.98)	(55.37)	(36.12)	(60.49)	(38.55)	(22.90)	(23.69)	(7.68)	(23.18)	(41.33)
a_{iK}	0.6045	0.5536	0.2763	0.5370	0.7952	0.7010	0.6230	0.6211	0.6078	0.8165	0.4286	0.6788
	(172.99)	(47.85)	(8.15)	(65.92)	(106.02)	(136.65)	(60.99)	(64.49)	(37.07)	(47.87)	(22.38)	(112.97)
b_{iLL}	-0.1562	-0.3215	0.2255	-0.1527	-0.0846	-0.1427	0.1843	-0.2687	-0.2165	-0.2232	-0.4679	-0.1561
	(-7.32)	(-4.713)	(1.01)	(-4.35)	(-3.50)	(-5.71)	(3.96)	(-3.33)	(-3.06)	(-3.05)	(-3.69)	(-4.18)
b_{iLK}	0.1037	0.3244	-0.2227	0.0081	0.0326	0.1742	-0.2634	0.1890	0.0487	0.2385	0.4180	0.1006
	(5.51)	(5.20)	(-1.20)	(0.21)	(0.96)	(7.03)	(-5.06)	(3.49)	(0.59)	(2.76)	(3.98)	(3.08)
b_{iKK}	-0.0386	-0.4375	0.2331	0.3009	0.0513	-0.0740	0.2678	-0.0590	0.1209	-0.4270	-0.3642	-0.0617
	(-1.99)	(-7.29)	(1.48)	(4.87)	(0.91)	(-1.83)	(4.21)	(-1.44)	(1.16)	(-4.09)	(-4.01)	(-2.11)

rentals being discounted at the real rate of interest i, plus the empirically observed depreciation rate d_i:

$$C_{iK}(p_m,p_b,p_v) = \Sigma_{t=1}\, r_i\,[(1-d_i)^{t-1}/(1+i)^t] = r_i/(i+d_i) \qquad (10.8)$$

The equilibrium condition for sector i labor is

$$a_{iL}[w_i,r_i,c_{iM}(p)]y_i = L_i \qquad (10.9)$$

where y_i stands for output in sector i. All goods except buildings are traded and therefore have their prices determined internationally once the trade policy is specified. The price of buildings, however, is determined by internal market-clearing conditions. Buildings are demanded by industry, individuals, and the government. In principle, it would be desirable to estimate private demand for buildings as a function of private income and to include this in the market-clearing conditions. However, there are insurmountable data problems because private housing demand responds to considerations that have fluctuated widely over the estimation period, such as the anticipated rate of inflation, the availability and the terms of finance, and the desire to hold wealth in a nontaxable form. Moreover, the government provides a significant portion of the housing stock, as well as all infrastructure that is included in the category "buildings." As industrial demand for construction has been a relatively stable proportion of the output of the construction industry, we shall suppose that, as a matter of social policy, the government targets the proportion of construction available to meet private and government demands. Our simulation sets this equal to the proportion that was observed in 1989, when the value of output in the construction industry was 500.3 billion pesos while industrial usage was 310.7 billion pesos. Thus, we set total demand for construction equal to industry demand multiplied by $F \equiv 500.3/310.7 = 1.61$. Of course, we can easily explore the implications of other values of F.

The steady growth stock of buildings in sector i is that implied by steady growth output:

$$a_{ib}(w_i, r_i, p)y_i$$

Steady growth investment in sector i buildings is that required to ensure that the stock of buildings grows at a rate g after depreciation d_i:

$$(g + d_i)a_{ib}(w_i, r_i, p)y_i$$

Thus, industry demand is $\sum_i (g + d_i)a_{ib}(w_i, r_i, p)y_i$, while total demand for buildings is assumed to be larger by a factor F. Thus, equilibrium in the market for new buildings requires that

$$F\sum_i (g + d_i)a_{ib}(w_i, r_i, p)y_i = y_b \tag{10.10}$$

There is no corresponding constraint on machines or vehicles because they are traded.

This model can be solved for steady growth outputs and factor returns. There are 12 sectors, including 3 capital-goods sectors. We assume that all goods (apart from buildings) are traded so that equations 10.7 and 10.8 comprise 24 equations in 25 unknowns (w_i, r_i for $i = 1, .., 12$, plus p_b, which is endogenously determined because buildings are nontraded). Equation 10.9 comprises 12 equations, and equation 10.10 comprises 1 equation, so we have 37 equations in 37 unknowns. Thus, with exogenously given labor forces, the model can be solved for steady growth outputs and factor returns.

VII. Optimization of the Sectoral Labor Forces Under Steady Growth

Instead of requiring the sectoral labor forces to grow exogenously at the rate g of population growth through the beginning of year T (the steady growth phase), we allow deviations within specified bounds (f_i, h_i) while forcing the *total* labor force to grow at the rate g. Thus, in solving for the steady growth path starting at time T, we impose these constraints:

$$(1 - f_i)(L_{io}/L) < L_{iT}(1 + g)^T L$$
$$< (1 + h_i)(L_{io}/L) \text{ and } \Sigma_i L_{iT} = (1 + g)^T L$$

and choose the L_{iT} to maximize steady growth gross domestic product (that is, domestic output net of input costs) *valued at domestic prices* in order to duplicate the effect of market choices in face of domestic prices. We then compare the steady growth value of gross domestic product (GDP) at *world* prices under free trade and under current tariffs. The next section provides a rigorous welfare interpretation of our empirical results.

VIII. Production and Consumption Gains from NAFTA

If a country practices free trade at world prices p and its GDP is r(p), then its welfare u^f is given by this income-expenditure identity:

$$e(p, u^f) = r(p) \tag{10.11}$$

where $e(.,.)$ is the country's expenditure function [Dixit and Norman (1980)]. If the country imposes a vector t of ad valorem tariffs and therefore faces internal prices $p_i = p_i(1 + t_i)$ for good i and its GDP at these prices is $r(p)$ while its tariff revenue is R, then its welfare u^t is given by this income-expenditure identity:

$$e(p, u^t) = r(p) + R. \tag{10.12}$$

Suppose that the expenditure function is multiplicatively separable (that is, consumer preferences are homothetic) with the form

$$e(p, u) = I(p)f(u)$$

where $I(p)$ is the exact consumer price index and $f(u)$ is "real income." Then the expenditure required to ensure free trade utility u^f at internal prices p is

$$e(p, u^f) = e(p, u^f)I(p)/I(p)$$
$$= r(p)I(p)/I(p) \quad \text{by equation 10.11} \tag{10.13}$$

Thus, a GDP of r(p) in face of world prices p yields the same welfare as a

GDP of $r(p)I(p)/I(\mathsf{p})$ in the face of tariff-ridden prices p. Thus, NAFTA increases domestic real income by the factor

$$f(u^f)/f(u^t) = e(p,u^f)/e(p,u^t) = r(\mathsf{p})/[r(p)+R] \cdot I(p)/I(\mathsf{p}) \qquad (10.14)$$
$$= \frac{r(\mathsf{p})}{\Sigma_i p_i y_i(p)} \cdot \frac{\Sigma_i p_i y_i(p)}{[r(p)+R]} \cdot I(p)/I(\mathsf{p})$$

For example, if this equals 1.09, then without NAFTA, a 9 percent increase in income would be needed to achieve the welfare level attainable under NAFTA.

Both production and consumption gains are included in this calculation. In equation 10.14, the term $r(\mathsf{p})/\Sigma_i p_i y_i(p)$ is the factor by which GDP increases as a result of NAFTA, when output is evaluated at world prices. This measures the *production gain* from NAFTA, that is, the increased value at world prices p of the country's output when internal producer choices are made facing world prices rather than the distorted prices obtaining under a tariff. In equation 10.14 the term $\Sigma_i p_i y_i(p)/[r(p)+R] \cdot I(p)/I(\mathsf{p})$ measures the *consumption gain* from NAFTA, the gain arising when internal consumer choices are made facing world prices rather than the distorted prices obtaining under a tariff so that consumer needs are met at a lower foreign exchange cost. Exploiting the homotheticity of consumer preferences, an elementary calculation (see appendix B) shows that

$$\frac{\Sigma_i p_i y_i(p)}{[r(\mathsf{p})+R]} = 1 - \frac{[\Sigma_i \gamma_i t_i}{(1+t_i)]} \qquad (10.15)$$

where γ_i is the share of consumer expenditure on good i. Equation 10.15 gives the impact of a unit increase in domestic expenditure on the foreign exchange cost of the goods consumed. This is less than 1 because some the expenditure increase is returned to the domestic economy as tariff revenue. Thus, the consumption gain from NAFTA increases welfare by the factor

$$\left[1 - \frac{\Sigma_i \gamma_i t_i}{(1+t_i)} \right] \cdot I(p)/I(\mathsf{p})$$

that is, the percentage consumption gain from NAFTA equals the percentage increase in the cost of living due to the tariffs minus the percentage of domestic expenditure that would be returned to the domestic economy as tariff revenue.

Cobb-Douglas preferences imply that the expenditure share γ_i on each good i is fixed and that the expenditure function has the form

$$e(p,u) = hp_1^{\gamma_1} p_2^{\gamma_2} \ldots p_n^{\gamma_n}$$

so the tariffs t_i increase the consumer price index by the factor

$$I(p)/I(\mathsf{p}) = (1+t_1)^{\gamma_1} (1+t_2)^{\gamma_2} \ldots .(1+t_n)^{\gamma_n}$$

Estimating Mexican demand parameters assuming Cobb-Douglas preferences, we find that NAFTA would reduce the cost of living by 3.59 percent, while 3.36 percent of domestic expenditure is returned to the Mexican economy as tariff revenue. Thus, the consumption gain from NAFTA is about 0.23 percent. This is very small compared to the production gains reported below, indicating that it is hardly worthwhile making more sophisticated estimates, for example, with more flexible functional forms or nonhomothetic preferences. Thus, we henceforth focus on production gains.

IX. Steady Growth Outcomes

The results in Table 10.7 were obtained for steady growth gross domestic product at world prices. The long-run effect of NAFTA is a substantial increase in Mexican gross domestic product, even at current real interest rates. The gains are even greater if NAFTA reduces Mexican real interest rates, as we would expect for the reasons given below in Section 11. Our analysis indicates that this could well be one of the most significant benefits of NAFTA to Mexico. These results assume that each sector's share of the labor force can deviate from its current share by 30 percent either way.

Table 10.7. *Effects of NAFTA on Steady Growth Mexican GDP at World Prices (billions of 1980 pesos)*

Sector:	A: Tariffs, i=15%	B: Free Trade, i=15%	C: Free Trade, i=12%	(B-A)/A %	(C-A)A %	(C-B)/B %
AGR:	32.69	32.51	33.4	-0.5	2.2	2.7
MIN:	5.54	5.5	5.7	-0.8	2.9	3.7
OIL:	27.78	25.25	33.77	-9.1	21.6	33.7
FOO:	39.03	35.63	38.93	-8.7	-0.2	9.3
TEX:	14.96	7.73	8.25	-48.3	-44.9	6.7
CHE:	15.92	15.46	18.18	-2.9	14.2	17.6
MET:	11.58	12.54	11.1	8.3	-4.2	-11.5
MAC:	11.47	10.54	11.67	-8.1	1.7	10.8
VEH:	8.95	11.26	10	25.8	11.7	-11.2
BUI:	47.53	37.75	49.57	-20.6	4.3	31.3
SER:	430.45	473.53	504.01	10.0	17.1	6.4
MIS:	29.86	29.01	31.49	-2.9	5.5	8.6
GDP:	675.76	696.71	756.08	3.1%	11.9%	8.5%

X. The Transition to Steady Growth

This section sets out the equations governing the transition to steady growth beginning at time T. At transition times $t = 0, \ldots, T-1$, the rental r_{it} on sector i capital satisfies

$$p_{it} = c_i(w_{it}, r_{it}, p_t) \qquad (10.16)$$

The equilibrium condition for sector i labor is

$$a_{iL}(w_{it}, r_{it}, p_t)y_{it} = L_{it} \qquad (10.17)$$

The equilibrium condition for sector i physical capital is

$$a_{iK}(w_{it}, r_{it}, p_t)y_{it} = K_{it} \qquad (10.18)$$

The equilibrium condition for buildings is

$$\Sigma_i\, a_{ib}(w_{it}, r_{it}, p_t)I_{it} = y_{bt} \qquad (10.19)$$

where I_{it} is the time t physical investment in sector i.

Time 0 ($= 1989$) physical capital in sector i, K_{i0}, is obtained from the data. Its value at $t = 1, \ldots, T-1$ equals the depreciated value of time $t-1$ physical capital plus the time $t-1$ value of physical investment:

$$K_{it} = (1-d_i)K_{it-1} + I_{it-1} \qquad (10.20)$$

Thus, if we know sectoral physical investment at $t = 0, \ldots, T-1$, then we can deduce the capital stocks for $t = 0,..,T$. Given the sectoral labor forces during the transition, at any $t = 0,..,T-1$, equations 10.16–10.20 comprise 37 equations in 37 unknowns ($w_{it}, r_{it}, y_{it}, p_{bt}$).

We suppose that the total labor force grows at the population growth rate g, but in each period we allow deviations (fi, hi) in the growth rate of the labor force in each sector i. Thus during the transition, we impose the constraints

$$(1-f_i)(L_{i0}/L) < L_{it}/(1+g)^t L$$
$$< (1+h_i)(L_{i0}/L) \text{ and } \Sigma_i L_{it} = (1+g)^t L$$

we then set GAMS to choose the L_{it} and sectoral physical investments ($I_{it} \geq 0$) during the transition to maximize the value of gross domestic product valued at domestic prices in order to duplicate the effect of market choices while constraining the time T capital stocks to equal the levels required to begin steady growth at time T with the population exogenously specified for time T.

The Second Fundamental Theorem of Welfare Economics indicates that this maximization duplicates the market outcome when investors can sell their time T sectoral capital stocks at prices equal to the Kuhn-Tucker multipliers I_{iKT} associated with the constraints on these capital stocks. Investment at time $t < T$

would then satisfy the following market equilibrium conditions for time t positive investment (with complementary slackness):

$$C_{iK}\,(p_m, p_b, p_v) \geq \sum_{\varphi = t+1}^{T-1} r_{ij}\, \frac{(1-d_i)^{j-t-1}}{(1+i)^{j-t}}$$

$$+ I_{iKT}\, \frac{(1-d_i)^{T-t-1}}{(1+i)^{T-t}} \quad [I_{it} \geq 0]$$

Time t investment in sector i is positive only if the time t price of a unit of new sector i capital equals the time t present value of the rentals which that unit would earn through time T (when steady growth commences) plus the time T value of the depreciated capital.

Von Neumann's Theorem on the optimality of balanced growth indicates that if the transition and the steady growth phases comprise an optimal program, then I_{iKT} equals the price p_{iKT} of sector i capital emerging from the steady growth solution. Thus, the discrepancy between I_{iKT} and p_{iKT} indicates whether the transition phase has been set long enough such that the above procedure is close to maximizing the present value of domestic output at domestic prices, thereby duplicating the market outcome.

Our simulation used 11 periods, leading to discrepancies between the values of I_{iKT} and p_{iKT} that were always less than 0.5 percent and average less than 0.3 percent. This suggests that little accuracy would be gained by increasing T.

At real interest rates of 15 percent, NAFTA increases the present value of national income over the transition and growth phases by 2.5 percent. The comparison between the present values of national income at different interest rates is dominated by the effects of discounting at these different interest rates, but the last column of Table 10.8 shows that the drop in the interest rate from 15 percent to 12 percent leads to substantial increases in GDP in all periods (except the first).

XI. The Economic Gains from NAFTA

This section provides an intuitive idea of the economic gains from NAFTA that are captured in our model, contrasting them with the gains captured in earlier models.

Equalization of Effective Rates of Protection: Static Gains

Consider three sectors A, B, and C, each protected by a nominal 5 percent tariff. If each sector used only Mexican inputs that are themselves unprotected, then their effective rates of protection would be the same, and there would be no misallocation of resources across the three sectors, although there would be a misallocation between these sectors and sectors producing nontraded goods. The latter misallocation would be small because of the low

Table 10.8. *Mexican GDP at World Prices during the Transition*
(billions of 1980 pesos)

Year	A Tariffs, i=15%	B Free Trade, i=15%	C Free Trade, i=12%	(B-A)/A %	(C-A)/A %	(C-B)/B %
1993	549.5	558.9	558.1	1.71	1.57	-0.14
1994	561.4	569.5	605.0	1.45	7.77	6.23
1995	583.9	590.3	626.7	1.11	7.34	6.16
1996	585.1	595.3	627.9	1.74	7.32	5.48
1997	597.1	614.8	644.4	2.97	7.93	4.82
1998	610.5	626.0	676.2	2.54	10.76	8.02
1999	623.5	640.9	689.4	2.79	10.58	7.58
2000	636.0	653.7	700.3	2.78	10.12	7.14
2001	648.7	670.3	714.8	3.33	10.19	6.64
2002	661.7	682.8	738.3	3.19	11.58	8.13
2003	674.9	697.1	755.5	3.29	11.94	8.37

level of the nominal tariffs. By contrast, suppose that the free trade percentage of the final product price representing value added from Mexican sources is 90 percent in A, 50 percent in B, and 50 percent in C. Suppose also that A and B use inputs that are imported freely, whereas C uses inputs that are subject to a 20 percent tariff. The standard formula for effective rate of protection measures the percentage by which the domestic value added exceeds the equivalent value at world prices. This implies that the tariff structure has increased the value added from Mexican sources by $+5.55$ percent in A, $+10$ percent in B, and -10 percent in C, severely distorting the allocation of these resources between these sectors even though all enjoy the same nominal protection. Moreover, relative to nontradeables, the value added in sector B has increased by 10 percent, while that in sector C has fallen by 10 percent, suggesting that NAFTA would move resources from B into nontradeables and from nontradeables into C. Thus, removing modest nominal tariffs can significantly improve the efficiency of resource use. The gains from eliminating a complex tariff structure can be estimated only within a CGE model that captures all intersectoral resource flows; there can be no presumption that low nominal tariff rates imply low welfare gains. Indeed, as the above examples illustrate, *low* nominal rates of protection of a final good sector tends to imply *high* negative effective protection when combined with moderate tariffs on inputs. Thus, models with highly aggregated input structures that fail to capture the impact of NAFTA on traded input prices could well miss important efficiency gains.

Equalization of Effective Rates of Protection: Dynamic Effects

Machinery and other capital goods are currently subject to substantial nominal tariffs on the order of 16 to 20 percent. We pointed out above that a sector whose inputs are highly protected suffers negative effective protection and ends up too small relative to sectors enjoying positive effective protection. This effect is stronger, the greater the share of the final product price absorbed by inputs that are subject to tariffs. For goods whose production requires substantial investment, the relevant "final product price" is the *present value* of the future revenue generated. The very high real rates of interest currently obtaining in Mexico imply that in highly capital-intensive sectors, the cost of capital goods is particularly high relative to the present value of the revenue stream generated from investment in those goods. Thus, highly capital-intensive sectors suffer particularly high negative levels of effective protection. The tariffs on capital inputs act like a tax on capital accumulation, slowing economic growth by raising the perceived cost of producing for future periods and cutting off investment projects that would enhance labor productivity. The efficiency losses imposed by the tariffs on capital inputs are cumulative, reducing the rate of economic growth.

Efficient Input Use Within a Sector

Tariffs not only misallocate resources across sectors but also prevent each sector from using the input combination with the lowest foreign exchange cost. Models with highly aggregated input structures could bypass the potential gains from NAFTA arising from the more efficient use of inputs *within* a sector. For example, within a broad category such as "materials," the removal of tariffs on different types of materials will lead sectors to choose combinations of materials that cost the country less foreign exchange, but these cost savings will not be captured in a model that treats all "materials" as an aggregate. Indeed, unless the model captures the full impact of the removal of tariffs on the internal prices of the aggregative inputs, it will not even fully capture the gains from the use of more efficient combinations of these inputs.

The detailed modeling of intersectoral flows in our model should capture more of the gains from more efficient input use within each sector. The prevailing high real interest rates imply that these gains will be particularly great because they exacerbate the inefficiencies in input use within a sector that result from tariffs on capital goods. Faced with high rates, an entrepreneur will economize sharply on capital goods whose prices have been raised by tariffs, resulting in production techniques that are inefficient for the country as a whole, given their actual opportunity cost.

A Fall in Real Interest Rates

The free trade agreement with the United States represents a very public, internationally binding commitment by Mexico to a certain path of economic development: that of an open market economy with stable, predictable policies. It also makes clear and stable the terms of Mexican access to the U.S. market. Whatever the complexion of future governments, the access provided to U.S. markets will provide a very substantial reason to adhere to the agreement and to the policies that permit Mexico to benefit from this access. This removes a great deal of risk from investment in Mexico. With a great deal of the perceived potential risk locked out, we shall see a surge of investment, yielding substantial economic growth. Instead of demanding a payback period of just a few years, investors will be willing to accept returns over much longer time horizons, which will result in projects that make a much greater contribution to the long-term health of the economy, instead of "fast buck" projects. The effective interest rate will be substantially reduced as the risk premium falls. Access to international capital markets and the terms of international loans will be greatly improved as the international financial community removes the "political risk premium" from the interest rates that they charge for investment in Mexico.

Our analysis indicates that this will be one of the NAFTA's most important benefits, contributing a 8.5 percent increase in gross domestic product. As real interest rates fall, industries will switch to more capital-intensive techniques (see Tables 10.9 and 10.10), increasing the productivity of the existing labor force and raising GDP.

XII. Increases in GDP and Changes in Welfare

Critics pointed out that if all additional investment induced by NAFTA were foreign, then a large portion of the gains in GDP will be gains to foreign capital owners. If this were the case, then the gains in GDP will be an upward-biased indicator of changes in Mexican welfare. This concern is shared by Mexican citizens who perceive that investment in Mexico will be dominated by foreigners, resulting in a loss of Mexican sovereignty.

Important evidence to the contrary has accumulated in the last few years. The conservative financial policies followed by the Mexican government have led to a major inflow of capital, which has kept the exchange rate stable. What is the source of this inflow? Mexican citizens are repatriating their capital from abroad in a reversal of capital flight. Mexican citizens got the news that their government was following sound policies much earlier than foreigners. After all, they live there, whereas foreigners have to wait until their observers write reports, submit them to the central office, and have them read by the board of directors at the next meeting before a decision is taken.

Table 10.9. *Capital Stock at World Prices in the Steady Growth Path (hundred millions of 1980 pesos)*

	A: Tariffs, i=15%	B: Free Trade, i=15%	C: Free Trade, i=12%	(B-A)/A %	(C-A)A %	(C-B)/B %
Capital Stock:	657.0	640.4	810.4	-2.5	23.4	26.6

Table 10.10. *Capital-Labor Ratio in the Steady Growth Path (thousands of 1980 pesos per worker)*

(thousands of 1980 Pesos per Worker) Sector:	A: Tariffs, i=15%	B: Free Trade, i=15%	C: Free Trade, i=12%	(B-A)/A %	(C-A)A %	(C-B)/B %
AGR:	5.7	5.6	5.9	-2.3	3.9	6.4
MIN:	33.2	32.3	35.1	-2.7	5.6	8.6
OIL:	1249.4	1071.1	1630.3	-14.3	30.5	52.2
FOO:	27.7	24.1	27.9	-12.8	0.8	15.6
TEX:	8.9	8.2	9.3	-7.8	4.3	13.1
CHE:	96.5	91.1	119.7	-5.7	24.0	31.4
MET:	61.8	68.7	58.0	11.1	-6.2	-15.5
MAC:	30.6	26.1	31.9	-14.7	4.0	21.9
VEH:	34.7	44.5	38.1	28.3	10.0	-14.3
BUI:	2.4	2.6	3.5	12.4	49.6	33.0
SER:	13.4	14.3	16.8	6.8	25.3	17.3
MIS:	27.1	25.6	29.8	-5.7	9.8	16.5

At the moment, increased investment in Mexico by Mexicans has been mainly in the financial economy, but with the increased certainty about long-term prospects that could result from a free trade agreement, this investment will switch to the real economy where the returns are much higher. However, this information will take longer to penetrate abroad and even longer to be acted upon. In the meantime, it will be acted upon by Mexicans who are already poised to take advantage of the improved investment climate. The enormous funds held by Mexicans abroad (where did the funds from the oil boom go?) will provide a major portion of the requisite financing. The enhanced credibility of Mexico on international financial markets will facilitate further investments with international financial backing but controlled by private Mexican citizens. Much of this will take place before the foreign investors in real projects react to the improved investment climate here, after having commissioned the requisite studies and convinced their boards of directors of the new situation. Just as Mexican citizens have been the first to take advantage of the improved financial returns available in Mexico, so they will grab the lion's share of the most attractive real investment projects.

References

Bachrach, C., and L. Mizrahi. 1992. "The economic impact of a North American Free Trade Area Agreement between the United States and Mexico: A CGE analysis." KPMG Peat Marwick, Washington, D.C.

Balassa, B., and Associates. 1971. "The structure of protection in developing countries." Baltimore: John Hopkins Press.

————. 1982. "Development strategies in semi-industrial countries." Baltimore: John Hopkins Press.

Brooke, A., D. Kendrick, and A. Meeraus. 1988. "GAMS, general algebraic modeling system." World Bank, Washington, D.C.

Corden, M. 1966. "The structure of the tariff system and the effective rate of protection." *Journal of Political Economy* 74:221–37.

————. 1975. "The costs and consequences of protection: A survey of empirical work." In *International trade and finance: Frontiers of research*, edited by P.B. Kenen. Cambridge: Cambridge University Press.

Dixit, A. K., and V. Norman. 1980. *Theory of international trade*. Welwyn: Nisbet & Co.

Young, L., and J. Romero. 1990. "International investment and the positive theory of international trade." *Journal of International Economics* 29:333–49.

Zellner, A. 1962. "An efficient method of estimating seemingly unrelated regressions and test for aggregation bias." *Journal of American Statistical Association* 57:348–68.

Appendix A: Data

Data Sources

1. Gross production, value of inputs, gross profits, total payments to workers and employees (including contributions to social secuirty programs), indirect taxes minus subsides, and private expenditures, all at constant and 1980 prices: INEGI, "Sistema de Cuentas Nacionales de México," 1970–89.

2. Gross and net investment and capital stocks (as well as its composition) at current and 1980 prices: Banco de México, "Acervos de Formación de Capital" 1970–89. Survey of capital stocks by Gerencia de Informatión Económica.

3. Input-Output Matrix: INEGI, "Sistema de Cuentas Nacionales de México," Matriz de Insumo-Producto de México, Ato de 1980, México," 1988.

4. Inflation rate and nominal interest rates: Banco de México, "Indicadores Económicos," April 1992.

5. Rate of population growth: CONAPO, "Informe sobre la Situación Demográfica de México," 1990.

6. Tariffs on Trade: Dirección General de Política de Comercio Exterior, Secretaría de Comerecio y Fomento Industrial.

Additional Data Tables (Constructed Data)

Table 10.11   Prices (1980 = 1)
Table 10.12   Nominal Wages
Table 10.13   Rentals
Table 10.14   Price of Materials (1980 = 1)
Table 10.15   Price of Capital (1980 = 1)
Table 10.16   Share of Labor in Total Cost Output
Table 10.17   Share of Capital in Total Cost of Output
Table 10.18   Share of Buildings in Total Cost of Capital
Table 10.19   Share of Machines in Total Cost of Capital
Table 10.20   Technical Coefficients (from the Input Output Table)
Table 10.21   Private Expenditure Shares

Table 10.11. *Prices (1980 = 1)*

YEAR	AGR	MIN	OIL	FOO	TEX	CHE	MET	MAC	VEH	BUI	SER	MIS
1970	0.21	0.13	0.17	0.22	0.21	0.27	0.21	0.24	0.22	0.18	0.21	0.20
1971	0.22	0.12	0.19	0.25	0.22	0.28	0.21	0.24	0.23	0.18	0.22	0.21
1972	0.23	0.13	0.19	0.25	0.24	0.29	0.22	0.26	0.24	0.20	0.23	0.22
1973	0.28	0.16	0.23	0.29	0.28	0.31	0.23	0.28	0.26	0.21	0.26	0.24
1974	0.36	0.22	0.32	0.38	0.34	0.37	0.31	0.35	0.29	0.27	0.32	0.31
1975	0.41	0.24	0.33	0.42	0.38	0.42	0.36	0.40	0.33	0.34	0.37	0.35
1976	0.49	0.29	0.35	0.51	0.46	0.49	0.43	0.47	0.38	0.41	0.44	0.41
1977	0.61	0.44	0.46	0.68	0.51	0.64	0.54	0.61	0.55	0.52	0.57	0.53
1978	0.72	0.50	0.50	0.76	0.66	0.70	0.64	0.69	0.66	0.62	0.67	0.62
1979	0.85	0.72	0.65	0.84	0.78	0.81	0.80	0.81	0.80	0.77	0.80	0.76
1980	1.00	1.00	1.00	1.00	1.00	1.00	1.00	1.00	1.00	1.00	1.00	1.00
1981	1.27	0.95	1.01	1.25	1.20	1.23	1.24	1.25	1.25	1.28	1.26	1.26
1982	1.87	1.57	1.91	1.96	1.85	1.98	1.98	1.99	2.01	2.05	2.05	1.94
1983	3.63	3.42	6.01	3.58	3.81	4.35	4.10	4.04	4.18	3.66	3.76	3.97
1984	6.40	4.10	8.87	6.26	5.94	6.95	7.38	6.61	7.13	5.79	6.05	6.51
1985	10.41	7.46	11.77	10.02	9.25	10.65	10.72	10.22	11.12	9.13	9.50	10.29
1986	18.82	14.91	17.00	18.12	16.67	20.56	19.74	19.10	21.75	16.69	16.66	19.00
1987	41.79	36.64	49.86	41.44	43.36	53.01	48.79	48.84	54.00	38.48	39.08	47.02
1988	84.36	77.17	81.23	85.40	86.97	107.32	107.64	99.31	97.70	79.99	80.41	97.12
1989	109.90	91.06	74.39	100.26	97.11	117.15	117.38	109.65	108.11	88.60	103.70	108.82

Table 10.12. *Nominal Wages (millions of current pesos)*

YEAR	AGR	MIN	OIL	FOO	TEX	CHE	MET	MAC	VEH	BUI	SER	MIS
1970	0.003	0.014	0.057	0.018	0.019	0.029	0.027	0.026	0.032	0.018	0.011	0.021
1971	0.004	0.015	0.057	0.019	0.019	0.031	0.030	0.028	0.036	0.018	0.016	0.023
1972	0.004	0.017	0.060	0.022	0.022	0.036	0.032	0.030	0.039	0.021	0.019	0.025
1973	0.005	0.019	0.069	0.025	0.025	0.040	0.037	0.031	0.042	0.022	0.021	0.028
1974	0.006	0.025	0.084	0.033	0.031	0.051	0.047	0.043	0.054	0.029	0.027	0.037
1975	0.007	0.030	0.100	0.040	0.038	0.060	0.058	0.055	0.066	0.037	0.033	0.045
1976	0.008	0.040	0.123	0.049	0.049	0.073	0.072	0.070	0.085	0.047	0.042	0.057
1977	0.010	0.050	0.158	0.061	0.062	0.093	0.096	0.090	0.114	0.063	0.053	0.072
1978	0.012	0.056	0.198	0.071	0.072	0.106	0.112	0.107	0.132	0.072	0.062	0.084
1979	0.015	0.067	0.250	0.084	0.088	0.122	0.135	0.124	0.157	0.087	0.076	0.099
1980	0.018	0.084	0.315	0.103	0.108	0.148	0.165	0.152	0.183	0.105	0.095	0.124
1981	0.023	0.124	0.387	0.134	0.136	0.199	0.220	0.200	0.244	0.124	0.131	0.162
1982	0.033	0.179	4.065	0.201	0.208	0.301	0.358	0.324	0.375	0.174	0.197	0.250
1983	0.055	0.285	0.730	0.311	0.334	0.467	0.566	0.503	0.591	0.285	0.310	0.402
1984	0.086	0.428	1.093	0.485	0.512	0.738	0.890	0.784	0.884	0.442	0.488	0.627
1985	0.137	0.659	2.146	0.757	0.805	1.198	1.379	1.229	1.459	0.694	0.765	0.972
1986	0.256	1.116	3.378	1.290	1.353	2.072	2.360	2.134	2.496	1.156	1.271	1.695
1987	0.551	2.497	8.000	2.899	3.024	4.695	5.541	4.986	5.776	2.586	2.880	3.833
1988	1.020	4.733	17.138	5.881	6.381	10.425	11.774	10.792	12.609	4.798	5.540	7.974
1989	1.160	5.628	21.423	7.598	8.276	14.043	15.220	13.938	16.033	5.350	6.827	9.899

Table 10.13. *Rentals (millions of current pesos per each hundred millions of units of capital)*

YEAR	AGR	MIN	OIL	FOO	TEX	CHE	MET	MAC	VEH	BUI	SER	MIS
1970	1.8	1.3	0.2	1.6	4.3	0.6	0.7	1.0	1.2	3.9	1.9	1.3
1971	1.8	1.0	0.3	1.8	4.5	0.6	0.6	0.9	1.0	3.3	2.6	1.3
1972	1.9	0.9	0.2	1.9	4.5	0.6	0.7	1.1	1.2	4.2	2.8	1.3
1973	2.1	1.2	0.3	2.1	5.2	0.7	0.7	1.4	1.5	5.0	3.2	1.5
1974	2.5	1.5	0.6	2.6	5.8	0.7	1.1	1.7	1.6	5.7	3.8	1.9
1975	2.7	1.4	0.6	3.1	6.0	0.8	1.3	1.8	1.3	6.3	4.2	2.0
1976	2.9	1.5	0.4	3.6	6.4	0.9	1.5	2.2	0.9	7.3	4.6	2.2
1977	3.7	2.2	0.7	5.2	9.3	1.4	1.5	2.9	1.7	8.1	5.8	2.9
1978	4.6	2.3	0.5	5.9	11.5	1.7	1.9	3.8	3.5	9.7	7.2	3.8
1979	5.9	3.4	0.6	6.6	13.6	2.1	2.8	5.5	4.6	15.2	8.7	5.2
1980	8.0	4.5	1.0	10.0	16.2	2.7	3.5	7.0	5.6	23.0	11.3	7.5
1981	10.3	3.4	0.8	13.1	20.3	3.8	4.2	8.4	7.0	32.5	15.3	10.5
1982	15.6	5.5	1.8	20.8	29.6	6.2	6.0	10.7	7.5	53.3	23.0	15.5
1983	28.1	14.3	9.4	40.0	62.0	16.6	11.7	18.9	12.0	67.4	43.6	29.4
1984	48.6	20.3	11.7	72.5	100.9	28.3	24.8	33.3	30.3	119.6	70.3	53.2
1985	82.5	31.4	14.7	127.5	172.8	41.0	37.4	58.1	56.6	223.4	106.2	93.9
1986	144.5	62.2	16.4	241.4	299.4	79.8	74.2	101.6	83.3	373.6	185.5	171.4
1987	371.3	166.7	54.6	593.4	789.1	248.5	208.1	276.2	253.0	944.1	374.2	449.8
1988	839.6	342.6	57.3	1213.4	1712.2	515.2	505.5	630.8	502.7	2610.0	811.6	962.8
1989	978.4	405.2	45.6	1456.7	1914.1	620.1	560.0	733.1	629.0	2873.0	1097.8	1158.8

Table 10.14. *Price of Materials (1980 = 1)*

YEAR	AGR	MIN	OIL	FOO	TEX	CHE	MET	MAC	VEH	BUI	SER	MIS
1970	0.22	0.19	0.32	0.23	0.22	0.27	0.23	0.25	0.23	0.19	0.22	0.21
1971	0.23	0.17	0.34	0.25	0.23	0.27	0.23	0.25	0.25	0.19	0.23	0.21
1972	0.24	0.18	0.35	0.25	0.24	0.28	0.23	0.27	0.25	0.20	0.24	0.22
1973	0.28	0.23	0.44	0.29	0.30	0.30	0.25	0.28	0.27	0.22	0.26	0.24
1974	0.36	0.33	0.59	0.38	0.36	0.38	0.33	0.35	0.31	0.28	0.33	0.33
1975	0.41	0.33	0.56	0.43	0.40	0.43	0.38	0.41	0.36	0.33	0.39	0.37
1976	0.48	0.40	0.63	0.52	0.49	0.49	0.44	0.47	0.42	0.39	0.46	0.42
1977	0.61	0.60	0.64	0.67	0.58	0.65	0.54	0.62	0.58	0.51	0.61	0.55
1978	0.73	0.62	0.71	0.76	0.67	0.71	0.66	0.70	0.68	0.60	0.69	0.64
1979	0.86	0.82	0.88	0.86	0.80	0.81	0.81	0.82	0.82	0.76	0.81	0.78
1980	1.00	1.00	1.00	1.00	1.00	1.00	1.00	1.00	1.00	1.00	1.00	1.00
1981	1.24	0.98	1.12	1.24	1.18	1.22	1.22	1.25	1.24	1.27	1.24	1.23
1982	1.85	1.63	2.07	1.84	1.83	1.95	1.93	1.97	2.00	2.02	1.99	1.87
1983	3.81	3.59	2.61	3.49	3.83	4.29	4.02	3.98	4.15	4.06	4.08	3.80
1984	6.59	5.35	4.14	6.14	5.98	6.93	7.17	6.56	6.91	6.60	6.88	6.18
1985	10.55	7.78	8.49	9.78	9.26	10.70	10.34	10.01	10.68	10.50	10.67	9.75
1986	19.04	15.60	16.25	16.97	16.89	20.68	19.07	18.82	20.89	19.24	20.09	18.02
1987	43.83	37.88	36.06	38.88	44.28	52.18	46.30	47.79	52.10	45.00	43.72	44.55
1988	100.75	77.92	88.51	80.86	86.84	104.03	101.01	96.21	96.97	96.37	98.79	92.25
1989	126.90	90.08	81.71	97.33	96.52	113.76	110.43	105.62	106.74	103.92	116.23	102.96

Table 10.15. *Price of Capital (1980 = 1)*

YEAR	AGR	MIN	OIL	FOO	TEX	CHE	MET	MAC	VEH	BUI	SER	MIS
1970	0.20	0.19	0.18	0.19	0.23	0.19	0.21	0.20	0.20	0.21	0.18	0.20
1971	0.20	0.19	0.19	0.19	0.23	0.19	0.22	0.20	0.20	0.22	0.18	0.20
1972	0.21	0.20	0.19	0.20	0.24	0.20	0.23	0.21	0.21	0.22	0.19	0.21
1973	0.23	0.22	0.21	0.22	0.26	0.22	0.24	0.23	0.23	0.24	0.21	0.23
1974	0.30	0.30	0.28	0.29	0.33	0.29	0.30	0.30	0.30	0.28	0.29	0.30
1975	0.35	0.36	0.34	0.35	0.37	0.34	0.36	0.36	0.35	0.35	0.35	0.35
1976	0.43	0.43	0.42	0.43	0.47	0.43	0.44	0.43	0.43	0.45	0.41	0.43
1977	0.61	0.60	0.55	0.60	0.72	0.60	0.64	0.62	0.62	0.67	0.54	0.60
1978	0.69	0.68	0.64	0.67	0.79	0.66	0.72	0.70	0.71	0.75	0.63	0.67
1979	0.81	0.81	0.77	0.80	0.88	0.80	0.84	0.82	0.83	0.84	0.78	0.79
1980	1.00	1.00	1.00	1.00	1.00	1.00	1.00	1.00	1.00	1.00	1.00	1.00
1981	1.23	1.23	1.29	1.24	1.21	1.22	1.22	1.22	1.23	1.22	1.25	1.22
1982	2.23	2.18	2.11	2.17	2.41	2.17	2.33	2.26	2.26	2.45	2.05	2.17
1983	5.55	5.44	5.06	5.24	6.12	5.29	6.03	5.59	5.62	6.38	4.93	5.32
1984	9.13	9.28	9.33	8.83	9.26	9.10	9.61	9.01	9.12	9.50	8.52	8.84
1985	14.89	15.44	15.78	14.37	14.89	14.49	15.77	14.61	15.04	14.89	14.25	14.31
1986	29.74	30.29	29.05	27.54	32.67	28.17	33.31	29.08	29.09	32.53	27.36	28.06
1987	68.43	69.29	66.04	65.04	75.14	66.27	76.01	66.48	64.76	74.23	64.41	65.05
1988	129.94	133.04	132.91	128.15	133.92	129.58	138.53	125.77	121.82	133.10	126.25	126.26
1989	143.83	147.86	144.48	141.38	148.92	143.78	154.54	139.34	134.44	149.33	138.49	139.58

Table 10.16. *Share of Labor in Total Cost of Output*

YEAR	AGR	MIN	OIL	FOO	TEX	CHE	MET	MAC	VEH	BUI	SER	MIS
1970	0.20	0.21	0.21	0.09	0.18	0.17	0.16	0.22	0.15	0.30	0.27	0.20
1971	0.20	0.23	0.19	0.09	0.17	0.17	0.17	0.24	0.16	0.30	0.28	0.21
1972	0.21	0.26	0.18	0.09	0.17	0.17	0.17	0.23	0.16	0.32	0.29	0.21
1973	0.20	0.23	0.16	0.09	0.16	0.17	0.17	0.23	0.15	0.31	0.29	0.20
1974	0.19	0.23	0.13	0.09	0.17	0.17	0.15	0.23	0.16	0.31	0.30	0.19
1975	0.18	0.25	0.15	0.10	0.18	0.17	0.17	0.24	0.17	0.32	0.32	0.20
1976	0.18	0.27	0.17	0.10	0.19	0.17	0.18	0.25	0.21	0.35	0.33	0.21
1977	0.18	0.23	0.16	0.09	0.18	0.16	0.18	0.24	0.18	0.35	0.33	0.20
1978	0.18	0.25	0.18	0.09	0.18	0.16	0.16	0.23	0.16	0.35	0.32	0.19
1979	0.18	0.21	0.18	0.09	0.18	0.15	0.15	0.21	0.15	0.33	0.32	0.18
1980	0.18	0.21	0.11	0.09	0.18	0.15	0.15	0.21	0.14	0.31	0.32	0.17
1981	0.19	0.28	0.14	0.09	0.18	0.15	0.16	0.21	0.17	0.31	0.32	0.16
1982	0.18	0.26	0.11	0.09	0.18	0.14	0.17	0.22	0.18	0.29	0.31	0.16
1983	0.16	0.18	0.05	0.07	0.14	0.10	0.13	0.18	0.16	0.28	0.26	0.13
1984	0.14	0.19	0.06	0.06	0.14	0.10	0.11	0.17	0.12	0.28	0.26	0.12
1985	0.14	0.19	0.08	0.06	0.14	0.10	0.12	0.16	0.12	0.28	0.26	0.11
1986	0.14	0.16	0.09	0.06	0.13	0.09	0.10	0.16	0.12	0.27	0.25	0.11
1987	0.14	0.14	0.08	0.06	0.12	0.08	0.09	0.15	0.10	0.26	0.24	0.10
1988	0.13	0.13	0.11	0.06	0.12	0.09	0.08	0.14	0.10	0.24	0.22	0.10
1989	0.12	0.13	0.13	0.06	0.14	0.10	0.10	0.16	0.11	0.26	0.21	0.11

Table 10.17. *Share of Capital in Total Cost of Output*

YEAR	AGR	MIN	OIL	FOO	TEX	CHE	MET	MAC	VEH	BUI	SER	MIS
1970	0.52	0.39	0.16	0.21	0.24	0.24	0.20	0.23	0.19	0.18	0.49	0.27
1971	0.52	0.39	0.21	0.22	0.23	0.25	0.18	0.21	0.15	0.16	0.53	0.27
1972	0.50	0.36	0.18	0.22	0.24	0.25	0.19	0.23	0.18	0.17	0.51	0.26
1973	0.52	0.38	0.18	0.21	0.25	0.26	0.18	0.25	0.19	0.17	0.52	0.28
1974	0.53	0.37	0.26	0.21	0.23	0.24	0.19	0.24	0.17	0.17	0.50	0.26
1975	0.53	0.38	0.26	0.20	0.24	0.23	0.19	0.22	0.13	0.17	0.48	0.26
1976	0.53	0.36	0.19	0.20	0.22	0.22	0.19	0.23	0.09	0.17	0.47	0.25
1977	0.53	0.37	0.33	0.22	0.25	0.25	0.20	0.23	0.14	0.15	0.47	0.26
1978	0.54	0.37	0.29	0.21	0.26	0.25	0.21	0.24	0.19	0.15	0.49	0.28
1979	0.53	0.42	0.26	0.21	0.26	0.25	0.23	0.26	0.19	0.16	0.48	0.29
1980	0.54	0.43	0.24	0.24	0.26	0.26	0.23	0.27	0.20	0.17	0.49	0.31
1981	0.54	0.33	0.39	0.24	0.28	0.28	0.23	0.27	0.19	0.17	0.46	0.34
1982	0.54	0.35	0.46	0.26	0.28	0.29	0.23	0.26	0.19	0.19	0.47	0.35
1983	0.54	0.41	0.77	0.27	0.30	0.34	0.26	0.30	0.21	0.16	0.51	0.38
1984	0.56	0.40	0.72	0.27	0.30	0.33	0.28	0.31	0.26	0.15	0.50	0.40
1985	0.57	0.41	0.61	0.28	0.31	0.32	0.28	0.33	0.27	0.14	0.50	0.40
1986	0.56	0.43	0.48	0.30	0.31	0.33	0.31	0.33	0.27	0.15	0.49	0.41
1987	0.56	0.46	0.60	0.30	0.32	0.36	0.32	0.35	0.29	0.16	0.49	0.42
1988	0.52	0.47	0.39	0.29	0.33	0.35	0.33	0.36	0.27	0.17	0.51	0.41
1989	0.55	0.48	0.36	0.28	0.32	0.34	0.32	0.35	0.26	0.16	0.54	0.41

Table 10.18. *Share of Buildings in Total Cost of Capital*

YEAR	AGR	MIN	OIL	FOO	TEX	CHE	MET	MAC	VEH	BUI	SER	MIS
1970	0.41	0.57	0.56	0.39	0.21	0.34	0.26	0.46	0.42	0.16	0.73	0.35
1971	0.40	0.54	0.55	0.39	0.22	0.33	0.26	0.45	0.40	0.16	0.72	0.35
1972	0.39	0.51	0.55	0.39	0.19	0.31	0.28	0.44	0.39	0.17	0.72	0.34
1973	0.38	0.49	0.56	0.39	0.18	0.30	0.26	0.42	0.38	0.17	0.70	0.33
1974	0.37	0.47	0.55	0.38	0.18	0.30	0.27	0.41	0.36	0.14	0.70	0.32
1975	0.36	0.44	0.56	0.34	0.17	0.29	0.28	0.39	0.37	0.11	0.67	0.31
1976	0.35	0.42	0.55	0.34	0.17	0.29	0.27	0.38	0.37	0.11	0.64	0.30
1977	0.35	0.41	0.58	0.34	0.17	0.29	0.34	0.37	0.36	0.11	0.63	0.31
1978	0.35	0.41	0.54	0.35	0.17	0.29	0.32	0.37	0.35	0.10	0.60	0.31
1979	0.34	0.40	0.54	0.35	0.19	0.28	0.32	0.33	0.35	0.11	0.58	0.30
1980	0.35	0.40	0.61	0.36	0.17	0.27	0.33	0.33	0.35	0.11	0.57	0.30
1981	0.36	0.44	0.73	0.37	0.17	0.27	0.34	0.33	0.35	0.10	0.55	0.28
1982	0.36	0.45	0.75	0.37	0.18	0.27	0.34	0.32	0.34	0.10	0.52	0.28
1983	0.36	0.46	0.76	0.38	0.18	0.28	0.33	0.33	0.33	0.11	0.52	0.28
1984	0.37	0.44	0.78	0.39	0.19	0.29	0.34	0.33	0.33	0.13	0.52	0.28
1985	0.37	0.45	0.79	0.38	0.20	0.26	0.34	0.33	0.33	0.16	0.52	0.29
1986	0.37	0.44	0.81	0.38	0.20	0.27	0.33	0.33	0.32	0.16	0.51	0.30
1987	0.38	0.44	0.75	0.41	0.21	0.28	0.33	0.33	0.32	0.19	0.57	0.29
1988	0.39	0.45	0.76	0.41	0.22	0.30	0.35	0.33	0.32	0.24	0.57	0.29
1989	0.39	0.47	0.74	0.43	0.22	0.32	0.35	0.33	0.33	0.26	0.57	0.30

Table 10.19. *Share of Machines in Total Cost of Capital*

YEAR	AGR	MIN	OIL	FOO	TEX	CHE	MET	MAC	VEH	BUI	SER	MIS
1970	0.57	0.39	0.38	0.57	0.78	0.65	0.72	0.53	0.58	0.76	0.26	0.63
1971	0.58	0.41	0.40	0.57	0.78	0.66	0.73	0.54	0.59	0.75	0.27	0.63
1972	0.58	0.43	0.39	0.57	0.80	0.68	0.71	0.55	0.60	0.74	0.27	0.64
1973	0.59	0.44	0.40	0.56	0.81	0.69	0.72	0.57	0.61	0.73	0.28	0.65
1974	0.59	0.47	0.40	0.56	0.82	0.68	0.72	0.58	0.61	0.75	0.28	0.66
1975	0.60	0.50	0.40	0.60	0.82	0.68	0.70	0.59	0.59	0.79	0.31	0.66
1976	0.61	0.52	0.40	0.60	0.83	0.69	0.69	0.60	0.58	0.79	0.33	0.67
1977	0.60	0.53	0.37	0.59	0.82	0.69	0.62	0.61	0.58	0.79	0.35	0.66
1978	0.61	0.54	0.40	0.58	0.81	0.69	0.65	0.60	0.58	0.81	0.37	0.66
1979	0.61	0.55	0.41	0.57	0.79	0.70	0.64	0.63	0.56	0.82	0.40	0.66
1980	0.61	0.55	0.34	0.56	0.80	0.71	0.63	0.63	0.57	0.83	0.40	0.67
1981	0.60	0.52	0.24	0.55	0.81	0.71	0.63	0.61	0.59	0.83	0.42	0.67
1982	0.59	0.52	0.22	0.52	0.81	0.69	0.64	0.61	0.61	0.83	0.42	0.68
1983	0.59	0.51	0.21	0.51	0.80	0.68	0.65	0.61	0.61	0.82	0.43	0.68
1984	0.59	0.53	0.20	0.49	0.79	0.67	0.65	0.60	0.63	0.81	0.43	0.68
1985	0.58	0.53	0.19	0.49	0.78	0.67	0.65	0.60	0.63	0.77	0.43	0.68
1986	0.59	0.53	0.18	0.50	0.76	0.67	0.65	0.61	0.65	0.77	0.44	0.68
1987	0.59	0.52	0.24	0.51	0.76	0.67	0.65	0.61	0.65	0.75	0.39	0.68
1988	0.57	0.51	0.23	0.51	0.74	0.65	0.63	0.61	0.65	0.67	0.40	0.68
1989	0.56	0.48	0.24	0.49	0.74	0.62	0.63	0.62	0.65	0.64	0.41	0.66

Table 10.20. *Technical Coefficients (from the Input Output Table)*

	AGR	MIN	OIL	FOO	TEX	CHE	MET	MAC	VEH	BUI	SER	MIS
AGR	0.4192	0.0000	0.0000	0.2848	0.0514	0.0083	0.0000	0.0000	0.0000	0.0000	0.0017	0.0032
MIN	0.0030	0.4888	0.0142	0.0004	0.0000	0.0302	0.1509	0.0128	0.0019	0.0617	0.0004	0.0414
OIL	0.0349	0.0148	0.7379	0.0074	0.0024	0.2543	0.0035	0.0034	0.0029	0.0200	0.0742	0.0198
FOO	0.1690	0.0001	0.0001	0.3353	0.0012	0.0873	0.0000	0.0000	0.0002	0.0000	0.0098	0.0137
TEX	0.0143	0.0014	0.0013	0.0139	0.3340	0.0057	0.0015	0.0026	0.0082	0.0024	0.0130	0.0162
CHE	0.1250	0.0602	0.0183	0.0174	0.2511	0.2296	0.0395	0.0436	0.0248	0.0302	0.0623	0.1733
MET	0.0233	0.0414	0.0181	0.0297	0.0085	0.0202	0.5046	0.3084	0.2020	0.2715	0.0247	0.0488
MAC	0.0085	0.0087	0.0192	0.0017	0.0021	0.0018	0.0100	0.0680	0.0067	0.0356	0.0137	0.0051
VEH	0.0052	0.0143	0.0010	0.0019	0.0022	0.0024	0.0057	0.0099	0.2199	0.0000	0.0308	0.0040
BUI	0.0000	0.0000	0.0000	0.0000	0.0000	0.0000	0.0000	0.0000	0.0000	0.0000	0.0000	0.0000
SER	0.1826	0.3450	0.1855	0.2706	0.3020	0.2733	0.2619	0.4584	0.4650	0.2942	0.6846	0.3516
MIS	0.0150	0.0253	0.0045	0.0369	0.0451	0.0870	0.0225	0.0930	0.0685	0.2845	0.0849	0.3229

Table 10.21. *Private Expenditure Shares*

	AGR	MIN	OIL	FOO	TEX	CHE	MET	MAC	VEH	BUI	SER	MIS
%	7.3	0.0	1.5	20.8	6.1	2.7	0.6	0.0	1.2	0.0	54.5	5.2

Appendix B

Derivation of equation 10.15

Tariff revenue R satisfies

$$R = \sum_i \frac{p_i \tau_i}{(1+t_i)} \cdot \{d_i[p, r(p) + R] - y_i(p)\}$$

Given homothetic prererences, the share γ_i of expenditure on good i is independent of income, so

$$d_i[p, r(p) + R] = [r(p) + R] \gamma_i / p_i$$

and we then have what becomes

$$R = \sum_i \frac{p_i \tau_i}{(1+t_i)} \cdot [r(p) + R] \gamma_i / p_i - \sum_i \frac{\tau_i p_i y_i(p)}{(1+t_i)}$$

Therefore

$$r(p) + R = r(p) + [r(p) + R] \cdot \sum_i \frac{\gamma_i \tau_i}{(1+t_i)} - \sum_i \frac{\tau_i p_i y_i(p)}{(1+\tau_i)}$$

and:

$$[r(p) + R][1 - \sum_i \gamma_i \tau_i / (1+\tau_i)] = r(p) - \sum_i \frac{\tau_i p_i y_i(p)}{(1+\tau^i)}$$
$$= \sum_i \pi_i (1 + \tau_i) y_i(p) - \sum_i \pi_i \tau_i(p)$$
$$= \sum_i \pi_i y_i(p)$$

Equation 10.15 in the text follows immediately.

11

Toward a Dynamic General Equilibrium Model of North American Trade*

Timothy J. Kehoe
University of Minnesota and
Federal Reserve Bank of Minneapolis

I. Introduction

The current tool of choice for analyzing the impact of the North American Free Trade Agreement (NAFTA) on the economies of Canada, Mexico, and the United States is the static applied general equilibrium model. Examples of such analyses include Brown, Deardorff, and Stern (1991); Cox and Harris (1991); Hinojosa-Ojeda and Robinson (1991); KPMG Peat-Marwick (1991); Sobarzo (1991); and Yúnez-Naude (1991). They all tend to find small, but favorable, impacts of such an agreement.

Static applied general equilibrium models can do a good job in analyzing, and even in predicting, the impact of trade liberalization or tax reform on relative prices and resource allocation over a short time horizon. Kehoe, Polo, and Sancho (1991), for example, assess the performance of a static general equilibrium model of the Spanish economy that had been constructed to analyze the impact of the tax reform that accompanied Spain's 1986 entry into the European Economic Community. They find that the model was able to account for more than two-thirds of the variation of relative prices that occurred between 1985 and 1987. (It would be interesting to do similar ex post performance evaluations of the analyses of NAFTA.)

Typically, however, this sort of model predicts small changes in economic

* I am grateful to Karine Moe for diligent and energetic research assistance. The views expressed herein are those of the author and not necessarily those of the Federal Reserve Bank of Minneapolis or the Federal Reserve System.

welfare [see Shoven and Whalley (1984); Whalley (1989)]. One reason for this is that these models do not attempt to capture the impact of government policy on growth rates. For this we need a dynamic model. Anything that can affect the growth rate of a variable like income per capita or output per worker, if only slightly, can have a tremendous impact over time.

Currently, there is no model that analyzes the impact of NAFTA on growth rates. This paper outlines some of the issues that confront a researcher interested in building a dynamic applied general model to assess the potential economic impact of NAFTA, including the impact on growth rates. A dynamic model can capture the effect of government policy on capital flows, and these are very important. Yet, as we argue in the next section, a low capital-labor ratio cannot be the only, or even the most important, factor in explaining the low level of output per worker in Mexico compared to that in a country like the United States. We must look elsewhere for explanations for the differences in levels of output per worker. It is here that the new, endogenous growth literature, which follows Romer (1987) and Lucas (1988) and focuses on endogenous technical change, is able to provide potential answers. This literature is still at a tentative, mostly theoretical level. By developing a disaggregated dynamic general equilibrium model of the three countries of North America, we could go a long way towards making this theory operational. A model could be calibrated, and alternative versions of the theory could be tested by applying them to past experience. The present paper uses preliminary empirical work at an aggregate level to estimate the impact of free trade on growth rates in Mexico.

Although our calculations are fairly crude, they suggest that the dynamic impact of NAFTA could dwarf the static effects found by more conventional applied general equilibrium models. Similar kinds of suggestive calculations are performed to estimate the dynamic gains from the European Economic Community's 1992 Program by Baldwin (1992). Unlike Baldwin's analysis, however, the results presented here are based on theories and empirical estimates that deal with trade directly. Baldwin obtains his numbers by multiplying estimates of static gains from trade obtained by other researchers by a multiplier derived from a highly aggregated growth model with dynamic increasing returns but without any explicit role for trade. It is worth pointing out that the analysis in this paper does not take into account phenomena like unemployment or underutilization of capacity. It is possible that a free trade agreement would provide dynamic gains based on a more traditional macroeconomic analysis; see Fischer (1992) for some suggestive results in this direction.

Although the endogenous growth literature is still at a tentative stage, the intuition behind it is fairly simple. Increased openness can alter the growth rate in clear ways; economic growth is spurred by the development of new products. New product development is the result of learning by doing, where experience in one product line makes it easier to develop the next product in the line, and of direct research and development. On the final product side, increased openness allows a country to specialize more, achieving a larger scale of operations in those industries in which it has a comparative advantage. On the input side, increased openness allows a country to import many technologically specialized inputs to the production process without needing to develop them itself.

It is worth noting that the analysis in this paper pertains to the benefits of free trade in general, not just in the context of NAFTA. Because of their relative sizes and geographical locations, Canada and Mexico do most of their trading with the United States; see Figure 11.1. For them the concepts of free trade and NAFTA are inextricably connected. Although Canada is the United States' largest trading partner and Mexico its third largest, about three-quarters of U.S. trade is with countries outside North America. Nonetheless, NAFTA represents an opportunity for the United States to commit itself to a free trade policy, and for this reason the progress on NAFTA is being closely monitored throughout the world.

II. Capital Flows

A major impact of NAFTA would be on capital flows. One would expect capital to flow from relatively capital-rich Canada and the United States to relatively capital-poor Mexico. Indeed, it is by exogenously imposing a substantial capital flow of this sort that static models such as that of KPMG Peat-Marwick (1991) are able to show a significant welfare gain to Mexico. It is worth stressing two points about capital flows, however. First, differences in capital-labor ratios between Mexico and its northern neighbors cannot be the sole explanation of the large differences in output per worker between these countries. [See Lucas (1990) for a discussion and calculations similar to those below.] Consequently, simply equalizing capital-labor ratios cannot be the solution to the problem of eliminating income differences. Second, when modeling the savings and investment decisions that determine capital flows, we need to take into account the significant differences in age profiles of the population between Mexico and its neighbors. This point is discussed further in the next section.

To illustrate the point that differences in capital-labor ratios cannot explain the differences in output per worker observed in Mexico and the United States, we carry out some simple calculations using aggregate production functions. Suppose that each economy has the same production function

$$Y_j = \gamma N_j^{1-\alpha} K_j^{\alpha}$$

Exports

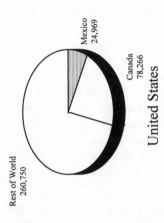

Canada

United States
89,550

Rest of World
30,250

Mexico
525

United States

Rest of World
260,750

Mexico
24,969

Canada
78,266

United States
27,590

Rest of World
11,179

Canada
1,434

Mexico

Imports

Canada

United States
78,266

Mexico
1,434

Rest of World
44,292

United States

Rest of World
375,782

Mexico
27,590

Canada
89,550

United States
24,969

Canada
525

Rest of World
15,245

Mexico

Figure 11.1. Direction of Trade 1989 (millions of 1989 U.S. dollars)
Source: IMP, *Direction of Trade Statistics Yearbook,* 1990.

where Y_j is GDP, N_j is the size of the work force, and K_j is capital. In per capita terms, where $y_j = Y_j/N_j$ and $k_j = K_j/N_j$, this becomes $y_j = \gamma k_j^\alpha$. The net return of capital is

$$r_j = \alpha \gamma k_j^{\alpha-1} - \delta$$

where δ is the depreciation rate. In 1988, according to Summers and Heston (1991), real GDP per worker was \$14,581 in Mexico and \$37,608 in the United States. Suppose that $\alpha = 0.3$, which is roughly the capital share of income in the United States. Then, to explain this difference in output per worker, we need capital per worker to be larger than that in Mexico by a factor of 23.5,

$$\frac{k_{us}}{k_{mex}} = \left(\frac{y_{us}}{y_{mex}}\right)^{1/\alpha} = \left(\frac{37,608}{14,581}\right)^{1/0.3} = 23.5.$$

Suppose that $\delta = 0.05$ and $r_{us} = 0.05$, which are roughly the numbers obtained from calibration. Then the net interest rate in Mexico should be 17.2 times that in the United States,

$$r_{mex} = (r_{us} + \delta)\left(\frac{k_{us}}{k_{mex}}\right)^{1-\alpha} - \delta = 0.10(23.5)^{0.7} - 0.05 = 0.86.$$

During the 1988–90 period, the real return on bank equity in Mexico (and banks are the major source of private capital in Mexico) averaged 28.2 percent per year, as compared to 4.7 percent in the United States [see Garber and Weisbrod (1991)]. Because 28 percent is far less than the 86 percent that we would expect if differences in capital-labor ratios were the principal determinant of the differences in output per worker between Mexico and its neighbors, we must look elsewhere for this determinant.

There are at least two objections that can be raised to the above calculations: First, a comparison based on per capita GDP in U.S. dollars using the exchange rate to convert pesos into dollars would suggest that y_{us}/y_{mex} is much larger, about 7.9. Second, calibrating the capital share parameter α using Mexican GDP data would yield a larger value, about 0.5. These two objections work in opposite directions, however, and our calculations can be defended as being in a sensible middle ground – income comparisons based on exchange rate conversions neglect purchasing power parity differentials; per capita comparisons rather than per worker comparisons neglect demographic differences; much of what is classified as net business income in Mexico is actually returns to labor; and so on.

Moreover, that differences in capital per worker cannot be the sole explanation of differences in output per worker across countries is a more general point. It is supported both by historical evidence, such as that of Clark (1987), and by even more extreme examples of differences in output per worker:

According to Summers and Heston (1991), real GDP per worker in Haiti in 1988 was 4.9 percent of that in the United States. The same sort of calculations as those above would suggest that interest rates in Haiti should be over 11,000 percent per year if differences in the capital-labor ratio were the sole explanation of the differences in output per worker. Furthermore, historical evidence does not indicate that Mexico has always been starved of funds for investment. The problem has often been that investments abroad, particularly in the United States, have been more attractive. Between 1977 and 1982, for example, $17.8 billion of private investment flowed into Mexico, while $18.7 billion flowed out [Garcia-Alba and Serra-Puche (1983), p. 45].

Although capital flows cannot provide all of the answers to Mexico's problems, they are important. If capital flows could lower the net interest rate in Mexico from 28 percent per year to 5 percent, we would estimate that the capital labor ratio in Mexico would increase by a factor of about 5.5:

$$\frac{\hat{k}_{mex}}{k_{mex}} = \left(\frac{0.28 + \delta}{0.05 + \delta}\right)^{1/(1-\alpha)} = 5.5.$$

This would increase Mexican output per worker to roughly $24,300, which would close the current gap with the U.S. level by about 42 percent.

A dynamic applied general equilibrium model would be an ideal tool for analyzing the capital flows that would result from NAFTA. With some sectional disaggregation, such a model could account for differences in total factor productivity in the United States and Mexico that differ widely across sectors. Total factor productivity in some sectors in Mexico is similar to that in the United States, whereas in others it is much lower [see, for example, Blomstrom and Wolf (1989)]. The calculations of the impact of capital inflows reported above are based on aggregate production functions and ignore these differences. A disaggregated model would enable us to capture the various impacts that capital flows would have on different sectors.

If a model is to explain the impact of large capital inflows on the Mexican economy, it should be able to answer this question: If the post-NAFTA interest rate in Mexico is to be so much lower than the pre-NAFTA interest rate, why is the pre-NAFTA rate so high? One possible answer is that a high interest rate in Mexico is the result of closed capital markets and of inefficient, oligopolistic financial intermediaries. If this is the case, we would want to model imperfect competition in the financial services sector and to model explicitly the way in which NAFTA would lower the interest rate.

Another potential answer is that the gap between the pre-NAFTA interest rate in Mexico and the U.S. interest rate represents a risk premium: International investors demand a higher rate of return in Mexico because they fear that a financial collapse and maxidevaluation like that which occurred in 1982 would wipe out much of their investment. By locking Mexico and its two

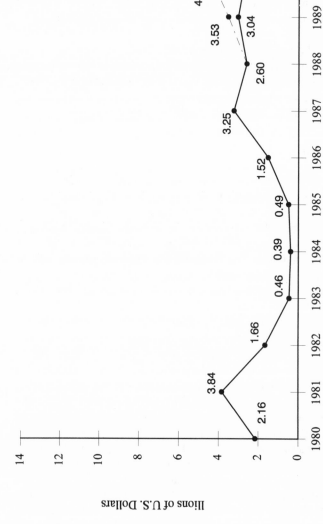

Figure 11.2. Foreign Investment in Mexico
Source: Banco de México.

Millions of U.S. Dollars

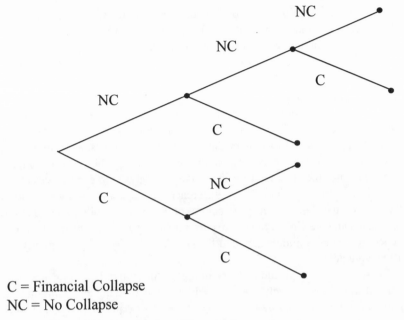

C = Financial Collapse
NC = No Collapse

Figure 11.3. Introduction of Uncertainty

northern neighbors into policies that would help guarantee economic stability in Mexico, NAFTA would lower this risk premium and thereby lower the interest rate. Foreign investment in Mexico has increased dramatically in recent years, as seen in Figure 11.2. Some of this increase has been due to the liberalization of Mexican laws regarding such investments, and some has undoubtedly been due to improvements in expectations about Mexico's economic future.

It may be possible to model the process by which NAFTA would lower the risk premium in a simple way. Figure 11.3 depicts an event tree for a dynamic, stochastic general equilibrium model in which there is a probability π_{ct} of a financial collapse in period t and a probability $1 - \pi_{ct}$ of no financial collapse. In simulations, we could concentrate on the path in which no financial collapse actually occurs. Even so, in principle, we would have to model what would occur at every node of this event tree. This would subject us to the "curse of dimensionality" associated with an expanding-state space typical in this type of model. To simplify the analysis, however, we could model what happens if a financial collapse occurs in a simple enough way so that we do not have to move further out on branches in which a financial collapse occurs to compute the equilibrium outcomes. Even though we would not need to model in great detail what happens if a financial collapse occurs, lowering its probability

π_{ct} could have a significant impact on equilibrium outcomes along the branch of the tree where there is no collapse. To make this approach useful, we would need to model the interaction of π_{ct} and NAFTA in a way that is tractable but also captures the impact of NAFTA on economic stability in Mexico.

III. Demographics

To successfully account for capital flows, a dynamic general equilibrium analysis of NAFTA would have to model consumers' savings decisions. In modeling savings decisions in Canada, the United States, and Mexico, we must take into account demographic differences among the countries. Figure 11.4 illustrates the stark contrast in the population growth experiences of the United States and Mexico. These differences in population growth manifest themselves in differences in age structures of population; while the populations of Canada and the United States are currently aging as the postwar baby boom generation reaches middle age, half the population of Mexico is currently age 19 or younger.

These differences would be very important in an overlapping generations context in which life-cycle consumers dissave when young and build up their human capital, save during the middle of their lives, and dissave again when old during retirement. An example of an applied general equilibrium model with overlapping generations is Auerbach and Kotlikoff (1987). This model has a single country with a single production sector. A model with a similar dynamic structure but with several countries and multiple production sectors could be used to capture the impacts of NAFTA on capital flows in North America.

Modeling demographic differences in an overlapping generations framework would be especially important in a model in which the accumulation of human capital, as well as that of physical capital, plays an important role. The alternative modeling strategy is to assume that a bequest motive links generations in such a way as to produce families that act as if they were infinitely lived consumers. Empirical evidence does not seem to clearly favor one approach over the other: On one hand, a large percentage of wealth seems to be the result of bequests [see, for example, Kotlikoff and Summers (1981)]. It would be essential to account for this phenomenon in Mexico where wealth is very concentrated. On the other hand, while bequests may be important in some families, they are not important in others [see Altonji, Hayashi, and Kotlikoff (1992)]. Consequently, an applied dynamic model should be able to incorporate both families linked by bequests and other families who engage in life-cycle savings. A theoretical version of such a model has been developed by Escolano (1992); it should be possible to implement an applied version of this model.

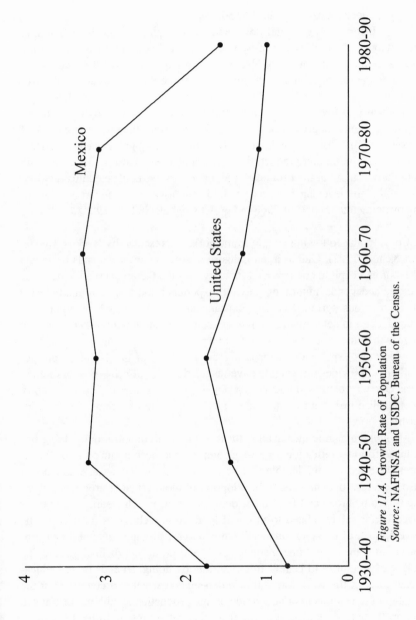

Figure 11.4. Growth Rate of Population
Source: NAFINSA and USDC, Bureau of the Census.

IV. Specialization in Final Products

Incorporating capital flows and demographics would be essential in any analysis of the dynamic impact of NAFTA. Even more essential would be to account for the impact of NAFTA on growth rates in the three countries. Studying the recent economic performances of the Philippines and South Korea, Lucas (1992) concludes that the key to understanding growth is what economists call *learning by doing*. The potential of learning by doing to account for economic growth has been recognized since the pioneering work of Arrow (1962). The microevidence has a long history going back to Wright (1936), who found that productivity in airframe manufacturing increased with cumulative output at the firm level. Later studies have confirmed this relationship at the firm level and industry level. Recent research that incorporate learning by doing into models of trade and growth include Stokey (1988) and Young (1991).

Consider the following simple framework, as presented by Backus, Kehoe, and Kehoe (1992): Output in an industry in some country depends on inputs of labor and capital, country- and industry-specific factors, and an experience factor that depends, in turn, on previous experience and output of that industry in the previous period. Keeping constant the rates of growth of inputs, the crucial factor in determining the rate of growth of output per worker is the rate of growth of the experience factor. Output per worker grows faster in industries in which this experience factor is higher. The level of growth of output per worker nationwide is a weighted average of the rates of growth across industries. One way increased openness promotes growth is that it allows a country to specialize in certain product lines and attain more experience in these industries.

Modeling dynamic increasing returns as the result of learning by doing is a reduced form specification for a very complex microeconomic process. It captures the effects of the learning curve documented by industrial engineers. It also captures, to some extent, the adoption of more efficient production techniques from abroad and from other domestic industry. The learning that takes place is not solely related to physical production techniques but also to the development of complex financial and economic arrangements between producers of primary and intermediate goods and producers of final goods. The ability of a country to benefit from learning by doing depends on the educational level of the work force. It also depends on whether a country is at the frontier of development of new products and production techniques or if it can import these from abroad; it is easier to play catch-up than to be the technological leader.

The challenge that lies ahead is to build the concepts sketched out above into a calibrated model of North American trade. To appreciate some of the issues involved, consider a simple analytical model in which value added in industry i, $i = 1, \ldots, I$, is produced according to the function

$$Y_{it} = \gamma_i A_{it} N_{it}^{1-\alpha_i} K_{it}^{\alpha_i}$$

Here Y_{it} is real value added of industry i in period t, N_{it} is labor input, and K_{it} is capital services. The variable A_{it} measures the external effects of learning by doing. We assume that

$$A_{it+1} = A_{it} (1 + \beta_i Y_{it})^{\eta},$$

where β_i and η are positive constants. Thus, the rate of increase in learning is proportional to total output. This is slightly different from the standard experience curve, in which productivity is an increasing function of cumulative output, but has the same flavor: Current production raises future productivity. Defining $y_{it} = Y_{it}/N_t$ to be real output per capita and similarly defining n_{it} and k_{it}, we obtain

$$y_{it} = \gamma_i A_{it} n_{it}^{1-\alpha_i} k_{it}^{\alpha_i}$$

which implies that the growth rate in per capita output is

$$g(y_{it}) = \frac{y_{it+1}}{y_{it}} - 1 = (1 + \beta_i Y_{it})^{\eta} \left(\frac{n_{it+1}}{n_{it}}\right)^{1-\alpha_i} \left(\frac{k_{it+1}}{k_{it}}\right)^{\alpha_i} - 1$$

If we consider a balanced growth path in which the capital stock in each industry grows at the same rate as output and the fraction of the labor force in each industry is constant, then we can calculate

$$g(y_{it}) = (1 + \beta_i Y_{it})^{\delta_i} - 1$$

where $\delta_i = \eta/(1 - \alpha_i)$.

The aggregate growth rate is the weighted average of growth rates of individual industries, with weights given by shares in aggregate output:

$$1 + g(y_t) = \sum_{i=1}^{I} (Y_{it}/Y_t)[1 + g(y_{it})] = \sum_{i=1}^{I} (Y_{it}/Y_t)(1 + \beta_i Y_{it})^{\delta_i}$$

If, in addition, $\beta_i = \beta$ and $\delta_i = 1$ for all i, aggregate growth is

$$g(y_t) = \beta Y_t \sum_{i=1}^{I} (Y_{it}/Y_t)^2$$

We refer to the summation in the above expression, a number between zero and one, as a *specialization index*. Its product with aggregate output operates as a scale effect on growth. In general, that is, with $\delta_i \neq 1$, the appropriate specialization index is based on other powers of the output shares Y_{it}/Y_t, but this simple measure captures the dispersion of production across industries that the theory suggests is important.

V. Imports of Specialized Inputs

Increased openness allows a country to import more specialized inputs to the production process. Stokey (1988) and Young (1991) have proposed models in which new product development is still the result of learning by doing but where the primary impact of learning by doing is in the development of new, more specialized inputs. Trade allows a country to import these inputs without developing them itself. Aghion and Howitt (1989), Grossman and Helpman (1989), Rivera-Batiz and Romer (1989), and others have proposed similar models where it is research and development that leads to the development of new products. (Here, of course, the relationship of trade and growth is more complicated if one country can reap the benefits of technological progress in another country by importing the technology itself without importing the products that embody it.)

Suppose, as in Stokey (1988) and Young (1991), that learning by doing leads to the development of new or improved products. Final output is produced according to the production function

$$Y_t = \gamma N_t^{1-\alpha} \left(\int\limits_0^\infty X_t(i)^\rho di \right)^{\alpha/\rho}.$$

There is a continuum of differentiated capital goods (or intermediate goods), with $X_t(i)$ denoting the quantity of capital goods of type i, $0 \le i \le \infty$. The parameter ρ is positive, allowing output even if there is no input of some capital goods. This type of production function embodies the idea that an increase in the variety of inputs leads to an increase in measured output.

Growth arises from an increase in the number of available capital goods. In period t, only capital goods in the interval $0 \le i \le A_t$ can be produced. Production experience results in the expansion of the interval, the development of new products,

$$A_{t+1} = A_t(1 + \beta Y_t)$$

The resource constraint on capital goods is

$$\int\limits_0^{A_t} X_t(i) \, di = K_t$$

If the production functions for capital goods are identical, then the most efficient allocation of resources results in equal production of all goods that are actually produced. Let us assume that all goods in the interval $0 \le i \le A_t$ are produced in equal amounts. Under suitable assumptions, this is the equilibrium outcome [see, for example, Romer (1990)]. Letting X_t (i) $\bar{X}_t, 0 \leq i \leq A_t$, we obtain

$$\bar{X}_t = K_t/A_t$$

which implies

$$Y_t = \gamma N_t^{1-\alpha} K_t^{\alpha} A_t^{\alpha(1-\rho)/\rho}$$

The growth rate of output per worker is

$$g(y_t) = (1 + \beta Y_t)^{\alpha(1-\rho)/\rho} \left(\frac{k_{t+1}}{k_t}\right)^{\alpha} - 1$$

If we assume, in addition, that the capital stock grows at the same rate as output, then growth is simply a function of the scale of production:

$$g(y_t) = (1 + \beta Y_t)^{\delta} - 1$$

where $\delta = \alpha(1-\rho)/[\rho(1-\alpha)]$. Again, there is a scale effect at the country level: Countries with larger outputs grow faster.

The most interesting aspect of this theory is the perspective it gives us on trade and growth. In the previous section, the natural interpretation is that technology is embodied in people and is not tradeable. Trade may influence the pattern of production, including both the scale of production and the pattern of specialization, and in this way affect growth. In this model, technology is embodied in product variety, and there is a more subtle interaction between trade and growth. Recall that increases in the number of varieties of intermediate goods raise output. If these varieties are freely traded, a country can either produce them itself or purchase them from other countries. By importing these products, a small country can grow as fast as a large one. When there is less than perfectly free trade in differentiated products, we might expect to find that both scale and trade in differentiated products are positively related to growth.

A commonly used measure of the extent to which a country engages in trade of specialized products in the Grubel-Lloyd (1975) index. The Grubel-Lloyd index for country j is

$$GL^j = \frac{\displaystyle\sum_{i=1}^{I} (X_i^j + M_i^j - |X_i^j - M_i^j|)}{X^j + M^j}$$

Here X_i^j is exports of industry i; M_i^j is imports of industry i; X^j is total exports; and M^j is total imports. Backus, Kehoe, and Kehoe (1992) find a strong positive relation between the Grubel-Lloyd index for all products at the three-digit

S.I.T.C. level and growth in GDP per capita for a large sample of countries. They also find a strong positive relationship between the Grubel-Lloyd index for manufactured products and growth in manufacturing output per worker. Trade in category 711, nonelectrical machinery, might consist of imports of steam engines (7,113) and exports of domestically produced jet engines (7,114). Simultaneous imports and exports of these goods provide the country with both and leads to more efficient production.

VI. Some Empirical Estimates and Illustrative Calculations

Using cross-country data from a large number of countries over the 1970–85 period, Backus, Kehoe, and Kehoe (1992) analyze the determinants of growth. Various other researchers have used similar cross-country data sets to estimate the parameters of endogenous growth models; see Levine and Renelt (1992) for a survey. Typically, researchers in this area find that their results are very sensitive to the exact specification of the model and the inclusion or exclusion of seemingly irrelevant variables. Backus et al. (1992) find, however, that, in explaining rates of growth of output per worker in manufacturing, results related to the theory sketched out in the previous two sections are remarkably robust. Using their methodology, we can estimate some parameters for a model in which both specialization in final output and the ability to import specialized inputs foster growth. Details concerning the data sources and methodology can be found in Backus et al. (1992).

Consider a relationship of the form

$$g(\bar{y}^j) = \alpha + \beta_1 \log \bar{Y}^j + \beta_2 \log \sum_{i=1}^{I} (\bar{X}_i^j/\bar{Y}^j)^2 + \beta_3 \log \bar{G}\bar{L}^j$$
$$+ \beta_4 \log y^j + \beta_5 \text{PRIM}^j + \varepsilon^j$$

Here $g(\bar{y}^j)$ is average yearly growth of manufacturing output per worker in percent form from 1970–85; $\bar{Y}^j$ is 1970 manufacturing output; $\sum_{i=1}^{I} (\bar{X}_i^j/\bar{Y}^j)^2$ is a specialization index based on exports at the three digit S.I.T.C. level; $\bar{G}\bar{L}^j$ is the 1970 Grubel-Lloyd index of intraindustry trade; y^j is 1970 per capita income; and PRIM^j is 1970 primary school enrollment rate. Bars above the variables indicate that the variable deals with the manufacturing sector only; the specialization index and the Grubel-Lloyd index, for example, are computed for manufacturing industries only.

We include total manufacturing output and the specialization index to account for the impact of specialization in production of final goods. One motivation for using export data is that specialization is most important in the export sector. Another motivation is purely practical. The trade data permits a more detailed breakdown of commodities, and the export specialization index can be thought of as a proxy for the total production specialization index; if exports are proportional to outputs, then $\bar{X}_i^j = \varepsilon \bar{Y}_i^j$ and $\Sigma_{i=1}^{I} (\bar{X}_i^j/\bar{Y}^j)^2 = \varepsilon^2 \Sigma_{i=1}^{I}(\bar{Y}_i^j/\bar{Y}^j)^2$ and the two indices are proportional. The Grubel-Lloyd index is included, as we have explained, because it captures, in a loose way, the ability of a country to trade in finely differentiated products, which our theory implies is important for growth. We include initial per capita income and the primary enrollment rate partly because they are widely used by other researchers in this area, such as Barro (1991) and partly because they may be relevant to our theory; the inclusion of per capita income allows for less-developed countries, which are playing catch-up, to face different technological constraints. The inclusion of the enrollment rate allows for differences in countries' ability to profit from learning by doing because of differences in levels of basic education.

A regression of the above relationship yields

$$g(\bar{y}^j) = \frac{2.602}{(5.686)} + \frac{0.743}{(0.259)} \log \bar{Y}^i + \frac{0.309}{(0.113)} \log \sum_{i=1}^{I} (\bar{X}_i^j/\bar{Y}^j)^2$$
$$+ \frac{0.890}{(0.410)} \log \bar{GL}^j + \frac{-0.172}{(0.799)} \log y^i + \frac{2.421}{(2.271)} PRIM^i$$
$$\text{NOBS} = 49 \qquad R^2 = 0.479.$$

(The numbers in parentheses are heteroskedasticity-consistent standard errors.) Notice that in this regression the coefficients all have the expected signs and that the first three variables, total manufacturing output, the specialization index, and the Grubel-Lloyd index, are all statistically significant.

To illustrate the dramatic impact of trade liberalization possible in a dynamic model that contains the endogenous growth features discussed in the previous two sections, let us suppose that NAFTA allowed Mexico to increase its level of specialization in production of final manufactured goods and imports of specialized inputs. The average values over 1970–85 of the specialization indices and Grubel-Lloyd indices for the three North American countries are listed below. The values of the same indices for South Korea, a country with about the same output per worker as Mexico, are also included for comparison.

	$\Sigma_{i=1}^{I}(\bar{X}_i^j/\bar{Y}^j)^2$	$\bar{GL}^j$
Canada	7.10×10^{-2}	0.638
Mexico	5.93×10^{-4}	0.321
U.S.	1.92×10^{-3}	0.597
Korea	5.43×10^{-2}	0.362

Suppose that free trade allows Mexico to increase its specialization index to 0.1×10^{-2} and its Grubel-Lloyd index to 0.6. Dramatic increases of this sort are possible: In 1970, for example, Ireland had a Grubel-Lloyd index for manufactured goods of 0.150; in 1980, after having joined the European Economic Community in 1973, this index was 0.642. Over the same 1970–80 period, earnings per worker in Ireland rose at a 4.1 percent annual rate.

Using the above regression results, we would estimate the increase in the growth rate of manufacturing output per worker of 1.430 percent per year:

$$1.430 = 0.309 \log \left(\frac{1.00 \times 10^{-2}}{5.93 \times 10^{-4}} \right) + 0.890 \log \left(\frac{0.600}{0.321} \right)$$

$$= 0.873 + 0.557.$$

It is clear that much is at stake in the issues discussed here. Suppose that Mexico is able to increase its growth rate of output per worker by an additional 1.430 percent per year by taking advantage of both specialization and increased imports of specialized intermediate and capital goods. Then, after 30 years, its level of output per worker would be more than 50 percent higher than it would have otherwise been. By way of comparison, if Mexico's output per worker were 50 percent higher in 1988 than it was, then output per worker in Mexico would be about the same as that in Spain (again, this comparison uses Summers' and Heston's 1991 data). Our earlier calculations suggested that Mexico could increase its output per worker by roughly 66 percent by increasing its capital per worker until the rate of return on capital is equal to that in the United States. Admittedly, these calculations are very crude, but they suggest that there is a significant impact of increased openness on growth through dynamic increasing returns. Furthermore, the dynamic benefits of increased openness dwarf the static benefits found by more conventional applied general equilibrium models.

Obviously, this is an area that requires more research, and even a crude disaggregated dynamic general equilibrium model of North American economic integration would make a substantial contribution. More empirical work also needs to be done. Notice, for example, that the Grubel-Lloyd indices reported above fail to capture the observation that Korea is fairly closed in final goods markets but open to imports of intermediate and capital goods.

Our analysis suggests that Mexico has more to gain from free trade than do Canada or the United States. Both are already fairly open economies, and the United States is big enough to exploit its dynamic scale economies. Mexico, however, has a smaller internal market. To follow an export-led growth strategy, Mexico must look to the United States, as the trade statistics in Figure 11.1 indicate.

Endogenous growth theories can be used to support industrial policies that target investment towards certain industries and trade policies that protect some final-goods industries. At the level of aggregation used here, our results have little to say directly about such policies. Two warnings about such policies are worth making, however. First, with regard to industrial policies, the learning-by-doing process discussed in this paper, and innovation in general, is something that needs to be modeled at a more advanced microlevel. Whether the government can do a better job than market forces in directing investment in the presence of this kind of external effect is an important question that is left open by our analysis. Second, with regard to trade policies, open access to U.S. markets for Mexico means open access to Mexican markets for the United States in the context of NAFTA. It would be politically difficult, if not impossible, for Mexico to pursue selective protectionist policies like those of Korea.

VII. Aggregation Issues

One problem that confronts a researcher interested in constructing a dynamic general equilibrium model to analyze the impact of NAFTA is what level of aggregation to use. There is evidence that some disaggregation is necessary: Echevarria (1992), for example, finds that although changes in total factor productivity in the OECD has been negligible in recent decades in agriculture, it has been significantly positive in services but less than in manufacturing. Simple regressions of growth in income per capita on the initial composition of output – that is, on percentages of output in industry, agriculture, and services – account for more than 22 percent of the variation in growth rates. Furthermore, differences in total factor productivity between Mexico and the United States differ substantially across industries. The growth effects of NAFTA are, therefore, apt to vary across industries. The empirical results of Backus, Kehoe, and Kehoe (1992), which finds that the simple endogenous growth models presented in this paper do well in explaining productivity growth in manufacturing but not growth in total output per capita, further suggest that some disaggregation is necessary if endogenous growth theory is to be successfully incorporated into an applied general equilibrium model. Yet disaggregation has its costs in terms of data requirements and potential computational difficulties.

A further problem in applied modeling of trade and growth at a disaggregate level is that the objects in theoretical models that stress the development of new products do not have obvious empirical counterparts in the data. [We should note that work such as that of Brown (1987) and Watson (1991) indicate that the disaggregation of goods typically used in static trade models has problems in terms of capturing the degree of substitutability between imports and domestically produced goods.] Various approaches have been used to reinterpret trade data disaggregated using the S.I.T.C. in terms of these sorts of themes, for example, Feenstra (1990), Havrylyshyn and Civan (1985), and this paper. This is obviously an area that needs more research, particularly research with a high imagination component.

References

Aghion, P., and P. Howitt. 1989. "A model of growth through creative destruction." Unpublished manuscript, Massachusetts Institute of Technology.

Altonji, J.G., F. Hayashi, and L.J. Kotlikoff. 1992. "Is the extended family altruistically linked? Direct tests using micro data." *American Economic Review* 82:1177–98.

Arrow, K.J. 1962. "The economic implications of learning by doing." *Review of Economic Studies* 24:155–73.

Auerbach, A.J., and L.J. Kotlikoff. 1987. *Dynamic Fiscal Policy*. Cambridge: Cambridge University Press.

Backus, D.K., P.J. Kehoe, and T.J. Kehoe. 1992. "In search of scale effects in trade and growth." *Journal of Economic Theory* 58:377–409.

Baldwin, R. 1992. "Measurable dynamic gains from trade." *Journal of Political Economy* 100:162–74.

Barro, R.J. 1991. "Economic growth in a cross section of countries." *Quarterly Journal of Economics* 106:407–44.

Blomstrom, M., and E.N. Wolff. 1989. "Multinational corporations and productivity convergence in Mexico." NBER Working Paper no. 3141.

Brown, D.K. 1987. "Tariffs, the terms of trade, and national product differentiation." *Journal of Policy Modeling* 9:503–26.

Brown, D.K., A.V. Deardorff, R.H. Stern. 1991. "A North American free trade agreement: Analytical issues and a computational assessment." Unpublished manuscript, University of Michigan.

Clark, G. 1987. "Why isn't the whole world developed? Lesson from the cotton mills." *Journal of Economic History* 47:141–73.

Cox, D., and R.G. Harris. 1991. "North American free trade and its implications for Canada: Results from a C.G.E. model of North American trade." Unpublished manuscript, University of Waterloo.

Echevarria, E.C. 1992. "Sectoral composition and its relation to development." Unpublished Ph.D. dissertation, University of Minnesota.

Escolano, J. 1992. "Essays on fiscal policy, intergenerational transfers, and distribution of wealth." Unpublished Ph.D. dissertation, University of Minnesota.

Fischer, S. 1992. "Growth, macroeconomics, and development." *NBER Macroeconomics Annual* 6:329–64.

Garber, P.M., and S.R. Weisbrod. 1991. "Opening the financial services market in Mexico." Unpublished manuscript, Brown University.

Garcia-Alba, P., and J. Serra-Puche. 1985. *Financial Aspects of Macroeconomic Management in Mexico*. El Colegio de México.

Grossman, G.M., and E. Helpman. 1989. "Product development and international trade." *Journal of Political Economy* 97:1261–83.

Grubel, H., and P.J. Lloyd. 1975. *Intra-Industry Trade*. London: Macmillan.

Havrylyshyn, O., and E. Civan. 1985. "Intra-industry trade among developing countries." *Journal of Development Economics* 18:253–71.

Hinojosa-Ojeda, R., and S. Robinson. 1991. "Alternative scenarios of U.S.-Mexico integration:

A computable general equilibrium approach.'' Discussion Paper 609, University of California at Berkeley.

Kehoe, T.J., C. Polo. and F. Sancho. 1991. ''An evaluation of the performance of an applied general equilibrium model of the Spanish economy.'' Research Department Working Paper 480, Federal Reserve Bank of Minneapolis.

Kotlikoff, L.J., and L.H. Summers. 1981. ''The importance of intergenerational transfers in aggregate capital accumulation.'' *Journal of Political Economy* 84:706–32.

KPMG Peat Marwick/Policy Economics Group. 1991. ''Analysis of economic effects of a free trade area between the United States and Mexico: Executive summary.'' Washington, D.C.: U.S. Council of the Mexico-U.S. Business Committee.

Levine, R., and D. Renelt. 1992. ''A sensitivity analysis of cross-country growth regressions.'' *American Economic Review* 82:942–63.

Lucas, R.E. 1988. ''On the mechanics of economic development.'' *Journal of Monetary Economics* 22:3–42.

———. 1990. ''Why doesn't capital flow from rich to poor countries?'' *American Economic Review,* Paper and Proceedings 80:92–96.

———. 1992. ''Making a miracle.'' Unpublished manuscript, University of Chicago.

Rivera-Batiz, L., and P.M. Romer. 1989. ''International trade with endogenous technological change.'' Unpublished manuscript, University of Chicago.

Romer, P.M. 1987. ''Growth based on increasing returns due to specialization.'' *American Economic Review,* Papers and Proceedings 77:56–62.

———. 1990. ''Endogenous technological change.'' *Journal of Political Economy* 98:S71–102.

Shoven, J.B., and J. Whalley. 1984. ''Applied general equilibrium models of taxation and international trade.'' *Journal of Economic Literature* 22:1007–51.

Sobarzo, H.E. 1991. ''A general equilibrium analysis of gains from trade for the Mexican economy of a North American free trade agreement.'' Unpublished manuscript, El Colegio de México.

Stokey, N.L. 1988. ''Learning by doing and the introduction of new goods.'' *Journal of Political Economy* 96:701–17.

Summers, R., and A. Heston. 1991. ''The Penn world table (Mark 5): An expanded set of international comparisons, 1950–1988.'' *Quarterly Journal of Economics* 106:327–68.

Watson, W.G. 1991. ''Canada's trade with and against Mexico.'' Unpublished manuscript, McGill University.

Whalley, J. 1989. ''General equilibrium trade modelling over the last five years.'' Unpublished manuscript, University of Western Ontario.

Wright, T.P. 1936. ''Factors affecting the cost of airplanes.'' *Journal of Aeronautical Sciences* 3:122–28.

Young, A. 1991. ''Learning by doing and the dynamic effects of international trade.'' *Quarterly Journal of Economics* 106:369–406.

Yúnez-Naude, A. 1991. ''Hacia un tratado de libre comercio norteamericano: Efectos en los sectores agropecuarios y alimenticios de Mexico.'' Unpublished manuscript, El Colegio de México.

Index